With love to
Jane + Bob Everts

Elizabeth W. Brown
Sept 1989

INTERVAL IN AFRICA

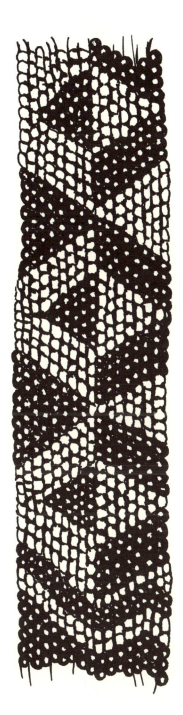

INTERVAL IN AFRICA

by
ELIZABETH
WIBBERLEY
BROWN

Protea Publishing Company
Canterbury, Connecticut

Library of Congress Catalog Card No. *88-92784*
ISBN *0-9621538-0-*x
First Printing
Printed in the United States of America

To Roy

Who made it all possible

ILLUSTRATIONS

CONTENTS

Author's Note

Each time we went to the movies in Gaborone, we encountered the Interval; a break after the shorts and previews when the whole theatre emptied into the plaza and milled about in the cool of the evening before returning for the main feature. A pleasant and memorable custom.

So I have called this book "Interval in Africa". It is the record of a memorable two-year break in my established Connecticut life; an experience so strong that it is still in my heart and mind, daily.

Prologue

Roy came home from work one day, seemingly as usual, but he handed me a sheaf of papers and asked, "How'd you like to go to Africa for a couple years?"

My throat was struck by some strange paralysis. No words would come out, no pros, no cons, no opinions of any sort. Frozen would be the only word to describe me then, and it has taken me weeks to begin to thaw.

That sheaf of papers he brought home is lying on the sideboard and I'm supposed to be reading them over, studying the details of the project, the plan of the city on the desert where we might live, the suggestions as to what should be shipped and what would be furnished; what and what not to bring.

I have been avoiding that thick brochure as though it were a coiled cobra. I skirt it with a sidewise glance, all the while pretending it's not there. I've done this for weeks and still have nothing to say when I'm asked if I have read it.

I know, just as well as I know my own name, that no logical or illogical arguments, no tears or good sense will have any effect on Roy. He has that keen light in his eye and spring to his step that means he's got a new idea that he's enthusiastic about; one that will release him from the daily drudgery of the long drive to the State Tax Office and its routine. He sees where he can make some money and at the same time, have his family go along on a great adventure.

I know already, although I won't acknowledge it, that before many months have passed, I will find myself in a strange land somewhere in South Africa; uncertain and yes, afraid, too. Once again getting used to a new life.

I was younger when these proposals came up before. When preparing for a flight to the Far East, with a babe in arms, a toddler, and two school children, someone asked, "You're going to Korea? All alone?", and I casually answered, "Oh no. The children are going with me."

Then, ten years later, when Turkey was the place the letters came from, the anticipated homecoming never materialized. Rather, "You and the kids come along to Germany. I'll meet you there and have quarters ready. We can spend three years, right in the middle of things."

Of course we went and enjoyed it all. We camped from Copenhagen to Pisa, climbed the Eiffel Tower, peered over the Berlin Wall, were rained on in Spain and returned to Venice again and again. We loved getting acquainted with the map of Europe but when we came back to our old colonial home we had been slowly restoring and renovating through so many years, I made a vow; a determined vow that now I was home, I'd *never* embark on another such episode of travelling.

By now, this house is shaping up, though never finished and always demanding. With the threat of leaving it, I've felt as though my days were numbered and I have frantically shopped for wallpaper and embarked on all those projects I had been putting off. I worked around the papers on the sideboard, vigorously wielding the paste brush and slapping new paper on the walls between the wainscoting and the beamed ceiling. The front hall, too, is transformed by a unique wall design picking up colors from each of the adjoining front rooms. It looks great.

This frantic activity has helped me to adjust my mind to what I know is coming. But I still can't talk about it. When it's mentioned, my throat clamps tight which automatically forces out tears, so I turn away, which irritates Roy and frustrates him to the point of screaming, "Damn it! What's the matter with you? I can't get anything out of you but tears!"

I don't like to pull up my roots, and I know that life will never be the same on returning, if we do go. We'll never pick up at the same place, for we will be different people and the family will have changed. Joel, now in the sixth grade, will more than ever be an "only" child, separated from his five adult brothers and sisters for two years.

It's easy for Roy to move. He welcomes moves as his roots are never very deep. His attachment to this house was greatest when he was in the midst of reconstruction, with the suspense of getting the roof covered before a downpour, or a side back on before the deadline of heading back to work after a leave. With big projects completed, he's always ready for new fields and he searches for them.

But I can understand Roy's fascination with this package; a great escape and also a challenge. I keep thinking one should have a great passion for helping people, in order for something like this to succeed, but we shall see.

Well, the house will wait. It won't go away. It's stood here about 200 years, so it'll survive a few more without my constant care. If I can think that, maybe I am all cried out and uglied out. I suppose I shall have to switch from this frenzy of foolish activity and face the responsibility of getting out the footlockers, must repair and paint them, start seeing about shots and making wills and changing addresses; start thinking seriously about what to pack. I'm sure the acceptance call for Roy will be coming any day now.

The first thing, I guess I'd better go pick up that brochure and see what it has to tell me.

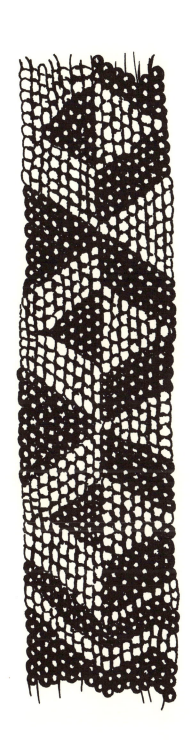

1

To A New Continent

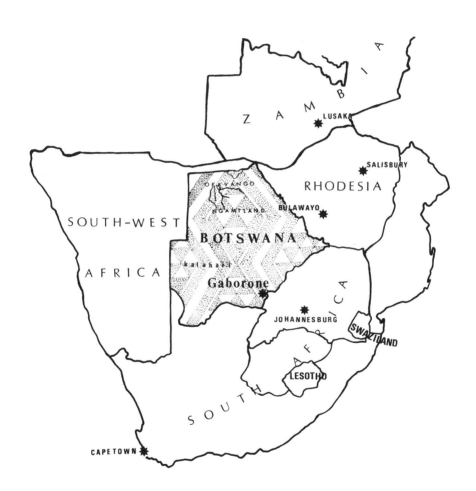

It is exactly five months to the day, since Roy brought home those papers about Botswana. We are high above the Kalahari Desert, in a forty-passenger South African Airlines plane, peering anxiously to catch the first sight of Gaborone, the end point of all this upheaval.

We are flying low, and in this clear, pure air, visibility is infinite. An hour ago, we took off from Johannesburg where we looked down on the flat-topped mountains of yellow-cake from the gold mines that rim the southern edge of the city and then on a mosaic of red roofs and blue swim pools set in the bright green expanse of the northern suburbs. Beyond them, immense highways snaked out over the vast and rolling farmland.

I have kept my eyes glued to the ground, not wanting to miss a thing. It's good to be in this small plane. When we left New York, we were packed into a 747 night flight and then a long delay in Rio de Janiero confined us to a hot waiting room. The last long haul had been at great heights over the Atlantic, without much to see. However, in the middle of the night, just before we landed, Joel stared out the window at lightning flashes within huge banks of billowing clouds; one bright pink explosion after another, softly diffused and reflected. He was impressed and mystified and finally whispered,

"Do you suppose that's Heaven?"

Now the roads down there look as if they were drawn by a ruler. Red clay, straight for miles, then angled in another direction, still straight. Once in a while there's a little hill, cone shaped, seeming out of place in all this barren flatness. I'd thought the Kalahari would look like the Sahara, but it is grass covered and dotted with thorn trees.

Here I am enjoying myself, and have been, ever since making that final break. Joel and I had waved from the train at New London after a warm and rollicking family send-off; no tears. We waved and waved to our dear family until they were lost from sight and that was the point at which I gave myself up completely to whatever was ahead. We were then, indeed on our way.

We joined Roy in New York, where the four members of the Tax Team and their families were already assembled for orientation. Comparative strangers united in this venture, we were all very open with each other and voiced all our misgivings, pooled our fears and concerns, and bolstered each other as we were given reams of advice and reassurance from men who had already served a tour in Botswana.

"We've sold our house in Stockton," Juan Kudo said, "And sent our household goods on to Francistown. There's no turning back now." But Juan was flat on his back; a back that had rebelled. His wife, Suzu, and daughter Mimi, hovered over him as he spent the week in bed. We wondered if he or his back would win the argument, but felt he would never make the flight we would take the next day.

Ben Webb said his wife, Vi and daughter Damaris were still in Portland, Oregon. "They'll be ready for the trip in a month or so." He had spent four years in Tanzania, at one time, so didn't have the same air of entering the unknown, that we had.

Jerry and Alice Pahl with their seven children, were embarking on their first trip beyond Minnesota. Alice expressed her concern about "taking all these kids out of school three months early. Jeannine will miss her graduation, but she is ready for High School. I'm hoping there's an opening at Maru-a-Pula. Danny and Tony are right on her heels, going into seventh and eighth; John and Patty haven't started yet, but Mary and Peggy will be fine. I know there's Thornhill Primary School for them."

"Anyway," she confessed, "I was in such a state there, for a while, with Jerry giving up his job with the State, storing our stuff, renting the house, not knowing what waits for us and wondering all the time if we were doing the right thing, I was so bad off I couldn't go to church and see Danny get his God and Country award for Scouts. I finally went to see a psychiatrist; didn't think I'd make it! But he assured me my anxiety was normal, and here I am!"

"Well, I was a mess. I cried for weeks!"

"You! I thought you'd done lots of travelling. Roy said you had lived all over the world. I didn't think you'd have been upset."

So, we got acquainted and the youngsters became fast friends.

The kids, pressed against the windows, are excited now; that is, all of them who aren't air sick, and Danny yells,

"There's the city!"

"Hey, it's bigger than I thought it'd be."

"And here's the field. We're going to land!"

"Hey, it's smaller than I thought it'd be," comes from another.

We are down, rolling along. We reach for some of the mountain of coats and jackets which have burdened us ever since Rio, gather our bags, rouse the sick children and help them up, ready to get off.

As we wait there, apprehensively, I wonder if anything in the next two years will be "the way I thought it'd be."

"Well, this is home," Roy said, as we turned into the yard of the small pre-fab house on Elephant Road. The house looked neat with its fresh coat of paint. The crew of workers still milled about; most sitting in the shade of the sprawling thorn trees. The yard was overgrown. Thorn branches, trimmed from somewhere though I couldn't see where any were missing, grass and just plain junk had been heaped in two gigantic mounds. The knee-high grass over the whole lot met the lower branches of the thorn trees and all were laced together with a rampant vine that crept on to the top of the wire fence on the perimeter. It was a big yard and every inch was screaming for attention.

Studying this layout, as I sat in the pick-up truck that we had just acquired, I was startled by someone leaning in at the window; open of course, in this stifling heat.

"Here," a big dark girl said, "I want a job. Working for you," and she offered me a piece of paper.

I was not ready yet to deal with the selection of a maid. We had been told we must have help, as the local people need the work. I glanced at the paper and found it said that Pauline Sedimo had worked two and a half years for a man who had moved to Rhodesia, then two years as a cleaning girl and kitchen helper at the University of Botswana, Lethoso and Swaziland. We had seen the campus, as we rode in from the airport after our warm welcome there by a delegation of the Tax Department who scooped us up, bag and baggage and deposited us at the Inn, for some rest and recuperation before "settling in" our quarters.

I hesitated, and evaded the problem by saying, "I'll talk to you tomorrow," and she disappeared.

"This is one of the Tax Department houses," Roy said, "It hasn't been occupied in over a year. Took them so long to recruit a new team. Come on inside and look it over."

The head painter proudly displayed the rooms, saying he had selected the colors himself. The robin's egg blue in the living room-dining area wouldn't have been my choice, but we smiled and complimented him. It was a nice house, well designed. As we walked through the three bedrooms and saw the bright kitchen with big windows onto the overgrown yard, we were startled by strange creaks and tappings. It sounded like rain, but we looked out into brilliant sunshine. This was our introduction to the constant expanding and contracting of the metal roof during temperature changes. We heard later it had terrified some new arrivals during their first night; they were up constantly, searching for intruders.

The painter assured us he would be done the next day. We did wonder why they had such a late start on the project for our arrival date had been known for months. We were still staying in the Inn and during the past week there, as Roy got underway at the office and located the small pick-up, most of us had been catching up on sleep, with the kids enjoying a few days of the pool before starting school. One afternoon when Joel picked up his towel, a small cobra slithered out from under it and moved along the terrace by the pool. At his yells, a gardener had come running with a hoe and chopped it up. The kids were more thrilled than scared, for they now had a good story to tell their friends at home.

As we left the house, with the painters back under the trees again, we glanced across the road at Joel's school. It looked like a California school; long, low white concrete-block buildings tied together by covered walkways and gardens. There was no way to pick Joel out of that surging mass of blue; the student body was blended, as one, in slate blue safari suits and grey knee socks, the girls in lighter blue dresses and white blouses. Here and there was a splash of royal blue, the school sweater. Joel had been petrified the morning we took him in to register, but the Headmistress, Mrs. Dixon-Warren, with the rolling r's, was gracious and friendly and very understanding. She deals with a constant flow of students from many lands and told us that twenty-nine countries are represented at Northside Primary; about one third of the 450 being local boys and girls. Joel was lucky to have his school so close and some of the students proved to be next door neighbors.

When Roy arrived at the house early the next morning with key in hand, he found Pauline waiting on the porch. She grabbed the bucket and cleaning supplies from him and went straight to work scrubbing floors.

"She seems to be energetic," he reported as he picked me up later, "and is doing a good job."

He dropped me and our luggage at the house and I worked along with Pauline as he went on to unravel the paperwork at the airport in order to get the footlockers.

Pauline had the place frighteningly clean by the time we unpacked. I liked her; she worked well from the beginning and didn't slow down.

I had once said that the only kind of maid I'd like would be one who was deaf, dumb, and blind but still able to get the work done. Pauline hadn't said a thing but "Aye, Aye", to whatever I asked her—she almost filled that bill!

When Jerry and Alice stopped by one day and exclaimed over the sparkling house, Alice asked,

"Did you find out if Pauline has any children?"

"Well, I asked here if she had any family."

"Yes, but did you ask if she had any children?"

"She said she wasn't married, that she didn't have a father, only a mother."

"Well, that doesn't make any difference. Just wait."

Alice and family were still at the Inn. Our house may have been a bit behind schedule, but there was no housing for the Pahl's big family. A possibility is to use one of the Agriculture Department houses out at the College six miles north of the city. This doesn't do much for Alice, a city girl who didn't even want to live in the suburbs of West St. Paul. No knowing when they'll get out of the Inn, but I could see she had been getting advice about how things might be; that help would get well started and sure of the job, then spring a large family that would settle in the little house at the back of the lot.

I paid Pauline each day for some time. She knew she was on probation, but the suspense was too much for her and one day she asked me for the key to the maid's house.

"Mr. Brown will take care of that", I told her.

The next day I heard a truck come into the yard and the murmur of voices. I looked out to see a motley crew squatting under the carport in the shade, kicking beer cans around as they emptied them, and saw Pauline plowing through the tall grass toward the little house; one energetic young man with her.

After the gang had departed, she came in and told me that they had brought her the key.

"I didn't ask for it. They just brought it."

Then I was puzzled by her saying, "I need Cobra". I kept questioning her and discovered that she had a good command of English far beyond the "Aye, Aye" I had heard so much of, and I ascertained that Cobra was a brand of floor wax; she wanted her concrete floor to shine.

So, I gave her the wax, a wash basin, and an empty footlocker to use for her clothes, and she attacked her cleaning with even more vigor than she had mine. She showed me later how the floor shone; that she had hung a bright cloth for a curtain. There was one room, furnished

only with a cot, a shower and toilet room and a porch, with a small
stove on a ledge. It seemed bare and poor, but I realised why she was so
delighted and why she had been so anxious for the job. Housing is
scarce. Here, she has a solid concrete block house, a shower and flush
toilet, and a source of hot water nearby. Practically palatial compared to
living in the bush, or in a good Rondavel in a village, where water might
be at some distance.

That afternoon at the Mall, we found Pauline standing by our
pick-up loaded with bundles and her blankets. A cousin was with her,
"Who is going to see where I live!". They piled in the back with our
groceries and my quiet maid was now a chatterbox. She talked and
laughed all the way home.

A day or so later, we noticed an increase in traffic up and down our
drive; young women, old women, some with babies on their backs, and
little children. Alice's warning came to mind when Roy went down to
give Pauline her pay one evening and came back saying,

"There's a whole crowd down there. All eating."

Girls kept stopping by each day at my back door. They would peer
into the distance somewhere over my shoulder softly saying,

"I wantt a chobb", or "I am asking for a chobb", and I had to tell
each one as she came,

"I already have a girl."

Yes, I had a girl. She was a smart one, as she had kept close watch
on this house so she'd be on the spot when the new occupants arrived.
She had been there with a big, warm, smile and her request the first
instant I had been in the yard, and she had started working before I could
even consider accepting or rejecting her. She was a smart girl and she
became an integral part of our household. Through her, I learned about
the Botswana life upon which my life as an Ex-Pat was superimposed.
And, I found her to be one surprise after another.

MARCH 30

"Funny," Alice said one day, "I thought we were doing something
unique; that these people would be excited that four Americans were
coming into their country to help with their Tax System. Now I find
we're just part of a constant flow of ex-pats, coming and going."

"Yes," I agreed, "I don't think there's a day that someone new
doesn't arrive and someone else leave. Some serve short advisory tours,
others stay two or three years, then often extend."

"Ex-pats" we were and there were thousands of us. The black

population of this new city, built to be the capital of Botswana when Bechuanaland gained its independence from Great Britain, is diluted by the Europeans, Canadians and Americans here in a helping capacity.

The British dominate, of course. Many have been in Zambia, to the north, still earlier in Uganda, Kenya or Malawi, moving down as politics dictated. Some say they have lived in East Africa over twenty-five years. They dash back to U.K., on leaves, send their children home to boarding school, but don't dream of going back permanently. One such lady asked if I had been overseas before.

"Yes, with the Army, in Korea and Germany."

Then after talking a while she said, "I can't tell from your accent if you're Canadian or American."

"American . . ." and before I could get out another word, she said,

"Of course. The Canadians don't go around sticking their noses into other people's business."

Luckily, I didn't come up with an apt retort. In the same vein, Roy was introduced at a bridge club one evening as "A chap from the Colonies". It seems the film strip of history can be stopped at any frame, in the minds of people who don't care for the rest of the show.

I could see that the Batswana had long ago learned to take the flow of ex-pats as casually as the change of seasons, but I could see, too, how our presence might change some of their traditional ways of life.

As I was finishing preparations for dinner one evening, soon after we had "settled in" as the British say, Joel wandered across the yard and struck up a conversation, through the fence, with some of the boys who live next door. A few minutes later, I saw them stream into our yard; three boys with a couple of younger girls tagging along. Joel brought the biggest boy into the house saying,

"We're going to ride my bike," and went to get it from the bedroom.

"What's your name?", I asked.

"TuTume."

When I tried to say it as he had, he laughed and said,

"Kenneth."

"O.K. Kenneth. I can get that right." I had been surprised at the names when I got here; as Dorcas, Ivy, Benjamen, and Robert, but found quickly, that each also has a Setswana name, too.

Kenneth sailed off on the bicycle grinning delightedly. When the bike came back, I went out with three Frisbees which are always fun and take no special talent. They started right in, squealing at the unpredictable funmaker. The girls hung back and I had to go out and tell Joel to give them one. He did, and they ran and squealed and had as much fun as the others.

When Joel came in to dinner, he said,

"Do you know how old that boy is?"

He was shorter than Joel so his age of fourteen was a surprise.

"And he doesn't go to school. I asked him what he does and he said he hangs around, like he's doing now."

He seemed quite puzzled about a situation where a person didn't go to school, or couldn't.

"Not everyone can go to school," I said, "Their parents have to pay and some can't afford it."

He seemed pretty quiet for a while and I knew he was picturing what his life might be if he hadn't had a chance to enroll at Northside Primary, get his uniform, play soccer at breaktime and ping-pong in the afternoon, to say nothing of getting acquainted with all the kids his age.

"Kenneth knows my friend Thomas, who goes to Northside; he lives in the house next to him, over our back fence. Boy . . . he just hangs around", his voice trailed off and he was quiet again, thinking.

"Well, I can give him one of my Frisbees. He can have fun with that."

We continue to call the house "Kenneth's", but find it holds a myriad of people who may take shifts with the space available. Joel says the boys have a room of their own but they are not allowed to go into it in the daytime; then it's the girl's study room. There are always old people sitting under the thorn trees in the yard. One old lady lives in the garage space, and even what would be maid's quarters if an Ex-Pat were living there, are full and overflowing. . . . It seems to be a good example of the extended family, where if there's a roof overhead and food in the house, one must be taken in and cared for, if related, at all.

Joel, Kenneth, Shinga, Edwin and Thomas are good friends and never lack for something to do. Shinga's sister, Vivian and Thomas' sister Charla join them, and they borrow cards and sit in the sun playing until the cards are grubby and worn.

The boys are always making something. Lately, it's been cars and musical instruments; banjoes from floor wax cans or guitars from salad oil cans. Then they sing, and Joel tapes.

Kenneth and Edwin talk in Setswana and repeat in English and roll on the floor when it's played back to them.

"Some songs can't be translated," Kenneth says, "They are just about how you feel."

Some are about the Cattle Post. Botswana life is fluid. The families stay in the villages or here in the city during school sessions, and the day school is out, the youngsters go to the Cattle Posts.

"We don't dress up or wear shoes there", Kenneth says. "We even just wear a skin around us instead of pants."

Another time of year, they are at the "Lands", where crops are raised. I can't get the boys to pinpoint these places.

"Far away. On the train. Far away."

Earlier I asked Joel if there weren't some of his other school-mates nearby to play with, thinking he should spend more time with Ian, the British boy down the street. Then I saw how mistaken I was. Joel has made real friends and is finding out faster than we are about the way people here live and what they are really like.

Yesterday we realised it was quiet in the next bare yard; only old folks and young adults about. Joel went over after supper and Edwin's mother told him, "They won't be back for a month." The Exodus to the Cattle Post had taken place so quickly the boys hadn't even stopped in to say good-bye.

APRIL 2

Yesterday was quite an April Fool's Day. We had forgotten that it marked the beginning of Winter and ushered in a new time schedule. All rushed off to school and office at 7:30 and then wondered what had happened to the rest of the world.

Pauline, too, was here early and I told her to come back later, reminding her of the new schedule. Then, she said,

"I brought my child, last night." and held out her hand to indicate the height of a toddler, not a babe in arms.

"What did you say?" I asked unbelievingly, and sure enough, I had heard correctly.

She was a little late coming back and I began to wonder if she planned to leave a child alone down at her house, or bring it up here to the kitchen, and what my reaction would be to either. I went on repotting my plants and then turned to rake the newly mowed grass in the back yard.

I looked up to see a young woman coming around the corner of the house, from the front, carrying a little girl. At first I thought it might be someone looking for work, but just then Pauline stepped out the kitchen door and grinned.

"Who's this?" I asked.

"Thandi."

I smiled at her, admiring the little leather choker around her throat, the silver loop earrings, and talked to her. She clouded up and I said, "Don't cry!"

Pauline said, "Even with me . . ." indicating that she too, is a bit of a stranger to her own child. I felt sorry for her. Her baby has probably been cared for by aunts and cousins while she is off working.

"This is my sister Catherine. She is the youngest."

"How many sisters do you have?"

"Four. Marcielle is married and at the Lands, Lillian, Vivian and Catherine."

"Brothers?"

"Oh, one. Robert", in a tone indicating men weren't that important.

Catherine took Thandi off to the little house and Pauline went on with her work, hanging the wash in the bright sun where it would dry quickly enough to iron and put away before lunch.

So Alice was right. After about two weeks of getting settled in, Pauline felt it was all right to start bringing out the family I had questioned her about; to which question she had parried an answer. Pauline's little girl did not stay with her. When I asked she said, "Oh, she went home yesterday, to Molepolole."

APRIL 7

Pauline, is a lovely girl; soft spoken, bright and a hard worker. You never have to give her many instructions. She does everything well and goes beyond what is required. I do my own cooking, from preference, and I don't have her come back into the house after she finishes the lunch dishes as I treasure my privacy over any amount of help. Her little house is bare, but today is our Susan's birthday, and as there is no way to send her something up there in Maine, we will get some gifts for Pauline instead.

Right after lunch, Joel and I headed for the Mall and the Chinese hardware store where you can buy anything in the world except food, but we stopped at the USIS Library, on the way and I read my first newspaper since leaving New York.

Joel was enthusiastic about our expedition to the Mall as he had been back and forth a few times, by backyard paths and devious routes past tennis courts, certain fences, certain blind dogs, and a myriad of landmarks and points of interest he wanted me to see. He anticipated everything coming up and then proved he was right by what we did see.

We missed a lot; couldn't stop in the National Gallery, or in the Tourist Office where we could see they had posters and maps we'd like. Carrying our plastic bag of Pauline's cookware, two pads of typewriter paper, the camera and our dark glasses, we hurried along home enjoying the change from the usual route on the road.

We are impressed with the design of our new home city. It is an oval laid against the side of the north-south Francistown Road and the Rhodesian Railroad.

Government buildings fill the area at the upper edge and under them is a cluster of Banks and offices from which the wide Mall runs straight down the center. The Mall descends in a series of shop-rimmed squares, from the Post Office and Theatre at the top, to Trinity Church and the Cathedral at the bottom.

At this point, one main road circles the city and farther out, another encompasses the whole. The spaces between are cut by radial streets into residential sections of varying density. The city is designed so the Mall is accessible, on foot, from any of these areas.

Late in the afternoon, Roy took us all to the Camp Store, out in the Village, the site of a Boer War Camp.

It seemed a hazardous trip, with masses of pedestrians spilling onto the roadway, unpredictable bicyclists, the leftside of the road system to remember and some of the most erratic drivers ever encountered.

At the store, Pauline chose what she needed, starting with a 12.5 kilo bag of Mealies, the nation's staple, then cooking oil, a box of tea and some dishes. When we got back, Joel took her all the things we had bought at the Mall, as well as a bag of oranges, salt, sugar and some flatware.

She came tapping at my door a few minutes ago to thank me for the presents . . . I told her that my Susan was 26 today and she grinned and said, "I am 23."

APRIL 9

Because we have heard ever since we arrived, that it's a good idea to go down to Zeerust, South Africa, once in a while to do shopping in large quantities, Roy has been anxious to make the trip. He was all for going the first Saturday we were here, but we heard enough about how bad the road was to put it off until after our initial settling in. Then, he made up his mind that Saturday would be the day.

The evening before, we stopped to see an old-timer who has just completed 36 months here; a training officer at the Tax Department. He lent us a cooler and gave us a lot of advice. But he went on interminably about the rough road. "Oh, terrible. Almost ripped off the exhaust pipe, not from the back but from the front—Oh, terrible!"

"It's thirty-six kilometers of that dirt road, so you can measure it off as you go."

Well, during the night the rains set in again. Not just a light drizzle, but driving rains. All night it beat down; it seemed I woke a half dozen times and listened to it, visualizing what it was doing to a red dirt road.

On waking at 6 a.m. Roy said, "We'd better not go." I agreed, too enthusiastically, reeling off a long list of alternatives for the day.

"Well, we could go as far as Lobatse, and we could see how the road is. Maybe it didn't rain down there," he countered.

So, up and out in a hurry and we were off, driving along roads that were new to us. We hadn't ventured any distance from this town since arrival, except about six miles out to see where our friends the Pahls finally got temporary quarters.

We passed acres of shanty town on the edge of the city. It's so easy to be unaware of it when your life is encompassed by gardens and shrubs in the nice area of the city. In the rain it looked its worst. As soon as we were past that, we could admire the landscape. It was flat and sandy, dotted with thorn trees, and beautiful mountains rose against the horizon in the distance. Stray goats wandered near the few small villages we passed and cattle were being driven along the road by herd boys with raggy coat-tails flying.

I kept pointing out how the water was running in torrents in the ditches beside the road, but we kept going.

Near Lobotse, after an hours drive, we checked through the Border Gate out of Botswana and went on a short way for entry to the Republic of South Africa. I cast a discerning eye on the cars coming this way, looking to see how muddy they were or any signs on the drivers' faces of utter disgust. I didn't anticipate being stuck in the mud on this road.

Finally, Roy came back with his sheaf of papers and said,

"They gave me a break. Our visas aren't for going in and out for shopping. They're just transit visas for passing through. But they let us go this one time, and gave me application blanks for the other kind."

So, we were off down the road, which wasn't too bad to start with.

The first sign was "Speed Limit 90 km". I thought that was a laugh. Luckily, there wasn't too much traffic, so we could veer from one side to the other, choosing the least rough areas. It was a wide road, but that's about all you could say for it. Many places were muddy, and I felt that Roy maintained too fast a speed for the areas that were full of holes and puddles; thought the springs would surely be broken. When I suggested he hit them at a slower speed, he retorted, "This is a 90 km limit road!"

Well, 35 kilometers later, we sighted a lovely, lovely surface of asphalt and inside a half hour, we were in the neat little South African city of Zeerust. The stuccoed concrete-block homes with red tile roofs had prim little yards filled with flowers and shrubs. Main street wasn't hard to find, but harder to find was a rest room which was imperative.

While searching for it, we saw a Beverage store doing a lively business. But, it had two entrances, plainly marked "White" on one and "Black" on the other, and not ten feet separated them. Goods from the same shelf of stock were being dispensed to two separate lines of people. Joel couldn't believe it! This was apartheid in action. We turned away quickly and went to buy our necessities.

We were some of the last out of the stores when they closed at noon, and we loaded all in the back of the pick-up, redoing some of the things in Glad bags, such as my curtain material, spread the scrap plastic from the furniture store over the rugs as well as we could, securing it with bags of potatoes and fruit, put some in the front under our feet and braced ourselves for the return trip. Rain kept up—or down, rather, and we swerved and splashed all the way to Lobatse.

We stopped to explore it's "downtown" which looked like any poor shopping center on the wrong side of the tracks, but on an upper road, the big meat packing plant was a beauty, with carefully landscaped and groomed grounds which didn't of course, eliminate the slaughter-house odor.

Cattle is Botswana's mainstay, economically. This place packs, freezes and ships as much as 5,000,000 lbs. annually. We saw a cattle holding pen on the hill opposite the slaughterhouse, filled with a herd of beautiful dark red animals, their big horns shining in the rain. Later, we noticed many cattle loading areas along the railroad as we drove on home.

Joel fell asleep halfway, so he missed seeing us almost hit some kind of wild animal that dashed across the road in front of the car. It looked like a big red fox, but its back had long hair on it, standing up in a ruff of grey and white. I don't know what it could have been, and will look up an animal book when I get to the Library.

In spite of my dire predictions, our load of "junk" was all right when we finally arrived home. After the two and a half hour drive, we were muddy and dirty, aching in every joint, tired and sleepy and the truck was one solid mass of red mud. My good tan suit was red from top to bottom, but it all came out in the wash. I'll have to admit that it wasn't too bad a shopping trip.

We are making great inroads on our yard project. Grass cuttings and vines have been carried to a remote corner to start a compost heap. The rest of the stuff in front of the house must be burned.

This was a surprise to me; to see people burning outside. My first reaction was, "Don't they have an ordinance against outside burning?" No. Burning is the accepted way of ridding yourself of trimmed-off thorn tree branches and yard trash.

This mountain of stuff here can't be put in trash cans. I even tried forking it into the truck to drive it away, but that was too hard. We've started burning it, little by little.

As I was down near Pauline's little house at the back of the lot, with my compost material, I glanced at her doorway and was aghast.

For a girl who is so meticulous, personally so clean, and such a good housekeeper in here for me—and waxed her own floors so well, I couldn't believe what I saw. Her yard around her door was one big collection of paper and trash. It didn't make sense, especially since she had her girlfriend from Rhodesia visiting, and yesterday morning Roy noted that Pauline and her boyfriend, "didn't you see him, the big guy in the maroon turtle neck sweater?" had just gone up the drive.

So, today when she came, I told her she could have the big new wastebasket that Roy bought in Zeerust—to keep at her house and put her rubbish in. Later, her girlfriend came up to borrow a shovel and rake, so I guess they are going to neaten up the outside the way she knows how to neaten up the inside of a place.

The outside burning of trash and leaves is just one of the permitted activities here that have surprized me. At school, the teachers are permitted to slap students who don't shape up, and from Joel's reports, his teacher is kept busy shaping up a few every day.

A pleasant sight each morning is the sun birds. That's as scientific a name as I have for them so far. It seems a good one, as where the sun is, especially in the morning, there they are. They resemble humming birds, but they don't hover; they light on the stems of a rugged plant which has great orange globes of blooms, out of which the stem extends on upward through another globe, and onward up through another. Nectar in its flowers attracts the Sunbird with its long curved beak.

The bird is small, about sparrow size, and its back and neck are irridescent; brilliant green and turquoise changing to gold or reddish glints, depending on the sun and the birds movements. Some of them have white breasts and some orange. The constant sipping at the flowers is one thing that reminds me of the humming bird; the irridescence, the other.

Many little birds flock into the thorn trees in the back yard; sparrows and canary-like birds; some yellowish and some, probably the male, brilliant yellow. Joel marvels how they can fly into and light on the thorn trees, which are so treacherous to humans.

Yesterday afternoon, we drove out to Sebele, to the Botswana Agricultural College area, where the Pahl family is temporarily settled in a home.

We found Jerry out with a sack of fertilizer and a sheaf of garden seeds, even though it's now a bit late for planting. All over his garden plot were little tiny grey birds with bright blue breasts, great numbers of them. They blended in with the spaded ground, so that you didn't see all of them at once; just kept discovering more and more. Jerry was surprized we hadn't seen them before. He said they were the bird which is giving the farmers such a hard time. Perhaps they eat up all the planted seed before it gets to germinate.

Yesterday afternoon, I found out what "The" bird book is for Botswana. It's Roberts' *Birds of South Africa*. Roberts was a missionary's son and he classified all the birds of South Africa. The man who told me is from Dundee, Scotland, and has been in foreign service for 20 years. We talked a couple hours yesterday afternoon sitting in his yard under a thorn tree which had eight weaver birds' nests in it, now occupied by other birds. Weaver birds build nests like a Baltimore Oriole, and they build in a cluster community, eight or ten on a few branches. They'll be back in August and September and rebuild their nests which are now sublet to another specie.

I woke this morning to the shrillest of bird song. It was so unusual and so very loud I peered out to see if I could locate the big bird or birds it must be coming from. Roy stirred too and asked, "What's making that song?"

I went from window to window until I located the three big yellow birds with kite-like tails.

There is always birdsong in the air. Even though we are living in the city, there are so many trees and shrubs in all the yards there is plenty of place for birds and they trill and shrill at all times of day. Even the kids get interested as they hear a strange call, and get you out into the backyard to listen, until you've heard it too.

Joel called excitedly the other afternoon—"Run, run to the back of the house! Look, Look—a bird with two tails!" I never did see it, but it must have been one that had a tail, somewhat like a barn swallow, but long.

I didn't know we'd turn into bird watchers, but there are so many new ones to see, and are of the wild which we are interested in learning about. Those songs this morning were so loud that if I had switched on Joel's tape recorder in his room, the shrill notes could have been picked up.

I just went out to the kitchen; looked out to see what the neighbor's chickens are gleaning from my yard this morning, and there, for the first time, I saw a flock of the little blue birds which we had seen out in Sebele. The bright blue is all on their breasts and sides, the soft grey-brown is on their backs. That's why you have to keep looking to see how large the flock is. The big white chicken went right through the group and they didn't pay any attention. All of a sudden, they disappeared among some of the taller uncut grass, and there flew down a little red bird—red in all the places they had been blue. Just a tiny little bird and it came up near the doorway, pecking away at seeds and crumbs.

I have had to give up on planting seeds in my newly spaded beds. The chickens from next door are always here, and they scratch up the African Daisy and Bachelor Button seeds as fast as I scatter them. Kenneth and Edward, Joel's friends from next door look a little startled when I tell them I'm going to eat the chickens. They say, "There are many holes in the fence."

When Joel composed a letter to his class back home in Canterbury, he said "This isn't what I thought Africa would be. There are no lions, cheetahs or wild animals near."

That's true. This is not what either his Dad nor I had pictured Africa to be either, when we first considered coming.

It is more lush and tree covered than I expected, and of course much more attractive, in every way, with the lovely residential areas of the city, brilliant gardens, and flowering vines draped over the fences, to say nothing of the shops on the downtown mall offering every necessity and an abundance of "nice to haves". Not much relation to the wildlife anticipated.

An item in yesterday's Johannesburg paper noted that the unseasonal heavy rains have brought a great influx of snakes into Rustenburg, South Africa. That is quite a large city, about 50 kilometers east of Zeerust, where we shopped last Saturday. The paper listed a half dozen including Cobras, spitting cobras and other terrifying kinds that are in the suburbs and even seen in the city. Well, we'll not head for Rusten-burg in a hurry.

Our other "wildlife" is our friendly lizard population. So friendly it wants to live with us. There are always a half dozen or so sunning on the planter near the kitchen door, scurrying away when you go near, but there are many who want to scurry into the house. Pauline sweeps them out the front door with her broom, and we squeamishly brush them down off the curtains, or the window screens when we find them there. They sneak in under the door, but we don't mind them—much.

I have looked up the animal pictures and find that it was a wild silver-backed Jackael that dashed across the road in front of us as we were coming home from South Africa. Makes me feel more like I *am* in the Africa I anticipated.

APRIL 14

Pauline is full of surprizes. Surprizes, because I am so naive. As yet another facet of her existence flashes, I realize just *how* naive! Roy suggested we go over to the Holiday Inn last evening, to say good-bye to Oliver, someone who was flying out this morning to England. He's the old timer who warned us about the rough road to Zeerust, and sold us some of his household goods. He talked at length as we sat in the bar and listened attentively. Leaning past Roy to hear and not miss any-thing, I was unaware of two girls approaching us from the other side of the room until suddenly they were at my elbow and one took my hand. There was Pauline.

"Pauline! Hello!"

"I was over there and I saw you come in. I thought I should come and see you. I saw you from over there."

I said something, "This is my Pauline" to Oliver, and then she and her girlfriend from Rhodesia, went back to the far side of the room and sat in one of the semi-booths.

Oliver said, "Boy, our maid is an old crone about fifty, ugly as sin."

"Well, I don't know why she felt she had to come and report to me. I'd never even have seen her." I replied.

We continued to talk and several other couples stopped by to say farewell, too.

Soon, over came Pauline. She put her hand on my arm and said,

"I am going home, now," lifted her head a little defiantly and smiled, without showing her teeth, shrugged her shoulders a little and turned to leave.

I said, "O.K. We'll see you."

After she went out, her girlfriend stayed in the booth. Roy said, "Well, she seemed a little upset. I guess you spoiled her evening."

I didn't say it, but I was a little shook and could have said, "I think she spoiled mine."

Good Friday was a holiday—everywhere; offices, stores and banks were closed. Men were laying the rug in our living room the day before, and they worked straight through without a break. "If we take a break, we have to come back tomorrow", but tomorrow was Good Friday and he told Roy, "God wouldn't like me if I worked Friday".

His ethics otherwise were questionable—or understandable, I guess. He hadn't been working long on the job when he called me in to say, "Madam, I am a professional, and I enjoy my work. But I have found that I do my best if I have tea." So tea was made and served to the three of them. He later explained the "not working tomorrow" so I prepared lunch for the three, with tea and set it on the dining table on the front porch. All the furniture had been rushed out of the house in a hurry when they had unexpectedly arrived about ten, to work. A little later he began to describe a job he had finished the day before; "It was a good job. The lady liked it very much and she gave me a generous tip. She took care of me and I did a fine job for her".

I told him, "You should do a good job anyway."

They had tea again later, and toast and honey and cheese and they did work hard, finishing about 5 p.m. He brought up the tip bit again, and sighed and groaned about working hard, so I gave him some money after all. He went away happy.

It had been a hectic day as Pauline had just finished cleaning and polishing the rooms when they came and tore them apart.

This was also the day my yard boy turned up and I had to set him to work and advise him. He couldn't understand me very well and Joel and I worked along with him some of the time, and I demonstrated what I wanted. He cut branches off the thorn trees and did a great job on grass cutting with the scythe. Between taking him glasses of orange-ade when I saw him wilting outside, and fixing tea and snacks for the indoor men, I began to wonder, who was working for whom?

APRIL 19

We didn't accomplish much on the weekend in the way of yard improvement. One reason was the Pahl family invited us to come out to

Sebele for Easter dinner. Roy turned down their invitation once, saying their family was too big to have more people for the holiday, but happily, they insisted.

Along with the traditional baked ham, the Pahls furnished the warm family atmosphere around the long dining table, that kept us all from being homesick for our families, so far away.

Egg decorating was a bit of a problem but we had a creative time thanks to Bic Felt Tip pens. We did wonders with them. When Joel got exasperated at his results, he peeled the egg and ate it!

One of the children had a book on David Livingstone, so during this day, almost everyone read it. Botswana is his area, and the city Livingstone is just over the border—near Victoria Falls. Jerry pointed out that some of these children's books are a good source of information for adults, as they have many facts simply stated, and cover more ground in a short space than a ponderous book one might not have time to get through.

The kids also had purchased a Setswana beginners book, or dictionary. We all tried some of that.

We had been to a Setswana-English Church Service at 10:30 and our ears were still attuned to the "echo" of Setswana, as one pastor translated immediately, each statement spoken in English by the white-haired pastor.

The service had been in Trinity, a modern white structure whose great glass doors opened into gardens and rising tiers of steps under flower-covered arbors; giving the impression that with the doors open, the whole could expand into a greater church for a huge congregation—some inside, some out. It was ell shaped, with the altar at the juncture, and a choir loft rising up at the left. In back of the altar was a great expanse of wall on which was written in Setswana, in a beautiful script-John 15, 11 through 17. On it was superimposed a black wire cross, extending out somewhat from the wall in the upper left third of the inscription.

The church was packed. We were given a hymn sheet as we entered on which four hymns were written, in Setswana and in English. After initial announcements were made, in both languages, we sang the first hymn. I knew some of the people behind me were singing the English words, yet I could hear others singing in their language. There was a general uncertainty but the Pastor announced that all were to sing and asked that the choir members in the congregation take places in the choir, which they did and then everyone sang, each in his own language, to the same tune. The service was mainly the sermon. One must have something worth saying if another is going to translate it immediately into another language, leaving time for everyone to ponder on the sentence or phrase.

The acoustics weren't too good; I noticed that the roof above the wooden beams was corrugated metal. You had to listen carefully, as there was a tendency to echo—beyond the Setswana echo of the English statements. What a beautiful congregation, predominantly black, of course; fine looking families.

Joel had discovered the National Gallery and Museum; and wanted to show it to us. I had been looking forward to the Botswana Basket Show which had opened there, but Joel kept saying not to go without him. He was excited when we got to church at nine and found the service wouldn't be until ten-thirty.

"Come on over to the Museum—it's open today!"

The Gallery is only a block or two from Trinity; a new, impressive group of buildings so secluded by walls, trees and shrubs, it is easily overlooked.

It too is pure white, reminiscent of California or Florida—lots of windows and sunshine. We stepped up to the entrance, turned left through a huge doorway and were absolutely amazed by the sight of the great white room filled with soft beige and brown baskets—hung in clusters from the rafters, fastened in hundreds on the walls, which they shared with colorful hand woven rugs.

The rugs were of geometrical designs, and of pictures of home or tribal life—or commentaries. One showed a man milking a cow. The cow filled the greater part, the man leaning in front of it. The white streak of milk going in the pail was the only light touch. Above the cow was a calf. The comment posted was that the cow must share its milk with both child and calf.

Many rugs, in full color, showed the rondovals, with families standing as though having their pictures taken. Some big tapestries depicted a whole village and its festivals.

The baskets included current ones, many for sale, and rare ones such as those tightly woven, used for beer containers. They were about three feet high and bigger around than you could circle with your arms.

A potted palm of the type they use for the baskets stood in the center of the room with a description of the entire process. The basket show was enhanced by some striking printed cotton material hung from the rafters, just inside the entrance. I was pleased to see that the material they used was the one I had selected to buy at the Botswana Craft Shop, downtown.

I have yet to buy it, and hope it's still there. I heard yesterday that this combined display came about because neither group, the basket people or the weavers, were able to swing its own display—so they combined. They certainly complemented each other.

We stopped at home after church, to get the Easter eggs and the salads and drove out to Sebele to the Pahls.

Sebele is the Botswana Agricultural College site. After our dinner, we took a walk up through the residential area, occupied mostly by advisers, onto the main "campus", around and through some of their buildings. Jerry says they have quite a few citizens (natives) on their faculty, which is good. It will take a long while to make changes in their way of doing things, as the oldsters are reluctant to part with the traditional.

The boys played tennis, and I cut some hair. There isn't any barber service over here. One beauty shop would do men's hair I've heard, but I offered to do Jerry's, and later trimmed little John, who is six. We were having a good time in the sun just outside the kitchen door, and as John and Mary were standing there bug-eyed, mesmerized by my performance—I turned to them and said, "I'm going to sell tickets, I guess."

John took me seriously and wanted to know "How much are the tickets? How much are the tickets?" I explained I was only fooling, but later he came back, stood a while then piped up "I'll give you a penny for a ticket."

I had brought along a bag of wrapped candy, so the oldest girl hid it in the yard for the kids to have an "egg" hunt when we got back from the walk. That satisfied all of them, except for the ones who thought everyone should put everything they found in a pile and then divide it evenly!

All the Pahl children wanted to have a ride in our pick-up so they piled into the back and Roy took them around the "block" where there are plenty of big humps, ruts, and rough, rough road, to make the trip thrilling—to them. Then we gathered our belongings and headed home.

The Pahls are very happy out there in the country. Alice loves it now and will be very disappointed if they have to move into town. Life is family centered and they share in the work that has to be done and have a general good time. Alice says another thing is that all the residents out there are educators; interesting people, good for the kids.

APRIL 20

Roy had been wanting to go out to the Dam every since we got here so figured this Easter Monday afternoon would be a good time to go see the lake, formed by damming of the Notwane river, and to see the place where the boats are docked. We've seen a few boats around and heard about the "club" at the Marina.

Joel asked Thomas to go along and he got out his rod and tackle though I had reservations about him having anything to do with the fresh water here. Too dangerous; a fact reiterated often by the old hands.

We started without referring to the map but followed Thomas' instructions and were soon going cross-country on one of the worst roads I was ever on; red clay that had been rutted when wet and dried into concrete hardness. The boys were standing in the back of the pick-up and had to keep watch of thorn trees and do quick ducking. At one place water had to be forded. We veered to the right for some unknown reason, and came out fine on the other side.

Thomas was a little uncertain at times but we kept going, though I wondered if we'd ever find our way out again. Soon we saw a rondeval and another thatched roof house, rounded a curve and came to the end of the road. We were at the edge of the river, but there was a great expanse of reeds and marsh between us and the water. No fishing here!

This wasn't the dam area we were looking for, so we wandered off on another road even worse than what we'd been on.

We soon saw a "bridge" ahead of us which consisted of a series of culverts through which the water was rushing and over which there was freshly dumped earth. Roy hesitated only long enough to see that there were cars on the far side and went right at it. Another end of the line, with just room enough to turn around.

We stopped a while though, to see the beautiful stones; huge rounded stones and rocks that formed the channel for this river. Those below the culverts were full of people fishing in the water that rushed out milky grey, as though it were full of sand. We took a few pictures and one young guy stuck his big tongue out as far as possible while we focused on his group, then laughed when we were finished.

Well, the treacherous return trip was waiting, and over the bridge we went again, and then marked off the worst of the road as we covered it. We met a dune buggy and the boys wanted us to wait so they could watch it ford one of the big puddles—and we did.

Back to the original road, we headed to the Water Works; passed an agricultural station where the home grounds were beautifully planted and there were acres of nursery stock in sight. A short distance farther, the Water Works—another dead end!

Roy wouldn't give up, just drove along the outer circle of the town toward the Village, and kept going out the road toward Tlokweng—

supposedly a little village, and the place where there is a border gate to South Africa. He saw another turnoff, and though it said on a sign "Assembly of God Conference Grounds" he started down it—peering off in the general direction of the dam. The road was like a lane, and we soon found ourselves in the midst of a herd of cattle. They blocked the road and didn't intend to move. Big red bulls with horns spanning an arm's reach and others of assorted sizes stared at us. We honked and Joel reached out with his fish rod and poked a bit, and they ambled off docilely—thank heavens.

This was another dead end. We reached a gate, closed, where a lone young man was in the field near a small metal building. He called something to us as we turned around. Thomas reported, "He says, 'Where are you going?'", and we said "Tell him 'nowhere'".

APRIL 25

"Was there any mail?" is usually how we greet Roy when he comes home for lunch or after work. We never really expect any at noon, as the air mail isn't delivered until about 4 p.m. but ask anyway. This week, Tuesday he brought a telegram, but it was for Pauline. "I had to open it, to see if it was for our Pauline. It was addressed to the Department of Taxes," and he told her when he took it down to her, he'd had to open it. It was from her boyfriend, reporting that he had arrived home safely after the Easter weekend. She didn't go home to Molepolole, but her sister "brought my child down" the 66 kilometers—on the bus. Not an easy trip as it's a dirt road all the way. She said the baby hadn't been well, nothing serious though. They had all visited at her cousin's house, in town.

Pauline brought me a package about noon, that day; something long wrapped in newspaper. "This is a present for you." I opened it to find a barbeque fork and tongs. "You shouldn't do that, Pauline."

"Oh, it was part of a set and I don't know what that's for." I explained the tongs would be used to pick up a sausage and turn it.

Friday, I knew she was a little excited about something. She hurried through her work and about 11 a.m., she was running out to the clothesline and feeling if each article were dry enough to bring in to iron. She even ironed some and then hung them out again to finish drying. Then she buzzed around washing paint at doorways and doing extra polishing. Before we were through lunch, she was back in the kitchen washing up everything with a rattling and banging of pots and pans as fast as she could lay her hands on them. Joel had had an early lunch and gone off on a visit, and she polished up after that preparation so fast it made me hesitate to start another round.

Just as we sat down, she said, "I am going to my home this afternoon." I ascertained from her that she would go on the bus from the railroad station at 4 p.m. "But first, I am going to my cousins, in town."

It did occur to me that it was almost two o'clock already, but went on about some chore to do after lunch. All of a sudden she leaned over my shoulder and said, "I want to go to town, now."

I said, "O.K." Then to Roy, "You could give her a lift" and he said, "If she's ready in three minutes."

In two minutes, I looked out toward her house and said, "They're ready, Roy"—There was Pauline, hat and all, and her girlfriend from Rhodesia, with coat on and three suitcases and assorted bundles. The girl came up toward the house and said to me, "I am going home today, Good-bye."

So they piled in all their stuff, and Roy went the longer way across town to let them off near the cousins. How could you put two girls out with all those suitcases?

She knew all along she was going to get a lift at 2:05 and they were ready, right to the last stitch. Well, they'd be dumb if they didn't figure out being ready when a car was going somewhere.

Jerry Pahl drives in from Sebele, and back home to lunch every day too, and he has a number of people who have his schedule all worked out and they're on the spot, at one end or the other, morning, noon, and night. He says he knows he's being used, but he's a good guy and is happy to help them out. He just wishes some of them would take a bath once in a while, if they want to ride with him.

That afternoon there was another letter for Pauline. This one from someone in Lobotse. It's still waiting for her. We had a friend for dinner today who is going back to England, Friday. He laughed about the letter, said "Roy was pleased to have his name called at mail time, then one look and it was for the maid! Some letdown!"

Well she lives here on this lot. This is her address now so there's no reason she shouldn't get her mail through us. Going to be all right as long as she doesn't get more mail than we do!

Friday was a traumatic day for Joel. When Roy went out to open the gate at 7:30 to go to the office, there was a boy who came into the yard and wanted something. He couldn't speak English and Roy told him we have a yard boy, we didn't need any help. He didn't understand

English either, and kept saying something and pointing to the big stacks of thorn tree branches in the yard. Then I thought I had it figured out. He probably wanted the wood. Many people throw the branches over their fences, out in the space between fence and the street so people who want the wood drag the branches out and chop off what they want. I've often watched them do this and admired their pluck at wrestling the thorny branches. A few days earlier I had tossed a big branch over, as well as a sizeable stack of trimmed sticks. Toward evening, a truck stopped across the road and a well dressed man called to me and asked if he might have the wood. "If you need it", I answered. I didn't have time to say that he was more prosperous looking than I had visualized my taker would be, but let it go.

So, I made sawing motions questioningly, to the boy and he nodded. Still in my housecoat, I got out the saw, the gloves, demonstrated how to use the saw and he went to work. The regular boy, John arrived at 8:30 and looked a little puzzled at the other one at work. John doesn't understand a darn thing either; I have to have Pauline instruct him when I need to have him do or not do something.

When Joel went out, he joined the new boy and worked with him steadily. Toward 10:30 a.m., Pauline said "Madam, he doesn't want the wood, he just wants to work". The boy then had given up. He sat in a lawn chair near the kitchen door. I tried to have him take the wood. He wasn't interested. I got him two big slices of bread and jelly and peanut butter and made him orange juice, then went to get him some money. Pauline gets one Rand for all day; the garden boy gets one rand for 4 hours work, so I didn't figure he had one Rand coming. I gave him all the change I could scrounge up—60 cents. A few minutes later, Joel came in and said, "Boy, he wasn't very happy about that pay. He was almost crying." He stormed into his room crying and saying "Boy, everybody's not rich, you know!!" He was good and mad and called out, "I thought at least you'd give him a Rand". So I said, "All right, Joel. Take a Rand and go give it to him and get back the change." Though I explained again, the other's pay. He ran out and was soon back red-faced from the heat. "I'm going to take my bicycle and look for him". A crowd in the yard, especially John, who always loves to have something interrupt his grass cutting, pointed out which way they thought he had gone. Off went Joel, not returning until twenty minutes later. Still mad he couldn't find him. "Maybe he lives right nearby. He probably went inside somewhere. You'll see him again."

He was so upset he had lost all interest in plans he had to ride his bike to Roy's office at noon, ride with Jerry Pahl out to Sebele to visit his friends and come back with the family in the evening to Trinity Church where we would all go to hear the Messiah.

He finally cooled off a bit and decided to go ahead, and I was glad he did, as I felt if he got away from here he'd forget about the boy a little. He lost his way going to the office; probably travelled twice the distance he should have, and was exhausted by the heat when he did finally get there. Roy brought the bike home and Joel went on for a fun afternoon, though he had told Roy all about "it" as soon as he saw him. I guess he got so involved because he had worked with the boy, and because the boy wasn't much bigger than he.

Well, for a happy ending, all of a sudden right after breakfast Saturday morning, there was the boy and perhaps his mother. They gathered up two big bundles of wood; I got out some big plastic strips for tying up. Joel got 40 cents and ran out to give the boy. The lady said "Thank you, Joel" when they left. The boy had heard us calling him that while he was here. The lady popped her bundle of wood up on her head and they started away. Just then Joel disappeared too, though we were ready to go to town. Finally he came back—just in time to get reprimanded again—for disappearing. He had been intent on finding out where the boy lived. "It's somewhere out near the new housing area. She left the wood at a friend's house." It wasn't an area of abject poverty, so he felt better and I did too.

Yesterday afternoon, I sat and studied the crowds on the Mall. Most offices had closed and people were hurrying home, or doing last minute shopping at the places not yet closed.

Roy had brought me in, in the truck, to get fixtures for the drapes I was making. We found the gadgets, downstairs at the Hardware store. This place is unique. Anything in the world you might need for your home, yard, car, bike or hobby is there, somewhere; lovely bone china, every plastic container designed, kitchen utensils, doormats, paper products and firecrackers. Run by a Chinese family, it is on two floors and is one mad jumble spilling out into the aisles. Nooks and corners and alcoves are packed, but if you don't see it, you ask for it and they magically make it appear.

As the clerk handed us the package, Roy asked, "Oh, do you have kickstands for bicycles?" We wanted one for Joel's bike, but I hadn't noticed that many bikers used them. Without moving a step, the clerk bent his knees, reached under the counter and lifted out three varieties. I could hardly believe it!

While Roy went into another store, I sat on a low brick wall, the outer edge of a planter that encircles the whole plaza. The wall, filled with low blooming shrubs, has openings, here and there, where wide steps lead from the walks in front of the stores, to the open, dusty plaza. There are a few gnarled thorn trees towards the corners which lend shade for stalls that are sometimes set up for an open market. People sit on the wall, both inside and out, to rest, wait for friends, or just "hanging around". It's very convenient and pleasant with all the greenery and flowers.

I watched and listened to the varied crowd milling by. I could immediately spot new arrivals; the British couple in immaculate white shirt and trousers, she in khaki wrap-around skirt and good leather shoulder bag. There's a bearded American with rugged tanned legs, shorts, back-pack and sleeping bag. Girls in the gold uniforms of Maru-a-Pula High School, Indian shop keepers just closing up, Indian women in Saris, their girls in school uniforms, and well dressed business men. One unusually fat man, whose pants must have been a 50″ waist, with no belt. Just as he passed me, the pants slipped a bit, so he gave them a hike and let his stomach out a little, to hold them in place. There were mothers with babies on their backs, just the way the Koreans carried them; a blanket tied around, knotted in front or fastened with a safety pin. There were attractive fashionably-dressed girls, just leaving their office jobs, and many young men, all with close-cropped hair. A girl passed with a corn row hairdo, and something about her seemed odd. I studied her a minute then realised her scalp was white; she wasn't a black girl! I looked around to see how the other heads looked.

Then I realised that in all this whole country, I had not seen an "Afro" do. All the men have their hair closely cropped; the women have it close cropped or in a neat braided arrangement. I thought to myself, "If that isn't just like Americans, who always seem to overdo everything. The young blacks want so much to claim their African heritage, that they have all overdone and outdone the Africans."

Boy, I'm going to tell my yard boy to stay home a few days. I need a rest. He's all right to set at cutting grass with a sickle, if there's enough to keep him busy for hours, but if there are things to be done for which he needs instruction, it surely takes time.

We finally built a hugh fire yesterday afternoon and fed it with the now dried thorn tree branches. There was a real mountain of them, and they certainly detracted from the looks of the place, no matter how we improved the other areas around the house.

This morning all there was left was a heap of ashes. We got a wheelbarrow yesterday at last, and I showed John what to rake up of the leftovers, and to carry it all down into the back corner behind the storage shed.

A few minutes later, I saw smoke rising there, and flames—so had to run for Joel and Pauline, the hose and buckets all at once. He had begun his morning's work by shovelling up a wheelbarrow of hot coals and dumping them right on the side of the hay pile. Joel saved it in time, and we wet the area down and dragged the hot ashes and coals to one side. Of course there was bare ground nearby that would have taken them safely.

My mornings when I could close myself in this room and concentrate for a few hours are no more. I have to keep track of John every minute.

On the Mall, the other day, Joel rushed over to say, "There's a good picture" just as three or four young girls passed, each with a bag of mealie meal on her head. It was an especially good picture, with the repetition of the bag, at different heights and the girls dressed in bright colors. But they disappeared into the crowd and the scene changed as quickly as a kaleidoscope.

Each day someone has a story of what they have seen on a woman's head, thinking that the nth degree has been reached. But we still see new, unusual ones.

Roy and I were sitting in back of the house and looked up just in time to see a lady passing by with a huge sack of potatoes on her head. She was knitting steadily as she walked, holding her work up high enough in front of her to watch the stitches. It wasn't the first time I had seen someone knitting as she walked, but the first with a sack of potatoes on her head at the same time.

Alice Pahl reported, "I saw a girl down near White City, with a coffee table upside down on her head and it was piled with a number of other articles and some of her shopping."

Roy put in, "Well, I was down on the Mall yesterday and saw a girl carrying a watermelon on her head." We were all duly impressed by this accomplishment when he topped it with, "But it wasn't crosswise. It was up on one end! She just walked along with it balanced straight up!"

A group of people passed the house the other day all chattering pleasantly and one of the women had a metal bound box on her head which was fully the size of a footlocker. She turned her head in conversing with the rest, and though it pivoted once in a while, it never swayed too far in any direction.

Pails of water, tin cans, plastic bottles of kerosene, sacks of all kinds of food are some of the things casually carried, right here in the city, on the heads of the women, even some with babies on their backs.

One day Alice and I saw a young woman with the biggest suitcase in the world on her head. Alice spied her and said, as she was driving, "See if she has a hand on that." She didn't, but she did have a baby on her back, an umbrella in one hand to protect her from the noontime sun, while the other hand hung free at her side.

Every day brings a new version of a unique load on some woman's head and for each, I have only the deepest admiration.

APRIL 28

Last Tuesday I had a good time. Roy dropped me off at the top of the Mall as he returned to work after lunch. I had his camera and all afternoon, what was left of it, as it was now after two.

My first stop was the Botswana Book Shop. What a fun place. It had everything you might need for school, your desk, hobbies and crafts or study, along with reference books, best sellers, newspapers, and gifts. I was amazed at the wealth of material. I leisurely meandered up one aisle and down the other. By the time I got back to the beginning I had an armful of publications.

One, *Safari to Serowe* tells not only the history and life of Serowe, a tribal village north of us, but that of the whole country.

Serowe was a cattle post until Khama, tribal chief, made it the headquarters for his Ngwato tribe in 1902. This is the city that was a possible post for Roy but is the place that Ben Webb will be working when he arrives next month.

I found two books about Khama. He was born in 1838, son of the Chief of the Ngwato tribe. He was baptized a Christian in 1862. This led to complications, as the chief is responsible for carrying on the tradition of the tribe, many of which were performed by him alone. So his career as a chief for fifty years was a stormy one, but evidently he was a great and strong man and ruled well; was instrumental in preserving his country, as a protectorate of Great Britain when it could have been swept up as part of Rhode's South Africa Company lands, or made part of the Union of South Africa. He died in 1923. We saw a bust of him at the National Gallery on Easter Sunday morning and assumed he might be the father of the current President, Sir Seretse Khama. However, these two books don't note anything about his descendent other than his son Sehkoma.

I've enjoyed reading about him and surprizingly enough, today's

government Daily News was the issue of the week that had the letters
to the Editor in it. One impassioned writer covered the same facts that
I had just read; about the influence of missionaries Moffat and McKen-
zie on Khama, and their roles as policital advisers as well as spiritual, but
the conclusions and accusations were that it was all done as preface to
colonialism; a movement to make the people believe that the Setswana
customs and dress were evil, that only the western ways were good. He
was quite vehement in his opinion that none of the missionary influence
was of any good for the country. I had just been learning that there had
been a strong influence, through Khama, and was very impressed by its
long range effects, and then this letter expressed a contrary opinion.
Well, at least I knew what he was talking about and a week ago, I hadn't
even heard of Khama.

With these books, a compass for Joel's math work and a local paper
from Mafeking, I went on down the Mall to the USIS Library, near the
embassy, got a new book of short stories, read the newspapers and a
TIME, then went on to the Trinity Church, to take pictures of the
grounds and interior.

Although I have only used the USIS library, I know the National
Library, next to the Museum is really extensive. They have a separate
children's library and when the Pahls come to town, they make a bee
line for it and all seven children load up with volumes to their liking.

The day after this expedition, they all came in and we took an
excursion through the Basket Show and Museum and did the Zoo.
What seemed to cause the most excitement among the little ones was a
hugh spider web between two of the animal cages, with a great big ugly
spider. We all just carefully ducked under it and advised all to steer clear.

Later when we picked the youngsters up at the library where they
stayed while the mothers did a little grocery shopping, each wanted to
show the books he had selected. Little Patty, the youngest, had a skinny
book on which the bright yellow cover was inscribed with a big black
spider web and a hugh spider! We had a good laugh, knowing well why
she was drawn to that book.

Well, after I finished my roll of film, there wasn't much to do but
head on home. I came by all the back paths, as Joel had taught me,
recognizing I was on the right way by the yards and flower gardens I
had seen before. It's about a mile or so and was a hot sunny day. Pauline
saw me coming into the yard and hurried from her little house with the
key, to let me in my front door. Pauline never has to be told what to do.
She has good sense. I hadn't told her to lock up, but Joel was off playing,
and when she finished her chores, she locked up and watched for me.

When Margaret Rowe, our new British friend, ran into us right after Easter, she made a specific date for Alice and me to come out to her home in the Village for the morning. We had met her when we were all new arrivals at the Inn. The Village is the older, original part of this town, a short distance from where the new planned city is now built, but connected to it by one of the main roads.

Her home was fascinating. The long bumpy red clay drive circled on into the yard and we found ourselves passing masses of flowers, shrubs, rock gardens and hedges before we reached the front entrance, actually a side entry onto a porch. The house is a style they don't build any longer here, but I'm sure it's one of the coolest during the summer.

The entire perimeter is porches; actually rooms under the house roof, with windows screened instead of glazed. The bedrooms each open onto one of these "Khondas" as she said they are called in Malawi, but the rooms don't open into each other.

For security, each bedroom has to be locked, which is not too satisfactory with small children in the family, and, there is no way to the bathroom except first out into the Khonda.

The living room was a huge mausoleum in the very center; no windows except to the khonda at one end. The dining room proved to be the only cozy room but it was separated from the kitchen by a huge storage pantry; there was no possibility of having the storage room secure. It was designed to be cool and comfortable (though the cold is a problem in the winter season) and not for other kinds of efficiency. The khondas all had concrete floors, painted dark red and waxed. I thought it was pretty neat to have the khonda adjacent to each room but Alice thought she'd never be able to live in such a house.

Margaret gave us much practical advise on health matters, from her experiences in Malawi; all about tick fever, malaria, and belharzia and the necessity for staying away from all fresh water.

Margaret is really a unique person. She knows where everything is, what's going on, and she's in the middle of it all.

"Have you been to the craft center, in the Industrial Area? I'll stop and take you over when I go for the children's sweaters. I found I could have then knit over there at the BEDU establishment for less than buying them at the Mall." BEDU is a program of small business development under Dr. Chiepe, Minister of Commerce and Industry, the woman member of the President's Cabinet. Handcrafts of all sorts are encouraged; the government has provided space and materials and markets the things people can make.

When we left, she said, "I'll stop in and see you on Friday when I come to the school to pay the fees."

True to her word, Friday morning she and her young son appeared to pick me up. We arrived in a cloud of dust at BEDU, for the main roads down through the Industrial area are not surfaced. Three rows of pale blue concrete-block buildings, housed the work rooms. A bright sign on each identified the craft inside. First was "Sunday Clothes", then "Bokatela Fashions", then the knit shop, which we went into for Keith's sweater.

The room was about twenty feet square, had two small knitting machines and one large one on which a number of meters of grey knit was completed. Four or five women were at work hemmed in by stacks of open cartons of yarn. Huge spools in every color filled shelves behind the knitting machines. It was a jumble in close quarters, with the public coming in, also, to do ordering and buying. Shelves along the wall just to the left of the entrance, were filled to overflowing with "freshly knit" sweaters, all ranged as to sizes and colors of the various school uniforms. Royal blue of Northside was on the top, then green of Thornhill, and the maroons and golds of the other town and secondary schools, and the Camp school in the village. The lady pointed out the ones for Mochudi, which is miles away.

"Oh yes, we do them for schools even in Maun. My only problem, I can't get them to get me the orders soon enough ahead. The teachers wait until they collect all the money, send it at once and want all the sweaters. Here in town, they give me an idea, and I get a lot ready. Now, for him? She reached to the pile in the second grade size, "Oh, we're all sold out again." "Sold out! I was here on Monday and you said to come later in the week!"

"Well, lets see. Try this one. Sleeves are a little long. Here, she will fix it." She peeled the sweater off Keith, took it to the lady at the sewing machine behind a table piled high with luscious colored sweaters in all styles from babies to men's cardigans, in various stages of completion. I looked at the big cardboard patterns marked for different sizes, and the price list on the wall. Prices seemed determined only by size, not style; you made your selection and they made the sweater; one price.

Just then, the lady had finished resetting the sleeves and Keith tried it on again. It was fine.

We lingered at another shop to watch an older lady and girl creating wicker ware; their long loops of cane soaking in a huge tub. Much of it was done on a black wire base, making magazine racks, coffee and end tables; very attractive and not expensive.

The next room was jewelry and for a minute I thought I was back in Germany at Idar Oberstein. Just one young girl was working and she quoted prices of items on display while the slosh of the stone-polishing churn ground away in the background.

We went through several other rooms, and the morning was getting away. I bought a school bag, of natural cotton, stamped with "I support local industries, BEDU", as a souvenir for Joel.

There was striking material in the shop where they made curtains; the kind you can't find when you're looking for it for yourself. On the work table was spread a tablecloth, about two meters long of a blue and green design, with green fringe all around. Margaret asked, "How much would that cloth be?"

The man replied, "That's what I'm trying to estimate right now. See, it is double," and the girl flipped it back to show a plain green reverse.

"She can use it either side, and there's fringe all around."

"Well, in the vicinity of what?"

"About Rand 15, I guess."

We admired it and went our way. Funny thing, yesterday morning when the Pahls were here, I was telling Alice about our visit to the craft center, and she said,

"Oh, yes, I ordered a tablecloth and it should be done about now."

"Blue and green, reversible, with a fringe?"

"Yes."

"We saw it and asked the man how much it would be."

"How much did he say?"

Jerry looked around, aghast, and said, "How could you order something not knowing how much it's going to cost?"

We said, "Easy!"

MAY 11

My yard boy finally got the better of me. It wasn't a happy ending for either of us. I went to bed and sobbed; cried because I was sorry for him. I know how much the Rand 1 a day means to him. I know he was happy here—puttering along, stopping for a couple slabs of bread and jam mid-morning, then finishing up at noon with a day's wages pocketed—whistling off home. Later, he would breeze by the house, heading for town, wearing a white shirt and waving.

But there was work to be done. There were beds to be spaded. He didn't like to spade. He wouldn't touch a shovel or spade. He dabbled with a spading fork, raked and sprinkled. I demonstrated one day, how to spread the lawn clippings on the area under the tree, then take the spade and turn it over. "I will plant plants in it." He understood that, as I showed him. Two places were to be done and the pailful of ferns was waiting nearby. When I came home from shopping, after noontime, the two beds looked beautiful. "I can plant the ferns now!" I started to make a place to set one in and ran into concrete. I scraped back some of the soil and came to lawn clippings. They were spread on the ground as I had shown him, but over it he had spread some loose soil, maybe from close to the tree where it was less packed down. Determined to plant my ferns, I attacked the whole with my spade. I spaded till the sweat ran off me—on and on. That was on a Friday. Well, I'd just have to work along with him and keep watch. Monday I began early and spaded till I could hardly get lunch on. Next day I worked again, and as the yard and beds began to take shape, I was more and more enthusiastic. I had plants and showed him how to set them in, after my preparation, although I felt he was getting the "fun" part of the work.

Later, I showed him how to spade up a weedy place, shake off the dirt, put the weeds in the wheelbarrow and empty the wheelbarrow down in the corner. He used a hoe and cut them off, shovelled up more soil than weeds.

Alice stopped to take me to the Mall for groceries, mid-morning, so I told John to keep on weeding and to put into the shade a batch of plants a man had brought me.

Upon my return, I was aghast to find the new plants were lying in the sun. I was so mad I began again at top speed to spade the new area, get plants in and trim off the thorn tree branches. One huge one got caught in among its own branches and I struggled to exhaustion vainly trying to get it down. Later, Joel helped, and I cut off more small branches, standing on tiptoes, and we finally pulled with all our might, swinging on one until it gave way all of a sudden, both of us landing on the lawn—colliding with the front of the wheelbarrow.

Anyway, I kept at it, more enthused all the while by the cut edges of the turf, the newly designed drive, the stone edges, the grass seed in, and the lines stretched for cutting other lawn edges. Finally, on the point of exhaustion, I was ready to collect my tools and head for dinner making. Roy drove in and said, "I thought I'd do a little lawn mowing." My heart sank. I had just had Joel working with me to pull the weeds in the front lawn before they got cut again. So I hurriedly pulled as fast as I could, just keeping ahead of the mower—round and round. Then I moved the hose to the side yard, to get it out of the way of the mower, so watered the beds with it at the same time. Finally—in and to the dinner.

A quick cleanup afterwards and I hopped into bed by seven. I read but felt uneasy and made a cup of tea and later ate a pear. I woke at 4 a.m., my mind a turmoil over John. If he was to be of any use, I'd have to work with him all morning. Otherwise, there wasn't anything now he could do for me. Joel uses the mower, and should be doing yard chores, I would enjoy doing my gardening, at the times that were right for me. This way, my mornings were gone. I had no time for writing, and I hate to be paying him so much in front of Pauline, who really does a days work, who has common sense and is trustworthy. I feel sorry for him, but is he what my life is supposed to be dedicated to? On and on I tossed and turned and felt worse by the minute until I finally decided to make a try for the bathroom. I got there just in time to throw up, and when it was over for the moment, I couldn't get up again. My back was really conked out. The rest of the night was more of the same and I didn't seem to know where I was.

Thank God for Pauline. I told her she'd make a wonderful nurse. When she came in I was on my stomach, crosswise of the bed, hanging over a wastebasket. She knew all the things you need to have done for you in these circumstances. She held shoulders as you wretched, brought a glass of water, hauled me around on the bed and stuffed my feet back under the covers, changed the pillow cases and darkened the windows, asked me if I'd like a cup of tea. That I refused, as I told her, it was what I'd had just before I began to throw up. It was comforting to hear her working in the rest of the house.

I asked her to tell John not to come the next day. I wanted to have her say, "not ever again", but knew that was my job.

It was good to get some sleep and look forward to a day without a garden boy to supervise. I wallowed in my freedom and veered in my mind back and forth between getting rid of him permanently, or letting Roy have him on Saturdays or arranging a day or so a week. But I tried to put him out of my mind and rest. Of course it wasn't his fault that I get so involved in projects that I go faster and faster and can't stop. Alice said on Wednesday, "Come on out Friday with Margaret and spend the morning." I said, "Oh, I'll be deep in my yard work." and she replied, "Oh, that can wait. It'll always be there".

Little did we realise that by Friday, I would be laid out—all my own fault for not letting it wait.

I crept around Friday, by noon, and found that Pauline had everything spotless and had the table set for lunch in the kitchen. I even eased out the front door to see the garden progress and was disgusted to find that John had trundled the wheelbarrow away, leaving two big piles of weeds there in the garden. So, the balance was one sided again, way off to "Get rid of him". The town is full of competent boys asking every day for work, or I'll do my own.

Monday morning I heard John come. I had told Pauline to tell John he had done a fine job cutting the grass, but I wouldn't need him now. Everything was done. But, I joined her as soon as I heard her talking with him. He was taking out the tools from the pantry as usual and he stopped at the door as I said, "No John. All finished. No more work", and waved my hands, with spread fingers.

John, standing there in his khaki shirt and pants, Boer hat, and bare feet, practically went into shock. He stared at me with his great, big, black eyes, wide in disbelief and hurt. So I half relented and said to Pauline, "Tell him for weeks, there's no work. All done. Maybe later, a few days a week. I hired him to cut the tall grass and paid by the day and it's done."

I couldn't stand his eyes and plowed on back through the hall and went to bed and cried.

MAY 12

I was closing the front gate the other morning, after Roy drove out, and before I got the second half pulled around, there appeared under my nose a grinning little boy, seeming ready to burst.

"Kenneth!" I said, "Where did you come from? When did you get home?"

He kept on grinning, tickled to death to have surprised me.

"Come on in. Joel is getting ready for breakfast."

He walked in the front door with me, and Joel, coming down the hall, stopped dead in his tracks. He stared at Kenneth, speechless.

"Yes. It's Kenneth. He got home this morning".

I thought they'd fall into each other's arms. They looked and looked at each other and grinned and laughed.

Kenneth said, "We haven't only been at the cattle post. We went to Serowe to see my Mother. She works at the hospital there."

We were surprised that his mother lived up there, and never did know where his father lived; Kenneth once mentioned something about his working at the Teacher Training College. Batswana are so softspoken, one must listen carefully to catch all that's said.

At lunch, Roy told Joel he could take Kenneth and Edwin to the movies that evening as guests. Joel went to tell Kenneth and there ensued a flurry of excitement and activity as Kenneth's older sister had already started for town to pick up tickets for the boys.

"But my dad is going to get them!" Joel told him, and jumped on his bike and pedaled furiously towards the hospital where the sister was going to work; caught her in time to tell her the tickets would be bought by Dad.

As Kenneth and Edwin waited for movie time that evening, they sat poring over the booklets about Botswana that I had purchased on my first expedition to the Mall, especially the one about Serowe. They studied every page, and got excited about pictures of places and buildings they had just seen. They like to pick this one up, every time they come in. When I see these youngsters reading a book in English, I am overcome with admiration. Think how much they have learned; their own language, Setswana, the spoken language of about two million people, now written in our alphabet by missionary Robert Moffit, father-in-law of Livingstone, in the early 1800's, then they go to school and learn another one, English, and study in it. I have come to the conclusion that Kenneth has had much schooling and will have more; that this is an interim "hanging around" period.

When they came home from the movies, Roy was shaking his head. Not only had he taken the boys, but sisters of various ages had caught a lift with him too, which was all right, but after the show, "They all kept piling in the back of the truck!"

"I was in the front with Kenneth," Joel piped up, "And I watched through the window and counted all of them that got in. There were 15!"

"That back was so full", Roy continued, "That I just crept along and hung on going around curves; I had the feeling the front end was going to lift right off the road."

We never left the theatre without a truckful or later a car full of passengers. No matter how packed the parking lots on the outer rims of the Mall, or which one we parked in, invariably, when ready to leave, we would find a contingent of our young neighbors looking for a lift, and of course, we always gave it to them. Joel used to wonder who some of them were and if they did live near.

The extended family next door called on me often, for first aid, bandaids, aspirin, needles and thread, use of the phone, which we didn't have, or rides in emergencies. I didn't always recognise all the people who greeted me during the Interval at the theatre but I returned the smiles and assumed each was another member of the family next door.

Roy came home to lunch the other day all excited about a young couple who had come into the tax office that morning.

"They walked in, each carrying a motorcycling helmet; she had a long skirt, to the ground, and long dark hair. They came down yesterday from Serowe on a motorbike.

"Let's see—he's American, Joseph Whistler, and she's Canadian—Heather. He's teaching secondary school in Serowe, commercial subjects, and since he wanted to teach about taxes, decided to come down to the country's headquarters and get correct information and some forms and materials for his classes. He said she had been teaching, too, but they wouldn't pay her, so she quit."

"Boy, you have to hand it to them," he went on, "they found they couldn't afford the house they started out in, so now they're in a rondavel, with no electricity, and they carry their water some distance from a borehole."

I said, "That's sounds almost like camping".

"Yes, I think they're great. They really seemed enthusiastic and happy about their situation; said there's lots of good housing up there but few can afford it."

A couple days later, I dashed into the Co-op for some groceries. As I leaned over the frozen food case, looking for some orange juice, I caught sight of two motorcycle helmets moving past the other side of the freezer. I looked up to see a blonde young man and a husky dark haired girl.

"Oh, are you the couple down from Serowe, to visit the Tax Department?" I asked without a second's hesitation.

"Yes."

"Well, I'm Elizabeth Brown, wife of the assessor you talked with there. He told me about you; was very impressed with your situation."

They smiled and I asked, "How long are you staying?"

"Oh, three or four years, I guess," he answered.

She laughed and said, "Only a couple of days, here. That's what you meant."

"Yes, do you have a place to stay?"

"Oh, yes. We're on our way to friends for lunch, then to someone else's for dinner tonight. We're all set."

Then we talked about how "civilized" it was here in Gaborone; just doesn't take too much adjusting to. They agreed there was a great difference in being in Serowe.

"If you see something there, you have to buy it at once—you may never see it again. But we really enjoy it. No T.V. We enjoy the absence of things."

"Well, good luck to you." I said and they went on down through the store looking at things, but I didn't see them buy anything.

So that night when Roy got home, I told him that I had met his young couple from Serowe and I agreed with him that they were refreshing and admirable.

I can always tell when Pauline has some special plans. Instead of neglecting anything, to make a fast getaway, she works like mad. Rushes around scrubbing and then washing clothes and ironing with such energy, I tell her, "Pauline, slow down and have a cup of tea."

That was the way it was one day this week. I was still dragging, and lying on my bed reading a good many hours a day. Her cousin stopped in and sat in the kitchen while Pauline ironed. I thought Joel had said her cousin with her baby. So, I went out into the kitchen to see the baby, but it was no where in sight.

"Oh, I thought the baby was here", and they laughed and the cousin leaned forward and a little to one side, and there was the little doll, sound asleep, slung on her mother's back.

Later, I saw some other ladies going down the drive, but Pauline stuck to her chores to the last minute, with more than necessary accomplished before she hurried down to get lunch for her aunt and relatives.

Later in the afternoon, she tapped on my bedroom door and came in. She was dressed in jeans, a turtleneck and a denim jacket, and was carrying her cousin's baby on her back. The baby is Bonsho. It is the prettiest little girl with tiny gold loop earrings. I went out and took some pictures of Pauline and the baby; they were both so beautiful.

The day after I was so sick, when Pauline played nurse for me in the morning, I was roused by her tapping at the bedroom door. She was dressed to go out, and had a sheaf of papers in her hand.

"Could you help me with these?"

I took them and asked her to get my glasses. Things were a blur enough, even with them, at this stage. I read what she had. She had made application to a secretarial school here, to take elementary typing beginning July 19. They asked Rand 1 to submit this application; also had blanks to submit documentation of fulfillment of prerequisites. This was what she wanted help on. As they didn't specify any for the beginning typing, I gave her what advise I could, and told her to bring my pocketbook from the dresser. I only had a Rand 2, so told her she'd have to get it changed. She thanked me and I dozed off again and suddenly she was there handing me a crisp Rand 1. She had dashed over to the maid next door, made her transaction over the fence there, and got change.

I told her where to get a stamp, where Roy had been doing some letters, and she went off happy. First thing, I asked her, "Is this course in the day or the evening?" Then I noticed it said, from 7:45 to 9:45 p.m. I wasn't up to facing the possibility of life without Pauline.

I have started putting birdseed out on the patio each morning; no feeder, I just toss out a handful. The birds are already waiting for it. The first day, about 16 yellow birds came. I thought I'd take a picture of them, but decided I'd wait until they got used to coming and some morning I'd sit nearby, with the camera, and get a closeup. Well, birds have kept coming back, but not the yellow ones! The little blue ones do come though, and yesterday, I was happy to find they are not the culprits we had assumed they were. They are not the wicked birds who drive the farmers mad. I couldn't see how these pretty little delicate creatures, such a lovely blue green color could be a menace.

Friday's paper had a news item on the quelea bird about which we had been misinformed. Now we hear it is a bird about the size of a pigeon.

I have been collecting interesting stories from the Daily News, the government publication, mostly for the unusual expressions. Here is the one about the birds.

> Some Bokalaka farmers have abandoned their fields following a complete swoop on their crops by quelea birds. According to reports from the area those who still have some crops left are forced to harvest them before they are ripe, to save them from the notorious birds.

> Many sorts of methods are being used to try to chase the birds away—some people beat drums, others open their record players full-blast and yet others run from one part of the field to the other from 6 a.m. to 6 p.m. shouting their lungs out.

> They take their breakfast, lunch and evening meals at the fields. Some reports in fact suggest that the people have no time to cook their meals. And as if this were not enough, recent rains have added to the farmer's troubles—by causing the prematurely harvested crops to germinate or rot.

> The better-off people are those who planted more maize than

other crops. Other lucky farmers are those in the Northeast District where the birds have not yet come in as large numbers.

So far no one knows where the quelea colony is settled, although some people are busy trying to trace the birds camps in order to destroy them and hopefully scare them away.

Farmers whose prematurely reaped crops are not rotting—because of the rains—have been advised to buy insecticides—to save them from these other lurking destroyers.

We can appreciate the seriousness of the bird's destruction, but we had to smile at the way this describes the people shouting their lungs out—and it's not in the least bit funny.

MAY 17

When Roy came in Friday afternoon, he said,
"Does John live somewhere near here?"
"John who?" knowing full well who he was talking about.
"The garden boy, John."
"Perhaps." I didn't even want to hear John mentioned.
"I took Gaobakwe out to the Golf Club after work and I saw John working out there. He waved and grinned like an idiot when he saw me. I could see him talking like mad to a friend and pointing to me, and I smiled and nodded to him. He was wearing his Boer hat. So I gave him a ride to the Mall and then dropped him off out here at the gate."
I can't remember what I said to that, but no one knows how happy I was to hear that John was working somewhere, and that he didn't nag Roy for some work, or to come back. Margaret assured me the day I was so upset over letting him go, that he would get another job right away. This really makes my heart sing though, for if he is working I won't have to worry about him at all.
Today, when I was out poking in a few more ferns under the trees near the carport, I even grew so bold as to entertain thoughts of trying out another one of these boys who comes asking for work. I'll ask him if he can spade over some dirt, with a little muscle, and hire him for one day.

MAY 24

This was the day to be at the airport at 1:25. Right on the dot, the Zambia Airways plane came in from Lusaka. We were outside leaning on the fence in the bright sunshine, watching closely to see Ben Webb and his wife and daughter. Ben was in New York with us, but not his wife, so we were anticipating meeting her. Conjecturing ahead of time, Jerry closed off our women's discussion about what she might be like, by saying, "Ben's a fine man and I'm sure his wife will be someone you'll like."

I thought I saw an old friend, as they approached, and when Ben said, "This is Viola", and we all shook hands, both Roy and I agreed that we had never seen anyone who was such an exact replica of someone else.

"She's the image of June Hinz," Roy said—just what I had been thinking. Driving over to the Inn with their luggage in the back of our pick-up, he said, "Do you suppose she is Finnish?"

"Well, I'll bet she is. They just came from Duluth, Minnesota, and a lot of Finnish people settled there."

After arriving at the Inn in the company of Jerry and Alice Pahl, the Commissioner of Taxes, the Deputy Commissioner, Roy, Joel and myself, we all sat down to talk a while. Joel took their daughter, Damaris, into the dining room for lunch and we women had cokes and listened to reports of travels from Viola, while the men caught up on the Tax Department.

Inasmuch as Ben is black and she white, they did not come by way of South Africa; rather, landed in Abajan, Ivory Coast, the western side of Africa then went on to Tanzania.

In Dar es Salaam, where they had previously done a four year tour, they went to the beach and neglected to lock their car. Stolen were her bag, with billfold and charge cards, travellers checks, notes, pictures, addresses and jewelry. Also, Ben's new camera and I don't know what else. That would put a crimp in anyone's holiday. Damaris piped up on all sorts of details about it "all being in the trunk of the car and they didn't even take Daddy's watch which was in the car seat," etc. She's a little extrovert, full of life and chatting continually. They had gone then to Lusaka, Zambia and down here to Gaborone, where we all assured them, everything would be great. Of course, we don't know what their life will be in Serowe, but we thought we'd be encouraging anyway.

Sometime after three, the office force went to work, and the Pahls took the new family down for a quick tour of the Mall to see what's available. Roy dropped me off and I got my glasses repaired and shopped around, intermittently joining the rest. Joel and Dameris went their way buying firecrackers in the hardware and two little furry Baboons in the Botswana Shop.

Strolling along the Mall, I finally got a chance to ask Viola if she were of Finnish extraction.

"Why, yes I am Finnish."

"Well, you look exactly like a Finnish friend of mine, so I was almost sure."

"My name was Wainio."

"Well, our town in Connecticut has a great number of Finnish families", and I rattled off some names.

"You don't live near Pomfret Center, do you? I have relatives there." I told her it was just ten miles north of me.

There's never a time that you can discontinue saying the trite, "Isn't it a small world?"

The Webbs will be moving over here to stay with us a few days, until more space opens at the Inn. With Pauline here to keep everything clean and organised it shouldn't be too hard.

My Pauline is really something. Last Friday I was feeling lousy and the electricity was off. I went back to bed and read and slept. I had dozed off, but was roused by a tap on the door, and Pauline came in saying,

"Here is some coffee, madame." She had a tray with mug and cream and sugar, and handed me the instant coffee to put what I wanted into the boiling hot water. She had gone down to her little house and heated water for me on her parafin stove. I was just that weak and miserable that as soon as she went out, I cried. It just doesn't pay to do nice kind things for me—I dissolve.

We went shopping in South Africa that day; left home late afternoon. I was just about hauled together, but in a way I was ready. The sun was still bright and I was packed—in my handbag and Roy's zip case; the bare essentials. We were only going as far as Mafeking, (South to Lobatse 49 miles, then straight south another 49) and planned to window shop in the evening, stay at the hotel and have a good long morning in the stores. They all close at 1 p.m sharp on Saturdays. Well, when we were ready to go, Roy said,

"Mrs. Mawby in the office says, Lichtenberg is lots better than Mafeking; has more to offer. So, how about, as long as we're going as far as there, we could go another fifty miles to Lichtenberg."

After our overnight in Mafeking, we dashed down the highway towards Lichtenberg. The scenery changed drastically, now, as we left the hills and found ourselves on a prairie that stretched endlessly on either side of us. The horizons seemed farther away than was possible to see. Acres of corn, sorghum and sunflowers, were a surprize. In some places, the rows of corn and sunflowers alternated in the same field. So this was where all our sunflower oil came from. It's the only cooking oil available.

At intervals, there was a ranch house off to the side, with a tree lined lane leading to it, and windbreaks of trees clustered around it. Also, there were several groves of trees along the road. In one place, they were harvesting the rows, nearest the road. I haven't yet found out the name of the trees but there are forests of them. They resemble poplar, have a pretty leaf something like willows. They grow straight and tall, hardly any branches except near the top, and these are delicate. I have assumed that these are the trees they use to make the framework of the roofs of the rondavels, in preparation for the thatching. They are nice and round and straight, and can be "harvested" at any stage of growth, according to how large a "round" you need.

It continued to be flat and open for the whole fifty miles and we felt we were again driving out in Illinois. Lichtenberg was a nice enough city with a huge double square in the center with great parking areas surrounded by vast lawns, fountains, monuments and play areas. Trees provided shady parking spots, and in one area a farmer's market was under way with live chickens, fresh vegetables and exotic fruit.

Roy went his way as Joel and I assured him we'd come back to the car at intervals, but it was almost eleven when we got together, thus too late to return to Mafeking to shop further. However, I had bought some blankets, toys for Pauline's baby, a mirror for her and a tent for Joel. Roy had tools and other treasure to show us.

When we got home Joel wanted to give Pauline the things. He took her the bright yellow acrylic blanket and the mirror, which the girl had inadvertently wrapped as a gift—which was fine. When I was looking for blankets, I told the clerk I wanted one for my maid. When he heard that, he said, "Well, this is too good for a maid. Here, let me show you something." I said, "Oh, I want something pretty", not the old grey cotton things he brought out. In another store I got a bright yellow one, bound with ribbon and a turquoise one. Pauline was pleased with them.

I waited until the next day to present the toys to her little girl. She has never got used to me; clouds up and whimpers, then really cries if I come nearer. So, I have decided to bribe her; I give her a cookie or an orange anytime she's around. As Pauline started her ironing, her sister brought in the little girl and she promptly cried when she saw me, but I gave her the bright red and blue ball and the little teddy bear animal—

soft and cuddly. I looked in later and Pauline had set her on a chair next to where she stood ironing. There baby sat with the bear in her arms, but one hand holding her mother's skirts.

I asked Pauline if the baby had seen many white ladies in Molepolole.

"Not many. Once at the hospital when she had to get a shot." Well, that explains it somewhat. She may get used to me yet—if I don't run out of cookies.

Pauline's younger sister, seventeen, takes care of the baby and I guess they are permanently settled in the little house. It's good Pauline can have her with her. I often see Pauline heading out to town with Thandi, now 19 months old, on her back slung in the blanket and sound asleep. Pauline looks older than her twenty-three years—but happy and always smiling.

She brought me a sheaf of papers the other day; her receipt for the money I gave her for the school application and the letter saying only those who made the Rand 30 payment would be accepted for class. So, I gave her Rand 30 and also pointed out that there was another notice in the paper about typing being offered at the college for her to look into.

Everytime Alice comes over and sees Pauline in action, she exclaims, "You can't know how lucky you are to have a maid like her, with good sense." One day she drove in the yard to drop me off and saw Pauline out front washing the wall around the front door. She stopped the car and said, "She makes me sick! My maid wouldn't have sense enough to wash the front door if it was black unless I told her to. Then she'd probably use the bottle of wax instead of the Handy Andy!"

Latest news from Alice—"My maid is five months pregnant!" In addition to being inept at housework, although she is improving, she took the job without making her situation clear; now Alice can't fire her, but has told her she cannot keep the baby there. Alice has seven children; and she can't get over the fact that she didn't notice the maid was pregnant. Her neighbor had asked her the other day, "When's your maid expecting her baby?"

"What do you mean?" It really shook her up. Well, with seven kids and coping with getting work out of the girl, transporting kids to school and getting into town for the complicated shopping, she didn't have time to take notice, I guess. We are interested to see how this will work out.

When I was dissatisfied with my garden boy and wondering what to do, Alice said, "Well, Mr. Neilson out here couldn't take it any more, and one day he said to his boy, 'Here's two Rand. Take this and don't let me see you again', and the kid took it and left. He was afraid the boy's feelings would be hurt, but he saw him some time later and the kid grinned and waved and called 'Hi, Mr. Neilson!.'" No chance of her solving the maid problem that easily, though.

MAY 26

Roy and I were out at the airport for the 8 a.m. arrival of a plane from Johannesburg. Roy's niece, Debby Brown, in California, had written us that an Economics Professor from Sacramento State College which she attends, was coming to Gaborone for the summer. We found his arrival time was now 8:30, so we drove around, out through the old Village, the Boer War camp site, and located the homes of the people we knew. I showed Roy where Margaret Rowe lived and he pointed out the Tax Commissioner's house. Back at the field, a few more people were around, so we knew something was expected, although it was overcast. One lady volunteered that sometimes the planes arrive, don't like the looks and go off again.

Roy finally went to the desk and asked about the plane. The man reached over and said, "Let me see your watch." He looked at it, now at 8:40 and said, "Oh, it is late. It must be behind some of those clouds up there." That settled that.

It finally arrived; a small green and white Swazi Airways plane. We gave Dr. Curry a warm greeting and he was very happy to have us on hand. It only took a few minutes for him to pick up his one big bag; he was already carrying one small one. He said he appreciated Roy's letter, otherwise he wouldn't have known to bring warm clothes. "As it was, I froze in Johannesburg." He went on to say, "My travel agent told me I wouldn't need a visa for South Africa, consequently when I arrived there, yesterday—'Very sorry—but you can't leave the building'—but they were pretty nice, said there was a room upstairs that I could use, which I did."

"Well, you didn't miss much—just that short ride to the Holiday Inn and then back for your flight. The building at the airport was a beauty, wasn't it?"

"Wasn't it, though."

We came on home to sit around the kitchen table with Ben and Vi and have a few more cups of coffee before they packed and went back to the Inn, where rooms were now available.

Ben had gone to school at Eugene, Oregon where Dr. Curry had graduated and taught. They had many acquaintances in common and lots to talk about.

Dr. Curry was good about bringing us up to date on all the important developments at home; covered all the primaries and answered all our questions. He has had numerous articles published and his second book will soon be out. I shall be interested to read some of his papers.

He had Fulbrights to Africa twice; one to Liberia in the 60's and is proud that several of his former students from there are now getting their Ph.D.'s in Economics; another to Zambia, two years ago, teaching at the University in Lusaka. He was surprized the first evening at the Inn here, to run into one of his students from Lusaka. He loves Africa and I guess will be coming back intermittently—forever.

Dr. Curry told us his wife is Chinese. The next day, the Kudos came down from Francistown, the first visit here since they came from the States. So, when we got together, we had quite a crew. Dr. Curry who has a Chinese wife, Juan who is Japanese born in Peru, his wife from Japan, Ben Webb, a black from Oregon, and his wife a Finnish girl from Minnesota. Roy and I were the only matched pair of "plain people" at the table.

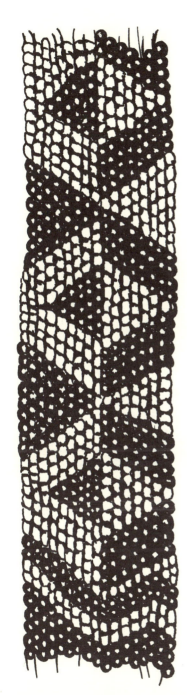

2

People and Places

Joel and his friend Thomas.

Just two days for a lull after all the activities of the previous two or three weeks wasn't really long enough for me to get in the mood and prepare for another long trip. Monday and Tuesday were to be holidays so that gave us a long weekend. We had planned to go to Rustenberg, which I thought was quite a long trip. After Roy traded in the pick-up on a comfortable station wagon and found it magically ironed out the bumps in the road that used to jerk us around in the truck, he felt we could travel as far as we wanted.

"How about getting as far as Rustenberg Friday evening, after work, then going on the next day to Kruger Park? We could spend Sunday and Monday there and come back on Tuesday?"

I really didn't have too much energy, but I was enthusiastic about getting to one of the animal parks. If we didn't, we might as well not have been in Africa.

We mulled it over, knowing all the while we would definitely go; would head east to where the Transvaal meets Mozambique.

We were packed and ready to take off when Roy came in from the office and within ten minutes, went down the road. The farther away we got, the better I felt. It was good to get out and see that there is a lot of world out there somewhere!

We reached Swartzruggens at 7:45 and stopped for petrol and Fish and chips, and were in Rustenberg looking for a hotel by 9 p.m. Just think, originally I had thought a trip to Rustenberg would be too far!

Just before we reached Pretoria the next day, we stopped for a while at a roadside park where there was a waterfall dropping into a deep gorge between steep hillsides.

"Here's your Victoria Falls", we jokingly said to Roy, as we watched the clouds of mist rising. Going over for a closer look, we found that the waterfall was gushing out of spillways in a huge dam between the hills.

Our narrow winding road snaked over the top of the dam and through a tunnel in the mountain and when we came out of that we had a view of the lake, its' marinas full of sailboats, mountains rising on the far shore and huge homes built into the hillsides.

The suburbs of Pretoria were impressive and we had no difficulty getting through the city. The huge Union building was red brick with a red tiled roof. It spread endlessly in two long wings, each with a dome and it looked like something in Italy, for great terraced gardens descended before it, for several blocks. There were tall cedars too, as in Italy; dark accent marks on the landscape.

A nice surprize was a mass of cloverleafs at an intersection of throughways, and for about a hundred miles, we were on a ribbon of concrete that rolled on over the open country where you could see so far it was awesome. The low hills of rich farmland ran on and on, seemingly forever.

We worked in a little suspense here. Roy had been warned there were no sales of petrol after noon on Saturdays, until Monday morning. He had a big tank and decided to fill it at the last moment, when it was nearest empty. It was getting closer and closer to noon, but he didn't stop off at the two towns along the way; he figured he'd be able to get to Witbank in the allotted time, if he could maintain a good speed. Well, we made it into the city at just 19 minutes until noon!

Crossing the road in front of a Mall after a short shopping expedition, we passed a palm-bordered park, to another square. On the right was a large lawn area, fairly dusty, with many benches, and it was evident that this was the area allotted to the blacks.

They are referred to as non-whites, or Bantu. There was a taxi station, all the cabs marked "non-white", a bus stop for them, an open market at the far side, and some take-out food places. We did see, on returning from our lunch, that a black bridal party was having photos made in the park against the palm trees, so I guess they were allowed to set foot on it!

We heard the crash of impact and shattering of glass just as we passed the non-white taxi stand, and saw that two fairly new cars had collided at the intersection above. It only took two seconds for a hundred or so people to congregate—Joel in the front row.

Later, he kept tabs on the accident from the balcony of a Chinese restaurant where we had lunch.

There were no more thruways, but the roads were fine and towns a long way apart; more roadside stands than anything, with bags of oranges, boxes of tangerines and avocados for sale. We stopped for a sundae at The Golden Egg in Machadodorp, from which there was a good view of the town; all the world like a German city near Trier. The view was beautiful, but inside, where we were being served, we saw that black people had to stand outside a window and ask for what they wished to buy, and it was handed to them. Enough to spoil our appetites.

The terrain soon became more mountainous, and we saw one impressive vista after another all the way to Nelspruit. Along here, in the orange grove country we became acquainted with "Mr. Hall and Sons" who seemed to own the greater part of the groves. They rolled on and on, with beautiful clipped hedges enclosing them; a deterrent I suppose, to people picking fruit as they walked by. It was sort of a joke from then on, as when we saw something especially fine, we'd say, "I guess that's Mr. Hall's" or "Mr. Hall's cousin's."

It was getting dark as we reached Nelspruit, where we had assumed we'd stay; the last big city before the park. Well, we scoured it and could find no hotel, so went on.

Soon we were in White River and spied a huge signpost for the Park, with the number of kilometers to each of a dozen hotels. While studying it in our headlights, we found we were right on top of the White River Hotel; were standing right in front of it. Roy got us a room, and when we went to it, we saw there were a number of Rondavels, also. A Frangipani tree bloomed outside our window, so the air was heavy with its perfume. The flowers are white, with a waxy texture like magnolia blooms, but are small, with only four petals. After a good dinner at the hotel, we window shopped a while and then got to bed.

One thing about this part of the world; most of it is in bed at 8 p.m. The towns and cities have nothing open. When the ordinary work day ends, everything just closes up.

In Gaborone, we think nothing of going to bed at seven or eight. Kids go to bed without having to be told. I thought it was strange when we first got here to have one of the men say he'd come to the hotel for dinner with us, but "I'm always in bed by nine". We soon learned that most people are, unless they have something special planned; the movie, or the Holiday Inn or its Casino.

At this point, we had travelled 1000 kilometers. Sunday morning as we started out after breakfast, I said, "I surely do hope we see a lot of animals, after coming this far." I was serious and felt a little apprehensive. In the 2,000,000 hectares of the park—as large as the state of Massachusetts, there was plenty of room for them to all hide out!

We were in the mountains here, but the whole area is referred to as the Low Veld. Not until we got our entrance papers at the gate did we realise we should have taken antimalaria medicine before coming. Well, we're all optimistic and no one remembers having seen or felt a mosquito.

We read all the rules of the park as we went along; there was a long list of them on the blue sheet verifying our entry fee payment. NO feeding of animals—*NO* getting out of a vehicle except at specified areas—*NO* parts of the body out of the car, and so on.

We strained and strained to see something in the underbrush or in the fields we passed. All of a sudden, there on the left was a family of wart hogs; Father, Mother and young one with a dark red ruff of hair down its back. What ugly creatures, but beautiful to us as we had finally *SEEN* some wild animals. Next there was a hugh snake stretched across half the road. Roy straddled it but I think the next car got it. Infraction of Rule #6.

We went down some side roads but didn't see much. We had a map, thank heavens, so we knew where we were. Then, all of a sudden, there were zebra; a whole group of them, to the left of us. We hurried up with the camera and got a good shot of the rear ends of six zebras. Now, we became expectant. What next? Down by a small lake on a side road three cars were parked; there must be something to see. Across the water, was a huge herd of Impala. We strained to see them and noticed other people had binoculars. Most entertaining was a bird or two in the parking lot. Just like those crazy dippy birds you buy in gimcrack stores. A real clown in action. Somehow, I just happened to drop a few crumbs of my cookie; as we had the windows open here. The common Yellow-billed Hornbill, proper name of this clown, scampered over in no time with the most ungraceful hopping and lurching, leaned back against his long black tail, then seemed to topple over from the weight of his long yellow curved beak, almost as deep as his head, and longer. He was black and white speckled and seemed like a Disney cartoon, especially drawn up to startle the newcomers to the park.

Soon we came to Pretorius Kop, a rest area. It is a fenced-in camp with space for tenters and caravans, but mainly vacation rondavals. We saw a huge ampitheatre, with screen, indicating movies or slides could be shown; a big main house with thatched roof, open rondavels with coal stoves fired up, and some with a number of gas burners, for doing your own cooking, also a restaurant, and gas pumps (closed). We drove around and decided one of these camps would be wonderful for overnight, but we continued with our animal observation, on toward the next camp.

Joel was the first to see a young Impala. It was close to the road and looked right at him! Then we saw what I thought must be some kind of a turkey—big and black with a lot of bright red wattly stuff on its head. It was a Ground Hornbill. The bird booklet says it has a booming call that carries for long distances. It must have carried beyond us, as we didn't hear it, though we saw many of them.

We saw more Impala as we went on to the next camp. There we unloaded and sat down to rest in the most unique camp we had ever been in. Our Rondavel was number 187 and near us there were new ones under construction. Some were in the final stages of having the roof thatched—all done but the trimming along the bottom edge. Some had only the framework up, of creosoted poles and the walls still only basic; no window frames in. The next morning I took some pictures of the various stages, and the stacks of thatching grass. There was a big building for registration, a gift and souvenir shop, post office, and bordering the riverfront, a restaurant and cafeteria with a huge open porch where you could eat and watch the Sabie River flow past—and see a family of Hippos submerging and rising, yawning or blowing spray. There was also a big library and a number of display boards with various horns of the antelopes, and some skeletons of other animals.

The Rondavel in Africa, is round with a thatched roof, as that way there is the least wind resistance and the building stands longer—no cracks as in the square ones. These of course were not just mud huts on reeds, but constructed of cinder block and plastered over. Each had a screened section, with chairs and table, and cupboards at the end. As inside, you were under an umbrella of the pole roof and thatch.

We had never been in a round room before and it was fun. Someone brought an extra cot for Joel, and it was good to look forward to having this "home" to come back to after our afternoon exploration. Actually, Roy would have liked to lie down on the bed and stay there, but he settled for a short rest and we then took off again, after having lunch down by the river.

We hadn't gone far when we were in the midst of a huge group of Baboons. They were on the shoulder of the road, in the bushes and in trees nearby. Friendly, too, and came close and looked at us interestedly. It's amazing, though, how quick the wild animals are. You think you've got the perfect shot set up and before you can press your finger on the camera, they have changed position or even turned their backs. Here now was when we began to see so many Impala, so many herds of them that we became saturated and began saying, "Oh, it's only Impala!" They wandered across the road, stood by close enough to touch, though we didn't of course. All sizes, but they are delicate and seem petite. The size of the horns was the way I judged the male age. Some were so small you'd think they were "babies", but I'm sure they weren't. More wart hogs were on the scene and then surprize of all, there were the giraffes! Three or four, standing there reaching to upper branches and calmly chewing away. Soon, we saw a group of nine. Once we rounded a curve and there in the middle of the road was a huge dark giraffe. We began to feel that we were lucky and would have been satisfied if this were all we got to see.

We were watching our petrol, as we hadn't yet ascertained if there were pumps at this camp, but we hoped there were. We were getting low, so planned our route on the map carefully.

The northern most point we could risk was where there was a "Tea Camp". It was a snack place with parking lot, grove of trees with tables outside as well as in the big pavillion which was built around a huge tree, which emerged from the peak, and spread its branches out over the roof.

We sat outside and were puzzled by a freaky looking stove, just beyond the tables. Big square stove bases sat on the ground with glowing coal fire making the heat waves rise; the tops of the stoves were huge kettles, with covers. A water pipe came up between them, with faucets piped over each kettle. Just remove the cover, run the water in, cover and let heat, then draw off the boiling water from faucets extending on pipes out of the sides of the kettles, near the bottom. It was a contraption that drew a lot of attention. Everyone seemed to go over and lift the lids and look it over.

They had some coal piles nearby, and also wood fires burning in cut-away oil barrels, with the unburned ends of the big logs and sticks extending out, propped on other oil barrels; perhaps they were going to barbeque something on them.

So, the back-to-camp drive started and our turnoff onto it was where we had first seen giraffes. There were more, not far down this road, and in a marshy place, all of a sudden there were Blue Wildebeest, three of them. I expected more and didn't take a picture of them. We strained our eyes. No wildebeest, but we were rewarded by big Kudu. Such regal antelope! Big and brown with lines on them like paint drippings, big round ears–huge horns on the bulls. They were good to see and we lost track of the count. Joel had the keenest eyes and he'd see them and yell for us to stop.

Another beauty was the Sable Antelope; huge and powerful and impressive. We saw just one pair. More baboons entertained us, a big batch of vervet monkeys swarmed around our car. Nearing the camp again, after more giraffes and impala and zebra, a number of cars were stopped. Holding up the traffic, was a big lion, lying insolently in the middle of the road, with three others nearby. We were right there to see them wander off. I had thought the lions were farther north, as the elephants are, so we were pleased to add another to our list. We then saw, perhaps because it was getting near evening, many flocks of Crowned Guinea fowl. Their heads were as bright as peacocks. Also, I saw a bright bird, purple breast and blue-green feathers. My little folder says it's a Roller; Lilac Breasted.

More Kudu and dozens of impala rounded off the drive and we were back at the gate about 5. They close at 5:30; all must be out of the park roads by nightfall.

We relaxed in our rondavel and Joel went out and met a wart hog family which had veered into the camp. I don't know how they got in, maybe they rooted under a fence.

Dinner was in the dining room of the restaurant, though Joel said he'd rather eat on the porch; he got his tray in the cafeteria. We had a truly elegant dinner on white table cloths, with an army of waiters rushing around to serve. The exotic call to mealtimes (not breakfast though) was a rhythmic beat of African drums for about five or ten minutes.

Joel was the first out on Monday morning, and he was no sooner out, then he was in; so excited he could burst, running in all directions for his camera. There were three impala outside by the car. He rushed off and got some good close-ups. I hope for his sake, that most of his pictures come out well. He was back again soon, almost terrified, for he had met a wart hog, face to face. "He was right there coming right at me, this close, and looking right in my eye, and the park man picked up some stones and threw them, to chase him off." He hadn't minded them the evening before when they just paraded through in a row, with their funny skinny tails standing straight up in the air, with the tassle of hair at the end hoisted like a flag. They were moving by, then, not facing him.

When we went down to the riverfront, on the way to breakfast, we spotted the hippos in the river, snorting and blowing spray and leisurely floundering around on the riverside, the far side, of course. I took a couple pictures, but I can visualise having to say as they are shown—"Look way over there—that ripple is where a hippo just submerged, and that black dot—way over there—is a hippo's nose". But I'm glad we took even those as our only disappointment of the park was about hippos.

We didn't hurry after breakfast, but visited the gift shop which was well stocked with good items for those with either 50 cents or $500, to spend. We bought some books, an Impala fur covered notebook for Joel, some animal printed cotton material and postcards. Roy and I went into the beautiful post office, with the mosaics of elephants at the entrance. As we waited for the clerk, I noticed a very unbeautiful wall on the far side. Dark green brick extended from the outside wall to past the counter and up to the rafters. Beyond it was the exit door, on the outside of which we had seen earlier, "Non-White" and "Bantu". It was enough to make me not want to buy and use their stamps. I shouldn't even have been there enjoying their park and their fine facilities.

"Just think, if Ben Webb were down here (of course he couldn't get inside the camp anyway unless he were a waiter), he would have to go around to that door to come in and have someone sell him a stamp."

It is a situation that I find untenable. There must be a word worse than that. I can't believe all I saw; that modern people in a so-called Christian country can accept and perpetuate such treatment of humans.

There was petrol; it was down the road past our rondavel and out of sight of the rest of the camp. We filled the tank, studied the map and plotted a course which would give us new routes, and head us out to the gate. We followed a river road as all points there led to the Hippo pool. Even big roads were named Hippo Pool Road. Our appetite was whetted, and Joel was saving his last few exposures for them.

There were many Kudu, baboons and monkeys, so our progress was slow. We stopped and watched their performances. It always seems as though monkeys are performing, and making fun of you. I read later in a little book from the gift shop, that the smell of petrol from the cars, as you drive through the park, eliminates all human smell, thus the animals do not pick up your scent.

Roy was keeping track of the kilometers to the place where the map indicated a short drive to the Hippo pool. We had passed a place that might have been it, but it had a barricade of branches across it. Finally, we were at a big stone marker, with an arrow pointing back toward the way we had come, saying Hippo Pool. We were really disappointed. At first Roy was going to go back, but we didn't, as there must have been some reason to have barricaded the road, maybe the water was low and there weren't any hippos there. Joel was disappointed, too, but we had seen a lot of wild life on the way out, and we planned to come back again, sometime, and go north to where the elephants and rhinos were.

As we approached the exit gate, there were some wonderful vistas of mountains, unique rock formations and sweeps of the valleys off to one side, but as soon as we got to a stopping place, it had all disappeared. I walked up a little ways, as Roy was checking out, but Joel called to me, "You can't walk up there into the Park!", and he was right. Anyway I'd have had to walk a long way to get that view again. There was a big mountain peak which we had seen as we approached and later left the park. It was high and craggy and the stones at the top looked like they had squirted out of the crest. Reminded me of frosting squirting out of a cake decorator. A big bouquet of squirts-all solidified.

Many of the mountains had freaky stone formations in the way of round boulders piled up on top of each other. Some looked dangerous, as though they might even topple off. In a feature on Rhodesia at the movies the other night, they showed formations something like these which are peculiar to that country too. Some grassy mountains had the crests covered with slabby rock, dark red, that gave you an impression of an overcrowded cemetery. There were endless unique mountains and mountain tops, but there was no opportunity to take pictures of all of them.

Some scenes I missed photographing were of great South African homes, surrounded by gardens such as a resort we passed, replete with tennis courts, pools and rondavels while just a few yards down the road was shanty town; tumble down, dusty and dirty, stones and rocks weighing down the roof coverings.

We pretty much unwound the way we had come. There was no more direct route and we were back in Pretoria by late afternoon.

We do not have pleasant thoughts regarding Pretoria. We were tired and hungry, and after Roy got a hotel room for us—with great problems of parking involved, we went in search of a place for dinner. At this time of night, one would think there would be a place. Nothing but "Take-Out" places, with little tables in the back. We drove round and round; parked near the Playboy Club Steak House, in front of which was the most beautiful yellow Jaguar I have ever seen. Brand new and Gorgeous. We walked for blocks and covered most of the downtown. They dedicated one block as a memorial to a former prime minister and we felt at the time, it might better have been used for a family restaurant! Seriously, it did seem a bit of waste of downtown space.

The block was completely paved, with flagstone, but it was walled, so you could only get onto it from one street. In one corner, was a bust of the renowned gentleman, on a pedestal. A great sweep of a canopy of concrete rose from another corner, went over the top about two stories high and came down to rest at the opposite corner. At each end, inside, there were searchlights which shone onto the bust (somewhat minimized by this great arc of concrete). Near it was another statue—four horsemen on prancing steeds, atop a fountain which spurted up toward the horses and flowed down in a big circular pool at the bottom, on which grey squares of stone were set at random; about brick size.

I wonder what the committee looked like that dreamed these up—or approved them. As the old saying goes, "It had to be done by a committee!" The searchlights also blinded you as you drove down the street next to it.

We finally gave up finding a place to eat—drove around again, even to the extent of getting on a throughway to Johannesburg. Back in the less desirable part of town, but desperate, we ate in a take-out place, and Joel kept running outside to see if the car was O.K., and we kept watching to see if *he* were O.K. We were glad to get through and get to bed. The movies were out of the question and we treated Joel to one after we got home, to make up for it.

The morning was memorable, too, as Roy went to the Chevrolet garage to have things done to the car. His program developed into a "half hour" and then "another half hour"—so Joel and I made quick shopping (that's a laugh!) trips downtown and hurried back, never stopping long enough to accomplish anything. We did that three times, then I went back once more to a delightful "Take-Out" to get some snacks for the drive.

So it was 12:30 before we were on our way and we had to get through the border gate outside of Gaborone, before 8 p.m. We hoped we'd not lose our way. They're not overly generous with direction signs and never post a sign of a distant city that might be your destination, in the long run. It's Podunk, Podunk, Podunk, then suddenly Metropolis!—after you get there. Keeps the tension up!

We were in the lovely orange grove section again and there were roadside stands every so often, with a little huddle of blacks around each. Sometimes there was a family, with a mother doing some sewing and the children playing around her. Sometimes there was a hut near. We bought some tangerines at one, from a young girl, then later some miles along, we stopped at a stand where there was an old man. He had huge sacks of naval oranges hung along the front and big signs, 70 cents.

We motioned for a bag and he ran over with one, put it in through the window, and Roy handed him the seventy cents. As it passed me, and I looked down at the coins, I felt he should have added more—but then, the man said seventy cents. But I felt bad, for about a bushel of the biggest oranges you ever saw!

He wandered back to his stand, but Roy hadn't started up, and I said, "He'd like those meat pies"; the too-much pastry pies, with the too-big meat ball in the center, that no one wanted any more of.

"Go ahead and give them to him!" I was so happy to have him say that!

I motioned to the man to come back and handed out the brown sack to him. I didn't care if one pie had a bite out of it and I knew he wouldn't care. He accepted the sack in both hands and bowed and bowed and kept saying, "Thank you, Madame. Thank you, Madame." Holding the bag, still in his two hands, which in this part of the world is the only polite way to accept a gift, he continued to bow and bow. I could have cried over his appreciation of the bit of food that we didn't even want.

I couldn't look back, to see if he'd extend his enjoyment by sitting and anticipating, or if he had dug right in. Joel looked back, and as it was flatland, could see for quite a distance.

"Yes, he's sitting down now. Now he's looking in the bag. Yes, he's trying them."

There wasn't any way that I could give some food to all the poor blacks that I saw. There wasn't a thing I could do. I just turned off my mind and admired the scenery and put my feelings away.

It was mid-afternoon when we got to Rustenberg. We did some hectic shopping and Roy met Jerry and Alice Pahl, who had spent four days at a park south of Pretoria. They too, had had rondavels to stay in. In that park, the animals had been fenced in and there had been enough to please the children. I would never encourage them to make the long drive we had, with their VW bus and the seven children.

"Well, I've got a parking place for an hour and a half", Roy said, and I wondered if he had taken into consideration the time we needed to get to the border gate, rather than available shopping time. The Pahls however, reminded him that it was almost a four hour drive yet, and they were going to get on their way. We finished up quickly and had a pleasant drive the rest of the way.

We took our shortcut after we got as far as Swartzruggens, drove along the beautiful Marico River, which as far as I can tell from map study, branches from the Limpopo, the river that separates Botswana from Rhodesia (and the top of Kruger Park from Rhodesia). I see the Limpopo is really fat and wide, in Mozambique.

Well, we took our shortcut, as I said, and the sun was just setting so we drove into a beautiful sky. There were pedestrians who reassured us every time we asked, that we were on the right road. "Gaborone, straight ahead." They were right. After an eternity, we were at the gate with time to spare.

We had no more than stopped in our drive than Pauline came rushing up from her little house, carrying the baby wrapped in a big blanket and calling, "You are home!" with great feeling.

"We've been gone so long", Joel said to her, "You must have thought we had gone back to America!"

"No, no, but I didn't go away anywhere. I stayed and watched so no one would steal anything". The baby then started to cry as I stepped near to talk, and Pauline instinctively threw a corner of the blanket over the baby's face—to cut off the offending view!

"Wait a minute, I'll get her some cookies", I said and rooted around in the car for some, and a few small oranges. She accepted them and they went on back to their house.

As soon as we got into the house, Joel's friends, Kenneth and Edwin came dashing over from next door.

"We had decided that we would not close our eyes until you were back tonight. So, when we saw the lights, we came right over." Later, Joel said, "There were two good things about that trip. The animals and coming home."

JUNE 13

Ben Webb, Vi and Damaris came down to Gaborone yesterday, after their reconnaissance trip to Serowe. They walked in looking bedraggled and weary. I was finishing a bath when they arrived, so called out to them, "How are you? You sound the same!", and Vi answered, "We'll never be the same again!"

"I have driven on worse roads", Ben said of the road from here to Serowe, but he intimated, "not much worse." "Some sections were fair, some were surfaced, but the real trouble spots were where there was sand. Sometimes that bus (a Toyota HighAce, 10 seater) just swerved from side to side and sometimes I thought I'd get stuck in the sand. It was rough."

Vi really looked beat. They left Oregon the first of May and have been on the road and in hotels ever since. They have the house in Serowe; Ben has the key, but they don't have furniture enough and no electricity, and won't have until he locates and buys a generator. The village of Serowe is just that, a village. Although there are over 40,000 inhabitants, it's still a village.

"What puzzled me, the other evening, was where to turn off the highway to my house," Ben said. "You just go off the road anywhere, off across a field to wherever you live. There aren't many roads." The paths of a cattle post and tribal village of rondavels, wander around; there's no definite center to the town. Vi pulled out a brown envelope and said, "This is my Bible, right now. Lokomo sketched this out for me so I could find my way around. It marks the post office, the Tax office, school, etc. I'd be lost without it."

Lokomo is now going to the U.K. for a while and Ben Webb is taking over the Tax Office from him. I have smiled over his name ever since I got here, for it is Conference Lokomo. He is "Conference" to everyone with no sign of a nickname. I asked what kind of a conference he might have been named for—of African states? of Nato? of a Church?

"A church conference. Methodist, I believe. His folks went to the conference where he was conceived, and that's what they named him."

He's been a help to them in getting settled up there, but when he requested beds, he didn't specify mattresses, so there aren't any.

First the Webbs entered their daughter, Damaris, in the government primary school, but with reservations about it. It was wall to wall debris, with wrecked furniture and general air of neglect. "Not", Ben said, "that Damaris couldn't sit on broken chairs, but I was afraid that the attitude evident in the physical appearance would be the same in the scholastic area. After some inquiries, we found there was a Catholic Mission school, St. Gabriels, so we retrieved her records and entered her in that." She is ready for fourth grade so it works out just right. The first three grades are taught in Setswana, with English as a subject. At grade four, all classes are taught in English, and the Setswana is continued as a language class. She won't have any problem anyway, as she reads through books faster than she can be supplied. Very bright.

Ben told us, when we mentioned having been in the malaria area and not being aware of it, that we should take the post-visit routine of medicine even if we didn't take it earlier. So we each took a dose and there are three to go. We were under the impression that the swamp area, north and west, and Serowe were the danger spots. We'll have to get on the ball.

Serowe is on a hill; hard to visualise, as we are really flat here. We are flat and high, with kopies in sight on the horizon, and we go between and over them to South Africa. But Serowe has some of the loveliest views. Ben says the one from the tax office window is the greatest and he plans to turn his desk around so he can face it. The village runs down both sides of the hill and spreads out in cowpaths—a maze of Kraals (which are groups of native rondavels) with fences around them. The fences are usually branches of thorn trees stuck in the ground. Those branches could stand up merely by locking themselves together by the thorns without even being stuck in the ground!

President, Sir Seretse Khama has his home there, on the hill. As you remember, I told you about Khama (his great grandfather), Chief of the Ngwato Tribe, and his moving the tribes to Serowe, from Palapye; Serowe is sacred to this tribe, as it is the burial place of their kings and chiefs.

In the book, "Safari to Serowe", it states, "Serowe is really a lot of separate Kraals clustered together like a bunch of grapes. Each is occupied by a different branch of the Ngatwo people. There are no streets or avenues, just trails made by the people to the main road and to their pastures and farmlands which may be more than twenty miles away."

It's hard for me to visualize a "city" of 40,000 designed that way but everyone says it's a must to visit. It is noted for its pottery and weaving. They have a system of Brigades. Brigades of weavers, carpenters, painters, brick makers; with a program to train people in various ways of earning a living and getting them in touch with the things that need doing.

I noticed that the Webbs, in discussing problems in getting settled, saying, "We could call the Brigade for that", or "I ordered the curtains made from the Brigade."

Well, we shall make a trip up there to Serowe before too long. It won't be in the rainy season, though, as we have been told that as soon as the road gets wet, it's as though you were driving on glare ice. There is an inviting section of road heading north, towards Serowe and Francistown, but not too far away the blacktop ends and you're on your own.

Today the Webbs will buy their necessities, on the Mall and in White City—at the stores of Indian Traders, and load in their air freight which is stored at the Tax Office, then drive north on that rough road again. They have to shop here as there is no way they can go to South Africa. Even if they could, they wouldn't want to. Ben is watching the South African papers closely, and keeping tabs on the Transkei Independence movement.

We studied the maps yesterday and finally located Transkei and Umtata. We had thought that this Tribal Homeland to which the Bantu will be welcome to retire to and be a citizen of—would be out in some undeveloped area, but it proved to be way south on the coast, above Port Elizabeth.

So, we will be keeping in touch with Ben and Vi and Serowe while the politics of South Africa—and Rhodesia—simmer along and control to quite an extent, just what we do each day.

JUNE 17

We can all breath a sign of relief now. Last night, Roy said, "I've about given up the idea of a trip to Bulawayo."

Getting to see Rhodesia has been uppermost in his mind since we were in New York. A few weeks ago, a Britisher from the office, took his family on the train overnight to Francistown, and went on to Bulawayo and up through Rhodesia, to Wankie Park for the animals, and north to see Victoria Falls. He had a fine trip, enjoyed all he saw, and it was without incident. But the Railroad up through there is the Rhodesian Railroad, and every so often there is an incident—derailings, accidents of different sorts, all with no discernible reason. Everyone knows they happen, but no one says so in print.

Perhaps yesterday's article on the shooting of the Botswana farmer who was retrieving his cattle that had strayed across the border, was what helped Roy make this decision. There's no use being in the wrong place at the wrong time, when you could be elsewhere.

So, we will proceed to take trips south, even though we don't care for South African policy on treatment of the blacks. South Africa's good roads fan out in all directions from Botswana.

Kimberly is within a week-ends travel distance, I think. Kimberly has a black triangle next to it, on the map, labelled Big Hole; the triangle denotes "Ruins—Things to see".

We can also go to Krugersdorf, just below Rustenberg, and stay in the Park. It has holiday rondavels and animals and wouldn't be too long a drive.

Some weekend, staying here, we can drive out to Molepolole, where Pauline's home is. It's a very old town and was there when Livingstone came through here. There is a series of watercolors in the National Gallery done by another missionary who stopped there on his travels. It amazed me to see them travelling in wagon trains—covered wagons such as we in the "colonies" travelled to our west.

Pauline must be lonesome today. After having her little girl, Tandi, here for a month, with her young sister Catherine as baby tender and housekeeper down in the little house behind us, she's alone. Last week, another sister appeared; Lillian, who is next younger than Pauline. She was helping Pauline polish the kitchen windows and I noticed she was a little more mature a girl than Catherine.

Little did I know that morning, that I would also meet Vivian. Pauline came rushing in to tell me she had bad news from home.

"My sister Vivian just came to tell me. I have a little house up there. No one lives in it now, but two got into it and lighted up and set fire and burned it all down. All down to nothing."

Naturally she was upset, but I could only sympathize with her and tell her I was sorry. So, now, there were four sisters and Tandi in the little house. I'm sure some of them went into town and slept at their cousin's home, though. I made sure they were all going to be around in the afternoon, Saturday, and got them all out on the lawn and took a picture of them together. There was a young boy in the group, too, about eight, and I have no idea to whom he belonged, but he didn't consider not being in the picture. Pauline blossomed out in a fantastic hairdo. I could imagine the sisters had a good time, doing each other's hair. This was a Bouffant Pouf, parted in the middle, so Pauline didn't look like herself.

When Alice Pahl stopped yesterday, she said, "I saw Pauline in town yesterday afternoon. She was the best looking woman on the Mall."

Sunday afternoon there was a knock on the front door and when I answered, there was Pauline, holding Tandi.

"My sisters want to go back home today, but we have no money."

"How much is the bus?"

"One Rand forty . . . 80 for Lillian . . . and . . ." she trailed off. When any Motswana asked for favors, he talks so softly it's difficult to understand what he wants.

"O.K. Wait a minute." Tandi was now crying at the sight of me, so I gave her a cookie and a small orange, then raided Joel's and my collection of change, and I gave her four 50 cent pieces. She thanked me and later I saw the troop going off heading for Molepolole.

Alice asked what I thought about how they felt.

"Do you think it hurts them terribly, the adults, to come to you and say 'I have no money' and ask, or do you think it doesn't bother them; that they figure you have so much, it doesn't matter?"

"I have no idea."

JUNE 21

Rhett is a Bushman who has made it. This week he will fly to Johannesburg, Capetown, Rio de Janiero, New York City, Washington, D.C., for a week of instruction, then on to the University of Southern California at Los Angeles, for a session in Tax Administration of 6 to 8 months.

"Rhett, you are brave and be warned that you are in for a culture shock!". I jokingly told him—kidding on the square. I really wouldn't care to be assaulting Los Angeles as a stranger, even with as much travel experience as I've had.

Rhett had never been out of Botswana, except to school in Lesotho, and this city of Gaborone is the largest place in this country. What's more, he comes from far to the west over the desert—the home of some of the Bushmen.

He had been in charge of the Serowe Tax Office, but came back here a while ago, and has been preparing for this trip to the States. Roy wanted to arrange some sort of a send-off party, and approached me about having it here.

"Why not? Fine with me. What do you want?"

"Well, I invited 12 for dinner and the evening—Saturday."

Good thing I had been agreeable to undertaking the party, or he would have been on the spot.

The next day, Thursday, he was checking on the number specifically, and asked Dennis, his other assessor here, if he were a married man.

"No, I'm not, but Rhett is."

"Rhett?"

"Yes, he got married yesterday. I was his witness."

So, that added a new dimension to the party and I got in the spirit of it quickly, with plans for a wedding cake and gifts. It took two days work, but everything was done ahead so the evening could be enjoyable and relaxing.

Alice gave me some pink roses and the day of the party, Roy brought home another bouquet of roses. Nothing like a lot of flowers for a wedding celebration.

There were a few surprises. Dennis, the bachelor arrived with a girlfriend. She wore a floor length light blue coat and tan stocking hat, neither of which she cared to relinquish. Girls and women here wear stocking hats more than any other style; bright colors and varied styles. Some are fancy crochet, some handknit, some striped and most just plain colors. They are acceptable indoor wear. Church and choir are full of them. Anyway, she was a shy girl, but enjoyed her dinner.

Gilbert Tedi, Higher Executive Officer is his official title at the Tax Department, of whom I had heard a lot since my arrival as he is influencial in the housing and furnishing problem, impressed me as a replica of George Jefferson—T.V.'s Saturday night character. Sharp dresser, same build and air. His wife, Margaret, in a navy blue stocking hat, skirt, sweater and plaid wool pea coat, which she too kept around her shoulders, was plump, round-faced, with a big smile showing widely spaced teeth. She was pleasant and talkative; works in Barclay's bank, on the books, not out front.

Then came the bride and groom. Susan, the bride, was a beautiful girl in a bright turban and denim dress—(the whole world is dressed in denim, it seems), and a coat, which she did not remove. Rhett, the proud husband, was average height, wore a plaid sport coat and had a frizzly beard of sorts. His face was broad at the eyes, and flat, without a high bridge between the eyes.

The wife of the Tax Commissioner arrived late, as she had worked late at school. The Commissioner is up north at Serowe and other towns, but we invited Janet to come. She is a beauty; tall and statuesque. She wore a deep green turtle neck sweater with long sleeves over which she had a soft heather green floor length sleeveless dress. Instead of her usual tightly braided hair, she had combed it in a soft fluff.

The two British men and their wives had arrived earlier and I liked both the women. One, who had just been in England for six weeks, got back this week. She had dark curly short hair, wore a turtle neck sweater, which she informed me in England is a "roll collar jumper", short skirt and beautiful T-strap high heeled shoes, of two tones of soft leather. She was vivacious and laughed a lot. Looked like twenty-five, but must be forty, anyway. Two children are in England, and one is here. She was Janet, too.

Marion, the other woman was a surprize. Blond with a reddish tinge, sort of a pompadour in front and neglected in the back. She wore a long dress that seemed to be busy, with a drapy shawl. She's an animal lover, and has a pet chicken and was enthused because she had found a chameleon. She gave the black girls the shudders, later, telling tales of how she pet it and held her hand where it could use the fingers for a ladder to get up the tree. As we women sat around the table after the men grouped together in the living room to talk of important things, I did not get up and clear the last of the cake plates and coffee cups, for if I had, everyone would have offered to help and it would have broken up the good conversation underway.

Susan was a quiet girl who told us she is studying to be a cartographer. All these people speak so softly, it's hard to catch all they say. Evidently, she is here in Gaborone, but her home is in Ghanzi, across the Kalahari, 400 kilometers as the crow flies, but about 750 kilometers to reach, by a route all the way around the desert.

Susan was especially pleased with the decorated wedding cake I set in front of her, at dessert time. She stood and cut it, giving a piece to Rhett, and cut a couple more, till I told her I'd finish the serving. Later, Roy took a picture of them, with her offering Rhett some, as we explained was a custom at U.S. weddings.

"Now, here's a gift for the bride." As I gave it to her to open, Roy gave something to Rhett also. He started right in, but Susan held her package on her lap, and handed it to Rhett, after he had looked at his, and let him open it.

While at the table, Roy impressed on Rhett that in the States he would find things extremely different. "One thing to keep in mind, if something is set for 10 o'clock, you *have* to be there at 10 o'clock!", and gave him a travel clock to help him keep track of the time. That may be difficult, as the time is the last thing of much concern here.

The shy girl sat by her boyfriend all evening, with the men, and missed all the women's conversation. Marion, as I said, is an animal lover and we told her she could talk about anything except snakes, which of course opened the conversation to every snake episode any of us could dredge up.

There is a snake living in the tree outside the fence that encloses Janet Gaobakwe's yard. She is worried it might come down sometime when the children are playing. "I think the Health Department should do something about it," she said.

Marion asked, "Why don't you have the tree cut down?"

"Well, there are trees all along the road. It could just move into the next one."

We reiterated the advice given us in New York, that when the hot weather comes, you must not park under a tree and leave any window of the car open. Snakes will come in and you might discover one after you've started to drive.

British Janet told us, "When I came last fall, I found a newspaper clipping, about a year old, with the story and picture of a python, out in Tlokweng (which is a small village, just past the Village part of Gaborone) that swallowed a goat. The picture showed it with the big bulge. Boy, that's not far away."

She went on to say, "There are monkeys out there, in the woods near the river. My yard boy said he'd bring me one for a pet, but I told him not to. And there are some families of baboons. We've seen them often."

Marion put in—"and remember that 12 foot snake they got out here, near Broadhust, where the construction was starting". That's the area Joel and the boys, and the Pahl boys were forever going out to.

They reported seeing snake skins there, but I didn't pay too much attention as they are always well dressed and shod when they go out. The law has been laid down now, though. No more going out to that old borehole.

"But, they cut the grass in the areas where the paths are, going to town."

"You don't mean to tell me there are snakes in those grassy places where I walk back and forth to town?" I gasped.

"Why not? Just keep to the path. There's no problem."

So, though this sounds scary, it is good to have someone put us on our alert and remind us that though we seem to be in a completely civilised little city, it is a small plot and the great wild bush is right out there in plain sight.

The party didn't break up until twelve, when the music on Springbok Radio switched from pop to a hymn on the organ, denoting Sunday had arrived. A mighty late night, for as I mentioned before, everyone goes to bed early.

The newlyweds collected their gifts, and they also took what was left of the wedding cake.

I was happy about the evening as no one had been shy about eating and all seemed to have a good time.

Now there will be more familiar faces, more people to say hello to in the Mall when I'm shopping. We may see Margaret at Barclay's, we may see Susan at the Post Office, looking for letters from California, and Janet and Marion, two more Britishers shopping for the makings of Yorkshire pudding, in the supermarket.

I mentioned before that I dissolve when someone does something especially kind and considerate for me all unexpectedly, as when Pauline went down to her house and heated water so I could have a cup of coffee when I was ill and the electricity was off.

Something that happened yesterday was even more surprising, although it was probably just one of many gestures of consideration by a person who is sensitive to other people, and acts on that sensitivity.

I went to church, at Trinity, to the United Service which is usually in Setswana and English. I was a little early and groups of people were standing wherever there was sunshine. It was a bit chilly, winter for them here, but crisply delightful to me. The difference between discomfort and not is the sun; out of its rays there is immediate chill. So I smiled to see the clusters in the sun in about six locations as I walked on to the doors. The sanctuary was completely empty, and I asked the pastor who was in conversation with someone near the entrance, if I were too early for the service.

"No, go right in."

So, I was the first to sit down, and chose a place far from the door, which I knew would be opening constantly, or propped open during the service as a welcome. I sat a few pews from the front, just below the choir stall rising up at the left, to sunny windows at the top.

The pastor moved about, shortly, carrying a folder, adjusting the sound system, and soon the congregation streamed in, all at once, from the steps and lawn. I noticed the pastor wore a gabardine suit, with belted back instead of his usual robe, although he had his clerical collar and a black v-neck sweater under his coat.

I had been impressed by him. He did the translation into Setswana on Easter, when we first attended. Then he had preached in English each Sunday since with various translators expressing his message in Setswana.

When Viola Webb and I went, there was a Baptismal Service. Prior to the sermon, the parents and their children to be baptised came up and stood together. All those to be baptised were youngsters, none babes in arms. One little girl, standing by her mother, began to whimper and cry as the first two were being lifted up to the pastor and as he marked a cross on their foreheads with the water he dipped from the fount. As her crying continued, the mother looked agitated, but didn't move to pick up the little girl. Then, an elder of the church—perhaps the girl's grandfather, stomped with determination out of his pew, down to the front, picked up the girl and elbowed in, holding her up to the pastor, as much as to say,

"Get on with this and get it over."

The screams of the frightened girl then filled the sanctuary. Though the pastor continued with the spoken parts and then dipped his hand to the water and marked her forehead with the cross, he seemed to me to be melting with love and sympathy for the little girl. It was just flowing from him. No one in the congregation batted an eye, just sat quietly, yet seemed to sigh with relief as the screams and then sobs subsided when the girl was placed in her mother's arms, and the officious elder returned to his pew in an air of self-satisfaction. I was impressed with the calm poise of the pastor and all that love flowing from him. There were eight little ones baptised and the remainder were done in blessed quiet. Viola said,

"I hope that little girl doesn't suffer from that traumatic experience."

I'm not sure of the Pastor's name. He is of slight build, but gives you the impression of bigness. His hair is closely cropped and he has a beard, mainly under the chin, which lends a triangular shape to his face, his forehead is broad and his cheekbones high; lean and light brown.

Well, I wondered if he were going to don his robe in time for the service. I glanced around, through the fast-filling auditorium to see if there were other expatriates here today. I didn't feel the need for their company, although I was looking to see if anyone I knew had come in, but I didn't see a single other white person. Just then, the choir which had been rehearsing out back came in and filed up into the loft pews and I saw the pastor go up with the choir, and that the man who had translated last week, was in the pulpit. I was noticing how full the church was, almost every pew occupied, and the three little children to the right of me; they kept peeking and smiling at me.

Just as the choir began the first hymn, and we stood to join it, the pastor came down the choir loft stairs, still singing, came up the outer aisle and stepped into the pew beside me and offered his hymnal to me to hold, with him. I indicated I couldn't read it and he said,

"I know."

But I put on my glasses and followed the words. The tune was familiar but I couldn't remember any exact words in English.

He sang like an angel, and hearing the words as I watched them on the page, I decided to try them. It didn't take long to figure out the sounds, and I enjoyed it.

When it was time for the pastoral prayer, he walked up the side aisle and stood near the front and then returned to the pew.

As the service continued, I realized that though there were some announcements in English, there was to be no translation of the sermon. The pastor beside me gave me the gist of it, at intervals. It was preached with a lot of fire and enthusiasm, and at the close of the service, I found they were starting a city-wide canvass, by sections; probably the reason for this especially fiery sermon.

There was no regular closing of the service; the pastor was up front calling out the leaders and workers of each group and directing them to different spots outside on the lawn and steps. I didn't even have a chance to say "thank you" to him for his graciousness, and he'll never realize how touched I was by his even noticing I was there, by his sensing that I might feel alone or disappointed not to be able to understand what was said.

There have been some chill days lately. Sunday was one of them, and Joel came in, in the afternoon, to say that Kenneth and Edwin next door, were cooking.

"Can you smell it on me?—some herb smell." He went on to say, "They didn't have any breakfast or lunch. No one is home over there. So they just made something to eat. They mixed flour and water and put spoonfulls into hot water and cooked it, and put in some noodles and some potato, then they put in what they called pepper. But it wasn't pepper, it was herb stuff. The smell made me sick." Then he added, "They were eating it up like mad."

He hung around a while and then said, "I think I'll make a cake." Which made me remark to Roy, "If you can't stand dough balls, you can eat cake." I didn't discourage him, but showed him how to use the mixer and he did a good job and watched it carefully as it rose and finished baking.

About 6:30 that evening Kenneth and Edwin came over. Joel let them in and they rushed to the electric heater. Little Edwin was shivering and didn't leave the heat for an hour. Kenneth was cold too, but perhaps he had on warmer clothes as he wandered around. Joel got some of his cake for them to eat and we had them stay until it was bedtime, to soak up the heat. Someone was coming into their house then, and perhaps they'd jump into bed and stay warm for the night. They have a fireplace in their living room, but they don't always have fuel on hand.

The winter chill is wicked for the families living in the shanty towns. Wind whistles through and they don't have rags enough to cover them or fuel to warm them. I felt sorry for Kenneth and Edwin, but they are of the more well-to-do group and live in a solid house.

Winter has brought us some new birds. After a very windy day last week I saw a number of new kinds and wondered if the wind and cold had something to do with it. Each day as I go out to the kitchen, the first thing I do is throw a handful of birdseed onto the concrete area under the clothes line. In just a few seconds, the crowd gathers.

There were numerous yellow birds, a few red-headed ones, a big group of "cut throats", soft brown sparrow-size birds with a red line from "ear to ear". Joel got excited one day and said there are a lot of "slit necks" out there. Flocks of bright blue waxbills rush for the seed and some mean doves, one of which I saw clamp onto the beak of a small bird who had just eaten a seed, and shake the little bird from side to side, the way a dog would do with a kitten. That was a sight I had never seen before.

The prize, when it comes to birds, are the big ones here now, supposedly moving north from South Africa out of the cold. They are bigger than pigeons, have a black and white body with a rust neck and head, crowned by a crest that shoots out backward. The bill is long and curved, and black.

When it is sitting on the ground and pecking at something, the whole body is absolutely still, and only the head hammers back and forth. Even pecking down into the ground, the tail doesn't move up a fraction of an inch. There have been many of them right in the back yard and in the thorn trees here and next door. When they fly, their wing span seems to be a yard wide! They are Hoopoes.

I have been describing the winter chill and the winter birds, and right in the middle of it, we have received an invitation to a reception at the American Embassy, July 5th, to celebrate the Fourth of July! More unusual than that, will be celebrating Christmas in the hottest of the hot season. Hot or cold, we'll celebrate what comes along and take the temperature in our stride.

JUNE 24

There was a chill wind blowing at the airport yesterday, but it wasn't the chill wind that made Susan sit and shiver, in the waiting room. Married just one week, she was here to see her new husband fly off to the United States for as long as eight months.

Roy had driven Susan, Rhett and his luggage, and some relatives out to the airport, quite early. It was almost too early—reminded me of getting to the hospital too early when you are expecting a baby.

Rhett was smiling nervously all the while although he must have been extremely . . . scared is the only word, and he seemed to mill around with his men friends, not spending every minute with his wife.

When Roy brought me out to the airport, he said, "Susan is inside, why don't you go sit with her?"

This I did, between her and a cousin, but she was shaking so, she couldn't keep her arms still, and I didn't want to embarrass her, so after talking a while, I suggested she walk around in the sun a bit, for warmth.

She wasn't wearing a hat today, just her button-down-the-front blue denim dress and a dark sweater. Her hair was tightly braided in a neat pattern and she had on grey hose and white sandals with extremely high soles.

There never was such a delayed departure. Finally, the plane came in from Johannesburg and it gave us something to do, to watch the unloading, refueling, and reloading of freight. Sacks of freight were tossed about; I thought at first it might be mail, but must have been small packages. When anything is sent air freight, it should be well insulated, as I think they practise on how far they can toss it. People have told us they think the goal is to have finally mastered tossing it the length of the field, having all contents broken, but the package intact.

A crowd from the office came to join the farewell. Conference Lokomo, who brought more relatives, Dennis the assessor, a crowd of other black young men, then the Deputy Tax Commissioner, who is British, of course.

Finally, one engine started and at long last, the passengers began to load. There was the final round of handshaking between the men. Rhett shook hands with me and showed me he had a nice little book in his inner pocket, "My Trip", which Susan had given him, and showed me that Roy had given him a pen, as he had forgotten one. Then he kissed the women, and I couldn't look when he told his wife goodbye.

She covered her face and turned her back to the room, trying to conceal her sobs, and mopped at her eyes and nose. I asked Roy if he had a clean handkerchief, but it didn't look very good to me, so I just looked the other way as she tried to keep her nose dry. Later, I saw she had a Kleenex, so some of her girlfriends must have come to her rescue.

We waved and waved, and Rhett was at the tail of the line boarding, when all of a sudden, he sprinted back into the building, off to one side. He hadn't been to the desk to check in and get his boarding pass. My heart sank. Poor Rhett, right off the desert and he hadn't even got through the right procedure in the little podunk he's starting off from. Eventually he was back, waving his little card, and this time, going on into the plane.

Well, it sat there, and before long the one roaring engine was turned off. Much rushing around and jabbering and we got the impression that someone scheduled to fly out hadn't arrived yet. After eons, a well dressed Britisher came flashing by with briefcase flying, calling "sorry, sorry", and ran for the plane.

It must have been an hour past scheduled takeoff time before it finally roared down the runway, and rose into the sky over the ridge of kopjes.

We all straggled out to the dusty parking lot, The other girls got into a pickup truck with Conference, and Roy and I waited for Susan to indicate that she wished to go along with them, but she turned toward me and took my hand and said, "I'll go with you."

As we got in, I said, "He'll be fine" (though my heart went out to him, with the phrase 'Babe in the woods' going through my mind) "because he'll be getting to Johannesburg and there he'll find out the procedure, and then at Capetown, and to Rio. Someone will tell him just what he needs to do, so by the time he gets to New York, he'll be an old hand at it."

Susan directed Roy to her part of town. The houses are very small and close together, and we drove a circuitous route, over bumpy roads, poor bridges, between houses and round about to her little home. The yard was completely bordered with cannas, the door was open, and all the chairs from the house were sitting outside.

"You had about forty at your party last night, huh?" Roy asked.

"Yes." She wasn't very talkative, but she didn't cry.

"Now you let us know as soon as you hear from Rhett" we said.

She thanked us and turned to the yard and began to carry the chairs into the so very empty house. The tall beautiful young girl walked now with her head drooping, like the flowers in the yard that had last night suffered their first frost.

JUNE 25

The other day, I went to the "Trinity Ladies". First, because someone had been kind enough to invite me, but secondly, with enthusiasm, because the speaker was to inform us about his work in translating the Bible into Setswana. I knew I'd learn something.

Dr. J. Derek Jones, when introduced, did not fulfill my picture in mind of a missionary who had been in the Boondocks of Africa for twenty years. He wore loafers, gabardine slacks, a bright pink shirt open at the collar, over which was a fine cashmere crewneck sweater. He was of medium height, rugged, had light brown curly hair with just a touch of grey, smooth rosy cheeks and a big smile.

"When I was asked to address you on this subject of translating, I planned to prepare a scholarly paper to present. Then, the manager of the Botswana Book Centre suffered several heart attacks; I was called in to help run the place, and so you have been spared the paper," was his introduction.

He had a lot to tell us, in an informal discussion, always open to questions as he went along, about his years of work in Botswana.

Setswana was not a written language until 1816 when Robert Moffat, British missionary, devised a system of spelling and began his translation of the Bible. The Setswana were the first to have a Bible, south of the Sahara and there are over 1600 languages south of the Sahara. In 1857 the printing was done in Moffat's house but the presses were later moved into a church.

Revising has gone on ever since then. The Setswana language is fluid and changing, but it is a rich language with no poverty of expression. There is no way translation can be done word for word or even sentence by sentence. Word for word can damage.

"The method I am using now is to get the kernel of the meaning of a passage, the root idea, and to get it into the Setswana language in idioms—in up-to-date expressions!

"Of course, there are many amusing incidents in the problems of communication. Once, a quotation, 'Alas! My Master, what shall we do?' was translated into Setswana as 'A girl! My Master, what shall we do?'

"There are minority languages throughout Botswana; Kalanga, in the north has the gospels and Acts in that language. They can speak Setswana, but won't admit it. In Maun, the Herero have the New Testament.

"But Setswana is firmly the official language of Botswana, in spite of these minorities."

He closed in saying that there are only a million and a half to whom Setswana is the language, and that is a small group, relatively, to retain a language, but the country seems determined to preserve it. More and more, in their ten years of Independence, they are emphasizing their own heritage. In spite of this determination, learning English is compulsory.

When Ben Webb came back from his visit to Serowe, he was excited about instances where he would be approached by an old man in tatters (sometimes a whole leg exposed) who would ask, in clipped British English, "I say, have you seen two oxen pass this way?"

I don't know why Ben was so amazed, but I think it was because he was in the native village, out on the open veld far from the city. It just didn't seem right to him to have every dusty, ragged, person straggling in off the bush, speak so well.

"Well, they are taught in school, Ben."

"How about John the garden boy?" Roy came back at me.

"I can't say. Maybe he never got a chance to go to school."

The advice you get about shopping when you first arrive here seems to make the whole operation more complicated than it turns out to be.

"You'll not have time on your hands. You can spend two hours each day, going from shop to shop" was the word from an old timer while we were in New York.

"Two hours a day! Never, with seven kids and all I have to do, I'll never use that system" was Alice's reaction.

Then when we got here, the British approach was—

"Now I get my butter in Food Town, because it's 74 cents there and it's 84 cents in Co-op. I'm not paying any ten cents extra. You can depend on anything you get in Food Town. But go out to White City on Friday early for the vegetables, and when you're there, go to Capri and get your bread fresh. I can't stand this in the Astra, and the Co-op after it's been slapped into these plastic bags when it's fresh, and then gets all soggy. Then, if you don't want to stop back at the Mall, you can just pick up your bags of milk at the bakery too. And, of course, there is the Butchery there in White City, too."

Well, I had no idea where White City was, or how I'd get there, and it was some weeks before I did get out there.

I started by going to the co-op store on the corner of the Mall. The first time, you notice all the differences between here and a supermarket at home. But all it takes is time. You have to get used to the names of things, and the weights.

Almost everything comes from South Africa, and it has all the information on the cans and packages in two languages, English and Africaans and weights in Kilos. I can't believe, now after I've gotten used to their stores, how perplexed I was to start with. Our meals seemed to be Maggi soups and sandwiches, with scrambled eggs for supper, for a while.

All the British Lady's advise confused me, for when I went into any one of the three stores on the Mall, I saw they had vegetables, a variety of bread and milk in the coolers.

Milk was and is still somewhat of a problem. It comes in plastic bags like a bag of frozen vegetables. Each holds 500 milligrams, with the bag having some expansion room in it. Thus, as they are all piled in the cooler case, the milk in each sloshes around, and the whole mass seems to be alive. Actually, buying the milk is not that much of a problem, except you have to learn to have a basket to carry it in. The bags are often wet, from some leakers, so if you try walking home with things in a paper sack—trouble. What took me ages to master, was handling the bags at home. You cut off one corner with scissors, and you'd better get it straight. If you can't lay your hands on the scissors and are in a hurry and jab a jagged opening with a knife, woe unto you when you pour it out. It may spurt in various directions, all unpredictable.

The partly-used sack, too, often tips, and leaks, and I began folding the opening down a couple times and clipping with a wooden clothespin. Great—to a certain extent. Finally, one day I studied the diagrams on the milk bag and they showed setting it in some style of a pitcher and then cutting. How dumb can you be! I got out a plastic square food container and began setting the open bags into that.

Friday is the best day to buy vegetables, as the big trucks come in then from South Africa, and they come first to White City.

This is an area of Indian Traders stores, around a dusty unpaved plaza spotted with thorn trees. The little buildings are a bit ramshackle, and there are about four stores which sell the same things, general merchandise, blankets, clothes, the usual run of basins and tea kettles. But the main point of interest to me is the vegetable shop with a wealth of varities, all the best I have ever tasted. Beside this store, on the "porch" (this area reminds me of an old western town, with the rickety porch along in front of the shops) is a man sewing on a sewing machine. He will make you a nice African shirt for Rand 2.75 if you bring him your material.

There are several "sewing centers" going full tilt around the square with mending and patching progressing and a huge box of rags and worn-out garments on the floor or ground nearby.

Down around the corner, past a few furniture places, with wares stacked outside, there is the Capri Bakery and Cafe with hot meat pies, ready to eat. It's just a small salesroom, with bread stacked on the shelves in back of the counter, special cupcakes and pastries in the cases, and stacks of bread in big boxes. You can smell the place before you get there—wonderful aroma and it's all as good as it smells.

Capri bakes all the bread sold in all the stores in town. Their bread is my downfall. Every week I determine I shall resist with greater strength and every week, I find my skirts just as tight.

The first time I went into the Butchery there in White City, I turned around and went out again. One, run by a Chinese is perfectly all right. It just takes a bit of adjusting to the smells, for the back regions are full of ugly carcasses hanging and blocks holding various portions of legs and rib sections, with the butchers in their dingy and blood-stained aprons whacking away at them.

Farther along the street, at the corner, there is a butcher shop that is even more odoriferous, and the meat hooks slide along a track right up to the cash register, where great hunks of tripe hang, avidly anticipated by the long line. The sight of it was enough to make a vegetarian of you.

There is another place to get meat—Wil-Flo-out on the edge of the Industrial area. It too has an odor, but as Alice remarked the other day, "After you're in here a while, you don't notice it at all." They have a good corps of butchers who work behind the scenes a little bit more, and have a regular display counter, with ready-cut pieces.

Here they grind your "Mince" by the Kilo. Mince is hamburger, as it is meat that has been minced. Sounds sensible. And you ask for Fillett, with the "t" well pronounced. Beef is very reasonable, as it is this country's biggest product, with the Botswana Meat Commission slaughter house only fifty miles away, at Lobatse.

So, once you find out where things are, the days of the weeks when the fresh vegetables will be best, and the local names of the products, and have transportation, shopping isn't too bad.

"It's a good thing Daddy didn't know what he was getting into, or he'd never have bought the tickets!" Joel whispered to me.

We were sitting in the Town Hall at Zeerust, Republic of South Africa, at eight o'clock on Friday evening and the dark red velvet curtains, had just parted for the beginning of what Roy had thought would be a movie.

He had talked us into taking another trip this weekend, even though things had been popping in South Africa. That's a very trite and superficial way of commenting on the tragedies of the week, but I don't really mean to minimize it. Joel said "No!". Said he was tired of taking trips and going places. "I just want to stay home." But, he like me, enjoys everything immensely, once he does get on his way.

Next Sunday is Fourth of July, with picnic and celebration out at Adume Park, near the Gaborone Dam and on Monday is the reception at the home of Ambassador and Mrs. Bolen. Also, the Ben Webbs will be down from Serowe for the weekend. Word from them is they are still in the Serowe Hotel which has no heat. Their furniture is still in central supply out here in the Industrial Area and he hasn't yet located a generator, and he's also freezing in his office. Temperatures dropped this past week to a new low, and no one has been overly comfortable, at any time.

These were some of the reasons Roy wanted to go down to Zeerust, Mafeking, Rustenberg or somewhere. He suggested Krugersdorp, to stay in the Park, but I countered we should postpone that until the weather is warmer again, for enjoyment. I wanted to go, as my larder was low, but wanted to go not too far, and take time to do and see something unhurriedly.

He said, "We can start right after 5 p.m. and be down in Zeerust, have dinner, stay in the Hotel, maybe see a movie, then after breakfast, shop at leisure." So that's what we planned and for the first time, I was energetic and raring to go when the day rolled around.

We were off and away even ahead of schedule and saw much of the Tlokweng road south, in the daylight. When it did get dark, we were startled by the glow of a huge veld fire, far to our left. It was raging so that the clouds above it were brilliant.

"Do you suppose it's riots?" Joel wanted to know.

"No, the riots are over for the time being and they're only in the areas where people are crowded together, near the city and the colleges," so he relaxed, though we kept an eye on the fire until we were climbing the last kopje; going down the last steephill into Zeerust.

The Grand Marico Hotel, on the main street along which all the shops and stores straggle, from the Indian shops at one end, to Checkers grocery at the other, was more Grand of name than of accommodation. It had an exotic air though, with its entrance a patio screened from the street by latticed brick walls interlacing at intervals so there was complete privacy for all the tables there. Boys in white jackets were on hand, hopping around to keep warm, and the girls serving in the dining room wore cream dresses embellished with bright red and gold border print and red head scarves tied at the back of the neck. The head waiter wore a red fez with tassel.

Roy ascertained from the desk that there was a theatre in town but the movie was in Africaans. However, there was a show at the Town Hall in English at 6 p.m. So we hurried through dinner and went on down the street about two blocks where a park ran down to the Town Hall, a block below. Plenty of parking space, and we joined the line for tickets, noticing that the hall was pretty well filled. It was a big hall, and high, and we saw banks of flood lights on poles at either side of the stage, which puzzled me a bit. But finally the curtains opened, and in a blaze of flashing colored lights there was the smashing opening of a four piece Rock Group!

Joel really came to life then but I didn't dare look at Roy. Rock isn't his favorite. But they were good—very good. This was the beginning of one of the best variety shows I've seen and it turned out that Roy enjoyed every minute of it too.

During the intermission, we had a good look at all the people sitting around or near us. There was a door nearby, and it let in frigid air from the outside, and we noted the people who opened and closed it. The next day, everywhere we went, we saw "the girl who sat in front of us", "the girl who sold us the tickets", "the man who was closing the door". We didn't feel among strangers.

"Doesn't this remind you of the place we stayed that time outside of Paris?" Roy asked, as we set our bags down in the frigid bedroom. I couldn't see any resemblance to the upstairs room in that lady's home in Rosey, except it dawned on me—he meant the cold.

He had turned on a wall heater before we went to the Town Hall, but it hadn't raised much heat. I didn't even unzip my bag—filled with robe, slippers, changes of clothes for everyone—stuff that had taken me a half hour to pack. I just turned down the covers and got in with everything I had on, except my shoes. That's the resemblance to the place outside Paris.

In the morning I peeked out into the courtyard and saw an Elephant Ears plant in a big Jardiniere that will never be the same again. It was wilted and yellowing already, crinkling in greater resemblance to real elephant skin.

Spartan Roy shaved. The electricity was off and soon a generator roared and sputtered into a drone, though we never could get the lights on again. In the dining room, we had a good breakfast, but no toast. Evidently the generator didn't get up that much power.

Out on the street so early, some shops weren't yet open. Then it was 11 a.m. and Roy said, "How about going on over to Mafeking?" That was great. I wanted to go and knew Joel would have fun with all the Pahl family on excursion there today.

"Let's go right now. I'll do the grocery shopping in Mafeking Checkers, and while I'm doing that you can hit the other places."

So off we went, and were in Mafeking, over good highway with no town between, by 11:40 a.m.

We found we had parked beside the Pahl's van in Checkers lot, so the conversation flew as we unloaded carts and packed in our stuff. The kids were all grimy—you don't know how dirty you can get on one of these expeditions—and Alice said she'd find some place for them to clean up then we'd meet at the corner restaurant on the square. Joel rode with them in the VW bus and he was happy—for sure.

Lunch was fun, as we all had to relax then; nothing else was open. They even locked the public restrooms on the edge of the square at one o'clock.

Alice had promised the kids they could have 20 cents apiece to spend in there after lunch. Little did she know what would develop. Although there was candy, cookies, funny books, etc., the first kid got a set of monster fangs to put in his mouth—a double set, top and bottom.

So, it spread like wildfire and in five minutes, there were eight kids with lips stretched over protruding teeth, with fangs sprouting in all directions. They trooped out onto the sidewalk and we started down the block where there was a vegetable stand still open. All of a sudden, Alice said,

"Look at that!"

There was a little black boy, about Joel's age, his eyes bugging out at the sight of all these kids with the teeth sticking out and he himself, unconsciously was drawing in his lower lip and sticking out his uppers—all the while with a puzzled look, like he couldn't believe what he saw.

Joel rode home with the Pahls and we arrived home just ahead of them. They had a story to tell as they piled into our yard soon after.

Somewhere between Lobatse and here, they had struck some kind of an animal. It was small, but had hoofs; might have been some kind of a little pig, but they had no idea. It had ended up hanging in a thorn tree. Joel said, "It made me sick. You should have seen it. Mr. Pahl thought two boys we had just passed might have thrown it at us, cause it came flying out to the car just as we passed them. The hub cap is all dented in. So, we had to go back and talk to the boys. When it hit, Mr. Pahl got jerked around, and his glass thing—in his eye—"

"Contact lens?"

"Yes, his contact lens fell out and they spent ten minutes looking for it. Finally found it though."

So that was quite an added excitement to the trip. Jerry had looked really beat when we had met him in Mafeking. Now he was more beat.

We asked them in for coffee, but they turned us down. Better to get the gang on home and unload the days shopping, as the dark would descend any minute.

They have things to think about, too, as they've been assigned a house in town, and will have to tear up from their "home" in Sebele, and resettle. But that's another story.

As I was crossing the lawn after church yesterday, where I had again been the only white person present, I heard someone call, "Mrs. Brown?"

I stopped and turned to see who could be there who knew me. and looked into the face of a thin black girl running up to me. At first I thought it might be one of the girls from next door, but in a second, I recognized Susan; the girl who married Rhett two weeks ago. I gave her a hug.

"I didn't know you went to Trinity."

She had her Bible and Hymnal in her hands.

We walked toward the car, parked across the street, and I said, "Come on. Mr. Brown will give you a ride home."

Then I recalled her little empty house, and added, "Or if you want to come over to our house a while?"

"Oh, yes," she answered with enthusiasm, so home we came.

Roy had the Sunday papers which she read while we had coffee, then I got dinner ready and she seemed happy to eat with us and was not so shy that she wouldn't ask for things to be passed at the table. She eats in a style that is prevalent here; holds the fork in the left hand, tines pointing down toward the plate and uses the knife in the right, to constantly cut and push food and load the fork, which stays in the left hand for all eating.

Now I had a chance to get out the Botswana map to have her pin point her home. It is way out on the western edge of the country, south of Ghanzi, and Rhett's home is twelve miles north of hers. I don't know how long she has been here in Gaborone; whether Rhett brought her down a few weeks ago or earlier.

Their home is not readily accessible from here, for the Kalahari Desert must be completely circumvented—there's no way to cross it directly.

So, it is amazing to me, that Susan arrived here from a tiny town, so far away, and she has her Bible, and her Hymnal and a fantastic command of English.

Roy gave her an aerogram to write Rhett when she had an address, in Los Angeles. She was engrossed in the new Time magazine, when Roy said he'd drive her on home, as he had to get to work on the car.

Her little house looked neat when we got there. I could see the door and the concrete floor of the "porch" were painted dark green and shining, and that all of the yards in this little cluster were planted with flowers; three with some sod laid, protected by a barricade of thorn bushes. No one will tangle with a branch off a thorn tree. I took a picture of her standing at her door and she was smiling this time.

Today she starts her work at the Surveys and Lands building. I'm sure she will do well and I hope she enjoys the work. She has a long eight months ahead of her, until her husband returns.

JUNE 1

We had a near disaster at the bird feeding area the other morning. Just as several dozen birds had begun to consume their regular breakfast, the big dog from next door sauntered in. First thing I knew was a big thump against the back of the house and when I glanced up towards the window, saw the flock of birds rushing up into the thorntree branches. I looked down where they had been and saw the dog with a bird in its mouth shaking it. I yelled at him and ran out and chased him. Luckily, he dropped the bird. I brought it in to show to Joel. It sat contentedly in my hand, and we spread the wings to see the markings. We smoothed its neck and patted it and finally I took it back out. At first it hobbled a bit and then sat so still, I went to pick it up again, and as I touched it, it flew quite a distance, over into some weeds. So I left it, and later we saw that it had gone. I hope it flew away.

This put a damper on the birds for a while. Not many hung around for more feeding that day. There was the regular crowd back again this morning, however, and some of the brightest yellow birds yet.

We keep seeing new kinds. There were sizable birds which reminded me of Siamese cats, in coloring. Buff with black heads and tails, and then I noticed a flash of yellow underneath at the base of the tail. They are Bulbous; red eyed or black eyed. Then one afternoon, six or eight big soft brown birds with speckled breasts came down near the back door. They ate around the base of the thorn tree.

Another new splash of color appeared on the lawn next door. The brightest red breast I ever saw. This was a crimson breasted shrike. Rich, velvety, brilliant crimson, the rest of the bird almost black. He was the size of a large robin, so was impressive to say the least.

We have seen a number of the clownish yellow billed hornbill, such as we saw in the parking lots at Kruger National Park. They are fairly common around here, and you can see them in the trees, outside the city. The cut throat finch, red headed finch, the blue wax bills, and a raft of yellow canaries or warblers are out there every morning to get the breakfast I throw out to them.

The sun birds are still in the big plants outside the dining room window. "Birds of South Africa", by Roberts, which Roy bought this week, lists twenty-eight in the Sunbird family, and the names include Bronze, Orangebreasted, Coppery, Purple-banded, Blackbellied, Yellow-bellied, White-bellied, Olive, Blue-throated, Violet-backed, Collared, and Scarlet-chested. So these names alone indicate that they are brilliant and colorful.

The most common one here is the Marico; a brilliant irridescent bird, forever hanging in those funny plants, darting its long curved bill in to suck out the nectar. The Setswana name for it is Senwa Borophi-Drinker of Nectar.

Roy and Joel drove out the Lobatse Road, south of Gaborone, to the Kgale Quarry. Roy had ordered some crushed stone for the drive-way, months ago, and they're always going to deliver "maybe this afternoon".

The quarry is back a short distance off the main road, and as they drove along, Roy thought he saw a man coming on a bicycle.

Joel, who has keener eyes, saw that it was a huge Baboon. As they neared it, a whole raft of smaller ones straggled along out of the bush to join him. It was quite a surprize to see them, even though people have said that they are around. This was more exciting than seeing them in the National Park—five hundred miles away.

They were on display again, on the return drive from the quarry. Perhaps they were as much the sightseers as Roy and Joel.

They are not to be toyed with. In *Jock of the Bushveld*, Fitzpatrick describes why he kept his dogs from ever tangling with them. A Baboon can hold its victim in four tight grips so there is no escape, and then he leisurely lies back and bites hunks out of it until he's had enough. Not so pleasant—for the victim.

I had heard about getting vegetables from the Prison Farm but that's all I knew. No particulars. Yesterday, Janet Stringer, whom I met when she came to our dinner and party for Rat and Susan (I was spelling it Rhett, the way it's pronounced) came over after lunch and asked if I'd like to drive out to the nursery. I was more than willing and grabbed my coat; we were away in the time it took me to turn off the stove.

"First, I thought we'd go to the Prison. Do you need any vegetables?" I didn't, but I wanted to see the place. It's just down the road past the Camp Cash Store; it's the end of the line.

She pointed out the residences of the prison personnel, and soon we were right beside the outer wall, with a watchtower up above. Through the fence, I could see a group of women sitting on the ground in the sunshine. I didn't know they had women here too.

We came to an open gate, after passing a football field on the left. "The soccer games here are something to watch. You can come out and see them, Sunday afternoons, I think."

"The gates are always open—no one runs away." she remarked, as we spied an open doorway, the wall beside it decorated with a bright picture of a wheelbarrow overflowing with vegetables.

They didn't have a great selection at this time of day; the men noted that the morning is the best time. I did get a big head of lettuce—and had to wait until the officer wrote out an official receipt, complete with my name as purchaser.

Janet pointed out that further along in the same building, there were several other doors, the first to the shoe repair shop; others to places you could purchase rugs the inmates made, and where you could bring anything that needed repair.

I turned then to take a picture or two, as we peered through the fence toward where the women had been—although I didn't actually have them in it. I took one of Janet, by the flowers, looking toward the watchtower. I should have known better; the matron came flying over and said emphatically there is to be no picture taking. Janet told her we only took one of her and the flowers, and we took off. I was embarrassed that I hadn't had more sense—putting Janet into such a situation, when she had been kind enough to come take me out.

I have mentioned the beautiful flowers for sale on the Mall. They are all fifty cents a bunch whether roses or carnations. Either of them seem to last almost two weeks in the house. When we were raving over them at the dinner party, Janet had asked, "Do you want to got out and see where they are raised? A Mr. Neilson has gardens out toward the river and he ships flowers all over the world."

So, this was where we headed now. Out over that terrible road toward the Gaborone Dam we travelled one Sunday looking for the Marina.

The road hadn't improved any. All of a sudden, we reached the brook across the road. Our fording of it that Sunday had been one of the high points of our ride. Janet had a small new car. She stopped in complete amazement. "Where did this come from? I don't remember it."

"You needn't go through it for my sake. I wouldn't have the nerve." It was wide, about three car lengths to get across, and the choice of places to cross was vast—far left, middle, far right and anywhere in between. We studied the tracks leading to it, and saw many far to the right.

"I'm going to go ahead. Let's go." she said.

In we dove, pretty much to the right, but we heard an ugly scrape halfway across. She was quite perturbed, but there wasn't a thing to do but keep going.

Not far down the dry dusty road there was a sign for the turnoff—"Sanitas Flowers" and she wondered when he had adopted that name and why. As soon as we stopped at the nursery, we both inspected the underpinning but couldn't see any damage—not even a dent, so we went on to give our attention to the flowers.

There were no "greenhouses" but what seemed acres covered with netting like a tobacco field. Carnations in bed after bed. Many women were working with stacks of clippings, fixing them just so, for planting.

They sat in a row on the ground, feet straight out in front of them, in a place where the sun shone. Each had a great stack of leafy stems beside her, and she picked up one at a time, pulled off some leaves, pinched off the stem and laid the prepared clipping in a big square plastic container which stood on end beside her. When one was packed solid, away it went and she started another. My first impression after the vastness of the beds was of the opportunity for employment here. Great for these women and a large staff of men.

We met Mr. Neilson, and Janet asked if he had a pink bougainvillaea and he said he'd locate one—that we were welcome to look around.

As we walked out through fields of carnations, where more women were cutting blooms, we began to see all the damage done by the frost of the recent cold week. At least it looked like a lot of damage to me. I thought Mr. Neilson looked calm in the face of it. Row after row of Rubber plants were now brown instead of green, though they were all carrying a great load of hay which had been scattered over them. Many small bright red plants were also touched by the frost though the roses seemed fine. We covered about all of it, a long walk, then returned to get the plant. I didn't buy anything as there was too much for me to choose from. Anyway, there's always a selection of his shrubs and plants available near the theatre on the Mall.

There was much searching for the right color, and he took us around onto his private grounds adjacent to his residence or offices, to examine the colors of some in bloom—then she finally made a decision and took one. How much? First, he said eighty cents then when she got out her purse, he amended it to sixty cents. I couldn't believe it. He had spent about half an hour of what must have been precious time—in the midst of the frost damage—for talking to someone and sixty cents!

"Mr. Neilson is always willing to take time. He's never in a hurry.

He came here quite a while ago and he decided to prove that you could raise flowers here successfully, and make a go of it. He does ship flowers all over the world."

We looked the car over again, and Mr. Neilson volunteered, "You must have gone too close to the middle. Stay more to the left going out. That place must be from some leak from the Water Works—I don't know why someone doesn't do something about it."

Just as we got to the water, a huge truck was crossing, but at the opposite edge we had crossed. We stopped a while to watch, then as it dripped off out of sight up the road, we made our plunge—so far to the left I thought Janet would get stuck in the mud bank, but she climbed out O.K. with no scraping sounds at all, much to her relief.

When we got to her home in the Village, she asked if I'd like a cup of tea, and how I like it.

"Oh, I drink it with milk, or just plain."

"Well, I heard once that someone was offered a cup of tea with lemon! I couldn't understand why anyone would spoil a good cup of tea by putting something like that in it."

We enjoyed a proper cup of hot tea well diluted with milk. There seems to be many ways of doing things, as the old saying, "The right way, the wrong way and the Army way". Well, here it's the right way, the wrong way, and the British way.

JULY 2

It must be that the winter chill has encouraged the snakes to come out to find some daytime warmth. Kenneth and Edwin saw a green snake near their front door and pitched bricks at it in a vain attempt to kill it; it got away and went up into a tree. Joel said, "They weren't scared of it; the kids said they'd like to climb that tree and go after it!"

Yesterday, on the school grounds, on a path out near the Soccer field, the custodian killed a big Black Mamba. At least the story always is that they are Black or Green Mambas, which of course are poisonous. Joel's class was allowed to come out and see it after the killing. The snake had evidently just eaten a big rat, as it had an obvious after-dinner bulge.

We have decided to be watchful, and someone—with a mean streak—suggested to be on the watch for them coming into the house at night, to seek warmth. You can be sure the doors and the screen door will be securely fastened!

Changing the oil in the car on a Saturday afternoon, Roy found he had the wrong size filter. No possibility of another until Monday, so we were on foot for the weekend. He was lucky enough Monday morning, heading for the office, to be given a lift by a man who lives only a few houses away, one who used to stop out front to pick up someone at Kenneth's house. He was on his way to Botswana Radio and Roy learned that his work is doing special feature programs which are aired at noon several days a week.

When Roy got home at noon (someone having given him a lift, with his proper size filter), he had much to tell. We put the radio on at the proper time and heard his fine interview with Dr. Gwendolyn Carter, Professor of Political Science and Director of African Studies at the University of Indiana, formerly of Northwestern, whom we had heard speak the week before.

She comes to South Africa every two years. The Botswana Society had invited her to speak at the Museum about the Republic of South Africa—whether it is an African State or a Colonial Power. The auditorium was packed; the door never was closed and people poured in and around the room all evening, leaning against the wall and sitting on the floor.

Although she had no "answers," she did give a historical resumé and much information on the plans for the Independent Transkei and the implications of it, from several viewpoints.

The most interesting part of the evening to me, and others expressed the same opinion, was to hear the comments and questions of the local people. They were happy to have a Forum and Dr. Carter told them they were free to make statements; needn't restrict themselves to questions.

Many had an amazing command of English and expressed themselves beautifully making valid arguments and moving statements. I smiled to myself when someone asked why the blacks in the United States were not more active in demonstrating for the ending of Apartheid in South Africa.

Even Dr. Carter smiled and said, "Well, for many of my students, we have to get out the Atlas and Globe and point out where Africa and the various African States are. The American Blacks have been pretty well caught up in their own concerns, in their own country." I am amazed at my own ignorance of the continent and the countries around me here, and have been busy learning about them and their history. Caught up in my normal routine of life at home, I couldn't have been less concerned about where Botswana was, or what the makeup or politics of South Africa were—not by purposely ignoring it, but because during normal life at that distance, it seemed irrelevant.

The evening reached somewhat of a climax after a session of impassioned speeches, when a drunk floated in, a bit smelly and tattered, decided to express his opinion loudly, and in no way would be deterred from either speaking or remaining. The whole room was for a while mesmerized by his performance. Even the emcee just watched and listened, forgetting his duties and not realising he had lost all control of the program. Eventually, he and Dr. Carter seemed to come back to the present, to the discussion, and more speakers were called on who attempted to put across their ideas, intermittently drowned out by the drunk. Eventually, the emcee wound things up and I guess everyone felt it had been profitable. Each must have learned something new and most had been able to speak if they had a statement.

The Radio interview with Dr. Carter was fine, and more informative than even her evening talk. The man did a fine job with his questions.

He had told Roy when driving him to work, that he is always on the lookout for people to interview so Roy told him about Dr. Curry being here, about his plans to do a study of an agricultural project up near the Okavanga Swamp, established by refugees from Angola, and that Dr. Curry has six former students now serving in the Peace Corps in Africa.

He told Roy to be sure and get in touch with him when Dr. Curry is back from that trip and he would interview him.

So, I said to Roy—"See all you'd have missed if you hadn't had a problem with the car. If all had gone well we wouldn't have had our good walks to town, you wouldn't have met your neighbor, wouldn't have taken such an interest in the Radio program—wouldn't even have turned it on, and he wouldn't have known about Dr. Curry."

JULY 6

I never dreamed that by the time the U.S. Bicentennial arrived, I would find myself celebrating it in the Republic of Botswana, in Southern Africa.

But celebrate it we did in both the traditional way and with a feeling for our own country that had been enhanced by seeing more of the rest of the world.

Who would have imagined that on the Fourth, we would be driving in a ten seater HiAce Toyota, with new friends, across a bumpy road leading to the banks of the Notwane River, where we would have a picnic with other Americans serving throughout Botswana. Who would have imagined, that as we crossed this area of thorn trees and tall grass, we would spy a bright red, white and blue sign—the beginning of a Burma Shave jingle erected especially for the day.

Nothing could have started out a day on a better note than Burma Shave.

Name tags, with states noted, helped the large group get acquainted quickly. We were happy to spot a "Rhode Island" tag and hurried to meet the Hopkins family, here for their second stay in Botswana, now in the village of Gabane, about ten miles outside Gaborone. Heidi is in Joel's class and the other two are younger. We found they had once visited friends in our home town of Canterbury.

The day was filled with games, competitions, food, music, and even speeches, under a big bright American flag.

When the day ends, it ends in a hurry. The sun goes out of sight and instantly it seems night, without a lingering twilight. Everyone packed up and moved out pretty quickly when it got near 5 p.m. You want to be home when it's dark, not driving across bumpy strange territory.

The Pahls, Webbs and Browns gathered on our porch with the house lights off, and Roy set off the big collection of rockets and fire-crackers purchased that morning at the Camp Store. There was noise and rocketry enough to warrant an investigation, but no one seemed to notice other than a few little boys, leaning on the front fence.

"American Madness" was the weekend celebration at the Holiday Inn—two nights of Red, White and Blue, and good buffets. The Webbs were staying the long weekend with us and we discovered that gala by accident, dropping by for a light supper.

That was topped by the lawn party at the Ambassador's Residence the next afternoon, with throngs of people to meet and exciting tales to hear. It was Tuesday afternoon before our house guests were off and we finally wallowed in some peace and considered the celebration over.

Later, Margaret Rowe said her daughter Helen got tired of hearing all about Botswana's Independence celebrations, and about the great picnic we had for our Independence celebration and she asked her British mother, "When are *we* going to get to celebrate Independence Day?"

JULY 7

The other night we gave Kenneth and Edwin a lift to the movies. Roy had bought tickets for two couples from the office—Dennis and his

girl and Gilbert and Margaret Tidi. The party expanded because the
Webbs came along, and the Pahl boys invited four friends including
Joel, and as long as their Dad had to bring them in, he brought along
four of his other youngsters and stayed himself, which is all beside the
point. As we drove away from the house, Joel said, pointing to a
woman walking in the same direction,

"There goes their maid."

"Whose? Kenneth's?"

Then Kenneth giggled and said something about going for a drink.

"Going for Chibuku?" which is a local cheap beer.

This made them giggle self-consciously, but he spoke up and said,
"We don't call them maids."

"What do you call them?"

"By their names."

"Oh, they just work for you like someone else would work in an
office?"

"In South Africa they have maids. In Botswana, no maids."

I thought this was pretty good for him to point out. There is no
aura of subservience anywhere here. There are the haves and the have-
nots, but anyone of them can move up as far as he wishes; there are no
racial bars. With more educational facilities on the horizon, really in
sight with the $9,000,000 windfall from the World Bank for schools and
furnishings announced last week, moving up will be a reality for many
more.

Roy met the young man who is in charge of purchasing the furnishings and software for these schools—World Bank Fund—and was
interested to find he had attended Annandale High School where we
once lived in Virginia. "He looks too young to me to be handling this
project, but that's the way more and more people look to me these
days!"

There was a cold spell recently. That's hard to believe, the way the
sun is pouring down today, but it was cold and miserable to say the least
for the people who don't have solid houses or fuel. Coal was not available, partly perhaps, as no one predicted the right amount that would be
needed. So, the Lions Club took it upon themselves to locate some coal
and have it brought in and sold at cost to whomever needed it. The day
for purchase was set as June 26th, a Saturday.

Janet Stringer said they went at 9 a.m. to get some. The man said,
"Would you mind coming back at ten?" so they went on over to the
Mall and did some shopping, returning at ten.

The man said, "Would you mind coming back next week?"

"Why?"

"We have lost the train."

Happily, I saw a notice stuck on a store window later in the week.

"The Lion's Club Coal is in! Sales will be at 9 a.m. on Saturday, July 3."

So they must have "found the train". It is now too late for the intense cold, but there may be more cool nights ahead when it will be warmly appreciated.

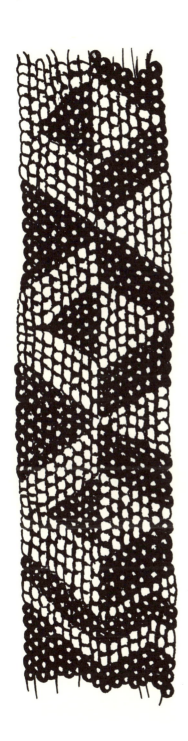

3

Rondavels

Pauline, with Fred and Thandi, at her Rondavel in Molepolole.

"What are you going to do this weekend, Pauline?" Roy asked her Friday after lunch.

"I want to go home. I am trying to build my house."

Roy had wanted to go to Johannesburg for the weekend, proposing it to me on Thursday, just two days after all my house guests had left so I was not enthusiastic. I couldn't face hurtling through the night down that rough dirt road, trying to make a couple hundred miles before bedtime, and if it were as cold a night and a similar hotel to the one at Zeerust the weekend before, I didn't feel it worth the effort. It would mean the rest of the trip into the city on Saturday morning, when the stores are only open to 1 p.m. I guess I looked stricken at the suggestion, as Joel piped up, "What's the matter with you?"

I finally said that I would prefer to go next weekend, and have this one a quiet one at home. I know Roy wants to get there to take his stereo down to where it was made, for repair. It's a neat radio and record player combination, slim and long on a black wire base. We have had lots of enjoyment from it.

Jeanine Pahl has used it several times to play her french records on, to tape them (she studies by correspondence course from the University of Nebraska), and one day she came over to tape new records. She put it on, listened and didn't hear a thing. I pushed every button and turned every dial, but still no sound. Joel tried—still nothing, and when Roy came for lunch—still nothing.

After supper, Roy pulled the cabinet out from the wall, tipped it up to take the radio out and found a fat brown mouse wedged in on top of the radio. I was relieved that a culprit had been found, and that it wasn't one of us. He took the problem to the radio shop and the proprietor assured him that it is a common problem; that mice do much damage when they're in there running around on crucial areas, especially when the radio or stereo is on.

We tried for a repair place in Zeerust, but when Roy saw the Indian Traders shop, where a heap of already-repaired radios was piled on the floor among stacks of other merchandise, with the clerks hopping over them, he wanted none of their supposed service. They said they could send away for parts, and it takes much time. Roy didn't feel they would be very skilled diagnosticians for his cripple so will take it down to where it was made, as I said before.

So, inasmuch as I had talked him out of that trip, I suggested,

"Maybe you'd like to drive up to Molepolole; we haven't been there yet."

"Hey, that's a good idea. Do you want a lift home, Pauline?"

She didn't seem to understand at first, but we said,

"We'll drive you up tomorrow morning and we can see the city and the Livingstone Hospital. Do you have some stores there?"

"Yes, we have shops."

We didn't get as early a start on breakfast as I had planned and Joel called from his room that Pauline was on the driveway, walking up and down.

So I told her to come in the warm kitchen and have some coffee. The minute she got in there, she ran dish water and was busy with the dishes and clearing up until we finally were ready to leave. I had a big cabbage in a bag for her, and a package of meat, so she'd have something special for her family when she got there.

Little did we know, as we started out the dusty road, 66 kilometers to Molepolole, what surprises were ahead.

The road alternated between rough gravel and beds of red sand; the kind of road on which you must drive every second. Not far out of Gaborone, we saw the two kopjes (small hills) which were made up of tilting rocks, all piled so they threaten to roll down any second, but never do. After that, it was flat flat land, always with a rim of kopjes in the distance. We remarked on how much longer it must have taken Livingstone with his covered wagon train to cover what we did in an hour or so.

A startling feature was a bridge over a dry river bed. The road narrowed at the approach, and the bridge proved to be a slab of concrete, with no fence or rail of any kind on either side.

"Do those big buses come over these?" I asked.

"Aay" Pauline said.

They were scary and we crossed three such slabs before we got to her home. There were no villages along the way, only scattered rondavels, fenced around with thorn branches, or sometimes a growing hedge. There were goats, burros pulling carts, and in one place, a big herd of cattle among the scrubby thorn trees on a hillside. It was hilly as we neared Molepolole, and we first sighted the village on arriving at the crest of a hill. It lay in a big shallow valley, but spread up over a low rolling hill. It was flat, as almost every building was a thatched roof rondavel.

The paved road started at the edge of the village, and was just a few miles long, ending at the farther side.

"There's a shop," Pauline said as we passed a dull stucco building with a high wire fence surrounding it.

Soon, on the left, there was another stucco-type square building and it was the Town Council Building and road equipment headquarters. Other than those, all we saw was round huts. We dropped off the pavement, down the hill to the right, and wound through them. The roads or paths were in bad condition and I was afraid we'd get hung up on some of the stones or our underpinnings scraped off as we sank into deep ruts.

You are not confined to driving on the "road"; you can drive anywhere you see it is open. In places where the roads through the huts met a main artery, you dipped down into the gutter and climbed the other side of it, up to the road bed.

Pauline kept pointing the way and just after we passed a building with a mass of children and adults swarming about it, the Community Center, she exclaimed,

"This is my home."

Roy pulled off into the grass in front of a tumbled-down wall, behind which, on the sloping hillside, was a bare swept yard where several little children were sitting in the sun, against another wall. The girls got up, the wind blowing the little cotton dresses which were all they had on, and seeing Pauline getting out of the car, they bent their knees, began clapping them together, and waving their arms in a little joyous dance. There was also a boy, and "Is that Tandi?" I asked.

She had been sitting by the boy, and she too got up, wearing only a little cotton shirt. They were all covered with a slight dusting of the red clay on which they sat, and which blew around them.

Pauline picked up Tandi, who began to cry as usual when she saw me, and her sister Lillian then appeared from the square house, to the right behind the little wall. The "home" was a complex of buildings. The square house on the right, which is probably used for cooking and eating in cool times, for they brought out four chairs from it; a big Rondavel just past it into which Pauline took us. "I live here", she said. It contained two beds, almost as large as double beds, had pictures hung on the wall, and the beds were neatly made up, with reddish chennile spreads.

Another large Rondavel was a little farther to the left, which was in use as a storage building. In it, Pauline had poles for a thatched roof, some bags of cement and two doors, in preparation for building her new home. She pointed out the area where her other house had burned down. I suppose it was some of these children who had played in there and set it afire. As I looked around, I was glad that none of the children had been caught in the fire, and wondered how they had been able to keep the fire from igniting the other nearby thatched roofs.

"Who are these girls?" Roy asked, of the two, looking to be about eight years old, both of whom had crusty looking eyes.

"Those are my sisters'."

"And who is this?" he asked.

"My boy, Fred."

"You never said you had a boy, Pauline." and she just laughed. I remembered now, that he was the boy who was down in Gaborone when all the sisters came, and I took their picture on the lawn.

"How old is he?"

"Five and a half."

"Oh, he looks about eight. He's a big boy."

"No, five and a half."

"Goes to school?"

"Yes, he has started Standard 1. The first session."

We left all the family there and Pauline came with us to drive around the village. It had thousands of inhabitants, but it's a village, not a city. Pauline pointed out the way. We drove downhill past the far end of the big building where crowds were still gathering, past a Bottle store, and then a beautiful big cream colored home, with big windows and fancy grill work and well-fenced yard.

"That man owns the Bottle store." It follows.

We passed a secondary school, with the primary school across the road; then a huge Congregational church, and soon came to the Hospital. It was a cluster of low buildings, with shrubbery and trees shading the walks to the various areas. There were staff homes, kitchen buildings and signs denoting the way to the various centers.

"Have you been here to stay, Pauline?"

"No, not for long."

"Where did you have your babies?"

"Here."

We passed a cluster of solid stucco buildings, not far from the hospital, and she said they were government buildings. There was also an Agricultural project with homes and big barns under construction, and then a Craft Center, which to my dismay, was not open on Saturday.

Pauline pointed to the two big dark buildings, off the path a ways and said, "There are shops." This was some time after Roy had asked where the "shopping center" was. Shops are spread around, where people can walk to them, not in a center.

These were Indian Trader stores, similar to the old-time General Store type; groceries, cookies and candy to the left—material straight ahead, clothes to the right, pots and pans, stacked on counters beside tea sets. All the necessities and treats were there.

"What do you need, Pauline?" Roy asked.

We bought sugar, several packages of cookies, and a big sack of mealies, the staple, candy to give the kids, and a bag of oranges.

We wound our way back to the house complex where we found the yard milling with people. Two big good-looking young women were just leaving. They said there was a concert beginning at the school. We could then see the horde of people disappearing into the building. A great troop of school girls then swarmed over the low wall and dropped their net bags, holding enamel pans (probably what they eat mealies out of at school) and tore down across the hill.

Joel unloaded the groceries and took them into the square building, and I saw that Tandi now had not a stitch on, and Lillian was lifting her out of a big pan of water, set on one of the numerous ledges or low walls in the yard. The wind was still blowing and I had on a sweater and coat. Lillian picked her up, popped her onto her back, as she herself was leaning over; picked up a green plaid blanket and threw it around Tandi and knotted it in front in one twist and scuttled back into the house, Tandi grinning happily.

Roy gave Pauline money for her return bus trip and we told them all goodbye. It was only quarter to eleven.

The terrain looked different, as it always does on a return trip, and we safely traversed the perilous bridges. I think it would be very easy to slide off, at the approach point, if it were rainy, or you skidded on the sand or gravel. We admired the odd rock formations again and before long we passed the turnoff to Gabane, where I plan to go out sometime to see the Hopkins family, and then we soon saw the water tower and government buildings of the city. There are centuries of contrast between the village of Rondavels, and the modern buildings of Gaborone ahead of us.

That evening, Joel said,

"I thought Pauline would live in something more luxurious than she does."

"Well, all the homes out in the village are like that."

"But. Now, you see Pauline. You see that house. Now, do you think those two go together?" He found it hard to accept.

This morning Pauline said,

"I am not going to build my house in the same place. I have been assigned a large stand, farther over, past the Community Center."

I had forgotten about being assigned places. She seems happy with another place, but I wonder if all her sisters and kids will go to her new place.

"I want you to help with the cement." She told me. I didn't understand her. I asked her to say it over again and it was perfectly plain.

"I want you to help me with the cement." In other words, give her enough money to buy it.

Now I realize what she meant when she brought me the paper about the secretarial school when she said, "I want you to help me with this." She didn't mean to read it and see if it were filled out properly, she meant to give her the money for it.

When Roy was having lunch, I relayed the message to him that Pauline wanted us to "help her with the cement."

"What?"

I reiterated and after a few minutes he said,

"What makes her think I should build her house for her?"

"I don't know. I'm just telling you what she said." "That could just be the tip of the iceberg," he replied.

He was gone when Pauline came back to finish her days work, and she didn't mention the cement again but the next day, at noon, I heard Roy ask her how much cement she would need. She said seven bags, so he told her he'd look into it.

JULY 17

We did some more "local" exploring Sunday. We drove up to Mochudi to see what's there.

Driving north, there is a sameness about the landscape for miles. Flat, grassy and thorntree covered, the sameness is broken only by towering ant hills, some herds of goats or a few cattle. The first signs of a village was about twenty kilometers up the road at Pilane. It was spread across a field in the shadow of one of those rocky hillsides with crazy piled up boulders that look as though they may roll down at any time. It was a poor looking village with many abandoned Rondavel sites.

We went on a few miles into Mochudi which was flat to start with, but spread up into rocky hills. We wound up the rocky paths to a fork in the road where we saw a sign "Please drive slowly through the Kgotla." We could see the enclosed area, up that road a ways, which was walled by trunks of thorn trees, in which the chief, his headmen and elders would sit and make decisions on community matters and altercations. We continued on through areas that reminded me of Korean villages; mud walls around groups of thatched roof buildings. On the way back to Pilane, in a cloud of dust, we noticed a grocery store with a porch and gas pumps of Caltex out front. It was a neat looking place, so Roy pulled in and disappeared inside.

He soon reappeared carrying some cold Pepsi's and said, "Conference Lokomo's father-in-law runs this place. Come on and say hello to Mr. Rompa."

I started to the door and met him on the porch. He was a charming man who spoke impeccable English, expressing himself well in just the casual idiomatic way we speak.

After a few preliminaries, he remarked on the problems of running this store all by himself.

"It's just too much for one person. My home is over that way about four miles, behind that hill. That's one reason it's hard for me to keep watch of this place. They break in all the time. I tell you, those kids are going to drive me to committment!"

He took us inside and showed us around the big area that is warehouse and storage space. "I need more room. I want to build on another shed off out that door to the back, but it's just too much for me." Here he pointed out a long worktable with shoe lasts and leather stacked, and said,

"I let someone use this area to work. See, he makes these slippers. It gives a man an opportunity to earn a living."

Just then an old man stepped in the door and looked at him enquiringly. Mr. Rompa said, "Go get yourself a cold drink, then we'll talk." The man put his hand in his pocket and started to say, "I haven't . . ."

"Who said anything about paying for it? Go get a cold drink!"

I'm trying to picture his face now. It is not what you'd call a typical black man's face. He was light brown, had a brown moustache, high forehead, high cheek bones, deep creases down from his nose to chin, nice bright, shining, friendly eyes. He wore an old shirt and bermudas, short sox, regular dress shoes and a beret, which is unusual.

We got back to the subject of Conference being away and that we had heard that Rat would be starting home in December.

"I wish my son were going to be here for Christmas."

"Well, he's not going to make it," Roy said.

"I don't mean Conference. I mean my oldest son. He's in Malaysia. He's a photographer—for taking X-rays in a hospital there. He wants to get home for Christmas, but his passport runs out in October. The British renew it and it takes a lot of time, so I don't know." He said his son had been there two years.

When I asked for his wife, he said, "She's over there going to church."

It was pleasant talking with him, but he had work to do, so we told him good-bye and went on, after returning all his coke bottles.

JULY 23

We shall drive to Molepolole tomorrow with at least seven bags of cement, to Pauline's house. We can't leave until after 10:30 as there is a Walkathon at the school in which Joel is walking and I am serving as a checker from 9:30 to 10:30.

"Maybe Pauline would like to go earlier", Roy said but my answer to that was,

"Beggars can't be choosers," and added,

"I guess maybe it's the money she wants to help on the house, not cement from down here."

"I'm sure, but if you buy the cement, at least you know what your money is going for; otherwise you wouldn't know what had happened to it."

"I'm sure you're right about that. You plan whatever you like and we can do it."

JULY 26

The Walkathon was organized to raise funds for BUCA, and for sound equipment for the School. BUCA means Botswana University Campus Appeal. President Sir Seretse Khama opened the drive, "One Man, One Beast", several months ago, striving for a million Rand by Independence Day, in September. This is be raised by the people, in cash or in animals which will be sold to get cash for the University. At present, they have reached about the halfway mark, and have found that the people in the rural areas have been more generous than those in the cities. The daily paper lists donors, and it is either heart warming or rending. For example, they list the names and after each, one beast or one goat, fifty cents, one bag maize, one chicken, two chickens or one sheep. Then there will be a speech reported in which such small gifts are decried. "Taking one chicken worth Rand 1.50 may cost the committee Rand 3 to take care of it until sale time."

The University was formerly of Botswanna, Lesotho and Swaziland, the second being small countries, near Natal, South Africa. The main campus was in Swaziland, which unexpectedly nationalized the school and left Botswana high and dry, with a small campus about like a Junior College.

I did my stint at the checkpoint with three others, stamping children's Long Walk cards. You stamped so quickly, you sometimes didn't look up to see the "whole" person, and twice I stamped Joel before I noticed a familiar shirt in front of me. The one startling event was when a boy laid down his card for me to stamp (they were about 5 × 7 when folded over), and I opened it to bang down my stamp and there was a dark grey mouse! He was carrying his pet around with him in the folder!

One of the men working with me was a teacher at the Vocational college. He was British, red headed and had a bushy red beard. "The trouble with these people", he said, "is that they all want to be white collar workers. They have this idea about learning to read and write, that it will get them a better job. Now *we* take a different attitude. Reading for the pleasure of reading."

"But you're not on the edge of surviving or not; starving or not. Why shouldn't they take that approach?" I asked him.

When I mentioned what he said to Jerry Pahl yesterday, Jerry said, "Why didn't you ask him to go down to the National Library and see how many locals are in there reading for the pleasure of it?"

Anyway, we had an interesting hour talking and watching the kids come thick and fast, redder in the face each time; the runners eventually slowing down to a steadier pace, and the rivulets of sweat dripping faster and faster, each time around.

Then we were off to Molepolole—after getting to town and buying the cement in the Industrial Area, and getting petrol at the railroad station area, where there was a big market underway, out under the thorn trees. I was too lazy to get out and buy anything, so just watched. Behind them were the newly finished market stalls into which they will soon move. I wonder if they'll be happy there. Most of the open markets are clusters of people sitting on the ground beside their boxes of apples and oranges or tomatoes, where they have a social time and customers can mill around at will. When they are all installed in under the metal roofs, each in his own cubicle, I'll bet there will be an adjunct to it—people sitting around on the ground, the same as ever.

It was a long ride out, and Pauline didn't seem too happy. We carried over 400 lbs. of cement, and used her wheelbarrow, when we got there, to load it and push it into her storage Rondavel.

The home site looked more dilapidated than ever. There were three little girls, dusty and dirty with shaved heads. Fred was there, but not Tandi. Catherine helped with the unloading.

Pauline said she wanted to come back with us, after Roy gave her a Rand 2 for bus fare. I guess she gave it to her sister, to shop with, and said she wanted to come back with us, "Now".

Roy couldn't understand why she didn't want to stay home once she got there, but I could. I'm sure there is no end to what she has to do up there, and as long as all her sisters are there taking care of things, it's far pleasanter to be down here in her nice little house.

When we got home, we found Joel soaking his feet and then creeping around like an old man, forcing himself to go on to the matinee as planned. He had walked thirteen kilometers and his pledges had totaled almost Twenty Rand.

AUGUST 5

The first Monday of August is a Botswana holiday, but not a South African one, so that seemed a logical time to make the trip to Johannesburg, some six hours away.

The biggest problem was Joel, who hates to go on trips. He had his bright written invitation to a birthday party for Sutu Beck, on Saturday afternoon. His first party, and they were to have a movie rented from the agency on the Mall. He wanted badly to go to it.

"I'm going to talk to Dad about it. I'm big enough to stay home alone. I can take care of myself. You two can go and do what you want. I'm sick of going somewhere every weekend. We never get to stay home. I just want to stay right here." He really cried over it, and then got that white pinched-up mouth and set face that indicated that he *hoped* he could hold out against the powers that be, but really knew he couldn't. After lunch I helped him fix his bike so he could ride over to a friend's house for a while, and thank heavens, by that time he was telling me what to "not forget to take along". He had reached the acceptance stage.

A few days later, we were gazing down at the city of Johannesburg,

South Africa, from the windows of the observation deck of the Strijdom Tower, 640 feet above the towering buildings of the city, with a view that included the distant hills, beyond the city itself. All of a sudden we noted a stadium that was obviously filled with spectators. I was sure it was full, but we couldn't see any movement, so Roy and Joel dropped a coin in the telescope, and peering through that, they saw that the stadium was indeed full to overflowing, and there was action on the field. This proved to be Ellis Park, with 65,000 people watching the New Zealand All Blacks, playing the Transvaal Rugby team. Later that evening, in a cafe pavillion in the City Park a block from our hotel, we saw the complete game on color T.V. It was the first Rugby game that I had watched, and I enjoyed it. It is a rough game and the men are handsome with their muscular legs in knee sox and shorts. No padding or shoulder protection as in our football; they are exposed to whatever comes.

The All Blacks of New Zealand, playing in South Africa, has had far reaching effects. Sports boycotting of South Africa seems to be one avenue through which other countries are attempting to let the Republic know their racial policies are not acceptable to the rest of the world.

In spite of the racial situation, Johannesburg is a wonderful place to visit. It's a beautiful city and it has everything. We kept comparing it with Pretoria, with Pretoria found wanting.

After four days of parks, museums, department stores, exotic markets in the Hill Brow area, movies and the Tower, Joel had to admit he had a good time. As we left, he said, "Boy, I wish we could stay longer."

Pauline is lucky that Roy got her that twenty litre can of "parafin" or kerosene, as we call it. Last week when Margaret gave me a lift down to the Mall, she said she was trying to buy a small amount of parafin to return to a friend from whom she had borrowed a few cups, to pour down the snake hole and burn. "There isn't any at Caltex", she said, "and they don't know when they'll have any." On Wednesday, Alice said, "I'm out of parafin so I'm going down to Caltex and pick up a big can." Of course, when she got there she didn't find any big cans of it.

Yesterday's paper had an article about the shortage, pointing up the fact that most of the poorer do their cooking on a parafin stove, unless they have wood. Since the shortage of parafin, the men with the donkey carts of wood have upped their price from Rand 5 a load to a high as Rand 10, and they don't want to sell it in little bits and pieces.

One place, down in the industrial area still has some parafin, and there's a daily queue there of eighty or more waiting. After work, when hordes more joined, he had to close his gates and serve only those who had been there for some time. His supply is supposed to be exhausted by today. The problem is that shipments haven't come up from South Africa—no one seems to know why. But this again, points up how dependent this country is for its survival, on the Republic of South Africa.

Botswana will have new currency, on August 23, Pula Day. This will be its own currency and beginning that day, Rand and cents will be exchanged for the new Pula, in 1, 2, 5, and 10 notes, just like our dollars; and cents will be exchanged for thebe, which also will be in denomination of 1, 5, 25 and 50. There will no longer be a 2 cent piece.

Specimen displays of the new currency have been posted under glass in places of business for several weeks and a program of information has been underway for some time, explaining the changeover to the people.

Pula was chosen as a name for the currency. Pula means rain, best wishes and all good things, so I suppose it's appropriate.

Friday morning, Alice stopped in early, looking fresh and "all dressed up" in a blue pants suit.

"I had to get to Thornhill School for the opening assembly. Tony was being inducted into the Red Cross, and they had a ceremony that the parents were invited to."

Tony had been working for quite a while to fulfill the requirements and he and the rest had been assured that when the induction did take place, Lady Ruth Khama would be there. Well, it so happened that Lady Ruth is with her husband, President Khama, on a trip to China, so the ceremony went along without her.

"Boy, those kids do well. I don't know if I could take school. It was really chilly and lots of the kids sat on the concrete floor. Poor Tony had to wear shorts. Just as he went to bed last night, I noticed that his only pair of school trousers were filthy—loaded with dust and rubbed in mud. I didn't know what to do, but Tony agreed he could wear the uniform shorts. We had to borrow a white shirt from Margaret. I knew Joel only has his one white uniform shirt, so didn't ask for his. Well, Margaret lent me a shirt of Helen's. When I told Tony to get his blouse on, he said,

"Please Mother. When I'm wearing it, it's a shirt!"

Then she went on to say,

"I was surprized at the religious emphasis at the assembly. Our kids go to Parochial School at home, but even theirs weren't like this. They opened with a hymn, then had a Bible reading, another hymn and then prayer, and then, I think, another hymn."

"Well, Joel says that's how assembly is over here. They have Bible reading and lots of hymn singing, and they're learning to sing the Botswana National Anthem. These are government schools, you know. Joel said the other night, 'Gee, Mrs. Dixon-Warren certainly is short tempered over the way we sing the hymns. She gets real mad and hollers at us! She thinks the choir sings all right, but all the rest of us, not good enough.'"

We went on to other subjects, noting that the final amount earned in the Northside Walkathon was well over 4000 Rand. Really great.

This brought to mind, Pauline, and our trip up to her home the day of the Long Walk, so I told Alice,

"Yesterday, Pauline excitedly said to me, right after lunch, 'Did you see Vivian? Vivian is down to visit me. She says the man needs 100 bricks to start my house with the concrete. I have used up all my money.' I didn't know what to say, so ascertaining that she wanted us to give her money for bricks, I told her she would have to talk to Mr. Brown about it. After thinking about it a while, I went out and asked,

'What did you do with the Rand 30 I gave you for your school? Did you give it to the school?' and she said, 'No, I . . . ' 'Did you just use it up?', I asked, and she said, 'Yes'. So I didn't say anything to Roy. I'll let her do her own asking."

"You'd better take it easy. There are still almost two years to go. Oh, I'm not telling you what to do. That's up to you. If you want to give to your maid and family, or some other way. Jerry says he wants to find out how he can help finance someone to the priesthood. It would be good to know you helped that way."

All the while we were talking, Pauline was working like mad in the kitchen. She had emptied the cupboards and was putting in shelf paper and fastening it with scotch tape, and rearranging things. I knew she was making a special effort, in light of her request. I was expecting Margaret over from school any minute to join us for coffee and I had a nice cloth on the table, with flowers, my new coffee pot, and the good coffee cups. It was cozy, with the heater on to take off the coolness of the morning. Alice finally said she really had to go along, and as we neared the front window, we could see Margaret coming from her car. We went out and talked with her a while, in the yard in the sun, and then Alice drove off. Margaret came in then for a cup of coffee, and walked into an absolutely bare dining room. The coffee, and everything else that had been on the table, including the cloth, had been all put away! It was one time that her extra special speed wasn't too well appreciated.

Just as we finished lunch, I told Roy about her extra bustling around, and her need for 100 bricks to get the house started. So he went out and I heard him talking with her, asking how much they were. She said she could get a hundred for Rand 21, and he gave her Rand 21 for a starter. So, we hope Pauline's house is underway. Roy says he's going up sometime and see how it is progressing—or if.

AUGUST 10

"Now there's no jack here in the car. It's in the house. I even keep my glove compartment absolutely empty. I don't have one thing in the whole car that anyone can take, and I leave it unlocked. You see, I have to go out to the dam everyday, and there are gangs out there of young thieves. If I locked the car, they'd just break the windows to get in, so I'm doing better to use my method."

Thus, Mr. Bayliss indoctrinated us on procedures, soon after we got here, as he was showing us his old Fiat station wagon which he had for sale. We have kept his advice in mind, since, but we haven't had occasion to park out at the dam. We couldn't even find the place—the so-called marina—when we did go in search. And any place out that way that we stopped, we stayed with the car.

All this information came back in a rush yesterday, when Roy came home for lunch and said,

"Guess what happened to the Pahls, when they went on a picnic out at the dam yesterday?"

"Oh, I knew they were going on a picnic with Margaret and her family, because she asked me Friday if we wanted to come along too. I told her we planned to go to the airport after lunch—well, what happened? She didn't say they were going to go to the dam."

"While they were away from the car (a new VW bus), some of the gangs out there pitched a huge rock through the window—the second one back—and then reached in and took six or seven jackets, sunglasses and I don't know what else. The VW was parked at the office today, but was all covered with dark powder the police were using to take fingerprints. Jerry said he pointed out to the police that there was a bloodstain fingerprint near the door handle, on the inside. But he said, the police didn't pay any attention to his comment. He figured that that print would have surely been of one of the thieves." With a family of nine using the car, they could get fingerprints for a long time without finding a culprit's print.

When Roy came home today, he reported Jerry had already had the window replaced, but he didn't have any other details for me, so I am anticipating Alice stopping tomorrow when I shall get the whole sad story.

AUGUST 9

Today I learned something about the Bushmen. Interest in the Bushmen seems always to be keen. When the announcement was made that a Miss Wiley would speak about the life of the Bushmen at Monday's meeting of Trinity Ladies, I don't think anyone realised how many would show up. Every seat was full, youngsters were given small chairs to squeeze in on, and the overflow had to have their cups of tea and treats out on the porch and on the lawn.

Again, I met an interesting person, Mrs. Betsy Wood, who sat next to me.

"You're not having a proper cup of tea," I said to her, noticing that she was drinking it without milk.

"Well, this time I just thought I'd be stubborn and insist on having it poured into an empty cup, and drink it my way."

Mrs. Wood, obviously an American, had just been Stateside to visit family and friends.

After telling me she had finished a study of tribal dancing I felt inadequate when she asked me what I do. At first I laughed and said, "I really don't do anything", and she said, "Oh, you look like you do a lot of something!" So, the only thing I could say was that I spend quite a bit of time just writing about what I see and feel here.

At this time, we got a surprise, as Miss Wiley, whom I had pictured would be a white haired woman in a dark cardigan and DAR shoes, turned out to be a 26 year old girl, with tight dark ringlets framing a pretty face with high cheekbones. She never hesitated a minute as she spoke; there was always another sentence coming, but she blotched red on the neck, and her cheeks stayed fiery for an hour, when she glanced at her watch and said "It's four o'clock!" and stopped short.

Miss Wiley, of New Zealand, had spoken to this group once before, but on the subject of the government development program for the Bushmen. This time, she said she'd talk about the way they live. I was impressed by the Bushmen "system" of bringing up their children—always knowing just where they fit in—always accepted, and always knowing just what they're going to be. Bushmen know where they live and they know what it takes to survive, and they assure survival by the way they bring up their children. These were her comments:

It is commonly remarked—"How stable are the relationships! How stable is the family unit! They are the same as they were hundreds of years ago." There is one major attitude and philosophy of the Bushmen. Tremendous pressure to *keep all equal*. Pressure to conform. Dealings are always fair, between families, extended families, bands with other bands. "We are equal." It is its strength and its weaknesses.

There is great care never to have open conflict. If there is a difference, those involved will move away from each other, in hopes that by the time they meet again, the difference will have disappeared.

If little boys get into a fight—they don't fight. They stand with arms raised and fists made, but only dance around in a threatening manner and never move into the hitting stage.

They believe there is no point in accumulating goods. If you were to have more than someone else, you would be obliged to share it, anyway. All must be equal.

There is a lack of competition. Games of children and adults as well, are non-competitive. They may be repetitive, and some attention on doing some throwing nicely, or good form, but no competing for "best".

There is a lack of specialization. There are few Bushmen who become doctors. Only those who have mixed with other tribes or people. Everyone hunts, all the men, and everyone gathers, the women, and everyone makes poison. Differences, uniqueness or originality are not valued; not magnified as great attributes, but downplayed.

This way of life and their beliefs are "fed into" the baby from the time of its birth. Birth is downplayed. No mention of it is made. The mother-to-be goes off into the bush by herself. When she returns, she may have now, a hump on her back instead of her front, but no mention is made of the happening. One does not enquire, 'Is it a boy? or girl? or name?' When the mother is assured the baby is healthy and will survive, is the time she will acknowledge to the rest that it is here, and she will begin calling it by a name, and then that will become common knowledge. The mother makes her presentation when she wishes.

It is obvious that they have some sort of family planning, as babies are spaced at three years. It is said they have a contraceptive, from some roots, that is as effective as the pill—that several years ago the root was not found, and there were 12 babies in one band; that was in 1973. Mothers nurse the babies up until the next pregnancy, which may have some effect. One anthropologist says that too fertile women have been bred out, as large families cannot survive. But it is clear that there is careful family planning.

Another myth, or supposed, is that there are so few Bushmen, that there must be much intermarriage. Contrary to that, the truth is that they have strict taboos on any blood relationships, much stricter than European.

When they name babies, they often use the grandparents names, so names reappear and several of the same family may have the same grandparent's name, with a few additions or diminutives. Families can easily be identified by this passing down of names. One place in the Northeast, near Angola, there are only 35 different names used.

For the first six months, the baby is never out of physical contact with its mother. It is either suckling, on her back, or lap or shoulder. There is total demand feeding up to three years. The baby—or child as it gets near that age, almost molests the mother—punching breast—or grabbing one and hanging on, when some circumstance might make it shy or afraid such as seeing strangers.

There is an extremely strong relationship between the child and its grandparents. It stays in the grandparents house, when it leaves its mother, about three, when it is displaced by a new baby. It has close ties with other children, cousins, old and young. It is never alone. In fact, no one is ever alone. No one goes on trips alone, or hunts alone, or gathers alone.

Young adolescents have made close ties to a friend partner, for life. They stay close to this partner for life, and it is not a cousin or sister.

When the mother is pregnant again, she impresses on the child of two or three that the exclusive rights to mother are over. "There's another one coming. I will leave you on your own". It is an emotional weaning. The child has had top priority for all his years; suddenly, it is finished. It is a critical period. The child must now walk, not be carried, and cannot nurse. It is a sudden rejection. But the grandparents now assume an important role. The child can say, "Well, if you don't love me, I'll go to grandpa's" so it does just that and the grandparents shower it with affection. Here then, they discover other three year olds and they begin their first visiting, going from fire to fire, listening to others and making bonds with new friends. They make dolls, or boys make spears.

Children always accompany parents as the mother goes gathering— or fathers hunting. Their learning begins at early age—where to sit by mother when she digs, what berries to eat, which not to eat, when they are identical except for the shape of the leaf. There is a continual learning process. The older sisters and brothers bridge the gap, too, at this time, and the little ones play making small houses and fires of their own. The three year old is given several months to be miserable, at having to be grown up—away from mother—but if he carries on longer, he'll be let know he has to shape up!

The pair groups now sift into groups of boys or groups of girls, the older ones dancing, flirting, teasing, etc. The younger ones reconsolidate into new pair groups. If the older girls are not happy with the selection of boys available, she may go off as far as forty or fifty miles to other bands, to go visiting. Boys can do the same.

Every several years, if there is a considerable marriage pool, there may be strictly social visiting between bands, for the purpose of arranging long time marriages. Other visiting may be done for exchange of weapons, food or poison. But the social ones are for the adolescents to have a good time.

From the beginning of life, a very important thing, there is never a time that you are just a child; there is no point where you are ever excluded from any area of life. Never excluded. There is no division between childhood and adulthood. Babies learn the Trance Dance steps from their grandparents, by following behind, when they are only two. It is unstructured, yet is orderly and they are constantly absorbing more learning—to be just what the parents and grandparents are.

They assume the child will be like themselves. They bring him up without lectures—he can see what he is to do. There is no emphasis on "don'ts". They grasp, someway, who is eligible as a friend, or as possible marriage partner.

There is a lack of abnormality among the Bushmen. There are no malformed to be seen. Some say that infantacide is practised. The Bushmen deny this. Yet sometimes, the mother may return from the bush without her hump, and with no hump on her back. No questions are asked. At some later time, she may confide in her husband or mother about the circumstances. No one else has a right to know anything about it.

Here, Miss Wiley called "time" and we were cut off as abruptly as a three year old Bushman baby from its Mother.

We all then walked down to the museum to see the film, *"Hunters"*, a movie made in the 50's by John Marshall, brother of Elizabeth Marshall Thomas, who wrote *"The Harmless People"*, a book about the Bushmen I read years ago, and which has since haunted me. The movie was about Twee, and Karl and other men of that book, showing vividly their hard life, and the methods of their hunting, for survival; the disappointments and some successes. It was a long movie and some people began to straggle out, especially those with children, but after it, there were still questions of Miss Wiley and a discussion session. The group gave her Rand 50 to be used in some way to help the Bushmen, not to go into government coffers, and she made two suggestions. Thinking about them later, I wonder if the development programs are going in the right direction.

Her suggestion was for some good hardy rams to help start some herds, or some seed to start planting where the government has dug some wells to give them a stable water supply.

I recalled the comments of Peter Matthiessen, in his book on Africa, about the difficulties of trying to make "farmers" out of a people who have been hunters for centuries. It is seldom successful.

AUGUST 10

John the garden boy—the former garden boy—keeps cropping up in my life. I see him riding by on a bicycle, often, and he waves wildly to me, with a huge grin. He has an exceptionally wide mouth, "just full of teeth" and when he grins, you know it.

I was in the Co-op grocery one afternoon, looking at the bottles on the spice rack, when his face appeared over my left shoulder. He was grinning and saying hello. Later, we got to the check-out at the same time, he right on my heels, so as the girl rang mine up, I said,

"Put that on too," pointing to John's box of Jungle Oats. Of course, he grinned some more, and I guess he was thinking, "Darn it. Why didn't I take the large size box!"

Yesterday as I was walking home from the museum, from our lecture and movie on the Bushmen, here came John toward me, on his bike, wearing a bright new red shirt embroidered in gold. In a minute or two, he rode up behind me, and said what I thought was, "Saturday, your husband at the golf course."

I had him repeat it twice, but still couldn't make any sense out of it, so asked,

"Are you still working at the golf course?"

"No."

"You are asking to work for me again?"

"Yes."

"Well, I don't need any help. Not yet. I'm sorry."

So, he grinned again and rode away. He looks prosperous enough to me as he keeps appearing in new shirts, so I'm not going to worry about him. Then it dawned on me that he had used a few English words. I hadn't ever heard him say that much before.

Later, I asked Roy and Joel about the golf course bit, and Roy said he had picked John up the other day and given him a ride to the Mall and back here. I wish he wouldn't stay on such friendly terms. I don't want him back in the yard to putter and drive me crazy. I'm having too much fun doing my own gardening.

Joel helped the other evening and we have two beds planted.

There is a proper way to plant and up to now, I have done it wrong. When I first spaded up beds, they looked O.K. to me, and I planted my seeds on top. The plants came up and promptly dried up, even with occasional watering with the hose. Then I began to look around.

In a yard where a gardener with some know-how has healthy flowering plants, and vegetables producing even in the dry season, I could see he had done a lot of "ditching". Deep trenches were dug with plants in the bottom of them. This way, dew will drop into the bottom of the ditch—or water from the hose will collect there. Flower or vegetable beds are lower than the surrounding surface, with a deeper ditch like a little moat on the inside edge; a place for a surplus of water to stand and slowly drain in toward the plants.

The ground, when dry, is solid as concrete; it's impossible to get the point of a shovel into it. When you soak it down, it's the greatest soil you ever saw. It spades up easily and is loose and a bit sandy. Now that we have our seeds in the bottom of ditches, within a bed like a bathtub, with the walk around it solid as concrete, we may have some success.

Someone also told me, that if you plant a bush, you must dig a BIG hole, and put in grass or mulch and have the surface lower then the ground level. Then you have a big "pot" for the bush to grow in, a place to run water into to keep it from drying up.

The general appearance these days, of lawns and gardens, is drab. It hasn't rained for months, but many gardens are blooming in glorious color, and even some lawns green. These are places where people have been here years, and they know the right way to do it.

Seeing the gardens in Johannesburg has encouraged us to get going on ours, and I'm afraid the day is nearing that we will begin again to shut our gate at night, to discourage the neighborhood dogs from having their fights and wrestlings in the middle of my flower beds.

AUGUST 12

When Alice arrived this morning, she didn't seem her old sprightly self; in fact, she was a bit bedraggled looking, and weary.

I said, "Come on in. I've been looking for you. Tell me all about . . ."

"Don't mention it! I'm trying to put it out of my mind."

She hardly noticed the especially arranged table for coffee, with homemade sweetrolls and fancy jelly scones. Too many things had been happening.

"First, we've been to Sports Day, for John. John won the three legged race—way out front, then he had a ridiculous time in the sack race with the sack down around his ankles, falling down every attempted step. But, Patti won the toddlers race, and guess what—I won the Mother's race! I'm sort of beat from that. And I did just what we always tell the kids not to do; I couldn't resist looking back to see where my competition was, and I almost got beat!"

Then she explained that when they went to the older kids Sports Day, Saturday, after being at the airport with us, she had bought a cake and put in in the locked car—all but one wing which just doesn't fasten tight, and when they came back, they found someone had been able to get that wing open and get the cake out. This was a little preface to what was to come on Sunday, when they went on the picnic with Bob and Margaret Rowe.

"We never heard anything about being careful out at the dam. But now I hear, it's a regular business; the thievery there.

"When we came back up the hill from our picnic, and saw what they had done to that car! They heaved a huge rock more than once, as they banged it up all around before getting the window smashed. And the rock went through so fast it smashed the inside of the car on the far side. I don't know how they carried everything. All our jackets and sweaters, a football, a soccer ball, Danny's new glasses, John's tin of matchbox cars, many years accumulation. The darndest thing was, that a man driving up to the marina, saw two boys coming down the road, carrying armloads of things, and almost stopped to challenge them, but they ran into the bush. There was a navy blue sweater dropped, though—mine, but even that had been picked up when he went to see if it were still there.

"Well, we were all in a state of shock at first, but later, a reaction set in with the little kids; they couldn't stop crying. They can't understand how anyone could do such a thing. We all went to Margaret's house while Jerry and Bob went to the Police. They were gone for three hours! To three different stations. No telling if anything will ever come of it though.

"Well, when we finally got home, the kids were all afraid someone would be breaking in there and didn't want to go to bed, but we all did, eventually, but I wasn't good for a thing on Monday. To think both the boys' good Hockey jackets are gone now. They prized them.

"Well, as I said, we'll just have to forget about it."

So we went to the Mall, shopped for Patti and her birthday party, and discussed the fact that they now must move to the new house. The keys are in hand, and if the furniture is brought out today, they will start the big process Saturday and Sunday. It will be somewhat of a new start, with all the advantage of being within walking distance of the Mall and the school, armed with all the wisdom accrued from the unfortunate happenings of the last weeks in their first home.

I think Pauline's cousin and her little Bontsho have moved into her little house. Now that there are two beds in there, there is plenty of room I suppose.

I had discovered that second bed, wedged in, when I took Pauline a tray when she was down with the flu. It had been delivered that very afternoon and I was perplexed how it could have happened without my hearing or seeing any of it.

The past few days, Pauline had little Bontsho up here at the house, mainly in the kitchen. She knows how I like little kids and when I discovered her here, Pauline laughed and I dug out cookies for Bontsho, and found a ball of Joel's for her.

Bontsho looked cute in her little patent leather shoes, a blue and white knit dress and a bright blue and orange crocheted poncho, with fringes and tassels and her gold loop earrings. I got a surprize though, when the little one-year-old bent over to pick up the ball and I could see her little bare brown bottom. She didn't have another stitch on besides the dress. Then is when I began to be a little concerned about her standing around near Pauline on the living room carpet, or those in the bedrooms. I lured her into the kitchen with some more cookies, and then she was soon out in the back yard near the flowers.

Late in the afternoon, I saw a girl coming up the drive with a huge cardboard box on her head. I exclaimed about it to Roy and we both watched her, and saw that it was full of junk which she was taking to the trash can, up under the shrubbery.

"Well, I guess they have had some housecleaning down there. I suppose her cousin and the baby have got settled in with Pauline."

The next day, Bontsho appeared again with Pauline, so I enquired if her mother were staying with her now.

"No, she is busy down there. Bontsho didn't want to stay with her."

"Are they living with you now?"

"They are staying a few days."

Bontsho was still as bare bottomed as ever and a little later, after she had cried about something, Pauline took her to the little house and she didn't come back here again. Perhaps Pauline thought I was objecting to her being there. Not really, other than being leery about the absence of diapers on the youngster and its possible effect on the rugs. It is cool and windy today, and I have glanced down toward her house and see there is quite a group sitting out in the sun, against the south side of the house, away from the wind. I guess they are settled in for a while.

I had remarked to Roy the other day, that if Pauline were ingenious, she'd rent out part of her house—to friend or relative, now that there are two beds there. I had only anticipated her by a little, as it appears that is just what she's done.

AUGUST 16

After Joel went on his bike hike yesterday, Roy decided to put some bushings on the shock absorbers so while he was busy at that, I cleared along our front fence, and clipped off the overgrown geraniums. I have clippings enough to plant a border from here to the Mall. Inevitably, when I putter in the yard, boys will step up to the fence and softly mutter,

"I want a chob," so softly, I have to ask them to repeat it.

I have a pat answer, now. I say there is only enough work for me and I do it for fun.

There were lots of people walking by as it was a sunny clear day, the kind you hope for when you wish to go to the beach.

Just after Roy finished working on the car and went in to wash up, a lady waved to me from the road as the man, called,

"Is the boss in?"

I waved back and smiled and said, "Yes, he just went in to wash. He'll be right out."

They both acted as if I should know them. I asked them in and by the time Roy came along we were about to the porch. He introduced me—one way introduction—'my wife' so I didn't know any more about who they were than I did before.

"Dr. Curry is back from his trip to the Tuli Block," Roy said, so I thought the man must be someone who worked with Dr. Curry.

We came in and sat down and when I asked him if he'd like something to drink, he asked for wine. I asked the lady if she drank wine. I knew she'd say no, and hurried to make us some orangeade. I have noticed that the ladies here rarely drink anything but orange squash or soda.

When I was squeezing the oranges, I asked Roy if they were friends of Curry.

"No. This is the man from the Radio Station who does the interviews. The one who gave me the ride to work."

"Oh, good." I knew where I was then and what we could talk about.

I found him an extremely intelligent man. He would have to be, to do his job. I told him I had heard his interview with Dr. Carter, and thought this program was better than her speech at the Museum.

"Oh, speeches. They can go on and on and on. But in an interview, you can have questions that lead somewhere and make a point. Did you hear Outlook this morning?"

"No, we weren't home."

His guest had been a Canadian Olympic Medalist who was visiting his brother here.

Olympics brought up our Ambassador, David D. Bolen, Gold Medalist some decades ago. We all exclaimed over the surprize of his having left. Bolen has been appointed Under Secretary of African Affairs, so it's a step up for him, and as Roy noted, a position where he will be able possibly, to do something for Botswana.

We told him Dr. Curry was busy this week; he must complete his four studies, going to Lobatse a couple days to do the Botswana Meat Commission and his typist is going on leave Friday, so he must be done by then.

They asked about Joel and remarked that they see him playing with Kenneth and Edwin and with Thomas. Everyone remarks on how happy Joel always seems here, and busy with many friends.

We talked about gardens and chickens. He has a batch of baby ones, with problems, so he was going on home to tend to them. They live just around the corner, just past Kenneth's house.

They were certainly a handsome couple as they went on out the gate and down the road. He was very tall, wore a beige safari suit, and she was a plump motherly type, with a bright head wrapping; a light skin, smooth and flawless, and a big bright smile.

When we told Joel they had been here, that they live around the corner, he said,

"Well, those are Thomas' parents aren't they? Didn't he have a pickup that he gave you a ride in? Was he real tall and have his nose sort of turn down at the end? Sure, that's Thomas' dad."

I said to Joel, "Well, if they are Thomas' folks, their back yard borders a little bit on the corner of ours. They'd better not let their chickens get over in our yard!"—only joking, of course.

I was alone in the house at noon yesterday, when a young boy knocked at the door. He appeared about fifteen, and I said,
"What can I do for you?"
"I want to know if you can give me something for this cut," he pointed toward his forehead. The sun was behind him, so I couldn't see him too well at first, but moving around, I could see he had a scraped nose and forehead and an ugly cut, ragged, over his left eyebrow.
"My head hurts, too."
"When did you do this?" I asked.
Thinking about it later, I don't think he gave me a straight answer, I thought he said 'just now' but the scrapes on his nose were not fresh.
"Where do you live?"
"Next door."
"At Kenneth's house?"
"Yes."
"Kenneth has gone to Serowe, hasn't he?"
He didn't make much reply to this, but I said to come in and I'd get some salve and a bandaid. When I went back to the bedroom for them, I was a little leery of leaving him in the living room alone, as I was still puzzled about the scrapes already being partly healed, and wasn't sure he really did live next door.
I got terramycin salve and put it on the bandaid, and on the ugly cut, then told him to take the tube of salve and rub some on the other places. He looked around as though for a mirror, so I told him to go to the bathroom and pointed the way—right past my typewriter in the hall.
"Now, here's some aspirin for your head. Take one now and the other later," and we went into the kitchen for a glass of water. He thanked me and went out and I didn't even watch to see what direction he went.
When Roy and Joel came home, I told them about it, and Roy said,
"You didn't let him into the house, did you?" and later laughed and said, "You're going to be picked up for practising medicine without a license."
I still puzzled over it, and even made a special move of putting all of Joel's radio and tape equipment into his closet and locking it.
Joel was off on a bike hike with his friend Ian, so I got the camera out, and Roy and I went out toward the quarry, where he had seen

baboons before, but we searched in vain. Roy said that perhaps they only come down and near the road in the morning, maybe for water across the road. We had a good ride. Sometime after we returned home, I noticed that Joel's food container and water bottles were in the sink.

"Hey. Joel's been home. I wonder how he got in."

"I came in through my bedroom window", he told us later, "Just stepped in. One of them wasn't locked."

So, I locked that, and went out again with the camera. Got a shot of the big blue lizard that lives in the tree next to the carport, and one of a couple doves in the thorn tree, but gave up on any other birds, deciding to wait until the first slides come back, to see what I'm doing wrong or right.

Dinner and the early evening got away from us and Joel worked to make up his day's reading assignment, just finishing when Roy called,

"Hurry up. It's time to get to the theatre. I don't have any tickets yet, so come on."

We rushed off in a hurry and it wasn't until later, when Duke Wayne and Bob Mitchum were well involved in shooting up the bad guys, that I realized I hadn't taken time to check the windows before leaving home. I had left the camera, complete with telephoto lens lying on the dresser; not returned to the locked closet Roy keeps it in. My pocket book was also out, in the bedroom with a sizeable amount of Rand in it.

This is a lesson on how to spoil a movie. I turned hot and cold back and forth, as I wondered if that kid had unlatched one of the living room windows when I was in the bedroom. They have a handle by which you push them out, by degrees depending on how open you want them, and when you close them, you pull the handle in straight toward you, then to the right to slip it behind a metal latch. The window can be closed without having the handle behind the catch; also you can latch them in two degrees of security. We never did get any household insurance. It's only Rand 15. I wonder what they'd take besides the camera and all the Rand they could find. Food, maybe. I hope they don't clean out the closets. I wouldn't want to lose all my coats. Why would he have said he needed something for the scrapes, when they were half healed up? I wonder how much the camera cost, altogether. I'd leave this movie and go home right now if I had my key for the car with me. I'll just have to stop being such a chicken about driving on the left side of the road. Just take the car and use it. Well, this will have to end sometime. Maybe Pauline will come home from Molepolole while we're here. We left a light on in the living room. They wouldn't dare climb through the front window with all the light there. If Pauline sees anything going on, she'll send them packing. This will probably be one of those times when Roy won't say a word, when we find the camera gone. It will be beyond comment. Even if that kid was casing the place, he would have changed his mind after I helped him out.

So, I went on and on, and it took the edge off a good movie. I was the first out of my seat and went to the car in a rush. We were stalled a while as three kids from somewhere in this area asked for rides home. Funny how they know us and where we live and what we drive, and they are anonymous faces and figures to me.

The house looked all right when we got there, and I was at the door in two seconds; rushed into the bedroom and saw the camera still lying on the dresser. Talk about relief! I made the rounds of the windows and found that at least four were not tightly closed. Several were pulled closed but not latched at all. I secured them all and no one seemed to notice what I was doing. I never mentioned how worried I had been, but I'll never leave again, rush or not, without a better check of security.

"Joel, is there really a fifteen year old over there at Kenneth's?"

"Yes, there are two bigger boys."

"Aren't there any adults there now, that would look out for one of them if he got hurt? Wouldn't they have some salve or a bandaid?"

"They..got..nothing!" he said spacing the words and accenting the 'nothing'.

"They got nothing but some kitchen stuff and I told you, the refrigerator is locked."

I was ashamed of being so suspicious. I was glad I had fixed the boy's hurts. I would have anyway, even if someone had been casing the place. I guess all these episodes of the Pahl's having things stolen has got to me. I shall send Joel over today to check on how the boy is and see if he needs some more salve or aspirin.

One day right after lunch, we saw a lady walking down the drive toward Pauline's house. We have wide windows in the living room, clear to the floor, and they have sheer curtains, so we can see all that's going on, in that direction.

It wasn't many minutes before Pauline came bustling in, all sparkling, with her hands full of an assortment of crocheted doilies, in sets.

"My friend from Rhodesia made these. She just came."

Each set was marked with a price, and I looked them over, but doilies aren't my bag.

"They're lovely, Pauline, but I don't use doilies. I just never use them. Is she going around to different houses trying to sell them?"

"No. She came straight to you first," she said with an intimation that I was honored or given prime consideration.

She was still quite enthused about the products, so I chose one that was unusual, and paid her for it, Rand 4.50.

We get many a smile out of the doily set. Pauline loves them and likes to have doilies on things. They don't spend much time in the sideboard drawer where I put them.

I may set a vase of flowers on the side table, with a bowl at the right—my own balanced arrangement under the picture on the wall there, but when I walk in the room toward noon, after the morning cleaning, the vase of flowers will be in the center of the dining table, on a white doily.

Another will appear on the coffee table in the living room, for an ashtray or bowl of flowers to rest on.

I never move them, except in general living, as setting the table for a meal. Then, if she has a little one at each end with a candlestick on, and the big one in the middle, I just leave them.

We smile over them, as they appear here and there, but I told Roy, "Pauline would love to have her own furniture, and a nice table like ours, to arrange doilies on, so let her keep on arranging them."

AUGUST 17

I was at Alice's house, standing at the ironing board, turning up hems on drapes. Six of them had to be lengthened and four of them shortened. The moving of her household of nine people had been accomplished and now the arranging, putting away and adjusting was underway.

There was a constant stream of applicants for the position of housemaid. I listened to the interviews as I worked out of sight in one of the bedrooms.

"Please write your name down on this paper. Then write down where you last worked. Now write down where you live now." After the writing was done, she found out how long they had worked at the last job, then I heard her ask,

"Are you married? Do you have any children? Are you pregnant?" There was no doubt about who was interviewing whom. Alice was in command.

"Now, I have had many applicants, and I will be making a

decision later. I want you to know, that the housemaid who is hired can live in the house in the back. But only she may sleep there. There can be a reasonable number of visitors, but *NO ONE* sleeps there but the maid."

As I brought out the drapes for hanging a few minutes later, I said, "Alice, you've come a long way since the night Maureen gave you a nervous breakdown just talking about the problems of getting and handling a maid."

"You think I did all right, huh?"

"Yes, I certainly do."

"Well, I'm going to set the requirements and I'm going to be fussy about what I get. Not like the last time, being intimidated by the first applicant, and having her extract a promise from me that I wouldn't hire anyone else until she had been tried out—and all the while she was pregnant and she didn't let me know. I'm in no hurry, I can get along without a maid for a while. There is plenty of time."

Alice added, "I am taking the advice I had from a nun working over here. She said that you must know what your job is, what you are supposed to accomplish. Then you have to draw the line and set limits. You have to learn how to say 'No' and maintain a condition in which you can get done the things you are supposed to do. You cannot feed everyone, or let everyone draw you water, or house everyone. You have to set limits."

This reminded me of what Vi Webb said when she was down from Serowe, explaining why she wanted to do so much of her household shopping while in Gaborone.

"It's not that I can't find things in the shops in Serowe, but there are so few Europeans there, and I'm conspicuous, especially in my big car, and to tell the truth, I'm ashamed of being able to buy so much." And she went on to tell about the garden boy they have, who begged after a week or so, to have them hire also, his cousin Benjamen who didn't have any work and needed bread. She said, "We only need one garden boy. You will have to talk to Mr. Webb.", but she went on to me, "There I stood at the sink, washing some wine glasses. I was washing wine glasses while they are asking me for work for bread."

When we had to get our initial supply of household goods—dishes, pots and pans, glasses, dish towels, etc., Alice went to the Hardware Store and made a collection of the basics for the family of nine. She said she had it all stacked on the counter and in cartons around her, in the cramped space, when a local woman walked by, looked at the purchases and sneered,

"Extravagant woman!"

Yes, we are extravagant, we have all we need and more. It's something each one will have to decide for himself; how he will live with his own possessions and what he will do to best help in the community. It starts with knowing you can't do it all, and also that you don't want to be ripped off or manipulated either. There are decisions along this line to be made every day.

When I relayed my dither about having the house broken into—imagined—Alice said,

"Boy, aren't we getting flaky? After our stuff was stolen from the car, I studied every face I saw—wondering if he might be the one. We'd better get hold of ourselves!"

Alice's former maid, Flora, showed up at the new house Monday, with a little slip of paper clutched in her hand; the house number written on it. She came in and sat in the living room, still wanting to stay with the family.

Alice had given her two months notice, but kept her on at Sebele, as the date of the move was postponed for a few weeks. They gave her some nice clothes and blankets for the expected baby. Alice gave her severance pay, and had impressed on her over and over that she would be through when they moved.

Alice says it was upsetting to have to go through it again. She feels sorry for Flora, and she said several times, "If she could just work better and more quickly; she's as honest as anyone could be. I can trust her completely. If she found as much as a penny, while cleaning, she'd always come straight to me and put it in my hand."

She told Flora that Jerry would drive her to her village when he came from work. This is when she broke Alice up.

They were helping her into the car with all her belongings, and as she was to get in herself, she turned and said,

"I will pray every day that God will take care of you all in every thing."

"It broke us up allright, and it was the most English we had ever heard from her. The only thing she ever had said that made sense. Jerry took her out to her village on the Molopolole road, but she may be back later, to show us the baby."

The maid Alice finally hired had worked for a man with an engineering concern here. She did all the housework and all the cooking, and was paid Rand 40 a month. The going rate here is Rand 26 a month plus housing. Then the man was transferred to Johannesburg and the family took her along to live with them there. They paid her Rand 75 a month. But she only stayed a short while.

"There is no life for me, in South Africa."

Roy was also surprized to find the other day, through a business talk with an Indian from South Africa, that he is in the same boat with the blacks. He too is living under restrictions; eliminated from the majority of public places.

So, we can see why the Holiday Inn here is swarming each weekend with Indians. Unrestricted is the way of life here. The best rooms, the luxury of the dining rooms and the Casino, are available to them all.

AUGUST 26

Joel has developed an intense interest in the yard. It started by his wanting to have a back pack and my telling him that he could earn it. At first that threw him, saying that it would take months, but when I asked how he figured that, we settled on a reasonable rate of pay and since then, there has been no holding him.

He is out of bed early and into the yard, while it is still cool and pleasant to work and has been accomplishing far more than I expected he would.

In the course of emptying the wheelbarrow loads of pulled weeds down on the "compost" heap, he discovered a nest with six eggs in it. A chicken from one of the neighboring yards has settled in, in the hay stack. There is a canopy of sorts formed by a piece of chicken wire on top of which hay has been stacked, and she's under that. A private residence with a nice view off her "porch". Joel was really excited about all the eggs, so he took a magic marker down and dotted each egg there, so the next day, he knew which was the fresh one. We told Pauline she could have an egg a day, as long as they were produced.

As I was working in the yard with Joel, by the fence which separates us from the back edge of a huge yard, a man was leaning on the fence, so I said,

"I guess you have a good garden boy there. Your yard looks good."

"Oh, this is my sister's place. I'm just here visiting; came down from Zambia. No, they had a garden boy, but he didn't show Saturday, so he got the boot."

"Well, I had a garden boy, but I was happy when he didn't show up! He drove me crazy—I had to work so hard myself to get anything out of him."

"We are going to South Africa now, to establish a new home. I guess I'll be starting a garden all over. We've been in Zambia twenty years, but can't stay any longer. There just aren't any essentials there any more. Can't get a thing."

"Isn't Rhodesia getting to be like that too?"

"No, because they manufacture a lot of things themselves."

I had heard from many, before, that Zambia is changing. They are more closely tied to the East than the West, I guess, economically. Zambia before independence, was Northern Rhodesia. We plan to get up through there, to Lusaka, at least.

Last evening I was sitting on the low brick wall bordering the Mall; sitting in front of the theatre waiting for Roy to get through the long line for tickets.

A young fellow was sitting about an arm's length from me, in fact had walked over there just after I had sat down. He looked at me a couple of times and then said,

"Hello!"

I didn't have any idea who he was, at first, then he pointed to his forehead.

"Well. Hello, hello. How's the cut? Better? Good!" I yakked away to make up for not having recognized him; my patient I had treated with salve and bandaids the week before.

"I didn't recognize you, at first. Hey, you're too young to be smoking!" I laughed.

He put his cigarette over the other side, a bit, but finished it, and another young man walked up to me and greeted me with a warm, "Hello. How are you?" so I greeted him warmly with, "Fine. How are you?" assuming that I knew him! I did know that he must be from next door too, at least part of the time.

I noticed how poorly "my" boy was dressed; an old poplin car coat that was too long, worn and not too clean. In my mind I ran through clothes at the house that might be spared, that might fit, and planned on what to pass to them when we're ready to go.

After the movie, we fought our way through the crowds and by the time we got to our car in the upper parking lot, there were the two boys standing beside it. How had they known which lot we were in?

"Hi. Would you like a ride home?" I asked just as though I didn't know why they were there.

After all these weeks of sitting through church services predominately in Setswana, we decided to go to one of the evening services, wholly in English.

We noticed that Susan was there. I had looked for her two Sunday mornings—armed with Time magazines for her.

"Where have you been? I've been looking for you."

"My Mother is around."

"From way across the desert?"

"Yes." she smiled.

"What do you hear from Rat? I have films at Bancroft's now and they should be done soon. I'm getting two of each so you can have some and we can send some to Rat."

She grinned at that, but said,

"I have to go now. The Pastor is having Bible Study now." and off she went.

AUGUST 27

Dr. Curry left in a hurry. No time for Sunday dinner here, and he had no interest in seeing the "radio man". He was bent on getting a flight and getting home to his wife.

I had started walking to the Mall, just as he came out of his drive and he opened the door for me to ride along. This was on a Wednesday. "I'm going down to see if I can't get a ticket to get out of here. I've finished my work so there's no reason just to wait around."

The next evening, he drove in just as we were having dinner. He joined us for dessert and coffee.

"I'm going out tomorrow afternoon. I found the airfield will be closed on Saturday, Sunday and Monday, for their construction work. Just think, if I hadn't got in there to see about an earlier flight, I wouldn't have been able to get out, anyway, till next Tuesday."

He went on, "I won't be coming back to Botswana next year after all. I know now what I'll be doing. I have a NATO Fellowship for three months. Dana and I will be in Sussex, England the whole summer. I'm thrilled about that. No more trips without her!"

He took Uncle Bob's phone number and said he'd call him, "And I'll be seeing Debby, anyway." He offered to take something to them if we wished, but I told him,

"Just 'hello' to them and tell them we are all fine."

We were out at the airport the next afternoon, and waved him off to California. We miss having him around.

AUGUST 31

At long last, I have figured out why I have never been able to get oriented here as to north and south. The only way I have been able to straighten out at all, is to get out the map and revisualize the layout of the city and the roads going north and south; rearranging it against my natural instincts. The problem has been that I didn't realize that I am south of the equator. The sunny side of things has continued in my mind to be south, and the shady, cool side, north.

Concentrating on it the other day, as the cool of the winter is now past and in the afternoons, you look for a shady spot, I finally woke up to the fact that the cool and shady yard is the south side, and the constant glare pouring in throughout the day is from the north.

I knew when I first came that the farther south you are, the cooler you can expect to be, and vice versa, but I forgot about it.

Now—I hope I know which way is up!

Sunday was Thanksgiving at Church; in August! See how confused even the holidays are, to say nothing of the directions of north and south.

The harvest arrangement was impressive Sunday; everything from baskets of seeds and grains to bouquets of carnations, a big watermelon, loaves of bread and fruit. Every seat was full and the American Missionary, Dick Sales, preached. This was good, as he repeated everything in English. I forgot to ask Susan after the service what his Setswana is like; if it's easily understood, if it has an "English accent".

Susan was on the lawn and rushed up to me returning the Bicentennial issue of the Time magazine which I had told her I wished to save. She also pulled out an envelope of color pictures to show us.

She and Joel and I sat down on one of the benches, in the shade, to look at them. First was one of a little black boy,

"Oh, that's my sister's youngest."

"She's your sister in South West Africa?"

"Yes, in Windhoek. This is her fourth." She had told me before that this sister is divorced—didn't say how long ago.

Then we got on with the pictures of Rat, from Los Angeles. Many were taken inside his apartment; a one room attractive place, with stove, refrigerator and sink combination which he would not have here in his little house that does not have electricity. There were group pictures of which I said,

"He's having too good a time!"

"Mr. Brown will pick us up at twelve. Do you want to come

home with us? I can give you the other magazines, and you can show Mr. Brown the pictures. Is someone expecting you home right away?"

"I would like to come with you."

"How about your mother. Is she still here?"

"Yes, she is around. Someone is preparing her lunch." I understood that she was visiting somewhere near.

"How did she get here, all the way from past Maun? By Bus?"

"Only by big trucks. That's all we have out there for transportation."

"How old is she?"

"I don't know when she was born, but she is old. And she is not well. She is here to see the doctor too. She has been, but will go again."

She wore a pretty tie-dyed short green dress with big "butterfly" sleeves. I told her how much I liked it; that I would like to draw around it for a pattern. "Did you make it?"

"No. I got it from the Brigades when I was studying. They had the Academic study and others doing things like this and I bought it."

"Are you working now?"

"No. I can't find work, so I am going to school each evening for a few hours. Secretarial school." She talks so softly, I can't get everything she says. I wondered which school she was going to, if it were the one Pauline has applied to.

Susan asked, "Did you see a few weeks ago, they came to Gaborone for sports, down at the Secondary School field? All the way from near my home. They were pure Bushmen."

I had seen big crowds and trucks and field events, but they are so constant, I didn't realise that there were actually a group of Bushmen there. There's never enough publicity on anything until it is over.

We had lunch in the back yard, under the umbrella, which turned out to be warmer than inside, so we came in to the cool dining room and she looked at the slides, in a small lighted viewer, taken here at the dinner right after her wedding before Rat left for Los Angeles.

I collected four Time magazines for her and when we let her out at her house, she said,

"Wait. Let me see if my Mother has returned and she can say hello to you."

"No, she has not yet arrived," so we drove away through the dusty unpaved area of the city, with Roy mumbling, "They ought to hold the Trade Fair and the 10th Anniversary celebrations here in this section! It's a crying shame they can't get these streets surfaced!"

"Yes. Maybe they could have spent some of the celebration funds on projects like that than building that fancy 'Arc d'Triumph' down on the end of the Mall—with it's Chinese top!''

AUGUST 31

We went down the Lobatse road at 5:15 Friday afternoon, heading for Mafeking, about a hundred miles away, straight south. Mafeking was the capital of Botswana, when it was the British Protectorate, Bechuanaland.

We noticed the difference in the length of the day, as we were still traveling in daylight when we were more than halfway there.

Just as we hit the dirt road, just outside Lobatse, we found it nicely wet down by a water truck.

"That's to keep the dust from settling into the town", Roy commented. But they didn't wet down very much of it. From then on, if you happened to catch up to someone ahead of you, it was visibility zero. All you could do was pull up along side the car, or almost to it to get a view ahead. If it was safe, you'd pass and miraculously find everything crystal clear—and the guy behind you now had to take your dust. It is a bit scary when it's that thick, for if you are travelling at any speed, you can run right into someone ahead of you going more slowly. We had one such scary time, after it was darker. The dust was solid—on and on, but we couldn't see anything that was raising it.

"It must be way ahead", Roy said.

"It can't be. Something is stirring it up thick all the while."

Joel and I leaned close to the windshield, straining to see something ahead. Finally, I spotted a tiny red light and yelled,

"Don't run into it!"

"I wasn't planning on it!" and Roy braked.

We were very close to it, though, and it was a huge truck, which pulled over to let us by. Good thing it had that one little reflector or tail light, as it would have been very easy to have overtaken it.

The driver waved to us, and we pulled out, finally, into clear air, with a view ahead.

It only took a short while at the border gates. We had anticipated a long session, as last week Botswana went onto its own currency, with restrictions on how much money you can have on you, crossing the border, but surprizingly, we went through quickly.

It took two hours to get to the city. We'll remember this trip for two things. The constant noise all night long, of carousing in the streets under our hotel room balcony, cars tearing around, and trains! (Joel said later that "they weren't very good ones as they try all the time to get going, but never do".) There was so much noise we seemed to be awake all night. Made us realize how quiet we are here, with most of the city asleep by 8:30 and no traffic out our way—or much of anywhere here. The second thing was a delicious dinner in the "Alley Cat", which looked like an ordinary drive-in, with car hop service. But there was an inside restaurant, in one end of this long thatched-roof building which was constructed as two Rondavels, bridged. We sat where we could look way up into the tip of the thatched roof. Well, better than the atmosphere was the food. We had grilled sole, on a bed of herbed buttered rice and a delicious salad, and our coffee was topped with whipped cream.

The good dinner, and the satisfactory shopping we did the next day made the scary drive through solid dust, worthwhile.

School resumes on Tuesday, September 7th. That means we will soon see Kenneth, Edwin, Shinga, Vivian and the other girls who live next door. They all made a quick exit as soon as school closed mid-August and headed for the cattle posts. Kenneth went to Serowe where his mother works, so he may not have gone to a post. It has been quiet here, with only the older group in the next yard. Fatso has been there all the while, though. He's the short-legged dog who likes Joel and follows him around, and waits for him to come home from school. He should begin to like me too, as I save scraps for him and call him over to the lawn for them. Beef scraps one day, and then he begged with his eyes so pleadingly, I threw him a hot dog. Last evening, he had some chicken livers. Living high, especially for a dog here.

The Tenth Anniversary celebrations are getting closer. I have a copy of the program of events which run from September 26 to October 3rd. We will be here for Sunday, Monday, Tuesday and Wednesday, but that afternoon, we plan to leave on a trip to Kimberly. Thursday is a National Holiday so Roy got leave approved for Friday, giving us a long weekend.

Perhaps it's just as well to be away. Alice said today she has heard rumors that some incidents may be planned—for either this anniversary, or at the Trade Fair which is on at the same time. It is reasonable to assume the possibility. Anywhere something big is underway, the more publicity to be expected from an incident. Yesterday's newspaper says the President of Mozambique has accepted his invitation to attend. Nyerere of Tanzania is coming, and Kaunda of Zambia. There will be a number of heads of state here, that's certain.

Some North Koreans are here now, training a group of the school children for a display in the Stadium. There are Concerts, Drama, Art Exhibits, Opening of the new building on Campus, Windup of the BUCA drive for funds, now at three quarters of a million, Ox Roasting, State Banquet and Choral concerts. I want to see the traditional dancing. Some is scheduled for the Airport, at times of arrival of VIPs, some at Trade Fair grounds, and others at Stadium, and Holiday Inn grounds.

They have been working hard on the preparations, and I hope it all goes well.

Today we had a letter from Rat, from Los Angeles. This is it:

Dear Mr. and Mrs. Brown,

I guess I have taken too long before writing to you. It's as always the case when one is trying to settle down and has to write to many relatives and friends—and one tends to forget some of one's friends.

I have now settled down in L.A. and have been touring the city and the coast. I have even had a chance to visit Gaborone's twin sister city, Burbank.

This Friday our class is taking a field trip to IRS's Computer Centre in Fresno, the trip will last about a full week. The itinerary will take us to San Francisco where we will spend the weekend, and proceed Monday August 30 to Lake Tahoe via Sacramento, and Tuesday we proceed to Fresno where we will spend two days touring the IRS Service Centre, after which we will return to L.A. We are almost through a third of the course and have been writing a long first examination paper of seven questions. We will be left with two more examinations to undergo.

After the end of this course, I will return to Washington, D.C., for a complimentary program with the IRS Headquarters for a week or two before I return homewards just in time for Christmas! And to see my dearest wife! Convey my sincerest wishes to all, Yours Faithfully, Rat

SEPTEMBER 5

Little did I realise when I moved from New England, that I would still be living in New England. Some time after I had been here, I read a letter in the paper, referring to this section of the city, where the houses are large, the streets paved and the gardens lush, as Little England, due to the high percentage of British residing here.

A while ago, as part of the movement to perpetuate their own language, the Town Council decided to give a local name to each section of the city, which up till then had been designated as Extension 6, 7, or 8, and Town, and Village. They announced that our section will officially be known as New England.

This may be New England, but it appears more like Florida.

Walking to the Mall or across town these days, one moves through clouds of heavy perfume. When the sweetness envelops you, you immediately search for the source. It may not always be near, and you can't be certain, even after looking for it. There are trees of all kinds now suddenly in bloom; some heavy with perfume and others just a visible delight. The white frangipani are definitely exuding a strong perfume, also a huge tree, completely rosy-orchid, just one solid mass of blossoms. The other day on one of the paths, Joel and I smelled the sweetness and I turned to what looked like a cherry or pear with small blossoms. Reaching up to get a good look, I found that it was not sweet, nor were the blooms like pear. They were little soft round clusters and it was a thorn tree in bloom. Strange variety of thorn, for those in my yard have no such blooms yet.

The poinsettias have been brilliant for months, in red, pink and even yellow. Just now is the time for the double reds, the brightest I have ever seen. They tower and you look up to see these huge scarlet blossoms, centered with a huge pom pom. They are impressive. A unique tree near the Mall has smooth shiny trunk and branches, no leaves, but set all over it, like Christmas decorations, are scarlet fragrant blooms. Each blossom seems to be shooting up in the air, the whole made up of several cups, successively smaller, all the pointed petals curling outward. We shall watch it to see what leaves come out later. Without doubt, they will be handsome.

Many trees are just trellises for bougainvillaea. Ever since March, the purple, cerise, pink or white clusters of their big blooms have been cascading over them. They have continued to bloom constantly, although there hasn't been any rain since April.

One of the many benefits of walking instead of driving is seeing all the gardens, drives, walls and hedges, with their great variety of blooms, and being swept by the great clouds of heavy perfume.

Joel, Tony and Danny Pahl have had two interesting hikes this week. One day they walked way out past the Francistown Road, back of where the new Brewery has just been built, and there in the bush, they saw several Kudu.

The boys were dripping with sweat as they straggled back, their canteen empty and their feet hurting in the heavy boots I insisted they wear, but they were so excited about seeing the animals, it made up for the discomfort.

I have never heard of Kudu being this close, but it isn't an impossibility. The boys made a bee line for the animal books from Kruger Park, to verify their claim. They should know, especially Joel, as he saw many and photographed them. They swore the horns were the same and the markings, so I will believe them.

Although we told them that the best time to see the baboons out near the quarry, on the opposite side of town, was in the morning, this didn't deter them from starting out at 1 p.m. That was the time they were free and ready for a bike hike, so that's the time they went.

It may be as far as six or seven miles out there. The most treacherous part of the trip though, was the noon traffic and the Road. Then, the scary part was riding past Naledi, the shanty town; a much different atmosphere from the inner town. Turning off the main road, they followed a narrow path through thorn trees toward the big Kopjes rising on the left, and got onto a big flat stone to survey an approach. Here they saw dozens of rock rabbits, and heard screams of the baboons up in the rocks.

They found tracks all over the sand, everywhere. Joel showed me what a track looks like, by finding a small child's footprint in the sand here, and rubbing out the heel impression.

They were wise to decide then not to go any higher onto the rocks. Wise, in that they had been told not to, to start with. Their own sense, at the sounds of the baboon screams up there, reinforced the parental warning.

The miles of biking back, in the intense heat, left them pretty tired and shaky. But they didn't mind, and they plan to go again some morning, when it's cool and the baboons may be down in the road.

A small pick-up truck drove into the yard at noon this Tuesday, and it took me a few minutes to realize it was the man from Mafeking, delivering the small freezer we bought when we were down on Saturday.

Luckily, we dropped into his store once and found he deals in all kinds of household equipment, and has the Caltex franchise all the way to Francistown. Also, that he comes to Gaborone each week and delivers to your home, whatever you purchase from him. Thus, we have a good washer from him, and now this freezer, with no transportation problems.

I went out to show him that Roy would move his car, so he could drive near to the kitchen door. I'll be darned—if instead of backing up, where there was endless space, he drove straight ahead, cutting between some of my newly planted gardens, a rear tire pounding down zinnia seedlings, and the front right tire, rolling over a hibiscus bush, having been nursed along since the first of May.

No complaints though. The seedlings will come along, and the bush had bent nicely and stood up again. Small price to pay for the free delivery service.

The Boss, and his assistant, were glad to sit down in the shade for a coke before going on, and we asked him if that "Alley Cat" restaurant was new. We hadn't noticed it the other times we had been down.

"A few years, it's been there. I own it—just bought it."

It is located at the end of the block, right next to his store. We let him know how very good the dinner was that we had there.

"The best ala carte restaurant in Mafeking is at the Protea Hotel down near the railroad station. Good food, but an awful noisy place to stay."

Then he went on to tell us,

"I just got back from the States. Went for two weeks, to Pennsylvania and Texas, buying good breeding stock. Brahma and Herefords. It cost me $1600 each to have them flown over here" and he told us about the man who flies animals over all the time.

"Does he take back animals for Zoos on his return trip?" I asked.

"Well, that's the problem. He tells us, the more return loads we could arrange, the lower our fee would be."

This man must have a lot of things going. We didn't ask about his own farm land, if he actually farms or is just doing the procuring for someone else—or maybe for an artificial insemination outfit. Guess he'd more than get his investment back, in any case.

Kenneth, who appeared Friday morning, says Edwin and Shinga will be back today. It will have to be soon, as school will begin on Tuesday.

Since Friday afternoon, Joel and Kenneth and others at his house, have been involved in an almost non-stop Monopoly game.

Friday night Joel begged to stay overnight at Kenneth's. I was hesitant, but he pleaded. They wanted to look at all the funny books he had bought from Ian, who is soon moving, and Kenneth was alone except for his big sister. "Please—Please."

So, I said O.K., and helped him put away his bike, bring it into the kitchen, and lock up the back door. Then he went out the front (it was about nine) and I went back to bed and to sleep.

Not for long. There was a loud rap on my window, just at the head of my bed, and a frantic cry—

"I can't get in !!!!!"

"I know. I'll open the door. Wait."

"Why didn't you want to stay?" I asked as he came in.

"Just cause I didn't." was all he would say and he dove into his own bed.

SEPTEMBER 11, 1976

Six months ago today, Joel and I took the train down to New York to join Roy to start on our way to Africa. Reluctant to go, then, I am now worrying that the time is going too fast, and I keep telling Roy to "stop talking about which way we will go home. We just got here."

To celebrate the occasion, Jerry and Alice Pahl, Roy and I are going to have dinner at the Holiday Inn this evening. We may do something for the whole gang, to celebrate too, when the 15th actually rolls around. Many changes, in us all, since we arrived at Gaborone Airport that day.

Yesterday I told Roy that the old hen was still sitting on those six eggs.

"I thought that by this time, they would either be hatched out, or she'd have given up. How long does it take, anyway? It seems she's been on them for weeks."

This afternoon, I went down to get a handful of hay for the garden; heard her clucking, so I glanced over where she was scratching through the hayseed, and there were four little soft chickies running around under her feet.

"You old son-of-a-gun!" was all I could say. That was some sight. I peeked under the hay into her nest and saw that there are two eggs left there. I wonder if they'll hatch. Wait till Joel comes home, he'll be really thrilled.

I went to get my camera, to take a good close-up of her in front of her hay house, but when I got back, with a handful of oatmeal to lure her close, she was in the nest. In no way would she come out. Didn't even investigate the oatmeal I threw to her. I'll try again when Joel is here. I can't recall how many years it has been since I have seen little chicks hatched out; by Mama, not an incubator.

The big news with Joel is that President Sir Seretse Khama will be coming to Northside School on Monday morning at ten.

"I'm going to shake his hand! He's going to shake hands with everyone in the sixth grade! We're going to have an Assembly. The President is going to come to the front car park, and he will go in by that entrance and go between the buildings, on the lawn there, and we will all be sitting facing him. We'll each have a flag, but we're going to keep it hidden until he gets there and then we're all going to pull them out and wave them and all yell, "Pula! Pula!"

"Are you going to sing the National Anthem, then?"

"Yes. And Mrs. Dixon-Warren is going to present him with the check for BUCA. Then he is going to make the prize presentations to the ones who won—you know, most money, most sponsors and all."

"Well, that will be exciting. Ten o'clock" I'll be right out here watching. I can see right up between the buildings."

"We had a practise today, for just what we'll do and where we'll sit, so we are all ready."

This was his biggest news and he has been spreading it. I hope he gets to shake the President's hand. He is really banking on it.

I have said a couple of times that weather is not a subject for conversation here, as it is always the same and it is always good.

Not so, according to Mr. Anderson, meteorologist, who has been here in Gaborone for 19 years. Weather is his subject and he can talk all day on it—even longer if someone would listen and his voice didn't give out.

He was the guest speaker this month at Trinity Ladies and he did have a lot to tell us, although I didn't catch it all. Somehow, I always get lost in those descriptions of high and low pressure areas and the reasons for varying weather.

Botswana has had three good years in a row. Something that hadn't happened in the last 70 years—and the three good years came on the heels of seven years of drought. He said he'd stick his neck out and predict; to say he thought the first shower would be on September 14—a little sample to whet our appetite for things to come; a good one on September 27 and then a big one on October 10. So we shall see— check up on how close he is in his predictions and hopes.

After a full background of basic information, there is still a gamble as far as weather is concerned; for farmers, especially, and for pilots. But great numbers of people are working, the world over, collecting infor- mation, to eliminate as much of the gamble as possible.

In Botswana, there are weather stations with staffs of from two to five people covering all of the country; Gaborone, Mahalape, Maun, Francistown, Ghanzi—the whole perimeter. They report every twenty-five minutes, from 2 a.m. until 8 p.m. to Gaborone, and this information is sent through Pretoria, then Nairobi the regional center, from where it goes to Melbourne, Australia, a world center. Another route is to Cairo and Moscow; still another, Lagos, Germany, Paris, Bretton Woods and Washington, D.C.

Every hour of the day, select stations, as Maun and Ghanzi, send through a report strictly for use of pilots, who are themselves meteorologists after dealing with unusual climate changes in other parts of the world.

He went on to describe Botswanas' situation, with all the moisture from both the Indian Ocean and the Atlantic, having been snitched long before it gets as far as here. Also, how when sometimes the rains finally come, there is too much and farmers view with horror the washing away of their precious topsoil and all the other damage that rushing high water can do.

All of us who heard his talk, and I must say he has a great enthusiasm for his field, and excitement about it, are reassured, and looking forward to another of those good years, when there will be enough rain, but not too much.

Yesterday I took Pauline's pay out to her in the morning saying, "Well this is the 15th". Later in the day, writing letters, I discovered that it was still the 14th. So we laughed over it.

As soon as we were through lunch, Pauline was right there, a bit early, and she was all dressed up.

"I want to go to the Industrial Site."

As usual, I can't understand requests—she talks so low. Finally, I got it through my head that she wanted to ride back with Roy when he went to the office; that he should drop her at the Industrial Site first.

"I want to get some windows and doors."

I had noticed the ad in the Daily News of a sale "first come first served, cash and carry" on window frames and doors, and had wondered at the time if it would be something she was interested in.

I asked her Monday, after she had been in Molepolole on the weekend, how her house was coming.

"It is up to here, ready for window frames. I made a deposit to the man who is doing the work. It will be Rand 300 when it is all done." She should have said Pula not Rand, but everyone is finding it hard to get used to the new currency names.

When I told Roy the sum total would be $300 or so, he could hardly believe it. He didn't think that was enough. But it's a round concrete block building and will have a thatched roof. She already has the poles, and the grass can be cut on the Veld.

Well, it was the hottest part of the day, but Roy went a little early, to drop her off, and gave her the office phone number, in case she needed help. She had her pay and also a P10 and another bill, in hand.

It wasn't too long before Pauline appeared at the office to tell him that she got a window and a door frame, and she would like to get a second window, but,

"I have no more money."

So, he gave her a P10, the only bill he had on him, and away she went to get the other window.

It was a very hot day and she didn't come back here in the afternoon. If she were able to walk back to town, to her cousin's from the Industrial Site, I wouldn't blame her if she sat down and stayed there until the cool of the evening.

If her doors and windows do come, maybe we'll drive them to her house Saturday morning.

I went to the Book Centre the other day to get the typing book, but unfortunately, they were out. I'll keep checking and get her started studying as soon as possible now, as the months are flying, and she must look ahead to the day when we will be gone.

SEPTEMBER 21

If I hadn't gone down to the Post Office just at that particular time, I would have missed one of the most exciting episodes of our stay here.

I had been planning to get a box off to Canterbury by mid-September with some small gifts for each of our children and grandchildren. I kept at in stages; collecting a few things, finding a box, deciding what would be for whom, wondering if I was evened out, getting the customs forms from the Post Office, discussing the perils of mailing with those who have had experience, and finally getting it packed. Now the box was ready, and I had learned the hard way that the only time to do anything is early; the earlier the better. So, as soon as Roy left and Joel was off to school, I picked up my box and headed for the Post Office. It was thirteen pounds, but that was O.K. as I switched it from hand to hand.

I hugged the storefront side of the Mall when I got there, to use every bit of the shade available. As I glanced over toward the Post Office, I saw a couple sitting on one of the new white benches that have been placed all around the edge of the square, as part of the additions for the Tenth Anniversary celebrations. I watched the couple, as they came into view each time I passed one of the flowering shrubs. They were young, were hemmed in by two huge rucksacks with aluminum frames leaning against each end of the bench, and they had other gear on the bench. The young man appeared to be feeling bad; was leaning over and the girl had her hand on his shoulder, in a comforting manner.

I went on past them, into the Post Office, and when I went to pay for the packages, I found I didn't have enough money! I had come away hurriedly, considered bringing more, but was sure I had at least a five and a 2 and some change. The new bills, Pula, are unfamiliar still, and besides that, I had glanced in without my glasses on. I was certainly disgusted and wasn't about to walk home again with the 13 pound box. Then, I realized that Alice was only three blocks away and I would go borrow from her. First, I'd check the box in a grocery parcel till I got the money.

In my disgust, I had forgotten the couple for a minute, but walked up to the bench as I headed for the store. The girl was alone and lifting one of the big rucksacks.

"That looks awfully heavy. Did you just get here?"

"Yes. A little while ago."

"Where from?"

"Maun, but first of course, from the States—California."

"The States! We're from the other end of the country, Connecti-cut."

Then I asked her, "What were you doing up in Maun, working there?"

"No, just seeing the Okavanga. Say, do you know of any camp site around here we could stay? We're heading for Johannesburg."

"Oh, we're going to Lobatse tomorrow—that's 66 kilometers on the way to Johannesburg. Why don't you come camp in our yard. There is plenty of room, and I haven't seen or heard of any camp spot around here", and added, "if you're up to another mile walk. That's about how far it is to the house from here. But first, I have to go get some money to mail this package."

"I'll watch it here on the bench for you if you like," she said. So I hurried off to Alice's where she had money on hand, and rushed back to the Post Office. Then I saw the young man sitting with the stuff—after I had finally got the package mailed—and he shook hands as I came up and said,

"Rika has gone to the bank to get some money, we only had 11 cents in hand by the time we got here."

He was a handsome blond young man, about thirty, I'd say. Semilong hair, a semi-short beard and moustache, beautiful dimples in a longish lean face; wore steel rimmed glasses. The lens were pretty thick and the gleaming frames were big and rugged; likely to withstand the rigors of travel.

We talked for a few minutes as we waited for Rika and we seemed to cover a lot of territory.

"Rika wants to go to the University to apply for a job. She's a biologist. We'd like to stay a while. We've been travelling for a year, this time. She may have to make an appointment for an interview, but we should be on our way too. We're behind schedule a few days. We had word from her sister that she will be on Madagscar to meet us around the 20th, so we'll never make that."

"My house isn't far from the University. You can shower and get organized and walk over easily."

"Where is the Princess Marina Hospital? I have a letter to give to the wife of a Danish dentist, there."

"We'll pass there on the way to my house. Everything is close here." And I pointed out where the Embassy was, and asked if he wished to go there now.

"No, we'll clean up first and start out and do it all later."

We even had time to talk a little about the general African situation and he had many definite ideas. Told some tales of Rika's experiences as a biologist working out of Nairobi, with a group of natives. "She about freaked out the way they went berserk, on a field trip, shooting everything in sight—pregnant animals, little or big, made no difference; they went wild with pleasure at the kill." He also mentioned a few places they'd been; Afghanistan, Iraq, Iran, Ethiopia, Greece, and the fact that he had gone in hospital after some time in Asia.

He had told me his name was Roger, and that he was British, from London, though his accent was somewhat modified. Not only had he fallen in love with an American, and married her, but I found, as I listened, that he had fallen in love with America.

It was beginning to get warm as we loaded up and started across the square and toward home. It's quite a while since I've walked the old route, as I go up past Alice's nowadays, so we wound around, past the Museum, the Secondary school and through an apartment house yard where I thought we'd come out near the Hospital, but we could see it, two blocks down to our right.

"Never mind, I'll get that later." and we went on, but I took a turn into a close one block early, and the path wasn't very pleasant as workers had things dug up. I lost my head, and we walked farther than we should have. They complained of the heat; that it wasn't this hot up north (remember, north is hotter and south is cooler here).

I kept encouraging them by saying—the house is "just up there" and finally, we did reach it.

They dumped their gear inside the door; I introduced them to Pauline, and we headed for the kitchen for coffee. Roger just plunked into a chair and sat, and Rika began to take food out of her luggage; bread, cheese, a jar of jam.

"There's bread here, and everything," I said, as I started to pour coffee.

"Just one," she said. "I'll get out some tea. He has a bad stomach."

"How about some scrambled eggs?" and Roger groaned with anticipation.

I put a cloth on the table right there, and as soon as the bacon was frying, in came Roy. Introductions all around, and he pulled up a chair and sat for coffee and talk. (There is no time that banks and stores are open at other hours than the office, so one must take a half hour or so about once a week to take care of some errands.) Before they finished eating, Margaret came in. I had forgotten all about her and that my original plan was to zip to the Post Office and back to go shopping with her. "I see you have company" she said as she stepped in. She joined them at the kitchen table too, and she and Roger compared notes on their British homes.

"I'm going to the Mall now, do you want to come along?" Margaret asked.

"Yes. I'd better go along; I need a few things. Here Rika, let me show you the bath and all. Here are clean towels, the shower, and here's the extra bedroom. Just put all your stuff in here and do what you like. I'll be back later. And let me get the city map for you. You can't do without that." I got the map and they were studying it, along with Roy, when we dashed off to shop. I knew they'd love getting into a warm shower. Camping is great when you don't have to do it; but only for so long. A year seems quite a stretch of it.

"It takes a special kind of person," Alice remarked later, "and they're special all right. They were the most exciting thing that has happened to me here."

We didn't see them again until supper time. I thought they might have got lost (Lost? after they have covered most of the world on their own?) I thought they might not have noticed the house number, or had got confused with the maze of streets. About 5:40, when I had dinner all ready, Roy said, "We'd better drive out and see if we can find them."

About five blocks away, between here and the Mall, there they were heading in the right direction. They hopped in.

"We were trying to trace our way back the way we walked this morning. I remembered Elephant Road, but I hadn't noticed the number."

"We were at the Embassy, for our temporary residents permit, and when he tried to put us off till Monday, I told him we were going to Johannesburg tomorrow, so he said come back at four. Everyone went to the Government buildings to see the President get an award, and then they didn't come back until after 4:30. Didn't have any luck at the University. Not being a resident, they wouldn't even talk to her."

When we got into the kitchen—where they wanted to know if they could help, but everything was ready—they were looking over papers and cards in various wallets and leather folders, and all of a sudden, Roger couldn't find his special card—residents permit of some kind verifying that he was married to a U.S. citizen. He was really upset and began nervously scrambling through everything, not seeing a thing.

"I just saw it" Rika said, "you had it here."

"That card is worth ten thousand dollars."

We all stood as though mesmerized, looking on, and then I woke up, and turned to get something out of the refrigerator. There at my foot was the card—he had dropped it when he was putting something in there, when he first came in. What relief.

"Surprize! Hold out your hand!" and then we got on—with more talking.

I don't think we stopped talking, except for three minutes as we were driving to Lobatse the next day, at which time I turned and said,

"Don't tell me we're finally talked out!"

Both took time to walk down to see what Joel was working on in the back corner of the lot—digging a fort—and to listen to his plans and tell him what a good job he was doing. We sat outside where it was breezy and they said they each have something in common with Joel. Rika's next oldest sister is 18 years older than she, and Roger is the tail end of his family, with nephews and nieces his age, to get the generations confused.

When Roy had come in, I asked him if he'd gotten the movie tickets yet; we were planning to go see Rooster Cogburn, with Duke Wayne and Hepburn. He hadn't, so asked Roger and Rika if they'd like to go. Of course, so he got the four tickets, for the 8:30 show. Late these nights, as Indians run the theatre and they are in the midst of Ramadan—fasting times.

The movie was a riot and we roared. We got there on time so they could see all our "commercials" and shorts and enjoy the "Interval"; about 20 minutes of break just before the main feature.

Jerry and Alice Pahl stopped by to chat—along with Jeannine. Mary, Peggy, Tony, John and Patty (Dan was at our house) and Alice asked if we'd like to come over to their house after the show. We would.

"What a nice family", Roger and Rika said. That's always without fail, the remark people make after meeting them.

So, it turned into a late night—but fun. Jerry whipped up some fancy ice cream treats and we all talked and talked some more. Roger is more talkative than she, but she kept reminding him of events and interesting occurrences to tell.

They had gone to Nepal to climb the Himalayas, but everything had gone wrong. Too much snow—fourteen feet, I think he said. Crawling through bamboo forests, under the snow, or trying to go on the snow in the nighttime when it was harder, they finally had to give up, as he was ill and getting emaciated. They went as far as Greece, and the hospital was so expensive, they got student fares and flew home to London to enter the Center for Tropical Diseases.

So, after recuperation—and medicine for maintenance, they started out again.

They have covered Pakistan, Afghanistan, Nepal, where they left some of their things, Turkey—where they say the east and west of the country is as different as if a line were drawn down the center and each half was a different country—Greece, Bulgaria, Ethiopia, all of Eastern Africa, where they have spent a long time. He's travelled six and a half years and used to work in Nairobi—or have I said that before?

He used to drive truck. As he has a phobia about snakes, he was telling us that "they say" if there's one on the highway—hit it with your brakes on with a good skid, as that will kill it. Otherwise, they are known to get caught up on the under part of the car, then when you stop and get out of the car or truck, they will bite you as you step down. "Whenever I stopped and got out, even if I hadn't seen a snake, I opened the door and made a flying leap, as high as I could jump."

"You should take the kids to the Okavanga. They'd love to see all the insects, the butterflies, the birds. It's a beautiful place" Rika said. Being a biologist, I'm sure she appreciated it all. They camped, of course, and hired a boat and boatman, for about ten days. I haven't studied the map, but they went up one side, by water, then across and down the other. They were warned to ration each days' food to the boatman, but thought that wouldn't be necessary. Then they found out that it's true. Everything available is consumed immediately with no thought for another day, and then it's gone. "It is gone". A big box of tea, enough for ten days, was gone the end of the second day.

Roger told of the eerie experience of going out on a crocodile hunt. "You know how the sky is at night; clear, bright with the stars so brilliant? Well, we were on smooth dark water, a perfect mirror on which were all the brilliant stars, identical to those above. I lost all sense of direction—scary—with the boat rolling a little and reeds sometimes brushing your cheeks." (I can't remember if they ever saw any crocodiles.)

Another something scary was that their boatman was continually taking a snuff—not tobacco snuff, but some herbs of his own that soon had him rowing with a madman, and splashing and dripping water all over them.

"We hope to write a book sometime, about all the things that go wrong. When we were in Nepal, they had built a dam. They kept building this dam, as it always collapsed. Each time something different was done wrong, and it was always taken for granted that it would be wrong. They were on the seventh construction this time. One of the supervisors asked me, "Have the Americans invented a way for constructions to be done now without foundations?" They believe in the miracles of our inventions. "Oh, no," I told him, "There always has to be a foundation."

"This time they are building without a foundation!"

He was reading a book. *"Blessed Be Small"*, I think was the name, by an economist, Schumacher, who has done wonders for many an undeveloped country here. His philosophy is that huge, complicated machinery and equipment should not be thrust on people, but small things, to help them—and he has invented and created many small helpful articles. I must locate the book and read it. Roger also recommended two books for must reading—by Gerald Durrell, *My Family and Other Animals,* first and then *Birds, Beasts and Relatives,* a sequel.

I said Roger loves the U.S. with a passion—says he's a colonist just 200 years late. He and Rika will travel a year in the U.S. after they finish in the Himalayas and whatever else they have planned. Then they will decide where they will live.

So, we are looking forward to their coming to the States after we're back there.

Well, we talked—and listened to adventures and opinions—until late at the Pahls. Needless to say, the little ones had all gone to bed right after the show. Reluctantly, we headed home, but sat down, had some iced tea, and talked some more, until after two. But there was another day coming, so we had to go to bed.

"I think there are enough blankets on the bed there", and they looked up and said, "Oh we thought we'd sleep in our bags."

I turned down the covers and said "Sleep in a bed, for goodness sakes!" So they did, and they didn't wake up in the morning. Didn't hear the all-night crowing of the roosters. Didn't hear the on-going dog fights and yipping and tearing around under the windows. Didn't hear a thing until I called for breakfast.

They showered and Rika washed her long hair. We had a barber shop on the back patio after breakfast; I took off an inch or two on Roger, but she did the finer touches. Roy's always telling that I'm a professional hair cutter, but that's not really so. I'm only utilitarian. Rika had had instruction, and I was happy to give her the scissors.

Eventually we got on the road to Lobatse, which is straight south. Roy gave them two South African border papers so they could have them made out ahead of time. We talked all the way—seeing first, the "other" side of the city.

They had a good view of Naledi—the shanty town just past the Industrial Site, and I told them the article in the newspaper said that "visitors to the city during the celebration should not be driven past Naledi." How about that!

They saw a bit of Lobatse, but we didn't drive all the way through the small downtown and past the Botswana Meat Commission; pointed them out from a distance, as we turned for the 5 kilometer drive to the Pioneer Gate, where they would check out of Botswana, into South Africa, and hopefully catch a ride to Zeerust, and on to Johannesburg. They were off to Mauritius, and then Madagscar—but would be back.

Just as we got unloaded, and had said our goodbyes—I could have kissed them and I could have cried, but I didn't do either—a huge truck drove up and before we knew it, Rika called to Roger,

"He says he'll take us as far as Zeerust."

"Hurry up then" Roy said, "Get checked through."

Joel kept asking, "Why do they have to go? Why can't they stay?" We did hate to see them drive away, and we've been thinking of them ever since.

I'll pick up their story again when they come back into our lives.

SEPTEMBER 22

It was all very well to be thrilled about the sweet little baby chicks being hatched out. They stayed in the hay pile area a while, but since then I could wring their necks.

Instead of going out to feed the birds, the first thing each morning, I now rush to the window, open it and scream at the hen to "Get out of there! Get out of there!", rush out back and pick up some clumps of dirt from near the ferns, throw them at her and send her scuttling out of my seed beds and struggling seedlings and newly planted treasures. She goes, and sometimes, she goes over the fence into the yard of the people who said they chopped off the head of a chicken who came in and pecked at their parsley.

I must take time to do something about getting her into her original yard, and seeing that she stays there. She needs her wings clipped, but I don't know how to do that. She can fly up and over the fence between us and Kenneth's house, and it is fully seven feet high.

The Moon Flowers, so carefully started to make a shade for the carport are in tatters, as are the castor bean plants I moved there for the same purpose. There's always something to undo everything you try to accomplish, be it man or animal!

The windows for Pauline's house were delivered on Friday morning, just when we were all busy with our two travelling guests. When we got back from the movie Friday night, we could see doors had been delivered; they were leaning against the storeroom. Two door frames. Roy had said something about taking them all up to her home, but Saturday morning was something else for us, with Roger and Rika here and our trip to Lobatse. Roy mentioned going up when it was cooler, so we settled on early Sunday.

He and I loaded in the windows and the two door frames, using lots of cardboard to prevent rattling and scratching. Company arrived for Pauline, and her sister was getting ready to go back with us too, and finally, Roy got exasperated, "I didn't contract to take all the relatives!". So I walked over to Pauline's window and called to her. "Let's go. We're ready!", as every minute the sun gets stronger. Vivian had to crawl in back and sit inside the door frame and we three got in front.

Same old dusty, bumpy road, but it didn't seem to take as long as sometime. There always seems to be a different cast of characters on arrival at Pauline's home stand! I don't know how they shift so quickly.

I asked if Tandi was around, and after the unloading was done and I had given them a bag of oranges and batch of candy bars for the kids, here came Pauline carrying Tandi. She had had her head shaved or clipped smooth; was wearing a little shirt and the little leather string with bead "apron" in front. Hers was of bright green beads mixed with white. One look at me and she set up her usual howl and buried her face in Pauline's shoulder. No getting used to me, in spite of cookies, candy, and oranges.

I could see there were fifty-two concrete blocks lined up in her yard. Roy had given her enough money for a hundred. He asked her where the new house was, and if we could see how it was coming along. She had indicated that it was ready for the window frames.

"They say you cannot pass there as there is a hole" was her answer. She pointed in the general direction of where it was supposed to be. So, he let it go.

She wanted to come back with us, and by the time we turned around and were passing her house again, each of the kids was beginning to peel his orange that Vivian had just passed out to them.

"My brother is building over there," she said, indicating a place about a block in back of her house.

"Oh, he's building here, and he works up in Francistown?"

"Yes, he lives here." It is normal to have a home in the home village but spend many months at cattle posts, in the lands, or off in cities at jobs. Then I began to wonder about the building projects going on. Do they use more than one door in a small Rondavel? Perhaps we are transporting building materials for other family construction. Well, we'll simmer down for a while and see what happens. The next time there's a request, we'll not make too much move until we see what is already done.

There seems always to be smoke rising somewhere. Veld fires are common and race along, some over thousands of acres. We don't worry about them as any personal threat, although I haven't seen any fire department here in Gaborone. They are grass fires, so just move along and a few weeks later, we can see bright green grass in the burned-over area. How can it be bright green when there hasn't been any rain since last April? A great puzzle. Spring is moving along here with things blooming and greening on schedule, with no rain at all.

Well, back to the fires. One evening, as it darkened, we saw the sky to the west of us, brilliantly lighted. Not just the sky; the flames were visible, licking up toward a few clouds which reflected the red of the fire, magnifying it all. The flames were so close Joel ran over and down Zebra (and that is pronounced Zeb-bra) Way to see exactly where it was.

He rushed back to say it was on the field next to Holiday Inn; between there and Maru A Pula (the High School). It was pitch black by now, except for the fire, so I said I'd walk over with him—"leave the bicycle at home".

Traffic had begun to get heavy in the area and pedestrians, like us, were gathering fast. About twenty acres were aflame, the breeze brisk and the flames racing but stopping at thorn trees for bigger bursts of dry branches and needles. A young couple was beating at the flames with sticks, doing their best to brush the flame back toward the burned area and stop its run farther south toward the Broadhurst development, probably where they lived. We got sticks and joined them, and actually did some good. But it was racing like mad and sometimes the strong wind blew great masses of flame and sparks clear across the road—to the residential side. I stamped out sparks here, and soon, up came a truckload of men; the truck said "Police Dept." and perhaps the men were from the prison. Great fun for them. They cheered and yelled and the crowds along the road, especially the girls, yelled and squealed and cheered as the men leapt over the fence into the burning lot and began beating with their sticks, some of which had some bags or rags fastened to the ends. Many of the men just milled around, walking down the road and asking for cigarettes, but most did a good job and soon you could see where they were getting the best of the flames.

Two more trucks arrived and spilled out their loads of men, who didn't do a thing; wandered around, wondered where the whistling was coming from, milled around in the dark, and jumped out of the way of the maze of traffic. The biggest job then, was reloading of the men and moving out.

Everyone straggled home; bunches of kids in pajamas, old and young, all relieved to see the brilliance subsiding. It had looked horrible, but now, all was well; everyone safe.

SEPTEMBER 29

Pula! Pula! At last the rain has arrived; just in time for the Tenth Anniversary celebration.

Flags are flying, workmen are still finishing projects, new signs have appeared denoting Machal Drive, Jawaral Drive, Mobutu Road. I had thought the road leading to the Airport had always been labelled

"Village" and was surprised to find it "Jawaral", but those who have more experience say this is normal. When Heads of State visit, there must be streets bearing their names.

Jawaral, President of Gambia, Nyerere of Tanzania and Dr. Kenneth Kaunda of Zambia are on hand. Kaunda has been a frequent visitor over the past ten years. We saw these Heads of State in an impressive and dramatic arrival at the Stadium with President Seretse Khama and entourage, for the Police Tatoo, opening the celebration, earlier this week.

The whole city turned out for this show of contests, motorcycles, flashing lights, fireworks and performances by the Police Band which at one point broke into traditional dancing, moving slowly toward center field in close formation. The crowd roared, for the players all seemed to have wet spaghetti legs, and moved rhythmically with their ankles folding and their knees "clapping", while still playing their instruments.

It was a good show. Roy and I were at the next-to-the-bottom step in the stadium, and Joel and the two Pahl boys way up in the heights. They didn't know it, but we had an extra show—a side show.

There wasn't room for everyone, and if we'd arrived a few minutes later than we did, we wouldn't have had any place to sit. That didn't deter hundreds more from trying to push in. They poured in and sat on the ground in front of the seats. The big tiers of concrete seats are in three sections, ranged along one side of the field. They filled all this space, and continued to press in. The steps up to the upper areas were filled in solid, but people still climbed up, on and over people to reach some spot they thought might hold them.

A woman sitting right in front of Roy, with her feet on the crushed stone of the ground, was the most aggravated person there. She was incensed that they kept blocking her view, that they kept climbing over her, seeming to think she was on the stairway section. She tried everything—in vain—to have a moment's peace. She ranted and raved and jabbered in Setswana. Although you couldn't understand a word, you knew exactly what she was saying. If she wasn't hollering at someone she was muttering to herself.

Tiring of the constant traffic in front of her, she tried a new tack. She'd grab some of the kids passing and push them down on the ground in front of her, attempting to make a road block of seated bodies. She almost succeeded, but the pressure of the crowd was too great at times, and there was almost an "incident" at one time, just as the lights went out for change of program. A fat lady and a man behind her insisted on coming anyway, and I was afraid a lot of people were going to be injured as the pushing and shoving got rough. The man next to me kept calling "Police, Police!" to the guard standing right in front of this ruckus, with his eyes glued on the field. When the lights came on again, the fat lady had disappeared. I don't know where she went, but I wouldn't have been surprised if she had been under the foot of this hussy on the seat in front of us!"

"She's certainly not overflowing with the milk of human kindness, is she?" I said to Roy.

She tried a new tack. When someone tried to go by, she grabbed them on the leg; on kids, she got a handful of jeans and a little flesh to boot, and hung on—berating them at the top of her voice. She hung on until a man sitting near reached in and removed her hand, and said, "Let her go, go along!"

If she just hadn't been on the bottom row, she would have been better off, but all the evening it continued—climbing over her, climbing down over her from above, across in front of her—forever spoiling her view and her evening. Her performance was almost as entertaining as the one on the field.

After a visit to the Trade Fair, I decided to walk home, not realising it was almost three miles. The noise at the Stadium, when I got that far, was an excuse to stop and rest.

It was worth the long walk, for a group of girls, clad only in skins, was doing traditional dancing. The crowd was close around them but I got a few pictures though I'm afraid they won't look very primitive, as I caught a huge B.P.Oil sign in the background of one.

As I was taking the pictures, a little old lady next to me turned and said, "Mrs. Brown?" Boy, was I surprised. "Yes", I answered. We talked a bit. I don't know where she came from—next door, some friend of Pauline's or a lady from church. I finished my film, then bought two apples from a boy near the gate, to get my strength up, and got on home.

A few days later, in Johannesburg, I read in the Rand Daily Mail, that Mobutu (of Zaire) did not arrive in Gaborone for this Tatoo at the expected hour of 5:30 p.m., after the President, seventy VIPs, the band, dancers, school children and Town Council had been out for the third time to welcome him. He arrived the next day, finally, but his plane ran off the runway and got stuck in the mud. I haven't been out to see if they finally got it unstuck. Yes, Mobutu still wears his Leopard fur hat.

The older children of Northside School were to walk to the Airport the morning after the Tatoo, to be part of the welcome for other Heads of State, but notice went out that they would go only when they had word on the definite arrival before noon.

It was raining that morning and when Joel woke and heard it he said,

"Well, there goes the Airport!" I didn't give it another thought and figured they'd stay at school. Well, nothing like a little rain would hold them up. Off they went, walked more than a mile and greeted the British Foreign Minister. His plane was interesting to the kids as it was an RAF plane, all camouflaged. President Khama was there too. There is great drama in appearances and movements of the President. The kids enjoy it. I was surprised to see them straggling back to school just after noon; some uniforms were quite damp, but they didn't seem to mind.

Alice first got in the swing of the celebration by accident. She drove out to Sebele, the Agricultural School area where they lived the first five months here, to see Jeannine's teacher, who supervises her correspondence courses. She found that visiting dance groups have been housed for the week in the empty classrooms; there were Bushmen and groups from Francistown and Serowe. The Bushmen were the ones who fascinated her the most. The dancing was underway and it increased in intensity all the while. Dressed in skins, decorated with feathers—chanting and dancing to drum beats, couples alternated in trying to outdo each other.

Alice said she happened to talk to one man, and found he was in charge of the traditional dancing; had run the elimination in the natives' villages, to select the ones to perform here.

He told her that the dances have real meaning to the tribe, but because he was of the tribe in which Francistown is located, he did not understand the dances of the Bushmen. She was so excited about it all, she urged us to go out there Saturday evening. She was sure they'd be dancing again. As it turned out, there was heavy rain Saturday afternoon and evening, and she got the flu and wasn't up again for a while.

So, I missed the Bushmen dances—but Joel said an old Bushman lady sat beside him at the Stadium Monday morning, in the first row.

"She was too old to climb up in the top of the stadium where the rest of them were sitting. Boy, was she old!"

The people are having a good celebration. Lights are strung with banners and pennants, so it's like a combination of Christmas decorations and Fourth of July.

The rain has topped it all off—in a positive way. Pula means rain.

Pula means all good things, and the best to you. So, Pula, the real rain can't be topped as a feature of the celebration.

Pauline came into the kitchen ostensibly to draw some hot water, but really to tell me something. She was troubled looking and said,

"You know, Bontsho, the little girl? Yesterday, she fell into a bucket", and she indicated the pail that was filling, "like this, but only bigger. She fell down in and she was bad. You couldn't see that she was breathing. They had to go to Maru A Pula for her Mother. She is in Hospital. Very bad. I don't know if she will get well."

Of course, I know little Bontsho—the little bare brown bottomed babe who has been here a lot.

Pauline said she was going to the Hospital to see her and I waited eagerly for some good word. It was good, as she was some better. The next day Pauline assured me she was improving "though yesterday she was serious", and added that she herself never expected the baby to get better. She is still in Hospital after a week, so she must have needed the care.

Monday, I went to a coffee, out at Margaret's in the Village; the first time I had taken the car and driven by myself. It was traumatic, for me and for Roy. I had practised in the yard, but was nervous, so when I went out to the highway, from the Tax Office, I stopped too suddenly, and for some unknown reason, the transmission goofed, and I couldn't shift into any gear. A girl going into work said, "Shall I call Mr. Brown?" so he came tearing out and it was good that it was movable, though it couldn't be shifted. He got it home, got a drop cloth to lie on, got the wrench and fixed it (it had happened when we first had the car), and we went back to the office. I started again. Same calamity. He was still in sight, so we went down the road to the bus stop and he did the routine again. Then the third time, I had it down pat, and made my get-a-way safely—and did my drive to the Village to the forestry where I picked up hedge plants and to Margaret's house to a good coffee all safely—as well as home again, and back to pick Roy up.

Oh, I forgot to say, after feeling fairly complacent about the success of the day after all, after left-hand driving, and through all the round-a-bouts, Roy came home wanting to know if I found his glasses. His good horn rimmed sun glasses dropped out of his shirt pocket sometime during the repair sessions. He had walked back to the bus stop and searched, but no luck. We haven't been able to find them in the car or anywhere else, so that was a truly expensive day. If I hadn't been so determined to start driving, I would have been better off to have hired a cab.

We sat glued to the radio Friday evening to hear Ian Smith's speech. Inasmuch as the short-wave antenna was down again—it has a recurring malady of dropsy—we listened on Springbok-South Africa Radio. The speech had no more than got a good start when the radio station went off completely. We still have heard no explanation. However, we were able to hear the rest of the speech by switching to Radio Botswana. We were elated at the speech and when we met Jerry and Alice and the Dunns (another American family) at the theatre at 8:30, Jerry said,

"Well, who knows? We may get to see Rhodesia yet!"

We have had some new birds. They are an everchanging show, for with the seasons, they move through the area, going north or south. As new varieties appear and stay a while, it is some time before we realise that some of our old friends are no longer around. We are not as conscious of the seasonal change here, as it's more a change in the intensity of the heat; also, birds go south to be cooler and north to be warmer. A bit confusing.

The other day I saw a slim black bird, about robin size, with a wide peach collar and some bright orange on his breast, with a little white here and there. The collar was such a decided peach—different from anything I'd seen on other birds, I thought I'd have no problem finding it in the book. Nothing matched, so I forgot about it.

A day or so later, looking out the front window, I saw a pair of these, sauntering around on the lawn. And the lawn both here and in back had been cut since I saw the first one. They were the same bird, but, I could see now, that they each had a long train of ruffly tail dragging along behind them. The tail had been obscured in the tall grass of the uncut lawn the first time. So, no wonder I hadn't found it in the book.

They are Wydah birds, and they are hampered by this long, long tail. When they fly, it drags them down, so they constantly undulate through the air; fly as though riding waves up and down.

OCTOBER 5

"Baboons are Dangerous. Lock all doors and windows on your car." This was the sign posted beside the road, about a half mile inside the Krugersdorp Animal Park. We followed instructions and began to look for the baboons. Just then we reached a fork in the road with a great mass of rocky ledge straight ahead, several huge trees in front of it and a bare space under the trees. There was a black man, with a staff, old hat and tan coat sitting on top of the rocks. We peered around looking for movement and Roy pulled up onto the bare space under the trees. Joel said, "There are some—on the rocks!"

They weren't on the rocks long. Before the car came to a halt, it was bombarded by, and swarming with Baboons. We were assaulted! They came flying over from the rocks, gave leaps and landed on the roof, where they ran back and forth, occasionally leaning over and peering in the windows; hopped up on the hood where they jumped up and down, using it for a springboard to the top of the car; ran around the whole car, window to window, using the "sill" of the windows for a walkway, stomped on the windshield wipers and hung on the rear view mirror until it sagged; never stable enough to be of much use the rest of the way home.

It all happened so quickly, the entire proceeding was hard to take in. We hesitated to drive off quickly for fear some would fall off or get run over. No need to worry. They rode as far as they wished, jumping up and down in delight, and bounded off into the road, heading back for a new model to smear with mud and try to scratch.

It was a good introduction to the wildlife there. This park is only 2800 acres, created for a "short stay" observation of a good variety of dangerous and entertaining creatures, with a sixteen kilometer drive from which you can see everything.

Soon after the Baboon episode, we followed a side road into the camp area. Here were about a dozen sturdy thatched-roof rondavels clustered in a little valley, a waterfall nearby; the view, a mini-Switzerland. The lawns were green, and even the fields and hillsides green. We drove through the camp area, past the swim pool—no swimmers as it was a rainy day—and back onto our animal trail again.

Krugersdorp is high, over 5000' above sea level, and hilly. Down in the little valleys there were lots of trees and we seemed to be driving through old familiar woods, following a rushing stream beside us, when we came to a tall wire fence and gate. Someone crawled out of the short Rondavel next to the gate—it was so short, most of it must have been below ground. Smoke was curling out of it—out the door—as we approached, and the black man emerged like a genie, and opened the gate for us to go into the Lion area. We drove for miles and miles but didn't see a lion until the exit gate where there was a pair in a breeding pen.

Later we saw a field, fenced, which held the rhinos. All other animals were loose, grazing at will. The roads looped and relooped, circled and switched back, so you got good views of herds of zebra, impala, eland—one of which came up to the car and kissed the windows, his dewlap wagging side to side. There were wildebeest, water buffalo and Kudu.

Here was our first glimpse of Ostrich. They are funny looking creatures, like something someone made up for a cartoon. Hard to believe they are real. After being excited about the first, and taking pictures at a distance—we later came out of a little grove of trees and found a pair, and five or six baby ones, right beside the road. We stopped and they came right up to the car, went around us and wandered down to a pond, eating along the way. It was a thrill to see the babies. They couldn't have been very old, as they weren't much larger than an ostrich egg.

After going through more droves of grazers, we stopped at the kiosk on the crest of a hill, also in a grove, and had something to eat, and bought a few souvenirs; beaded handled spear and either a "Tomahawk" or a drumstick, and a leather-bound quiver of arrows, and of course, two postcards. Joel climbed up into the observation tower, a rustic post built into a huge tree from where you could look down over a waterhole. As I said, it was rainy, so he held on to the bannisters tightly, both on the way up and down. He said it was slippery; you know how old wood gets when it is wet and a little mossy. There weren't any animals at the waterhole at this time though.

Later I asked Alce about the lions and she said there were loads of them in sight, roaming, in either early morning or late afternoon. Well, this was mid-day so that accounted for the empty (seemingly) lion fields.

We took a wrong turn here, and redid the whole route of the herds of zebra, the grove, and the Ostrich family, and this time saw the Rhinos. Finally, we were at the Baboon corner again, where we stopped on the road and watched the "show" on two other cars. They found us too, and Roy kept busy getting movies of them. He had dared to have his window down a bit while they were cavorting on the other cars, but was ready to get it up at the least sign they were heading his way. I hate to think what it would be like to have one of them get inside your car—with you in it!

So, we added a Camel, Ostrich, Bleisbok, Rhino and Water Buffalo to our list of animals. Time will tell when we ever see an elephant, but I'm sure we will.

Getting home was something else. The rains had come and there were detours on the Tlokweng Road. The rains didn't mean anything to us in Johannesburg or on the way home on the good roads, but when we got nearer to Botswana, Roy remarked, "The detour along the Tlokweng road is going to be something."

The road from Grand Marico River across the veld to the Tlokweng River was fine, nicely crowned, with puddles in the gutter where they belong. The road was hard and stony so no problem. There were also many kilometers of surfaced highway before we finally reached the place we had to drop off. Traffic in both directions shared the old trail running below the new road which was lined with boulders in mazes all over it to insure no one would sneak up and use it before they were supposed to.

On the second detour (there is a series of them, but fewer every trip) we were half-way through it, hugging the left side, when a bus came plunging along toward us, also on this left side, as the rest of the road was puddles and mire. He came on until we almost touched and the driver leaned out and said,

"Back up" and elaborated that this was a road where he had the right of way.

Roy suggested he continue on his side of the road; we were on the left where we belonged, but of course, the man wasn't about to drive his bus into that soup.

"You back up. There are cars behind me," the bus driver said.

We sat there a while, and then Roy did back up, far enough so there was some solid ground for the bus to pull around us.

The view revealed by the elimination of the bus and its tail of cars, was not good. There was a lake in front of us. No wonder the bus hadn't wanted to back up through it. We dived into it, not knowing how deep it might be, and stopped in the middle. Roy tried and tried to restart the car—each attempt jerking it ahead a little until the engine finally did start and we crawled up onto semi-solid ground. There was premature relief, for we soon were at the shore of a bigger and more ominous appearing lake. It covered the road and spilled into the "gutter" area in both directions. There was no estimating where it might be the most shallow, so we made a run for it, abruptly stopping right in the middle. Muddy water swirled around up to the bottom of the doors.

"Shall we get out and push?" I asked, thinking of my new shoes I was wearing.

"No. Wait a second." While I had visions of sitting there for hours and wondering who or what could ever pull us out, he miraculously got the car started, and we crawled out—again!

We were covered with mud. Fingerpainted designs by the Baboons completely covered the upper areas, including windows (though we had stopped once by a puddle and cleared the rear window) and great gobs of mud were built up over all the lower regions.

When we reached the border gate, the South African Officer on duty asked as soon as he saw us,

"Did you get stuck on the way?" and we gave him a little resumé of the problems, which were evident from the looks of the car.

We really felt sorry for all the cars and drivers we saw heading down the road; blithely whipping through the checkpoint with thoughts of getting down to home or holiday. There was no use giving them any warning. They were on the road and there was no other.

OCTOBER 7

Jerry had been stricken at work, with an attack of kidney stones—I don't know if "attack" is the word or not, but he was suffering, and not thinking clearly. He told his British superior that he was ill, was going home. However, all he had was a bike. It's somewhere between a mile and two to get home, and I don't know how he made it. He about fell in the door when he got there, almost passing out in pain. From then on, it was a mad rush to the doctor, to the hospital for x-rays, finally back to the doctor for a shot of morphine, and home to recuperate. The doctor said if things didn't improve in a short while, he'd have to go to Joburg, as no one could help him here. Well, it was tense times for them, except that this had happened before, so he knew what was going on. Thankfully, by mid afternoon, he was much better—far from normal—but better, and they both came over for the evening, to have dinner with us, the Webbs, and Juan Kudo, down from Francistown.

When Roy came from the Mall about 5:45 he said, "The Webbs are here, saw them downtown. They were late because they collided with a cow on the way. It kicked in the windshield on their new Toyota HiAce and smashed in the front a bit." Well, I could see it was going to be an evening of "can you top this?" with kidney stone pains vying with kicked-in windshields!

Vi told us later, "We got up at five, left about eight, stopped at the office, then went to the Brigades to pick up a lady to ride down with us, and promptly got stuck in the mud there. Then, the road from Serowe to Palapye is the very worst of anywhere—50 kilometers of that. When we got to the good new road, from Mahalape to Gaborone, wouldn't you know, it was just time for a dedication ceremony and we weren't allowed to drive on it; had to take the detour. After waiting so long for the road to be finished, it didn't do us any good." I missed all the details of the cow episode. It got up and walked away and there was no one anywhere in sight to report it to, so they just came along.

Ben reported that Serowe had celebrated the anniversary with a luncheon open to practically everyone in the Village. Juan said that Francistown staged both a car race and a motorcycle race. Jerry remarked that the day he watched the traditional dancing on the Mall, he noticed that every Bushman there was wearing a new pair of Adidas! Shoes for the needy will be appreciated long after the fireworks are forgotten.

"If they had only taken their allotment in Serowe and used it for some truckloads of gravel for that road out to Palapye" came from Ben. "Think how much help that would be!"

The next morning Pauline rushed around at a great rate, and about 9:30 she said she wanted to go to the station.

"Mama is coming through."

"Is your Mother here? Coming here?"

"Mama is coming through. From Molepolole. Going to Lobatse."

"Oh. Yes of course. Go ahead. Do you have anything to give her?"

I rummaged around and found a good tin of candy, a can of peanuts and a box of bacon crackers and put them in a plastic carrying bag. She went off and we didn't see her again until we were finishing lunch. She was very animated and smiling.

"My Mother said to tell you 'Thank you'" she said, and industriously went to work to make up for the morning excursion.

We had another letter from Rat yesterday, from California. He enclosed a color picture of himself on a beach with the Golden Gate in the background.

Dear Roy and Elizabeth,

Thank you for your letter of 19/9/76 and fabulous photos you sent me. They were very pretty and when I showed them to my classmates they remarked that Suzzie looks exactly like me and hence they said I must have married my cousin. Funny, this international class is, everytime one of us receives a letter they want to know about it and it has become a class policy to tell the class about nice news coming from home.

They have been fascinated by shirts sent by Susan and one has even asked for one as a souvenir.

I guess you are enjoying the celebrations and am looking forward to hearing from you about it. I also hope you'll send me some photos of the celebrations—my classmates want to see pictures of my country. They have been hearing a lot about it in the TV this week as some of the Five Presidents attending the celebration are mentioned in the Rhodesian situation.

We returned from a beautiful tour of San Francisco—Fresno—and I have sent Susan some photos of the trip. I enclose one for you to see. It shows the Golden Bridge of San Francisco in the background.

I am now Definite about my arrival there—it should be around 20th Dec. but my bookings haven't been confirmed yet. I hope to hear from A.I.D. Washington D.C. soon.

I haven't heard from Susan for about 2 weeks and I'm very much provoked. I guess her letters are piling up in some post office on their way to me.

Convey my best wishes to all.

Happy celebrations: Rat

I didn't see Susan at church yesterday, so toward evening, Roy and I drove over to her little house in new Canada to see if she were home, so we could show her the picture of Rat and let her read his letter.

The area looked shoddier than ever, but when we reached her little complex, dead-end drive with six little houses, all the yards looked fine. Each has a lawn protected by branches of thorn trees and flowers blooming.

Susan appeared from the back of the house, a few minutes after I had knocked on the front door. She was happy to see us and laughed a lot. She got in the car and laughed some more as she looked at Rat on the beach in San Francisco, and read his letter avidly. We talked quite a while; heard that Rat had had some things stolen from his room, including $57 which wasn't good. When we were about to leave, I asked,

"Did your Mother go back home?"

"She's around. Wait."

She went back into the house—perhaps to go out the back door. She was quite a while, then the two of them came out the front door.

Her mother wore a long gathered bright coral-red skirt, a head wrapping, a pullover black sweater, and had a shawl over her shoulders. She was quite plump, was barefoot and had a smiling face.

"Mellah" she held out her hand and shook mine, and went to the car and spoke to Roy, and chatted on in Setswana. We couldn't understand a thing except the tone of what she was saying. She seemed very happy to see us.

"You have a nice girl here," I told her, but Susan said she wouldn't understand anything I said.

Susan said her mother had been going to the doctor, that she will return home in about two weeks. "She is desperate to get home" is the way she put it.

OCTOBER 11

A beautiful cool morning. Soft breezes and not an iota of humidity, which is to say; it is a typical day.

Not too much has happened lately, but I have to mention that the bright blue lizards are really enjoying the springtime. There has been one huge one in a big old thorn tree, out by the carport, ever since we've been here, but lately, we see a lot of them. They all seem brighter to me, and they are like a prehistoric animal. Some are over 12 inches long and often you can see one crossing the lawn in front of the house. It goes along with its head way up in the air, the front legs being much longer than the rear, so the main part of it isn't even visible. It senses when you are near so if one is on a tree, perhaps going up it as you happen by, it only takes a second for it to be on the other side of the trunk. If you quickly step to the other side, to get a glimpse of it, it is back on the first side so fast you only get a flash of blue.

The best way to observe them is to watch through the bedroom window when one happens to be on the lower regions of the old thorn trees. The glass cuts their sensitivity to your presence and you get a good show. Their heads are bright teal blue, shading to another blue on the neck, their backs are beige, blending into grayish legs and tail. All are rough textured and a bit warty appearing, not a bit shiny or smooth. I took a picture of one once, but they are such artists at camouflage, it will take a lot of study to find the lizard in the picture.

As I sit here writing, there goes John, the former garden boy, in a checkered cap and a bright new yellow T-shirt—up the drive past this window. He has been down to see Pauline, I guess. Every so often we see him go up the drive. I suppose he feels he has some special attachment to the place since he used to work here. I have the feeling he's keeping tabs, and the possibility of having work here again is real. Not much—it isn't!

Yesterday afternoon, Joel and I played badminton—and he has the upper hand in that game with me now—and Tandi was sitting with her mother just behind her house. Anytime I came in sight, she cried. I'll just have to stay away from her, I guess. A little later, Bontsho was there to play with her. She seemed fine and was taking a great interest in Joel and his digging project. He has his fort done except for the roof, which he had better get done before it rains again, otherwise he'll just have a man-made well.

"I guess Tandi never will stop crying at the sight of me, will she?" I said to Pauline this morning.

"Oh, I think she is not feeling well," and she made churning motions with her hand in front of her, indicating perhaps an upset stomach.

Well or sick, I guess she's just established her reaction to me. Joel said, "Put on a scarf over your hair, or get a wig. Maybe that lady that gave her a shot at the hospital had dark hair like yours."

She'll probably be here a week. We'll see if a week changes the picture.

OCTOBER 22

Almost two weeks since I've written anything. Much has been happening, though. More rain, so the lawns are green, the plants growing almost fast enough to see, and the weather in general very cool. So cool all of a sudden, after a taste of what summer heat was to be, that Roy has had to wear a coat to work, and we got out an extra blanket.

There has been great activity in Pauline's area lately. For more than a week the little house has been overflowing. All the women there have had tools in hand and the whole back part of the lot has had the grass chopped off—carried away, and been planted to maize and other vegetables.

We were fascinated with the process. Nothing was spaded under—it was just cleared off by being chopped with the heavy hoe, and as I said, hauled off. Then the seed was dropped and stepped on. Perhaps ground doesn't need to be spaded up, for once the rain comes it is loose and pourous. Perhaps this is all that's needed.

Lillian is here; she's the sister next younger than Pauline, and if my eyes don't deceive me, she is quite pregnant. She did most of the chopping, while Pauline was working up here and she kept her eye on Tandi and little Bontsho.

The personalities of these two little girls contrast. Tandi, though older, is shy—cries when she sees me, stays close to whatever adult is there at the house. Bontsho is curious, sets out after anything she spies, rushes over to see what Joel is working on, gets bored down at the house and comes up to knock at the back door to be let in and see what Pauline is doing. She's only as big as a peanut, but every inch of her is on the go, all smiles. She lets you pick her up and hug her and she'll tag along after you anywhere.

She was standing at the corner of the house, Sunday afternoon, as we went out to get in the car. All she had on was the little bead apron loin string, so I rushed over to take her picture. Then, the only time I ever saw her shy or uncooperative, was when I said,

"Turn around now, so I can get a picture of your little bare bottom."

She dashed off, around the house. Perhaps she understands English enough to have grasped what I said—and wasn't having any of it.

That morning when Roy came back from getting the Sunday paper, he said,

"They must be having a convention down there."

Pauline and another girl had ridden into the Mall with him, got some groceries where they sell the papers, which he had brought home in the car, and they had waited until the gas station opened at 12, to get "parafin" to cook with. Cousins, friends and sisters milled around for days—and more and more of the lot had the grass chopped off it.

I finally went out and put in three stakes, along the edge of what I had laid out as the badminton court, so they wouldn't run right over that. Somehow or other, these people have the urge to immediately chop off any blade of grass which appears. This is protection from poisonous "snakes in the grass". There must be nice cleared-off smooth dirt. When I thought they had finished planting, there was Lillian, chopping away at the grass on the south side of the house—where we had mowed it—so I thought maybe they would have more garden there. No. She just wanted it clean and bare. I shall plant a border of marigolds or something across the edge, I guess, as a sort of boundary line and for better appearance. Their maize is already up. Perhaps they will bring in a big wooden mortar and pestle later, and grind it. Pauline will also have to keep her eye on that chicken and her young ones. I saw them out there early this morning heading toward her maize. The chicks are gangly "teen-agers" now. They stay away pretty well, but I see them in all the yards around here. I wonder how much damage they are doing, especially at this time of beginning gardens.

"Romeo and Juliet" by the London Shakespeare Group at the Gaborone Secondary School, Wednesday evening, was better than I anticipated. It was great and Joel enjoyed it immensely—sitting on the edge of his chair all the while. He had an aisle seat, and when the performance began, inched the chair out a bit and didn't miss a thing.

The costumes and lighting helped—with all the Capulets in yellow and the Montagues in red for easy identification, but even without the costumes it would have been great, for the actors were superb. You were really carried away in the story, and of course, the whole thing sweeping along in a two-hour production was so different from plodding through it by the page, in high school English class.

There were enough duels—"sword fights" to keep Joel alert, and he was really on edge, when the tragic developments began, with bodies falling from sword or dagger thrusts—and eventually, poison. I had wondered how he'd like it and was relieved that he enjoyed it all. He talked about it all the next day.

It was over about 10:30 and we had a ride home, although we had walked down—with our "torch", and Joel armed with a length of elephant grass (like bamboo) in case any dogs came after us!

NOVEMBER 1

The Geneva Conference is underway; tomorrow is the election in the States; yesterday we heard that people were killed in a resort hotel up at Victoria Falls. The Pahls went to Johannesburg last weekend, but were unaware that there were riots in Soweto—because that city of over a million is about twenty miles out of the city; and then we heard last evening that the U.S. has changed its AID policy. More A.I.D. men will soon be arriving and more money flowing in.

On top of all that, there's a new little baby back at Pauline's house. My eyes hadn't been deceiving me. Right out of the blue Lillian went off to the hospital and had a little boy. Not only that—before it was a week old, she came walking all the way "home" from the hospital, carrying it in her arms!

Besides that—Pauline went off Friday afternoon to go to Bulawayo, Rhodesia. She heard that her girlfriend up there was injured in a car accident and asked if she could have the day off. I gave her the end-of-the-month pay, but she was back next morning because the train hadn't gone. That was understandable, as the Rhodesia Railroad is far from predictable, and I told her,

"It's not good to go on that train now. Mrs. Pahl's maid told us that she had a bad trip coming down from Francistown this weekend. There was no water, food, or anything on the train. Its full of soldiers looking for Guerrillas. And, they say even if you get into Rhodesia, you won't be allowed off the train."

She sounded a little interested, but later in the afternoon, there was a taxi waiting out front, and she soon went up the drive and off in it.

"A taxi! Her pay will be gone by the time the weekend is over. There's never a thought for tomorrow" I muttered.

So, here it is Monday morning and no Pauline. However, her little girl, her sister and new baby, and a cousin are all in the little house—and coming up and drawing warm water—and white diapers are flying from my clotheslines!

The little baby is a doll; all pink and white, and as pretty as can be. I told Lillian he was beautiful!

"Mama" had arrived also, about Tuesday. I was interested to meet Pauline's mother. Pauline called her an old lady, but I doubt that she was much over fifty. Pauline's oldest sister was born in 1949, but she couldn't tell when her mother was born. She was a fine looking lady, with much resemblance to Pauline, and seemed to enjoy visiting and spending time with Tandi. There was a gang around for two weeks, with numerous cousins, little Bontsho, and Leng and Fred from Mole-polole.

I took pictures of Pauline's mother and I had Pauline take her in and show her around the house, so she could see where her daughter worked. Later, Roy took her and Leng to the bus station. The cast of characters at the little house changes constantly. A family always seems to have numerous members available at all times for baby tending and general helping out.

Just as exciting as the arrival of the new baby, was my experience Thursday morning. Playing nine holes of gold! I never dreamed I'd ever have the opportunity or the inclination. Early tomorrow, I'll be ready and raring to go, hoping to do better than the first time. Many of my acquaintances are beginning golfers, and if we go early enough we have the course to ourselves. So, that is quite exciting, and an interruption to my constant gardening, reading and writing.

NOVEMBER 4

There are more things happening than I can keep up with. Thank heavens now I have a morning, semi-locked in this room with the typewriter—and I can catch up on a few of them.

Seretse Khama has had a heart attack and is in the hospital in South Africa. The day he was struck by it, a staff of doctors evidently flew up from Johannesburg to take care of him, but the next day, he was flown down to have a pacemaker "installed".

When we first heard the news, I thought they wouldn't take him down to Joburg, because of the political situation, but when it's a case of life and death, you go where the help is. I sincerely hope he makes a good recovery and can continue for a long time as the head of his country.

There were rumors months ago that he wished to step down, but there's a problem of having someone who could successfully replace him. His Vice President has been in office ten years, but as someone said yesterday, the Vice President is not the son of a Chief.

Khama is unique in that he is the son of a Chief; great grandson of the Great Khama. He is well educated, in South Africa and Oxford, and is married to a British woman. He is the stabilizer in this new country and has a good representative system working. If he weren't at the helm, there might be some chaotic times.

When it was mentioned that Khama wished to step down, I was surprized, but Margaret said,

"He's a sick man. He's a diabetic, you know, and he has been under a lot of strain. We stood beside him at that party (during the 10th anniversary celebrations) and he looked grey, drawn, weary, with per- spiration beads on his forehead. He is really ill."

The past few months have been a strain for him, as he was in the middle of so much here at the time he had to fly off to Lusaka, and to Dar es Salaam for the Conferences, plus the strain of staying on his own tightrope. I guess the pace has eased a bit, but it never really lets up, for one in his position.

Lady Khama flew to England, with the twin sons, just before the celebrations, placing them in school; separated for the first time in their lives from each other. They are 17, and pursuing some sort of practical mechanical training. Reports are that the boys are not happy to be separated.

Pauline didn't show up on Monday but she appeared at the regular time on Tuesday. She got to Bulawayo all right, and I guess her friend hadn't been too badly injured, "she had some scratches on her face." I didn't ask about any details of the trip, but if there had been any inci- dents, I guess she would have mentioned them.

I say, I am slow to catch on to things. A long time ago I was surprized that a new bed had appeared at Pauline's house, and she told me, "It is Lillians'" and I wondered why on earth Lillian would want a bed here when she lives in Molepolole.

It finally dawned on me this week. The plans had been laid months ago, that Lillian would come here when it was time to have the baby;

that she would go to Princess Marina Hospital, and then move in here with Pauline, where there is running water—warm water from my house and the clotheslines. When I mentioned that to Roy, he just mumbled something about "the land of milk and honey".

They will get all the benefits possible, but I like to be on the giving end—and give at my own volition. I get irritated when I find I am being maneuvered.

I mentioned to Pauline a couple times that Lillian hadn't brought the baby up to show to Mr. Brown. Last night after supper, Joel and I played badminton an hour or so, and just as we wound it up, Pauline came along carrying the baby from her house. He was wrapped in a peach wool shawl. We came up to the house and Roy looked him over. I got to hold him, and we lay him on the dining table and looked at his little feet, and uncurled the tiny hands. His face was a tiny bit darker than when I first saw him, but his hands were still pink and white. He doesn't have any hair yet. He is a really beautiful baby; nicely shaped face and perfect little features.

NOVEMBER 13

It would be impossible to think up or create, no matter how hard you tried, the unusual situations and streams of events that seem to evolve of their own volition here. You laugh and retell them and dare your listener to be appalled.

"That follows, that follows", they will say, not at all surprised at the new heights of absurdity.

When Roy came home Friday, he reported that he had been invited to join a delegation from the Tax Office in attending a Memorial Service somewhere for a man who died a year ago, after being employed in the Tax Department over five years. He bowed out; just mentioned it in passing. And that was the end of that, or so we thought.

This being Saturday, morning was more leisurely than other days, but we had observed the new birds, looked up many in the book, had a big breakfast, worked some in the yard, and were ready to go shopping by 8:20. We spent time at the Mall and later went to the railroad station area where bicycle parts are available, and when Roy turned down the next road, past the Tax Department, someone waved from the yard and we saw that besides the guard on duty, there was a large group of people. One continued to wave and run toward us, so I called to Roy,

"They want you for something!"

Up they rushed saying, "The bus hasn't come! It never came. We have waited and waited,"

Richard, a man we know pretty well, then explained they were to go to the Church Service, then the unveiling of the tombstone. It was to have started at 9:30.

"Who arranged for the bus?"

"I did," Richard said, "I called BTC and they assured me a driver and Combi. But I have tried to call and I cannot reach anyone there. It is Saturday morning and no one will be in the office."

"Well, what time is it now?"

"Ten thirty."

"Is it too late now? Would everything be all over?"

"I don't think so. They would be at the house too, maybe several hours."

"Well", Roy said, "I can't fit you all in this car. There are ten of you here? But I can go over to tell Mr. Pahl and between the two of us, we can get you there. Where is it?"

"Ramotswa."

"That's down the Lobatse Road, and then off to the left at the crossroads," I volunteered, and I was getting interested and wanted to go along. We might never have another occasion to drive to Ramotswa.

"O.K. I'll go see Mr. Pahl—just wait." None of them had any desire to call it off as they were all dressed up, planning to go and had been impatiently waiting there for about two hours.

So, off we went in a hurry, with groceries to put in the house after we'd conferred with Jerry. He was willing to help take them out and could have taken them all in his VW, but I wanted to go, so Roy said, "Leave a few of them for me, and I'll be along as soon as I can."

Richard and another young man were our passengers, and we had a good ride on blacktop all the way and it was only about twenty miles.

After we got off the Lobatse Road and headed toward the village, we had to stop to let cattle cross the road, and a few times to weave through the ones who didn't bother to get off. Then we saw a cart being pulled by nine pair of oxen, eighteen big animals.

"Why do they need so many?" I asked Richard. "They can't have anything that heavy in that small cart."

"Oh yes, they need many. Very heavy."

Then there were men plowing in the fields off to the left with four pair of oxen pulling the plow. Goats were everywhere and I asked Richard about where they get the wool here for the weavers—do they use any from the goats?

"No, they import the wool for Oodi weavers. Goats are for hides", and of course—for meat. Not too much for milk.

We came to the village shortly, the center of it at the railroad station, and the road soon brought us in sight of a big church which looked like a mission establishment in California. There was no crowd near the church and we had passed the cemetery where Richard pointed out the new headstone, and he advised,

"Go straight on, to the house", which we did.

We spotted Jerry's car under a tree, near a group of houses set back from the road, and we approached by a bumpy dirt track across the field. It was an especially fine looking home site, where well over a hundred people were gathered.

Not far from the cars was a group of twenty or so men sitting in the shade of some thorn trees, eating. Beyond them, in the field, was a cooksite with six or seven great iron legged-pots over fires, and bones tossed out on the ground.

A canvas-covered temporary shelter inside the fence was a food serving center, with a long line moving in slowly; others coming out, with stacked plates; meat, pickled beets, corn and grey pasty semi-translucent "mealies". Just beyond, was the home stand which was entirely surrounded by a low wall, black on top and red on the sides. Three Rondavels and two rectangular thatched buildings composed the home. All the area around them and inside the walls were clean swept surfaces—looking like concrete—but composed of dirt and dung mixture. It was hard as a rock and decorated in a tile design by lines drawn when it was damp. There were a myriad of low walls all around different sections throughout the group of buildings. People sat on them and on ledges built out around the house.

Another "kitchen" was going out back of these, where women were in command, watching the big pots and dishing up big portions which were carried back to the serving area.

A group of children clustered together near what looked like a sand pile, and I wondered for a minute what was of such interest down at the center. All their heads were bent, and I thought they might have a game there. A closer look revealed a big pan of something, and each was dipping in her hands and licking them off. A bit later they had wiped it clean and one little girl held it high, upside down, up over her head.

We met the widow, and her uncle, a fine looking older man in a black suit. I asked his permission to take a few pictures of the attractive home and he said it was perfectly all right.

We learned from Richard, that Joseph, who was being honored, a well liked man, only forty-three when he died. "That's his boy there", and pointed to one about thirteen, pushing his bike by, wearing a tan khaki shirt.

He was taken ill one day, went to the hospital and three days later, he died. "Something in here", and he lay his hand on his chest. It was never definite what was the cause.

I tried to be inconspicuous as I got around and took some pictures but how inconspicuous could I be a lone white woman among them all? I put the camera in the car and came back to talk, and later noticed a large group of people behind one of the farther rondavels, eating together. They were all wearing purple and deep lavender. I enquired if they were of the family, and Richard said,

"Oh, that's the choir", from the church service. They looked beautiful with the sun streaming down on the mass of purple, under the green trees.

Just then Roy rushed up to me saying,

"Guess what! The bus IS out here. See over there under the trees? It's the bus that the Tax Department arranged for. Richard says it arrived out here for the 9:30 service just as the driver said he was supposed to do!"

Only problem, he had not bothered to pick up the passengers who were supposed to ride in the bus. Unbelievable!

After marvelling about that for awhile, Jerry and Roy suggested that as long as the bus was there, it could bring the group back to Gaborone when they were ready.

"But, before we leave", I said, "Be sure that driver *knows* he is to take them home."

Richard was gone for a while and when he came back he reported,

"That bus has been especially arranged for by the Tax Department so he will certainly see that all are returned to Gaborone," very straight-faced. No one could ascertain why the driver hadn't wondered why he didn't have any passengers coming out.

As I stepped up to one of the eight windows in the Post Office a young man ahead of me was asking for two 15 cent stamps. The clerk was telling him he could have 20 or 10 cent ones, but he didn't have any 5's, and sat there idly flipping the pages of his "album" in which sheets of stamps of various denominations are stored, handy for dispensing.

"I want two 15 cent stamps, or 5's and 10's to make 15 cents on a letter," he said again.

The clerk vaguely swept his hand in the direction of the windows, where other clerks were working.

"You mean there are *NO* 15 cent stamps in this whole Post Office?"

"Down there"—and he waved again. Of course, the other windows all had long lines in front of them.

"Well. How about *you* going down and getting me some."

"Oh. How many?"

"Two stamps."

In a few minutes, the clerk returned with two stamps, 15 cent ones.

"You should have had that episode taped," I said to him. He laughed and went away shaking his head.

This morning I had no more than got up, dressed, put on the tablecloth and fed the birds, than there was a knock on the front door. At 6:45 no less. Joel and I got there at about the same time, and found "Mr. Radio Man" standing there.

"Good morning. Are you having transportation problems?"

"No. I'd like to speak with Mr. Brown."

"Come on in and sit down. He's still shaving. Can I give him a message or do you want to wait?"

"I will talk with him."

So he sat a while and then he said, "I saw you in the garden yesterday, working very hard."

"Oh, I have a good time at that. It's fun for me. Come look at it."

So we walked around to admire what there is of it. At 6:50 in the morning!

Finally, Roy appeared, ready for the office and I went to hurry the breakfast preparations. It wasn't long, after a mumbled conversation that I couldn't make much out of, that he came into the kitchen and asked me if I had a 10 Pula anywhere. It just so happened that I did, and Roy gave it to the gentleman, and he dashed off.

"You'll have to set up office hours for your loans." I told him and laughed.

"Well, I keep a record of them at the office. I only have two out at present. Oh, he needed this money for his electric bill. He had some, but not enough."

Paying the electric bill is of prime importance, for they do shut off the power, without hesitation.

"Well, make a note of the date."

Roy had told me about the way they borrow at the office. The girls are not very good about looking ahead, and they love to order by mail. The Post Office is a huge merchandise mart, with boxes from mail order houses stacked to the ceiling—and all held for COD payments. So, sometimes that is a reason for a loan before payday; something important must be picked up at the Post Office. One day he said he had P37 out, all in small amounts, but he did say, "They do pay, when they get their check." I guess he is doing them a good turn. There's no way he can refuse them, if it's a reasonable request.

"I want Mr. Brown to drive some cement to Molepolole tomorrow. I need to get some at the Industrial Site."

"Drive up tomorrow? I don't know if Mr. Brown will. Can you buy cement in Molepolole?"

"It is 2P there and only 1P down here."

"But that's a hard drive. You'll have to talk to Mr. Brown."

Roy had been of the mind, the last time, to drive up a load instead of contributing money to the project. I then thought it was not worth the difference in price, but we drove anyway. It was the third time—and the charm. I guess he decided then—no more trips, as he got a stone caught somewhere in the shock absorber and had a sizeable garage bill besides the rest of the wear and tear. It's 66 kilometers or more on rough dirt and sand and sometimes rocky road.

"No, the cement is 1.70 here, so there's not much difference—not worth driving." I told Pauline, "No. Mr. Brown will not drive. I will give you a little money to cover the difference in the price."

She looked a little surprized, but said, "I will have to go home then and order it."

A little later she stopped in and said,

"I am leaving now."

So, I gave her P2 and said if the cement was 50 cents more for each bag, this would be enough for four bags. She didn't object, and off she went. She was back before Sunday noon, and I haven't had any new requests.

These family arrangements are something. Alice told me about her maid, Shanda. She speaks good English and is going to night school, studying typing. Alice thought she was living with four other girls, but that isn't exactly the picture. Shanda, has been going with a Policeman for several years and they had planned to be married in November, but lately changed to December.

Now, it seems she has been living with the boyfriend and taking care of five children of her boyfriend's brother!

"I am like a mother to them." They are in school, but range from first grade up to fifth. Shanda is helping with the rent, the electric bill and feeding them, and doing up the boyfriend's uniforms (starched stiff as a board), doing her own job at Pahls' and going to school.

"He must take care of his brother's children, because his mother says he has to; his brother has eleven children. She said he must help with these." Their home is a village way up toward Francistown.

"Where is their own mother?"

"Oh, she is up in their village. His mother says he must take care of these children but my mother says I should not be living with him and taking care of these children who are not part of my family. She says I should be using my money and my time on my own home." Shanda is about twenty-three. She says she will be moving into the servants quarters at the Pahls' residence soon. Presently, she uses it only as a place to change her clothes and to spend her lunch break. So Alice says, "If she moves in, I will assume there has been a break with the boyfriend. She says that he is afraid of his mother and must do as she says."

So, here no one has qualms about asking someone else in the family to take over their children, or some of them anyway.

NOVEMBER 18

As I neared Alice's house yesterday, on my way to the Post Office, I noticed the row of sturdy marigold plants outside her fence, bordering the road. Between them and the road surface was a good ditch a few inches deep, to retain water that might be sprayed on them, or to aid in collecting dew or rain from quick showers; diverting it toward the plants.

"Peter must have done that ditching", I thought, and wondered if he were coming every Saturday to work in the yard.

I had heard about Peter right after we got here. The Pahls found him, out in Sebele, sometime after they were trying to disengage themselves from a useless garden boy who wouldn't accept the fact that he was fired.

"This Peter is really sharp", Jerry told us. "He is quick and bright and on the ball. Hard to keep up with him. A good worker."

Soon after they moved into town, I was on the Mall with Alice one afternoon, when she exclaimed,

"Peter! How are you? What are you doing now?" and introduced me.

He had been working on the farm at the college. Alice got out a piece of paper and pencil saying,

"I am going to give you our new address. We're over near Thorn-

hill School. Now you come to us if you need to, if you need anything,"
and told me,

"I'd love to help get that boy into school somewhere. He would
like to go to school more, but his father says he must get a job and help
with the other children. He had to get some job other than a garden boy,
that's why he couldn't stay on with us at Sebele. It's such a waste that
he can't go to school. He finished Form 2."

Joel reported later that Peter had had lunch with them at the Pahls
on Saturday. It hadn't taken Peter long to locate their new home and
come to see them. It was soon understood that he should come every
Saturday and help get the new yard into shape.

"That Peter is such a nice boy," she said one day, "I'm getting a
shirt for him, and when I go to Joburg, I'm going to bring him something nice. He came the other day and asked if he could use one of the
servant's rooms. He is in training at Immigration, for work at the
Border Posts, and he has trouble getting into town each day from way
out at Sebele. He is a little nervous about his new job as he'll be stationed
way out somewhere, when he starts, and he's just a kid. But, I'm using
one of the rooms as a storehouse. All our luggage is in there; and too
many things for me to haul out and find another place for. And I can't
take the room away from Shanda. It's part of her wages."

Thinking about him, I went into the house after noticing how
much better the yard looked now.

"Is your mother here?" I called to Danny.

"Yes, she is," Alice answered. It was she, not her son, that I had
seen through the window, sitting at the dining room table. "I'm just
finishing this mending, then I'm going down for groceries. You can ride
along."

After enquiring about how Jerry was, and getting the latest developments about an appointment he was making with a doctor in Joburg,
Alice said,

"We had very sad news last night."

"What?" Thinking it was news from home about some relatives.

"Peter is dead."

"Peter? Your garden boy? What happened?"

"He was sick, went to the hospital and got a shot and then died."

Then she went on to say that she didn't know too many details, but
"I firmly believe that if he hadn't had that shot, Peter would be alive
right now."

That evening she and Jerry came over to tell us they had gone to
Immigration for the particulars and had also got his family name.

It seems Peter went for his physical in order to start work at the border post. They found he had Belharzia, so said he needed treatment for that.

He had the first shot—which is arsenic, according to Margaret, and he got progressively worse in the next few days, coming back to the hospital the third day, when he died.

Alice was very upset about Peter's death, and said she couldn't sleep the second night, but got up when all the rest of the family slept; got out her diary and wrote pages about him.

"He was one of the few locals here that I had a warm feeling for. I like Pauline and I like Shanda, but Peter was special. We talked together and I knew he meant what he said. There was no pretense and he was never trying to get anything out of us. He was open and warm-hearted and we really liked him."

NOVEMBER 19

The middle of this week, Roy came in with some mail—looking pleased.

"I'm going back to the Mall in a few minutes to get movie tickets, but I knew you'd want to see this, so came right home."

He held out the day's mail, with a post card on top—"From Roger and Rika!" At long last. They had left here the 18th of September and we had heard nothing.

Tananarive
(which we now know is the capital of Madagascar)
October 10, 1976

Hello All! We at last made it to Madagascar after hiking through intermediate countries, and it is so wonderful to be here. The people are some of the most friendly we've ever met, and they're always smiling! The variety and quality of goods in the marketplace, too, is incredible. Unfortunately, finding work here seems unlikely; as they are not exactly pro-West, but we'll still try. At the least, we'll probably stay till our three month visas expire. Then in the Spring I hope we can see you again. It was so wonderful of you to pick us up off the street the way you did and give us shelter for the night, as well as a movie on top of it all. We both greatly appreciate your openness and friendliness and look forward to seeing you again. Love, Rika and Roger.

When the Pahls stopped over after supper that evening, we passed

the card around, and recalled the fun time we'd had when Roger and
Rika dropped into our lives.

Tomorrow is Thanksgiving for Americans, and though all are
thankful, no one seems to have the seasonal feeling; there's no snow,
crisp fall weather or feeling that the whole holiday season is upon us. It
is mid-summer—or feels like it, although we know the heat will hit
higher temperatures yet, as we get into December and January.

Yesterday, Susan, Rat's wife, came to see me. She had three big jars
of Malt and Cod Liver Oil she wished to store in my refrigerator.

She is a skinny little thing, and this is supposed to help put some
weight on her. She said she was going to a doctor and he wanted her to
have surgery, the first part of December, but she is refusing as Rat
comes home on December 22. She had an operation over a year ago,
after she first started to lose weight. She had a pain in her right side; now
she has one in her left. I asked who her doctor was, thinking it might be
the one we go to. Dr. Letsunyane B.Sc. (Rhodes) M.B. Ch.B. Natal,
whose wife is Dr. Matthews, with offices in his building—whose
brother Dr. Matthews, also practices here.

She said no, her doctor is so and so, a gynecologist. It gives me the
creeps to think of someone doing exploratory surgery on her—especially if it ends up that she can't have children. A woman here who
doesn't have babies, is not in a good position. Well, I'm glad she has
postponed it so far. When her husband is home, maybe he'll have something to say about it.

Thanksgiving dinner has been postponed by Jerry and Alice as Jerry
is in Johannesburg for surgery for kidney stones. After suffering
through five of these attacks in the past month, he was immobilized by
another one on Sunday, and someone hunted up Dr. Matthews, at her
mother's home up the street two houses from Jerry's. She gave him pills
enough to tide him over for the trip and they put him in the back of the
VW and Alice set off at about noon for the long drive; too concerned
about Jerry to worry about finding their destination in the strange city
six hours away. Friends will look in on the family, left with fifteen year
old Jeannine at the helm.

Yesterday, about one o'clock, in staggered Joel, weak as a cat.

"Didn't you see us walking down the road this morning? And I
didn't have any juice bottle!"

"I know. I saw you had forgotten it, right after you left, but I
figured you'd dash over at break time and get it."

"We didn't have a break, and Mr. Williams wouldn't let me come get it. We had to go to the Airport right away after P.E. We started about 9:30, walked all the way, and it was hot. You should have seen those little kids that walked all the way from Thornhill. We almost died."

Which was a little exaggeration, but it was one of the intensely hot days.

"We met Sir Seretse's plane. He came back from Johannesburg. We stayed in the shade there, waiting. We all got under the planes parked along that edge."

"Did you have flags to wave?"

"Yep. We each had a flag, but they didn't last long. When you wave them hard, the thin sticks break and the paper tears."

"Well, I'm sorry. Of all the days not to have your drink bottle along!"

Sir Seretse has made a good recovery. We have smiled though, at the way they have twice printed it in the paper that "He was inserted a permanent stand-by pacemaker to prevent any future slow heartrate."

The team of doctors did insert a temporary one here at the hospital, but eventually decided to "insert him" a permanent one.

All was not cheers and flag waving on his return. As he came toward town from the Airport, he passed the University. Instead of a normal campus scene, there were riot police out in full regalia including shields. It was the second day of an upheaval which has ended with the University closed, all students sent home, here and to Swaziland and other African countries. Complaints of the students (better balanced meals, larger government allowance and longer library hours) hardly seem serious enough to have set off such rioting.

The Rector, when discussing the requests for more balanced meals said, "If the people could come in and see what is served, they would revolt, for few can eat as well."

This will not encourage the people to wind up their BUCA drive with any great push. The poor people who gave a goat or chicken to help their country—through education—might wish they had rather eaten it!

Our newest birds are Melba Finches. They have a moss green back—dull red tail and luminous red beak and face. They glow in the sunshine. The other afternoon we looked at the bird bath and there were sixteen Melba Finch in there at once, drinking and splashing. It was a more impressive sight than when there is a wide variety.

A great flock of birds flew over this morning—sailing in streaks, like jets; slim wind-swept wings and long, long sword tails. The birds are brave and fly down and wait for their food as soon as they hear me in the kitchen in the morning.

Several Wydah birds with their long trailing tails have come back; a pair of them ate with the others this morning. Literally dozens of brilliant yellow weavers, with black masks, vied with the blue waxbills for the seed. Of course, several big doves always have to be there to keep order and boss the rest around.

Joel and the other students at Northside are so engrossed in the production of Joseph and His Technicolor Dreamcoat, that it has taken on reality.

As he waited in the yard for his friend Pippin, who was coming for dinner this evening, two local boys rode past on bicycles. Joel waved excitedly, running after them a short ways, and I asked, "Who was that?"

"That was my father and Pharoah. Jacob and Pharoah."

That made me laugh. They have practised so much they are thinking of each other in terms of their roles in the play.

NOVEMBER 29

"Yuk!" let me wash my hands. I feel like I'm going to throw up!" Joel exclaimed as he came in from school Friday and tossed down his plastic bag holding a tin cake pan, fork, knife and spoon.

The kids had had a questionable treat; Independence Stew, at noon. During the Tenth Anniversary celebrations, batches of beef were donated to different sections of town, and to schools. A gift of meat to Thornhill and Northside Schools was to have been made up into stew then for a picnic day. But, it poured on the day for the outdoor cooking, so the manager of the Holiday Inn offered to put the meat into the Inn's freezer until another time was set.

"It was awful. It looked like it had chicken necks in it, like Kenneth and Edwin put in next door" and he went on to say he *HAD* to eat it. No one was allowed to leave his portion. He and Pippin discussed later how they had managed to secrete some, by wrapping it in a napkin.

"What did you think was in it Pip?" Joel asked.

"Guts. The stuff from inside by the stomach."

Even I could hardly stand the smell of his hands when he first came home. The women had probably done their best with the meat alloted them, but perhaps they should have had an equal portion of onions, celery, tomato, et al, to kill the taste of the old critter.

When Susan came to dinner Thursday evening, she handed me a large brown envelope and said,

"Here are the stamps."

I had mentioned to her earlier in the week that Joel was now interested in stamps and looking for some. That if she had a few on letters from her sisters in Windhoek, South West Africa, he'd like them. She had said then, "I have been saving them."

We opened the envelope and peeked in. It was packed full of corners of envelopes; all of Botswana. She had a second pack and said, "These are from other places."

"Susan. You don't want to give all these away. Let him take out some that are duplicates, and keep some yourself. You've been saving these a long time. Here's a Christmas, 1969!"

"I do not need them."

We began sorting them that evening. Joel went on to his swim club, but I spent a while after dinner, piling the Birds Series in one place, the Christmas in another, and the big stacks of duplicates elsewhere.

There were two from Russia so I asked,

"Who do you get letters from, from Russia?"

"My sister's boy is studying there. Engineering."

"Oh, your sister who lives in Windhoek! I didn't know she had children old enough to be away studying."

"She is my Mother's second born. She is old."

"How old is the boy. The one who is in Russia studying?"

"He must be 23. I am 22, yes, 23."

The things you learn when you begin to collect stamps!

Russia is most certainly involved in South West Africa, Namibia. Perhaps they are teaching her nephew more than Engineering.

Pippin Zeigler and his family took Joel with them Sunday for a picnic at the Livingstone Tree, at the site near where Livingstone and his family lived for three years; the longest in one place during their whole married life.

It was Pippins' Mother's birthday, so Joel took her some flowers. She was about thirty, as most of Joel's friend's parents are. They're awfully young.

The picnic turned into an all-day affair of climbing hills and rocks, playing games in the heat and tearing around, so when he came in about six, he went straight to bed, exhausted.

I just went over to the Pahl house to see how the kids are. They are keyed up about their parents coming home today. "It seems they've been gone eight weeks or months, not days" was Mary's remark.

Jeannine said when I got there, "Guess what! Our maid Shanda has problems. She got beat up. And guess who did it. Her boyfriend! She came to work today and did the wash, but brought a girlfriend along to help do the other work. Her boyfriend first wouldn't let her into the house when she came home from visiting her girlfriend; accused her of going out with some other man. Then when he did let her in, he beat her up and she had to get away and run a long distance to a place where she could stay." This may accelerate her breaking with him and moving into the quarters at the Pahl houselot.

DECEMBER 1

I pushed aside the curtain at the head of the bed and peered out into the nice cool morning. The sun was coming up, but the breeze was blowing and everything looked damp. There were kids in the yard next door and I could see a lady out washing the woodwork at the front door. Then I noticed the time—it wasn't 6:30 as I had thought, but 5:30. Well, Batswana usually get up early, but it seemed quite early for the kids to be out there.

When I did get up and open the windows all around the house to let in some of that nice cool air (makes me mad that because of security, I can't leave them open all night), I noticed a group of men sitting under the trees in the yard next door. Soon several cars arrived and groups of men, and then a man carrying a long case. Joel spotted that and added that it was a gun case.

"Oh, I know. Maybe some of them are going up to Maun today to the lion hunt." Roy had reported that there would be a four day hunt as Lions needed thinning out up there and he asked Joel if perhaps his friend Pippins' dad might be going, inasmuch as he is a Senior Game Warden. Well, off they finally went to work and school and after a few chores around here, I sat down at the typewriter to tackle overdue letters. Pauline came in and instead of beginning work in the kitchen, she came in here and stood—with that pent-up look, so I knew she had either news or some request. I look at her questioningly and she said,

"Last night in an accident, the owner of that house over there was killed. Two are in the hospital; one broken leg down here and one, broken up here", and she rubbed at her shoulder.

"Who is it? Edwin's father? Kenneth's? Does he have children?"

"He has six children" then she said, "They ran into a cow."

"I guess they must have been going fast when they hit it, to have killed one and injured the others."

I felt badly for them and all day I watched the people gather over there. Most of their friends and family seemed to have pick-up trucks and there were always two or three unloading or going in and out. Men gathered in large groups under the big canopy in front of the house, women gathered in the breezeway beyond the living room. You could look through the living room and see them on the other side. Then the rest of the furniture was carried out into the yard beyond the kitchen end—out toward the road and a mass of people have been there ever since.

They were singing hymns late in the evening. I looked out the window numerous times and groups were still gathered past midnight. Before five this morning, they were again moving around and then sitting in clusters. Such a large group of people, but even from a distance, from their stance and low talking, you knew it wasn't a celebration; it had an aura of sadness.

I got a sympathy card, yesterday, and asked Pauline what the custom was here. Do I take food? Flowers?

She said yes, food, flowers, money, cards. So I arranged a big bouquet of flowers from my garden, had Roy and Joel sign the card too, and baked a cake as soon as breakfast was over. Of course, I found I was low on frosting sugar, so had to walk to town for some.

When the cake was ready, I went over, and luckily too, a young woman with a good command of English greeted me, and asked me my name. I felt I could talk with her there in the dining room, as the crowds were mostly now, in the yard. I wanted to know whose father it was who had died, and where Kenneth and Edwin were; if they might have been along and injured as I hadn't seen either one of them.

"I see so many over here, I don't know them all" I said.

"Wait. I will show you the picture of the wife."

I was puzzled over that, but sat while someone else came with keys and finally this pretty girl came back with a sheaf of pictures.

I had also asked, "Was the wife tall? I know her."

She handed me a picture and then another and said, "This is the owner of this house that was killed. Here is her husband, and he is still in the hospital. He is bad."

"This lady was killed? Her? I know her. She was over talking to me the other day—asking to use my phone."

"Yes. She is the one. Here are some more pictures of her. And here is her daughter", putting her hand on the shoulder of a teen-ager standing there. She just finished her school exams, thank heavens, before this happened."

I couldn't believe that lady was the one. I had been looking for her amongst all the people milling around over there, to ask her about what had happened; and I'd been hoping that it wasn't her husband that was killed.

But she was Edwin's mother. She had worked at the President Hotel on the Mall. Edwin often took Joel up there to see his mother and she'd give them fancy snacks and let them use the bathroom when they needed.

There are dark days ahead for the family now. This Ford pick-up has finally done them in. It's one that had to have the new engine and Joel was concerned about them not having the money to get it out of the garage, that maybe they'd lose the car.

Little did they know it might have been a blessing if they had lost it.

With the hospital expense, the funeral, no car and now "the owner of the house" gone, I wonder what changes there will be for them and how it will affect Kenneth and Edwin and Vivian.

Night after night, the hymns of vigil continued, and I found, from Pauline, that one week is the tradition. On Saturday, the greatest crowd gathered and unfortunately, just as they had a huge fire going in the yard, a thunderstorm came up and a deluge poured down. Many people left but the rest squeezed into the house until the rain eased.

Early Sunday morning there was a service in the yard. People stood, of course, and the yard was full with at least fifty outside the fence, in the road and on the shoulder. At 8:30 I saw the crowd moving out and the vehicles starting. A blue pick-up pulled forward inside the yard and the bearers loaded the casket. Eight or ten women got into the back and ranged themselves on either side while two men sat on the cab roof.

A green sedan followed, as the pick-up left the yard, and in it I could see a lot of little heads, and their big sisters. Here was when I had to cry for all the little ones—Kenneth, Edwin, Shinga and the girls.

Soon there was only an old man sitting over in the yard under a tarp, and a young woman in the lawn area on the far side of the house, with some unhappy babies. It was a rare period of quiet before the whole two hundred people streamed back from the burial.

Three days have passed since then and the area is thinning out. Anytime now, there will be just the family, struggling along without its Mama.

Yesterday, Pauline said, "Lillian is going home to my people tomorrow." So this has been an interval, and she is going back to live under a bit more primitive conditions, where they have to walk to the water faucet some distance. It will be hard, after being where the water flows freely. The baby is beautiful and he seems healthy and happy. She came in with some color photos, and Pauline said, "One of them is for Joel." So, he has a nice picture of Lillian and the little fellow smiling. Joel is very good with little kids and he talks a lot with Tandi and teaches her words. This week, Leng, Fred and a cousin of Pauline appeared. So, we got acquainted with Fred, and he's a dear boy. I told Pauline he was just like her. He is lively and helpful and catches on fast. He followed me around in the yard and did more than my old garden boy! I knew he was dying to push the power mower, so against my better judgment, I asked him to come along. He grinned and pushed with me until he was exhausted, and I was very careful. There were no mishaps.

He threw off stones, and pulled weeds, and when I dug a certain kind of plant out of the lawn and replanted them along the edge, he immediately rushed around and located them for me. Not a word of English yet, but we got along famously without words.

This afternoon, we turned the corner of Elephant Road onto Zebra Way, and I spotted some movement in a driveway and realised I was seeing a snake. I yelled to Roy to stop the car and see it.

"I think it has a bird in its mouth—a masked weaver!"

He backed up and we could see the snake heading for the fence, which was thick with vines, and we got a good look before it slithered into the greenery. Clamped in its mouth was a bright yellow-green chameleon, wriggling in a vain attempt to escape. That was my first snake here, and I hope it's the last!

Saturday morning the birds were enjoying their breakfast out on the patio, and all of a sudden I heard one fly into the kitchen window with a dull thud. I was busy with breakfast and assumed that it had flown along. Then when I told Roy about it, he asked, "Did it kill it?"

"I didn't look to see." and went out and peered down. There on a small table right under the window, sat a little Blue Waxbill. It was immobilized and I thought dead. Ten minutes later, I saw it had moved a little bit, and after breakfast, the tray was bare. It had become un-stunned and flown away. Lucky bird. One flew at the window one day and broke its neck.

DECEMBER 16

Over a week since I have recorded anything new—as we left last Thursday afternoon for Johannesburg and I've been unwinding ever since.

The first evening there we went down to see if TV was available in the Kiosk and found that Joubert Park had been turned into a Christmas Fairyland. It was reminiscent of Tivoli in Copenhagen, but on a smaller scale. Lights sparkled, music played, crowds moved around to see the displays. The large green lawns had been encircled by metal picket fences. You could see the holes in the back-top walks for the metal posts, so you knew these were used often. Behind the fences were life-size depictions of every fairy story you ever heard. Cinderella, Three Little Pigs, complete with full-size straw house, twig house and brick refuge; Jack and Jill, House That Jack Built, Red Riding Hood, a Pirate scene with full-size ship, Jack and the Beanstalk—on and on. They were appropriately lighted—Scrooge and ghost eerie in lavender, and each scene had appropriate music. They were separated by the shrubbery of the park and each placed where there was a streetlight. A lovely manger scene was on the lawn at the Art Museum, and on one circular drive were four or five Tribal scenes of home and family life. The models of adults and children were dressed in native costumes, of the Bushmen, Zulu, Xhosa, and Nedebele tribes.

Japanese lanterns bobbed above, in some of the areas, and a scene near the center was a huge circus, with a tall center pole, lines of lights sweeping down in a tent shape. The softie man did a brisk business near the entrance gate, as did the men selling inflatable toys; plastic Santas, reindeer and animals. It was a gala scene and we were reluctant to leave it to see what was on the big screen.

Friday we accomplished most we set out to do; had the radio repaired, found a dermatologist for Joel who assured me his skin rash is just exzema—nothing infectious or anything that could get worse. He was a pleasant doctor whose son is in New York, associated with publishers—St. Martins.

He asked us if we were going up to the Okavanga, and when I said, "well, I suppose we might," he was indignant.

"What do you mean, you might! People spend $30,000 to come all the way from the States to visit it, and you're right here already."

So, I guess we should make the effort before the next year is over.

It was a five hour trip again—and a bit more, as we stopped midway for a half hour of snacks, ice cream and reading the Sunday paper.

The big story was the American tourist who had stepped out of his car in the Game Reserve in Angola, to take pictures, only to be pounced upon by a huge lion which tore his throat out in a second, was joined by others of the pride who devoured the man in front of his wife and two children. Other tourists on the spot had taken many gory pictures which were published. In a matter of minutes, there was only his watch, camera and clothes left.

When we got home, the Pahl children were all agog about that story and kept retelling that Jerry had done just that in Krugersdorps, taking lion pictures when there was a female with cubs, about fifty feet away. It sent the chills through them, realizing how that might have ended too. Pippin, at Joel's party, ventured that his dad, a game warden, said the lion should be shot, as it now would have the taste for human flesh.

Lillian and the new baby had gone back to Molepolole by the time we got back. Fred and Tandi were still here. Pauline was having Fred look after Tandi while she worked. No convenience of having a sister around to baby sit.

I asked Tandi, "Where's the Baby?" and asked Pauline, "Does she miss it?" Then I realized I had never found out what Lillian had named the little boy, so asked,

""Lovemore" she said. I thought I had misunderstood, so asked her to spell it.

"L o v e m o r e", she said.

I thought that was quite a name for the little doll with no father anywhere evident. We'll have to add that name to Conference, Englishman, Bias, and some other unusual ones we see and hear.

We had a good laugh as we neared home Sunday afternoon. Out along the Tlokweng Road, we approached a man standing at the road-side relieving himself. He was very polite—didn't turn his back on us, but waved vigorously. "Good thing he didn't try to tip his hat too" Roy said, "Or he'd have been in trouble!"

This is not an unusual sight. A couple Saturdays ago, some organization ran an afternoon of donkey races here at the Northside School with booths and carnival games too. Late in the afternoon, Joel rushed in calling for Roy to come again with the movie camera, for the donkey cart, loaded with kids was heading out the gate right towards us. Roy was napping at the time, so I got the Minolta and told Joel to use it, and then I decided to go too. It was quite a sight. There were three pair of donkeys pulling, and the cart was overflowing with little black children. It came out the gate and along the street in front of us and stopped. As I went out into the road to get a picture of the cart with our house in the background, I noticed why the cart had stopped there. Right across the road, in full view of all this gang and those leaving the grounds, was the driver—making himself more comfortable right into the gutter. He hurried back to the cart—buttoning up on the way!

One day, down on the Mall, right in front of the corner supermarket, a couple little boys about three, had to go so they competed a bit about how high an arc each of them could attain—no one paid much attention.

The most excited I ever saw Pauline get, was the other day when I was making a dress for her, and mentioned it was the kind of material that doesn't look good on me—a print. She went to the closet and pointed to a pair of long pants—green paisley and silvery pattern, and said, "How about that material?"

I pulled them down and said, "Do you want them?" I'm not going to wear them any more." They are floor length and look like a skirt. She accepted them enthusiastically and finished up her ironing.

Sometime later, I was still there working when she burst into the room wearing the long green pants and twirled around to show me how they looked—grinning and excited. She had on a white sleeveless top that was all right, but didn't quite match. So I said, "Here's the green top that I wore with them. You might as well have that too."

She whisked off the top she had on and much to my surprise, that's all she had on the top, but she was too excited to even think of it. She put on the green top and admired herself in the mirror and said,

"Thank you, thank you, thank you!" and rushed out and down the path to show the complete outfit to her visiting girlfriend.

DECEMBER 22

Rat Sethantsho returned to Gaborone today, from eight months study in Los Angeles, poised and confident, an experienced traveller who has covered most of the United States and shaken hands with President Ford. Bearing letters to be given to H.E. Sir Seretse Khama, Rat is the same smiling Bushman who left last April, but in some ways is a different person.

Last evening, Roy and I made a trip over to Susan's house to find out what the arrival time was and if she needed a ride. It's not a good idea to go anywhere after dark, but as this was the last evening before his return, we had to. With much difficulty, we finally located the house, but no Susan. A young woman was sitting on the lawn and to my enquiry of when Rat was to arrive said,

"We hope so", that he would arrive "tomorrow". She couldn't tell us when Susan would be back, so we wove our way out again, straddling the deep ruts and easing over the great ditches which ran crossways of the road in places.

This morning, early, we set off to Susan's house again and had no trouble finding it, and her. She was hurrying down the road toward the Mall to find a phone to call us. She was nervous, although she looked much better today than the last time I had seen her, and was all dressed up in a new leather skirt and bright Busham print blouse.

There were many changes at the Airport since the last time I was there; blacktopped parking area with curbs, enlarged building with ample space for processing and picking up baggage, with the public barred. The building is brightly painted now with many touches added at the time of the Anniversary. By the time we had looked around, a plane was landing, so the last few minutes were taken up by watching it come back from the far end of the field to unload and refuel. Although it was a small plane, there were about fifty passengers, so the tense moments were watching each one as he appeared at the top of the stairs until finally, Rat himself was there. Susan was so anxious and happy to see him. He came down the stairs, and we waved as he passed in front of us on the way to the Arrivals lounge, but he didn't come over, the ten or fifteen feet which separated him from Susan to hug or kiss her; just went along in line with a wave.

These men seem to be more open in their relationships with other men than with their wives. It's O.K. to laugh and hug and slap on the shoulder a man friend who is there to greet you. Three or four friends received from Rat the kind of response I'd think should have been made to her. When he did come out with his baggage, she ran to him, hugged and kissed him, and I guess he kissed her back, but he didn't show much emotion or much exclusive attention. After walking to the car with his big shopping bag of Christmas gifts and suitcases I made sure to open the back door and usher them in together. I didn't want him to get into the front seat and talk man-talk with Roy about Tax stuff and people he had seen.

We took them to the Holiday Inn for a cool drink and to sit and talk a while before going on to their little house.

DECEMBER 28

Christmas has come and gone. Not really gone, as we can always remember all of it; one of the best, in spite of being far from old friends and family.

There were Carols by Candlelight on Thursday evening—the night before Christmas Eve. Hundreds gathered on the Mall and each had been asked to bring a candle which enabled him to read the words of the carols from the good printed programs provided.

The evening was cool and a little breezy, therefore, all my attention was not on the carols. The family groups with children, found it hard to keep their candles alight. So, they used the printed programs for windshields, and once in a while, one of the sheets would catch fire. Also, there seemed always to be a girl with long hair standing in front of a little brother having fun with his candle, or just engrossed in his singing, while the candle wandered away in any direction. All was without crisis though, and no one was set afire.

The Christmas mood was at last descending having been held off by the intense heat and the abundance of flowers and lack of decorations we had become used to.

We sang ten carols, starting out with one I had never heard. Here, as in Church, the tunes to some were different. The British even use different words to the most familiar of all carols, Silent Night.

Little John Pahl spied that we were to sing Away In A Manger— and he sang it over by himself, during some of the intervals—when readings of scripture and announcements were being made, in both English and Setswana. No one noticed one little boy singing on his own. How puzzled his face was when they all began the old song; to a tune unfamiliar to him—and to me.

It was pleasant to be singing in the candlelight with so many people, with all our friends spotted, here and there. It made us feel that Christmas had truly finally arrived.

Janet Stringer came along with some young friends and little children. The first time I met her was when she came to the dinner and farewell party for Rat.

I greeted her and asked how everything was going.

"Well, I'm feeling better now. We've been having quite a time. My maid's boy was lost for three weeks."

"Three weeks? Where? Did they find him?"

"Yes. He got back himself. From Francistown!"

"Francistown? Over 400 kilometers away! How old was he?"

"Nine years old."

"You're kidding. How did it happen?"

"Well, we had reason to believe he was in Lobatse (66 km south), had been enticed away to there, and there was no other trace of him for three weeks. Of course it got us all down. His mother went around with a long face, and there wasn't anything I could do to help. But, I did go to the Police and I gave them a real piece of my mind. I let them have it and told them they were inefficient and so on. They got mad and asked if I wanted to get P.I.ed." (That means you become a "Prohibited Individual", banned officially.)

"My maid said she wanted to go to her Prophet, in Tlokweng Village. Later she told me all about her visit to him. She had to give him a Pula and he took a half hour or so with his ritual and rigamarole and then he told her not to worry; that her boy was safe and that he would get home safely. Sure enough, the boy got back; worked his way back somehow, all the way from Francistown on his own."

"How do you suppose he got up there from Lobatse? Did he get on the train?"

"Yes, I guess he probably got on and then fell asleep and ended up almost 500 kilometers north of where he got on."

"Can you imagine—all that at nine years old."

DECEMBER 29

We arrived at the Forestry out on the edge of the Village, about 2:45 on one of the hottest days you can imagine, to select our Christmas tree, dig it up and bring it back to the house to plant in the big African pot I had that morning scrubbed out, dried in the sun and spray-painted a brilliant white. The white Bougainvillaea that had been been thriving in it was now planted in the garden, not far from a thorn tree. Perhaps sometime in the future, it too would be cascading its blooms from the top of that tree, as we see so many of them do—but it'll be some years before that happens.

There wasn't any problem this time about having a "Revenue Man" on hand to receive payment for the tree. How many times our friends or we have been out there to select plants or shrubs; forced to leave them and come again as "No revenue man here today". Only one man is authorized to receive money, and I guess it's a good thing that various and sundry workers are not allowed to pocket the money, or pass it on. A very official receipt, resoundingly stamped with an official flourish (oh, how they love to pound that stamp) must be written out in triplicate. You'd better have the higher mathematics worked out too. This tree, at P2.50 a metre, was one and a half meters high, therefore, he wrote, $1 \times 1\ 1/2 = P3$, and he had said, one and a half metres at 2.50, that is Three Pula. That's what he told two others who got the same size tree, so we didn't argue.

I had taken a pail of water, as I knew from experience that almost all ground is concrete, but with water added, is very diggable! The Revenue man said that a couple of the boys would dig it for us, even though I had brought my own big hoe and spade. I poured the water around it, and they were soon down to where the water hadn't reached—solid concrete. One went then for a pick-axe, and wielded it in great heaves whacking down the ends of the branches. I had to holler to save the tree—we'd just paid for it. Luckily, being a small tree, it did have some sizeable roots still on when we lifted it out and stuffed it into a big brown sack, set the sack into a cardboard box and heaved it into the back of the station wagon.

I had a good laugh as we passed a VW onto which a family was tying a twelve foot tree just dug up. Exposed to the bright sun and intense heat was a little fist of root at the base, with about five fingers of root extending, fingers about the size of a man's hand. Few were the possibilities that the tree would ever grow when they planted it in their yard after Christmas.

The little plot of evergreens was alive with customers, pick-axes flying, shovels scraping and sweat pouring off the diggers. But already, in each place a tree was dug, a new little seedling had been planted. That was good to see.

Our tree suited us perfectly. We planted it in the white pot, flooded it with the hose and let it sit in the shade of the thorn tree a day before Joel and I wheeled it into the house in the wheelbarrow, to be decked with popcorn balls, strings of popcorn icicles, Reynolds Wrap tassels, fancy braid and bindings from the sewing basket, tiny packages, and then, to really make it complete, a string of tiny red lights—brought along by the Pahl family. They insisted they only needed one string, so we were pleased to have the lights—to transform the home-trimmed little fir to a glowing delight. How many hours we sat, late in the evening with only the tree lights on, just enjoying it.

Happily, the tree is still green and well watered, and there's hope that it will survive.

Many of the ex-pats we meet here lived in Africa most of their lives. One, of the Labor Ministry, told us his father had come to East

Africa in 1926, so that made him second generation ex-pat. He met his wife in what was then Tanganyika, and their children have homes in South Africa, or are in school in U.K.

While talking with them by the Inn pool one evening, the wife expressed the opinion that she is not sure it is right to be forcing the western ways onto the tribes of people here in Africa that have lived their own ways for so many centuries. Her husband added that there is too much pushing of too many changes—too fast. "Why do we think our ways of commercialism are so much superior to their close family and tribal system?" He agreed they need help in health and education, but "they don't need so many Malls, and mechanization."

"They have city planners here, laying out Malls and Industrial sites, and it's O.K. in a place like Gaborone, which is a new planned city—but to go into the villages, like Molepolole, and Serowe, and try to change things! They have planned their villages for years to suit their culture. The day they start replanning Serowe, there'll be disaster!"

Just this week someone told me, they *are* planning a Mall in Serowe!

We had asked Rat about the way the villages are planned. He said a man is allotted space for his home. When he has children, he can have added area, as much as is needed for his family to spread on out from him, and continue to have space allotted as the grandchildren set up homes. Thus the village grows as a bunch of grapes in family clusters. Family is always there, come what may, and people are supported in times of stress, or their children are cared for relatives if something happens to them, or they have to work in a different place a while.

Sounds like a fair enough system. Sometimes I wonder how Kenneth, Edwin, and Shinga like living in town like this, next door. The little boys are often trying to shoot the doves or birds in their yards to eat, and sometimes instead of bows and arrows, they have a BB gun—which is not too good with the houses and yards close.

Back to the poolside conversation—I then mentioned that I had been exposed to this family's vigil and pre-funeral services next door—when the mother was killed in the car accident.

"Yes, wasn't that frightful?" she said. "And he was driving, you know when he had no business doing it. It didn't happen the way it was reported in the paper. We heard about it at the Ministry. He may be charged yet."

"I suppose he was drunk and speeding."

"Well, when a person hits a cow in the road, he doesn't keep speeding on and hit another!"

So, that shed a new light on the loss of the mother next door from an unexpected source.

A couple of weeks ago, I was in the Book Centre and ran into Joan Keelin. She is from Newcastle, England, and her husband Tony is in Collections in the Tax Dept.

"We're off tomorrow for Bulawayo. Going up to see Victoria Falls."

"Well, you're brave."

"My folks are here, you know, and they are a bit nervous about the train trip, but I guess we'll be all right."

Then she went on to tell me about her folks' trip from England. The plane from the north was late to Heathrow, and they found that the flight to Joburg would not be held up for them, so they ran about a quarter of a mile across the field, and her mother tore the cartilege or tendons in her knee or leg, so after she finally did get on the plane, she couldn't walk. Eventually she was heaved about with a fork lift and moved in a wheel chair. Then during the flight to Joburg, something went amok with the stewardess' kitchen equipment in meal preparation, and her father reached up to hold something which was falling—and he got his hand burnt (British never write "burned"). Not only that, when they were to be served their meal, her mother "helped" pull her father's tray down and caught his fingers in it!

"So, it was disaster from the word go. My mother still can't get around too well, so we'll hope for the best."

"Sounds like they should have gone home and started all over again—Well, have a good trip and we'll see you later."

They did get to Victoria Falls, and back to Bulawayo, but when they left Bulawayo on the train, all did not go well. Luckily, the conductor had moved all passengers to cars at the rear and it wasn't too long before an explosion on the track derailed the first three or five cars. They, the Keelins, were in the ninth car back.

There was strafing of the cars up front and much rushing around by Rhodesian troops who were aboard the train. Much shooting after the guerrillas, but no one was killed or hurt, as far as the passengers were concerned. The train went back to Bulawayo; and the Keelins returned to Gaborone by plane.

All I can say is that some people want to see Victoria Falls pretty badly. We saw a beautiful movie of it in the theatre; that will do for me, unless the political situation changes drastically in the next year or so.

DECEMBER 30

This week the Neilson boys and the Pahl boys have been visiting back and forth, as the Neilsons, out at the Agricultural College are to go back to the States in a couple weeks.

While Danny and Tony were out there, they heard all about the scary happening of the evening before.

The Neilsons were going to be away, so decided to put their dog in the garage. The dog revolted and barked and carried on so badly, they relented and took him to a neighbors to stay. Returning, they picked up the dog and were again going to put him in the garage for the night. It again barked and—what, to their surprize, did they find in the garage—but a five or six foot cobra. Mr. Neilson killed it with a regular garden rake. He had a hard time too, as it eluded him—spitting and flaring its big head, slithering off to the edge of the garage, against the wall, and making it hard for him to get at it. He swore like mad at it, they reported—and he was careful too, but knew he *HAD* to kill it. Thank heavens he did—and then later killed a huge scorpion on his own lawn. He said the area back of the garage was open and he was surprized that the snake came in there. Nothing surprizes me, but I am glad we are living here in the "city" with paved streets, fenced yards, and lots of people, cars, kids and noise and commotion enough that a snake wouldn't want to be here. Of course, I did see one down at the end of the block—but at least it wasn't a Cobra!

Roy and I went to Zeerust on the last Saturday before Christmas in a search for gifts. We found a store that had some good small toys, books and stationery items and we picked up two armfuls, knowing they'd go somewhere but didn't decide that until we got home. We also selected a bright cerese parasol for Pauline.

It was one of the hottest days on record, and when everything closed at once, we stopped for a bite to eat, even though we thought the eggs might be poached in their shells in the car. One has to lock up tight, and that soon turns the car into an oven. So, it was a terrifically hot return trip; one wouldn't think we were returning from Christmas Shopping! The next day, Joel gave Pauline the big sack of wrapped packages I had ready for her and all her family in Molepolole.

She came in after lunch to do the dishes and then she was off like a flash up the drive, carrying the large zip bag—and holding the parasol over her head!

"Pauline. You don't wait for Christmas, do you, to open things!"

"No", she laughed and twirled the parasol. I wondered if she had opened everything—all my fancy wrapping—before she took it home to the children.

It didn't seem right on Christmas, not seeing the rest of the family. After breakfast, I said, "Now is the time that Charles should be elbowing at the door, looking sleepy, his arms full of brown paper sacks, rolls of fancy paper sticking over his shoulder, saying 'Just wait a minute—I have to get these wrapped up'''. We wondered what you all were doing, but then decided you were all asleep anyway, as we were six or more hours ahead of you.

After we opened our gifts, we straightened up and put on our new bathing suits. It was getting so warm, and Joel had in hand the flippers he had wanted, we locked the doors on the gifts and the roasting turkey and went down to the Holiday Inn and went swimming.

How's that for a Christmas celebration!

When we were on the Mall the day before Christmas, we saw Rat and Susan (he complaining that he hasn't had any rest yet after his long trip because of constant visiting with friends). I asked if they'd like to come to dinner and tell us more of his trip. They were enthusiastic, but I told Susan I wouldn't let them in if they brought any presents.

Roy picked them up and as I greeted them at the door; they were carrying a package. I reminded them they couldn't come in, but Rat said, "This is not a Christmas gift. It's something different. We had to wrap it in something, that's all". Then he said, "She has a paper there which tells about them."

So, we sat down to discover what it was and it was really something!!

To Mr. Brown:

This "Fly Whisk" is made out of a tail of a Wildebeste killed by me during my April–May 1976 leave. The "Fly-Killer" is also used by Witch Doctors to splash medicine water over the sick! It is also used as a "Rain Maker" during Rain making ceremonies! So Be Any!

Otherwise! For those whose years of existence are being a burden, it is used to fan away flies and mosquitoes!

A short stick is inserted in the skin above the tail end, and the skin is sewn around it with strips of leather, making a good handle for flicking it around. Rat had sewn and finished it himself.

To Mrs. Brown:
This Bracelet (she should have said necklace) was made in my home
village of Kule in the Ghanzi district! It was made by my uncle's
wife.
It is made out of small sand tourtoise! It is normally worn by adult
ladies!

The little turtle shell is covered with a flared square of beadwork
having a flap which buttons back over the opening in the top of the
shell. A chain is attached, so the beaded article hangs as a decorative
piece carrying money inside the shell.

We were pleased to have the gifts. They mean a lot, knowing that
they or their family had made them. We have shown them off to everyone who has stopped in since.

We were on our way to the Oodie Weavers, on a red dusty dirt and
sand track. Cattle wandered here and there in the grassy spots, herds of
goats trotted around, and the area was dotted with tall ant hills, one so
large that it went right up through some of the branches of a thorn tree.
I had read that numerous animals and snakes take refuge in abandoned
ant hills; I have never been keen to prowl around them much. Some of
them had recently been extended; the tops were a deep red of freshly
brought out dirt contrasting with the older dried out lower parts.

"Ten kilometers of this is not going to be so great" Roy remarked,
but there were interesting things to see along the way. All of a sudden
there were great masses of dark red rock, smooth and rounded, barely
protruding from the earth, surfaces big enough for a hundred people to
sit on for a picnic. Then, there was rock like that on the Molepolole
Road; piled up, in teetering round boulders.

We followed a Land Rover into the edge of the Oodie Village, and
we both turned at the white arrow painted on a small board; we assumed it would lead us to the weavers, and it did. There beside another
area of huge smooth red rock was a pretty Rondavel with thatched roof,
flowers around it, and a large building off to the left. The gate was
closed and the people from the Land Rover were reading—"If closed do
not hesitate to go over the hill in the back and rouse someone". As we
began to wonder what hill to go over, we turned to see someone come
out of the Rondavel; a man who ushered us in. This was the salesroom
with a dazzling array of beautiful rugs, table runners, spreads and a huge
rack of spreads hung like rugs displayed in a department store.

He told us the workers were not at the looms, as it was a holiday
until early January, but we were welcome to go over and look around.

"All the BEDU places in Pilane and Mochudi are closed now, too."

I selected a spread, after much consideration. I like the color scheme, basic gold tone, touches of aqua, purple and lines of black. I'm very pleased with it. All pure wool but washable, with care, and has a nice knotted fringe at each end.

We went over and inspected the workrooms. Sixty people work at the looms—although not all at once I'm sure. There were more than thirty looms though. Big tapestries were on display on the porch—the ones I had seen at the Trade Fair. This place is directed by a Canadian and when Sir Seretse Khama made his trip to the U.S. and Canada, an exhibit of the Weaving of Oodie was shown in Ottawa.

As we left, there were no little signs with white arrows pointing to Gaborone, so we passed a few forks mumbling "This is the way we came in, isn't it?" and spied a building ahead.

"Let's go see that store. Maybe we can get a cold drink." So inside he went, to explore the Indian Traders Shop. I attempted to take a picture of a herd of goats ranged on one of the big rocks but they melted away as soon as I headed in their direction.

"There's nothing in there but blankets on the back shelves and some other clothing," Roy reported.

"Well, there's no electricity out here, so they wouldn't have anything cold—that's for sure."

As we turned around and headed out, up from the left, out of a maze of huts and rondavels, came the Land Rover. We approached a "Y" at the same time, and they stopped and called,

"Are you going out? We'll follow you!"

"To Gaborone?"

"Yes. We've tried this way and it's not the one!"

We did get back to a few landmarks, and were soon on the main trail out. We hurried along to keep in the forward position so as not to have to eat blinding dust all the way back, and to get ahead enough so we could take the picture at the big ant hill. A huge herd of cattle deterred me a bit, as they milled around at that spot, but they didn't give us any trouble. I snapped the picture and dashed back to the car, as we saw the Land Rover approaching, and sped on home.

DECEMBER 31

Juan is getting restless in Francistown. Perhaps "restless" is not the best word. He reports the situation is getting tense and serious. He

wishes for someone to do a bit of revaluation of his position. I'm sure
he wouldn't mind at all getting transferred to Gaborone, and we'd love
it if that happened—but I don't know anything about those possibilities.
I was joking when I sent them Christmas Greetings "up there in the
Combat Zone"—but it's not a joke.

Alice's maid, Shanda, lives in a village about sixty kilometers from
Francistown, very close to the border. She said that her father was going
to come home for Christmas—no matter what. He is in Rhodesia, and
has been, a long time.

"My brother is coming from South Africa, and all the rest of the
family. The men will cook a goat. They will stay up all night. They
always stay up all night—singing and all, and eating the goat. In the
morning, we have presents. But they are not wrapped. The oldest one
gets to pick the gift he wishes, and on down through the family."

Then she told me about some "sibling rivalry"—how her sister is
so jealous of her as she is older and gets more things.

And she told about her brother.

"He has a seven year old daughter. He will come, but he lives with
a white woman—it is their daughter. She cannot come up to Francistown or the Village. What would people think? There would be no place
for her to sleep; there would have to be many preparations made. And
of course, she doesn't eat mealies!" That topped it off—for people sub-
sist on mealies. It's ground corn or maize which they cook up in a
variety of ways. Their mainstay.

"How can your brother and this white woman live together in
South Africa?"

"It is difficult. She lives in Natal and he works in Joburg. When
they get together for the weekends, she must be sneaked into his apartment and then she must hide there all the time and never come out."

Well, Shanda made ready to go to Francistown for the Holiday.
Alice gave her a fine umbrella or parasol and she was so pleased with it
she said she was not going to take it with her.

"If my Mother saw this, she would want it."

When she returned, not Tuesday as scheduled, but on Wednesday
morning, she said her father had not shown up for Christmas after all.
No one had heard from him.

She said things are not good up there. Even some shops in Francistown are already closed.

"My brother is not going to go back to South Africa until he gets
my mother moved from our village out to some place far; out in some

cattle post. It is not safe there anymore. The people with money have already packed up and left; they just built a new Rondavel somewhere else.

"People are afraid to go to the river for water. Everytime I went I saw soldiers. The Rhodesian soldiers, carrying arms, and many that I think are the Freedom Fighters—they wear black coveralls and their guns do not show.

"People are afraid to go into the fields to plow, so no mealies have been planted, many people are being injured, and some killed.

"My mother weaves baskets and when she went to where they get their best grasses, she found it had all been hacked down—cleared and burned, to expose the border area.

"On the train, the Police come through and talk to every person who gets on. First they talk in English. Later they talk in Setswana. If the person does not understand the Setswana, they must explain who they are, where from and what their purpose is. Many get on the train and maybe get off at different villages along the way. I mean if they are guerrillas. The police are trying to find them all the time."

So this is Shanda's report on her village—right on the border. Yesterday, Roy asked one of the staff who had gone to Francistown for the Holiday weekend, how it was, and she replied,

"All right. Just the same as ever. I didn't notice a thing."

Juan came down from Francistown. He did have much to tell us and it was not what I had expected.

Juan told us that things are tense. One night there was the stacatto of machine gun fire, practically in his yard. He dropped to the floor and lay immobile. The firing continued intermittently, but he said,

"Trip, trip, trip, out came Mimi, trotting to see what was going on and calling to me, then came Susi. 'Get down on the floor!' I told them, 'Get back into the hall!'—We all scooted into the hall and dragged some blankets in there and stayed several hours; the least exposed area of the house."

He went on to say that the Police Mobile Unit is so fired up that they have gone overboard. "I don't take a step anywhere without my passport in my pocket. If you get stopped and have no passport, heaven knows what would happen. A big gang would crowd around and grab you by the hair and chant, 'Smith's man! Smith's man!'. They have roadblocks set up and the other night a Peace Corps boy drove up to one and immediately had a gun stuck in his throat with orders to 'get out!' He couldn't get out as he had to turn off the key, and he couldn't reach it, with the gun in his neck and he was scared of having it go off. Eventually, he got the key off so he could get out."

"Then, you are in danger from the local Police more than any Rhodesians coming over?"

"I have never seen a Rhodesian soldier, all the time I've been there."

Then he said, "I've asked Susi if she wants to move down here to Gaborone, but she says, it's either stay there or go home, she doesn't want to move and settle again."

Juan asked for Pauline's brothers name. "It never hurts to know someone in uniform." He is a guard at the prison there, not a regular policeman.

Juan is a delight. Always smiling and his sense of humor helps him to take things in his stride. He always looks sharp and crisp and clean with nicely coordinated shirts and slacks. He is a hard worker; on loan from the California Tax Department.

Joel came home from the Mall last week saying he had seen Lillian—Lovemore's mother.

"Where did you see her?"

"Down near the Mall, on the road from Pahl's house. She says she's in the flats there—she pointed them out and asked where Pauline was and what she was doing. I told her she was home here working."

"You're sure it was Lillian?"

"Of course, she said 'Hello Joel' and asked for Pauline."

"Well, maybe she has a job."

I asked Pauline about it later, does Lillian have a job here? and she seemed not to know anything or have anything to say. I wondered why Lillian would be here and she not know.

Pauline went home for the weekend to Molepolole, and yesterday said, "Did you find out about Lillian? Is she working here?" and she said,

"She is living in the flats over there." So, I caught on, that she is not working at a job but perhaps the father of her baby has arranged for a "home" for them—I'm not sure, and Pauline doesn't volunteer anything. Perhaps she knew all about it, but didn't think we'd "understand" which may be another word for "approve".

The night we were at Dunns, Americans in the Agriculture Department, we got to talking about snakes again and Dunn told us there was a big Black Mamba over at the Ministry of Agriculture building, which is across the dirt road from the Tax Department. "The guards say it's a long one—they've seen it often."

Yesterday Roy came home at noon to say that the big Black Mamba had been killed.

"When Conference came to work—to park his car—he saw it hanging down out of the tree in the parking lot. So he ran and got a big piece of pipe or something and whacked on the tree to shake it down and then he mashed in its head."

"How long was it? Did they hold it up by its tail and show it off?"

"I didn't see any holding it up. It was long—longer than this dining room table."

We are glad to know that it is killed. I still haven't seen any snake except the one with the mouthful of yellow-green chameleon, and hope not to.

There are quite a few snakes out in Sebele—where the Ag College is. The residents there seem to be seeing more than they have for years. Perhaps it has something to do with the extra dry summer—who knows? One is always hearing about someone out there shooting or smashing the head off a Black Mamba or a Cobra.

The other night we were at an A.I.D. Officer's home, which had a small back patio, roofed with elephant grass over which a gravevine was flourishing. A man from Sebele was looking up into the foliage and it reminded him of the time he saw a snake at his house, up in some of his vines.

"I called the garden boy, as he had his sling shot in his hip pocket. He took that and actually hit the snake with a stone from it. He hurt the snake, but it got up into a nearby tree and that boy shot it again, knocked it out of the tree and killed it. Up to that time my wife had complained about the boys having sling shots. You know, they shoot birds with them, and Mary didn't like that. Then, another day, he killed another snake with his sling shot, so Mary tells me now—'Don't let those boys come to work without having their sling shots along.'"

The Sunday after we read the horrible story about the man being eaten by Lions at the Game Reserve in Angola, the Express printed a big story on it. It was a hoax. The pictures had been taken on a private game reserve, in Rhodesia, the owner under the impression they were being made for a Spanish movie. The "man" who was eaten, was a plastic dummy and it had been daubed with sheeps' blood and filled with sharp entrails for a realistic gory picture. The people who made the pictures then sold them to newspapers worldwide for huge sums, as the truth.

Even when one forest ranger found they were fakes, he thought they should let it pass—that it would be a warning to people who do get out of cars in Game Preserves.

JANUARY 18, 1977

This may be Joels' best school year. He has a teacher whom I have not yet met, but have formed an impression of as being strict, organized and demanding. She is preparing them for the Standard 7 exams which come in November, the most important of all exams over here; for if one does not rate "A" or "B" in them, they are not allowed to enter Form 1, the first year of secondary school.

Pauline came in Saturday with a couple notebooks, old ones, and said, "I want you to help me with these. I am going to study to prepare for my 7th Standard Exams. I need four books like this and two like this, a dictionary and an Atlas.

"All right, let me write that down. I have a dictionary, you can take mine, and I'll look for the rest this morning." By now, I have learned that "Help" means "Pay For".

They were out of Atlases, but I got the necessary notebooks and when I gave them to her yesterday afternoon, she almost squealed with delight. She starts tomorrow evening. If she doesn't have that Standard 7 exam on record, she's stymied as far as any further study.

Summer, in full intensity of heat and sun, is not conducive to energetic accomplishment. We are becoming accomplished in being lazy. Swimming at the Inn pool, sitting around talking or reading for hours, having leisurely meals, and going to the movies is not what a Puritan New Englander has been brought up to regard as ideal. It's hard to learn to be lazy, but seems to be getting easier all the time.

"Summer" is not word enough to describe the season we are in now. It is hot. A hot wind blows continually, all day, aiding the sun in the burning up process. The once green and flower-laden four-o-clocks are now pale and dying, mere skeletons of their early days. The life seems to be sapped from even the rugged old marigolds and they droop and fade, even though watered morning and night.

Old Fatso, the dog from next door who thinks he lives here, is constantly burrowing in under whatever green plants he can find in the shade, so because of the heat, even those are being destroyed. He lolls in the garden, panting, sprawled on a carpet of verbena, and rolls over once in a while onto the zinnias or slurps at the water in the bird bath.

I resent the sun burning up my garden over which I have labored, however contentedly, as there is no other work I enjoy more, but I am well aware that the heat is only doing superficial harm to me. I am comfortable and well fed here in this house where my air conditioner can within seconds cool and refresh the living room or my bedroom, where I may lie in comfort and read until late in the afternoon when, with the sun out of the way, the outdoors is once again inviting. In the coolness of the evening, I can wander over the yard, pouring new life from the gushing garden hose, and watch the limp plants revive.

But as I do, I think about the people here to whom the heat is more than the disappointment of unfulfilled blossoming. People who may go hungry because their maize has burned up long before maturing; who will have no grain to pound and grind in their mortars, so will watch their kids go hungry.

I can water the garden with precious water, for I can pay the water bill. It isn't much and even if it increased a great deal, I could afford it.

Although I'm disappointed at the slow but sure searing of the plants and realise they will never be what I envisioned, I don't feel sorry for myself. My desire for rain and my hopes that it will come soon is not just so it will rescue my flowers, it is for the people who have not even been able to plow and plant a crop, to say nothing of trying to harvest one. Their drought is most severe.

Because you cannot recall heat when you are chilly, or the chill when you are sweating, we are constantly being surprised. The air is cool and pure and pleasant in the morning and you feel the whole day will be the same. Not until past noon do you realise that "it is again as hot as it was yesterday!" Then, after the sun sinks and the breeze is cool under the most brilliant of stars in clear bright moonlight, you feel there never was a time that everything was more ideal. How distant the heat of the day! Had it really been hot? You can't recall. Everything is too perfect.

Day after day, the same fooling of the senses. The intense heat, the constant burning; then the refreshing intervals of morning, evening and night. Summer is the word for it, but it isn't word enough.

JANUARY 24, 1977

I was watering the garden in the late dusk, on a Sunday evening a couple of weeks ago; so late that it was almost dark, but there was already enough moonlight so I could see what I was doing. While holding the hose on some plants just inside the fence at the edge of the road, I saw a woman walking toward me. When she got to my drive, she stopped and called over to me,

"Mrs. Brown!"

"Yes?"

"Mrs. Brown. I am Thomas' mother and I am in trouble. I wonder if you can help me?"

"Yes. What do you need?"

"A friend of my daughters has been assaulted, by a University boy. I have her at my home and have been putting cold compresses on her. I want to take her down to the Police Station so she can bring charges against the boy."

"What you want is a ride down to the station right now?"

"Yes."

"Well, come on in. I'll get Mr. Brown."

She followed me in the house, and she said,

"Oh, not if you haven't had your dinner. We can wait."

"No, we are through. We can go anytime" and I explained to Roy what she wanted. She began to apologize for her appearance, and in the light now, I could see she had a housedress on and it was inside out with frayed seams flapping. That certainly showed how distraught she was!

Her house is just over the fence from Kenneth's although to reach it by car you would drive about four blocks, so she said they'd be over in a few minutes. Now, having met her, I realised we had been mistaken in thinking the Radio Man and his wife were Thomas' parents.

We had the car out in the drive waiting, when they walked in from the front. The person with the girl didn't look like the woman I had just been talking to, for she now wore a dark cotton flowing dress, to the ground, with matching head scarf wound around in a neat turban—though they don't call them turbans. The girl was a little slip of a thing wearing bright red and white check skirt and top, a white "Miss Muffet" hat, and sandals. Her face was swollen and her eyes puffy, and we didn't hear a sound from her.

"He said, 'I want to love you' and she said 'No' and he did it anyway" was how the lady had explained it to me earlier. He certainly had beaten her up and when I saw her later, in the evening, her eyes were almost closed.

We left them at the station, right on the Mall and Thomas' mother said, "You won't have to wait. We can get home. Maybe a friend of mine will give me a lift."

"Will they give you a ride home—the Police?"

"No."

"Well, we'll go up to the President Hotel a while. When you're through come back to the car here. We'll wait."

So, we went up to the Hotel balcony, where we had a view of the center of the Mall with the theatre across from us—milling with crowds just pouring out for the "Interval". When they went in again about nine, the outside lights "Capitol" went out. Scanning the crowd on the balcony where we sat, I wondered why we hadn't seen a friend from the Tax Department that we often meet when we stop here. Just as that thought crossed my mind, I looked up to see him coming out into the balcony, hand-in-hand, swinging like school children, with a young black man wearing a white T-shirt "Soweto".

To us, these men walking hand-in-hand seems unusual. But we were warned ahead of time, that it is natural here. Good friends hold hands. Men and boys walk hand-in-hand all the time. Young men meeting on the Mall greet each other, shake hands and sit down on the wall with hands clapsed and converse. They are very open and demonstrative with each other, but rarely do you see a man-woman hold hands; certainly not man and wife.

The friend stood and talked to us. He shook hands warmly with me, reported that he had missed a prize by "that much"—a few inches between his thumb and forefinger—at the Golf Course that day, but had won some balls—and as he talked, again held the hand of his friend, and they soon walked on down to the dining room.

We sat a while longer, then decided to see if the women were through at the station. No sign of them, so I went into the station and enquired, and I could see them in an inner room. "They are still making a statement", the officer said, so Roy and I did a round of window shopping—looking over all the fine expensive things in the Ishma Jewelry store, and all the skins, masks and such in the shop adjacent to it.

"Thomas' mother had said to me, 'there's a lot of trouble like this out at the University now'," I said to Roy.

"Yeah, you know it was printed in the paper that the Minister said in Parliament that the UBLS (University of Botswana, Losoto and Swaziland) was being known as the University of Booze, Love and Sex—and he wanted to know why."

"Yes, that was at the time they closed the University in November."

In a few minutes I saw the women coming over to the parking lot. The girl still didn't say a word and I didn't know what to say to her, so we just drove home.

I haven't seen her since, nor did I read anything about the incident in the paper. I suppose the boy weaselled out of any real punishment.

One thing surprizing here is that wrong doers are sentenced to a certain number of lashes. Never mind giving them jail sentences where the government has to feed and house them. If the crime isn't too serious, they are caned with a certain number of lashes—and it's over and done with.

I stepped out into the brilliant sunshine in the observation area at the Airport; a blazing heat in contrast to the dark semi-coolness of the waiting room inside.

A lady was sitting there on the wall, her daughter in prim school uniform—bowler straw hat, shapeless pale blue dress, white sox and hair in braids—I assumed she was returning to school in Johannesburg. I wondered what she would look like if her hair were out, she threw away the ugly hat and had sandals and a decent dress—she was all of sixteen.

"What is that in there? A special tour?" the lady asked me.

"Oh no. That's a group of friends here to see off a family who have been here a while. They're going back to the States."

Hers was a perfectly likely assumption. It did look like a great exodus was underway, but it was a sign of how well John and Anne Neilson and family were liked. They had a royal send-off.

"Boy, John really has a lot of friends," I remarked later to Alice.

"Yes. That's partly because John is one honest man. What he thinks, he says. If someone does a good job, he tells them so. If they don't do a job right, he tells them so. He is capable and good-hearted. He'll do anything for you; he's smart and practical. The locals really worship him because he can do so much and he never does a thing for any ulterior motive—he's no climber or freeloader. He gets off some awful jokes, and his language gets a little colorful at times, but I overlook that in light of all his good qualities and his good heart."

"Anne said the other day, they feel this is the time to go, but I guess they do hate to leave", she added, "but, they're going back to Idaho—Kendricks, Idaho, and he'll farm 300 acres." Anne said she had a letter the other day from the contracting organization, asking if she would write letters of assurance to prospective candidates for coming to Botswana—that it is politically a good place to come now—and she said that in all honesty, she could not write anyone that assurance—although she had been willing to do just that for the Dunns, a while ago. Things are changing fast.

The evening before, we went down to the Inn to say some semi-final goodbyes. When we arrived about 7:30, John was coming up the hall from their room with a gentleman.

"I want you to meet our Honorable Minister of Agriculture, Mr.

Masisi" he said, and we had the honor of shaking hands with him and talking a few minutes.

"Yes, I had to come and tell my friend John goodbye. I have worked closely with him the past two and a half years and he has done a fine job here—in typically American fashion."

When we got to the room, Anne was not at first to be seen, the room was so full of people, but we soon heard her say, "The Minister came at 5:15 and he just left!"

So, we sat on the bed and her boys pawed through newly packed suitcases finding certain pants and shirts to put on for dinner, and she retired to the bath to get herself dressed, as she was still in a light cotton dress she had rushed around in all day. As John, Jr., dug for his clothes, he pulled out a big Kudu horn—pinkish grey in a magnificent spiral, and he lifted it up and blew a blast on it, that should have brought the hotel staff running—but was ignored. This had been a gift from someone on the staff for John to take home to the Scout Troop.

Baden-Powell used just such a Kudu Horn at Mefeking during the Boer War. And Boer War sites are all around us here, a hill out toward where Joel saw the Baboons, still yields relics of shells.

After that exotic trumpet blast, they went on into dinner and the six of us visitors went out and sat by the pool in the cool evening breeze and talked of our kaleidoscopic life here—the design changing daily.

FEBRUARY 2

Everything gets overdone. When it's hot, it's too hot. When it finally rains, it rains too much. There has been a constant deluge since Sunday so that almost-dead plants are again crisp and green, the lawns are bright and lush, and everything is dripping like a rain forest instead of the edge of the desert. It is wonderful, except we heard on the news last night that rivers are overflowing and down in Soweto, as if they didn't have enough problems, people have had to be rescued by helicopter and many families have lost what little they did have. It's all plus here though, and we have been enjoying the coolness and the resurrection of the whole yard and garden.

Caught in one of these downpours yesterday, I dashed into the Museum for cover. I checked my basket and bundles at the desk and enquired about the new exhibits. Joel had told me they were unbelievable, but I wasn't prepared for what I found.

Making a sharp turn from the entrance hall, filled with stamps and first day covers, and passing through a dark hall, I came upon a startling bright diorama of the Bushmen Life. The freshly painted background, the lifelike animals and the weathered little Bushmen in front, gave an illusion of reality. I could visualize their bare existence in the heat of day and cold of night on the desert.

A group of youngsters viewing it exclaimed over the scene.

Next was a huge canoe of the Okavango area, loaded with all the necessities of life for a long water trek. I wondered if Roger and Rika's trip had been in such a boat. Under that window was displays of traditional articles of dress; wigs for ceremonies, implements of all kinds and weapons. A great scene of the Okavanga area was painted on a curved wall, and some animals were placed here and there before it; but there was wire screening across the front where the window would be when it was done. A fine job, surpassing even those large ones in the Museum of Natural History we visited in New York, as these are bright and new, and on the spot.

It still hadn't stopped raining when I came back to the entrance, but I ventured along—rain or no rain.

I keep forgetting to mention this, so will stick it in here. We are always interested to see the women carrying things on their heads, and Roy remarked several times that it is the funniest thing in this line that he has seen, when Lulu, at the office, goes to the ladies room with the roll of toilet tissue on her head.

Paper products here are expensive, so each one gets a ration of paper issued him at the office and it is guarded closely. "Nothing gets the attention and checking and rechecking that the list of toilet tissue does," Roy explained. "They don't bat an eye walking along with it on their heads."

He still thinks it's really funny!

There is always something moving here. Wherever you look, there'll be something alive. Out around the patio and back door, it's little lizards. They range from about six inches to tiny ones a fraction of an inch. Joel had one you could hardly see, a pale little tan thing.

The larger lizards are up and down the trees. Some of the blue-headed ones are over twelve inches long. Then there are the chameleons. Sometimes I lift a branch on a plant in the garden, such as when I'm cutting some flowers, and the branch will be very heavy—which will startle me, and then, the big scratchy yellow-green chameleon hanging on it will brush against my arm or hand and there's nothing I can do but jump and scream at the same time. Of course, they won't hurt you and are fascinating to watch. Their eyes are way out at the end of a mound of wrinkly skin, and each moves independently; each whirls around in every direction and you wonder how it can do it.

Birds are everywhere, and dogs too. Old Fatso stays pretty close and is always on hand at supper time. I keep a big pan of water out back all the time for him, and sometimes when it's quiet, inside, we hear a great "Slurp—Slurp—Slurp" and it takes a few minutes to analyse that it is not the refrigerator gone beserk, but Fatso refreshing himself. There are centipedes too, everywhere, even in the house. Hard and black, rust underneath, they roll, immediately upon being touched, into a tight corkscrew, so you can send them flying, without hurting them, with a flick of your shoe.

FEBRUARY 8

Shanda is moving into the servant's quarters at Alice and Jerry's house.

Last week Shanda said,

"I have given notice. I will be moving in here."

"What do you mean, 'given notice'?" Alice asked.

"I have given my boyfriend notice that I am moving out the end of the month. I told him, 'Don't waste any more of your time on me because I am not going to marry you'."

"Well, I'll believe it when I see you move in." Alice said. Shanda had "threatened" to leave him before, but she never made the break. Shanda went on,

"When I went home yesterday, I walked in the house and right past everything and went in and lay down. I didn't do anything. My boyfriend came home and he came in and said, 'there is nothing cooked to eat' and I said 'I know it', and he went and bought himself a loaf of bread."

Alice is hoping she will carry through on it this time. She told me it was understood when the brother's children went home for the break between school sessions, that they were not to return for Shanda to care for. But they did return. Not five of them, but six.

Her boyfriend was awarded an insurance settlement for an injury to his eye while on duty as a policeman. Ten thousand Pula! I can hardly imagine how he could have so much. He went immediately to Lobatse and bought a car. The rest I guess, he is fast drinking up.

"One of his friends talked to me the other day", Shanda told Alice, "and told me I should not marry him. He is the same as he has always been and will never be different. He drinks every day and he drinks very much on the weekends. He drinks much much money, and I only get P33 each month and have a hard time even getting my bicycle fixed, so I can come to work."

"Yes, I am leaving him. I said to him I am leaving and I said, 'you are going to feel funny when people ask you where is your wife and your curtains!'." (That's a line I shall never forget.)

Shanda actually moved into the servant's quarters. Alice gave her one pair of curtains, she brought some of her own, and Jerry helped her move her furniture.

After a day's settling she said something about her boyfriend coming over.

"He's not moving in here!" Alice exclaimed.

"Oh no. He will not bring any of his things. He will just come to sleep with me every night."

Her ideas of "leaving" and breaking with her boyfriend are indeed unique.

The secretarial school which Pauline had planned to attend had been in the news. It's closed at the moment. The students got ripped off, paying about P100 for elementary typing, with few classes, broken machines and no instruction. Someone is trying to get it sorted out—but the students are out many Pula. Good thing I didn't come up with the money for Pauline. I gave her P30, and she "lived" through that. We haven't heard a thing about her new house and how the construction is or isn't coming.

Lillian is here, off and on. When I ask Pauline if Lillian is staying with her, she waves her hand toward town and says something about "there . . .". But I often see the wash down there, diapers flying, and they've been here the past few days. Lovemore is a gorgeous baby. He's as beautiful as can be—clean, smiley and plump and soft. He is light colored, maybe a mixture. Joel said one day, "You know what? You know Lillian's baby, Lovemore? Well, I think he's an Albino."

Sunday, the Pahls decided to take a drive up to see Molepolole. Shanda appeared early in the morning to greet them, although she doesn't work on weekends, and mentioned she was taking a trip out to see some friends, in Molepolole.

"We're going out there too, today!" So, they arranged to pick her up, sometime between five and six, and give her a lift home.

"When you drive into the village, you will see a garage. Go a little farther and you will see some stores, and a place with lots of people hanging around and drinking Chibuku. Meet me there."

This of course was not too definite, inasmuch as the village was a new experience to the Pahls. They drove around the Livingstone Hospital and down some side roads and covered school areas and much of the village, which looks the same, no matter what section you are in.

They had a good time taking pictures—though frustrating. One scene of a gang of little kids sitting in the mud evaporated as soon as Jerry stopped and tried to snap it. The kids just took off. Contrary to that, in one area a large group were walking along carrying water pails, jars and boxes on their heads. When Jerry stopped to get a picture, all wanted to get into it, and quickly set pails and boxes upon the ground and rushed to "pose" in a group. He managed to convey to them he wanted a picture of them with the junk on their heads. Even then, the group expanded from about the six he started with to fifteen or so; all anxious to be photographed.

About now, someone heard a sissing sound, and they discovered a flat tire. While pondering the first move, a boy came running up to them and said,

"Shanda says to wait for her here."

"What did you say?"

"Shanda says to wait for her here."

"Shanda? Where is she?"

"Up there." and he pointed off up into the village of 40,000, toward a rise. Shanda did appear shortly. She had been about a quarter a mile away and had happened to see their VW bus come into the village and stop there. She was glad to have caught them, for the meeting point she had arranged was about four miles away, and she had been wondering how she was going to get there. She had sent the boy with the message, so they wouldn't drive on from this point.

The flat tire was indeed a problem, for they had never used the jack and could not figure out how it worked.

Shanda suggested that she and Alice and the boys lift it up by hand.

"The master will have to work quickly and put it on while we hold it up." !

However, a man happened by in a pickup who had all the tools necessary and helped them get rolling again.

While waiting and during the repair, a crowd of kids gathered.

Alice told me, "One little baby was far from well. It was being cared for, carried around, by a seven or eight year old. It had not a stitch of clothes on and it had diarrhea; horrible yellow-green. As it lay on the little girl's lap, as she squatted there watching, green ran all over her leg. It was a frail weak-looking little baby, and I told her, 'You'd better take the baby home'."

"There isn't any reason for them to be neglected there in Molepolole", I said, "as the hospital is there and I don't think they charge more than a few cents to be treated."

"I'm sure there is a lot of ignorance there, and poor situations. Shanda told us about her youngest sister. She is seventeen now and she is expecting her third child."

She went on to tell me that Shanda has tried to get her sister to come down into this area, from her village way up near Francistown, and get work, or especially to get to school.

"She cannot read or write."

"Doesn't your mother get upset over her having these babies?" Alice asked her.

"The first time she got really mad, because my sister didn't know who the father was, she had had so many boyfriends. But she didn't know anything anyway—why she was having the baby. Then the next time she got pregnant, my mother was not so upset because she knew who the father was and he provided for her and he liked her little girl and would have kept her for his own. But now he is in jail. He came from Rhodesia, so they have taken him and she doesn't have anything to live on from him. I was trying to get her to come down here with me after Christmas, but she said no, as she is going to have this baby now."

Alice may have qualms about having Shanda living in the same yard now, but time will tell what develops. I'll keep you posted!

FEBRUARY 15

"Come on. Hurry up. We want to be there on time because all of Thornhill and Northside will be there!" Joel urged us on. It was time for the start of the Gaborone Beavers Swimming Gala and he was raring to go. It was hot, which was good and the afternoon wasn't spoiled by any rainstorm. Families were asked to bring along food for the picknicking in the Interval between the swim events.

It was a long afternoon with twenty-five scheduled events and some of them had so many entries that they were in two sections with a run-off. So, the sun was setting when the last were completed.

There were ten events before Joel got into one, but he did well and came home with three first prizes; in the Backstroke, in the Family Relay, with Pippin and Pippin's Mother, and in the Rescue.

The pool is at Thornhill school, outside, with lawn around it and enough thorn trees nearby so there was shade in spots to move into when the sun became unbearable.

Joel was both exhausted and keyed up over it all and he went to bed at least three times, moving from room to room seeking a cool place, until eventually, he konked out.

Joel has something great to look forward to in the break after April 20. Sometime between then and when school resumes in June, he will go on a Student Holiday Safari, on the Kalahari for a week. There will be ten kids and one of the Northside teachers, along with the professional hunter guide. This is one of the Holiday Inn Safaris—arranged by the director, S.H. Youthed.

It should be a good expedition. All equipment, bedding, food and cooking, soft drinks and transportation will be furnished, but the kids will pitch in as at any camp, to help and are to take notebooks, cameras and binoculars, if they have them.

MARCH 2

A fantastic thing happened Saturday evening. Roy and I were sitting outside the kitchen door—having a cup of coffee after dinner, and Joel was playing around at something, when here came Tandi, striding up the path between the big marigold plants and zinnias. She came right up, almost to us, and perhaps she was looking at Joel or remembered all the "hand-outs" she gets from me. She hesitated a while and I said "Come on"—but Joel said, "Say 'Dock Wan'" so I did and she trotted over to me, climbed up onto my lap and settled down. She lay her head back against me just as if she were going to nestle down for nap. We were all amazed and remarked again about her "consorting with the enemy".

She lay there a long while and we looked her over! She has the most delicate little hands with long fingers. Fragile little things—all pale on the palms and her arms and shoulders luscious chocolate.

She was content to lie there, as we played with her hands, and Joel went and got some lollypops, made her say something in Setswana—gave her one for herself and one for a cousin who was down at the house. She excitedly ran down to deliver and that was all we saw of her that time. Then the next afternoon, I was down by the storehouse to get some tools, and over she came running—with Bontsho, who is still a tiny peanut of a little doll. Bontsho came running with her arms out and reached up for me, she's all extrovert, and Tandi came running the same way and hung on my skirt and leaned against my legs.

This after almost a year of her crying at any sight of me.

MARCH 3

"There's a new little coffee shop over in White City right next to Capri Bakery. We saw the ad in the commercials at the theatre the other night" Roy informed us. So on Saturday when we were over there, winding up our hunt for some fresh vegetables, he suggested we go in and try it.

What a surprise! The whole room was freshly painted white; had even been lined with new wallboard. There were brand new shiny tables and benches and toward the back, an area enclosed by a rustic fence, and thatched roof. Inside the door, to the right, was a sparkling display case with pastries, and much shiny new equipment; coffee maker and milkshake machine.

We had a good cup of coffee and chatted with the proprietress, a slim, attractive, vivacious black lady.

Yes, she came from South Africa. Her husband is head of the English Department at the University. Right now he was in U.K. finishing work on his Ph.D. She said she had a problem with the little shop in getting help. "Can't get anyone with class." Roy said he guessed she wanted someone attractive who would give good service, and that's hard to find.

Other examples of South African blacks who are easy to identify by their industry and being on the ball, are Mr. Rompa, Conference Lokomo's father-in-law who runs the Caltex station near Mochudi, and Mrs. Mawby, one of the most capable persons at the Tax Department.

Anyway, the ones with the zip and "know-how" are from South Africa. Life down there is just like Stateside and they're used to things moving and getting done.

In spite of all the inequities of life down there, a statement made the other day by some commentator in the paper was right. "No where in South Africa is there a place where the whites and blacks are not working or living together. There are great areas of cities in the U.S. where no one ever sees a black. There are no such areas in South Africa."

The only problem, in South Africa, when working hours are over, the blacks have to get on the trains and go out to their own townships.

I am reading *Robert Moffat, Pioneer in Africa* by Cecil Northcott, published by Lutterworth, London. It was 1817 when he arrived at Capetown and later went on north, getting acquainted with the Boer settlers. As long ago as that, their attitude was the same as it is now. I should say, that since those times, their attitude has not changed much. When Moffat asked them if their slaves could not come in for an evening service (they were the fastest in the west, at whipping out a Bible and having a prayer meeting) they guffawed, and asked, "Well, do you want us to bring some baboons in too, or how about calling in the dogs to listen?"

They are still the most "religious" of all people, strict, as no movies or plays or anything open on Sunday, but have a lack of charity.

The Boers run the country, but even the English in South Africa have a separate life from the Africaners, and of course, the Coloureds, Indians, and Blacks, each has its own. I wonder if they'll ever get together.

Joel's Spelling and English books are full of interesting stories. One is of Livingstone; three chapters about him marrying Mary Moffat— daughter of Robert Moffat of whom I am reading.

Three of their great-grandsons are Sir John Moffat, Leader of the Liberal Party, Northern Rhodesia (now Zambia), Sir Robert Tregold, former Chief Justice of the Federation of Rhodesia and Nyasaland (now Malawi), and Robert Livingstone Moffat whose father was first Premier of Southern Rhodesia (soon to be Zimbabwe—perhaps). I wonder where they are now and what their feelings are about the situation in Rhodesia. This book was published in 1961, and those men look to be in their 40's or 50's. It would be interesting to know.

There are shelves of books on Africa waiting to be read. I don't know how many I'll get through.

Oh, I have to end on a horrible note; another warning to keep me on my toes.

Joel said yesterday that Mrs. Hamilton, his teacher, said that she was out on the golf course with her husband and he said, "Now don't you move and don't you scream or do a thing when I say what I'm going to now. Don't look down or move. There's a cobra on the ground beside you."

She didn't scream. She didn't move. She didn't want to look down but she did see it slither away.

APRIL 15

It is the most beautiful April day imaginable. The sun is brilliant, the air pure and dry, blossoms everywhere and the sun birds are back, darting around the flowers in back of the house.

We didn't realise for a while that they were gone until anticipating Aunt Lois' visit, we suddenly found nothing around but sparrows—all dull—and knew that the sun birds, the weavers and most of the blue waxbills had rushed off to other climes. All was not lost, though, because while she was here, back they came. We saw a few weavers and waxbills and found some Wydah birds with the long long tails on one of our drives, so she didn't miss them all.

It is more than a month since I've recorded a word about our life here, and it's been a month overly packed with things to write about. Three weeks of fast-paced entertaining of Aunt Lois, a trip to see Victoria Falls—from the Zambia side, and the news that Alice and Jerry are expecting another baby in December!

Alice said this morning, "Did you ever see more perfect days than we have here in Botswana? Here you wake in the morning and see that brilliant sun and everything is perfect—you can't possibly feel down. This just naturally lifts your spirits!"

School closed and Joel was here on his own for a few days. "On his own" but melded into the Pahl family. It had dawned on us that our South African visas were about to run out, so I suggested we take our applications into Pretoria, hoping that we might pick up new ones the same day; if not, there'd be time for them to come by mail before Joel's school break was over. We hoped to drive to the Drakenbergs, to Losotho, Swaziland or Zululand; somewhere new and interesting. I'm not keen to go to Capetown as most people seem to be. Friends are going by train from Gaborone and it will take over thirty hours to get there. Driving takes days, and several of those are across the Big Karoo, a bleak desert without much to see. It's the same route that Moffat and his family came on from Capetown, in covered wagons and oxen.

In Pretoria there were no quick visas. "It will take much research and time", so we drove south to Johannesburg, on a new route for us, to spend the night.

It was a pretty drive and the distances we could see amazed me. Coming up over a rise we could see from horizon to horizon; rolling hills, distant kopjes, mining operations off in small valleys, and up front, the whole huge city; skyscrapers in the middle, the great sprawl of the city and the gold mines around it and then vast openness off in all directions. It was almost like seeing it from the air.

The thruway approached Johannesburg through luxurious areas of huge homes, richly landscaped. All the suburbs were ablaze with flowering trees and shrubs, or a mass of greenery. Shiny highrises appeared along one side and just then, a black woman walked across a modern overpass, carrying a cabbage on her head.

We walked down to Claim Street that evening to the movie. The theatre was typical South African. Luxurious, hung with a million miles of soft beige drapes, subdued lighting, cocktail lounge-type soft upholstered seats with much leg room, soft carpeting, sloping right up the the stage.

Before we left the city in the morning, I dashed up the hill from the hotel to a little shop to pick up some soft sliced bread; some for Juan who would be down this week from Francistown. As I paid for it, I told the man I was taking it to Botswana. "Botswana? That's where I come from. I kept the store in Maun for fifteen years!"

"Do you know anyone in Gaborone?", thinking most Indians have relatives or friends all over, keeping other stores.

"Gaborone? No, that's too far away." Of course, it's far away from Maun. I have to remember that Botswana is the size of France. One wouldn't expect someone in Biarritz to know someone in Metz.

It's always an interminable ride home and when we finally reached the point we could say "only three hours more", we took a break, for the last three hours are the worst; tense, with poor visibility in the stirred up dust.

We knew were were back in Botswana again, when we checked through the border gate, for there by the road, was a huge piece of road equipment resting for the night, and an enquiring herd of huge cattle were nosing all around it, straggling across the whole road. As we eased slowly through them, I warned Roy to roll up his window.

"That huge bull there with the long horns could hook into you!"
"He wouldn't dare!"

But it did glare with evil intent as we crept past, and I noticed Roy leaned over my way, as he kept his eye on those horns.

So, over the cowflops, where the cattle in that area love to spend all their time on the pavement, we carefully came home through the dusk, glad to have made it safely.

Joel greeted us with "Why are you home so soon? I've been having a ball!"

Remember the "Radio Man"? The one who stopped in here early one morning and asked for P20 so he could pay his electric bill? That was last October, and he has been conspicuous by his absence since. Months have passed and he's made no repayment—even a penny. He has waved once in a while passing in his pickup, but that's all.

One Sunday evening Joel went out onto the porch to see what was going on, as there was a rough exchange of voices, cars stopping in the road in front of Kenneth's and the air of something unusual.

"They're having a big fight" was his report. Later hearing a knock, I opened the door to the Radio Man and his wife. At first I thought they had come to repay the loan, they were so smiley and friendly. They wished to use the phone, to call the police to come settle, or put an end to, the ruckus out in the street. His neighbor—a good chap—was involved and the problem had something to do with the good chap's wife.

"I want to get the police, there could be real trouble" he said. I told them our phone was not hooked up, but they tried it anyway, with no success. In the meantime, Joel had been watching the fight and said he had seen one guy throw a bag of groceries that went all over the car, broken eggs and all.

"An Easter picnic for the dogs!" the Radio man's wife said.

They went off and we soon did see a Police truck come park in the school yard and policemen join the groups, now facing each other with headlights on.

Back came the Radio Man and wife and sat on the couch, facing the ruckus, the street scene visible through our front windows.

"We said, 'let's go back to our friends house so we can see what happens'. We went to the corner house and they called the police for us."

Roy said, "Sit down. Would you like something to drink?" I got an orange squash for the lady and the man said he'd like some wine—"white", so Roy got the bottle, opened it and set it on the coffee table, where the Radio Man continued to fill and refill his glass until it was gone. Toward 10 p.m. his wife made motions that they should go, but he impatiently poured himself something more and looked up to me, saying "Get her another coke", and passed me her glass. I couldn't help catching Roy's eye, as I passed on the way to the kitchen.

The fight had long since ended; the Police car followed one of the cars in the direction of town, and the other went off the opposite way.

They began to ask now if we'd sell them the wall to wall carpet in the living-dining room when we go. I said that was a long way off, but they countered that they would like to be working toward it. She also wanted the drapes and the glass curtains. Then she came to the bedrooms to see the rugs and the curtains and decided she'd want the turquoise rug and curtains, and called her husband to come and look.

They kept saying, "We want you to put us at the top of the list!"

I asked them how the people were getting along next door since the mother's death.

"That poor man. All he does is", and he pantomimed lifting a bottle to his lips. "I tried to talk to him once, telling him this is not going to help, but it doesn't do any good." Then he went on to say, "It's too bad, because if someone had been willing to stop that night when she was injured, she might have lived. Nine cars went past—whizz—when he was waving for someone to stop." He told again what a fine woman she was—so well liked by everyone.

After they went, I said, "They can never afford to buy all these things they want."

I still can't figure someone stopping for a $20 loan and then forgetting about it completely. We'll see what happens when we remind him of it sometime.

Discussing our determined daily sessions on the golf course with a girl from the Agricultural station, she startled me with,

"I hear there's a python out on the course; out on the back nine—way out, towards Maru A Pula."

"The back nine! That's where Alice and I always play."

"Yes, they say it lives out there."

I didn't quite believe her. There are tales that go around like Mrs. Hamilton and her husband seeing the cobra, and I thought maybe one of those stories had taken a new twist.

Later, by the Inn pool, "Did you hear that they saw a spitting cobra slithering across the ninth hole the other day? Someone went after it and beat it to death."

"The ninth hole! That's right near the club!"

Then I asked her, "Is that the same snake that someone now is saying is a python—living out there somewhere?"

"No. There's a python out there. It's way out back—towards the Maru A Pula grounds."

"It's this hot spell of weather, after a cool time, that has brought them out", she added.

Alice and I have decided not to look for any more lost balls in high grass out there.

I had another round with a garden boy!

One day, after I had been laid up for several weeks, and the grass had all got away from me, I snatched the boy who crept in whispering "I want a chob"—and put him to work. First I gave him a pair of shoes, showed him what to do, fed him a big snack at 10:30 and paid him well (more than I wanted Pauline to know he got). He did come the next day, and we got as far as the lawn mowing. What a time I had showing him how to use the "machine"!

I would show him how to push it—steadily—and then say "Go, Go Go"—and motion ahead. This startled him and he immediately pushed something to turn it off. Of course, I had filled it with gas and oil, and had started it for him. So as he couldn't get the hang, I ended up by holding the bar with him and walking along—pushing steadily ahead. Everything I said to him, about anything, he answered "Yes", so I decided that he didn't speak any English. But after pushing him a half dozen rounds and showing him how to turn the corners, he finally did learn and then there was no stopping him. His greatest thrill was when some acquaintance, or even stranger about his age, passed and saw him as master of this machine. Quite a crowd gathered at one time, and he was glowing with importance. He did keep on, and he finished everything and even went over some that had recently been done. I paid him well again. Told him to come back the next day after Sunday, to do it all again. The next evening, he and an Indian boy came back to talk to me in the garden and the Indian told me "He wants big job. Big Job." This I knew to mean he wanted to come every day and putter around. I explained I only needed help one day every week. "Come on Monday and use the machine again."

He never showed again. After shoes, food, cold drinks and good pay and the opportunity to preside at the "machine" for all the neighborhood to view—he passed it up.

I was working out back one afternoon, and all of a sudden there beside me was the girl from next door; where Edwin and Kenneth live.

She had her eyes on some spot off in the distance behind my head and spoke the soft tone used for asking favors, saying "I need a job. I have nothing to do. The people there said they could help me, but they haven't done a thing. I failed my J.C. so now I can't go back and try over, even if I have the money to pay for it. They never let you try again if you failed once. So I have nothing to do. I want some work. Anything."

"How old are you now?"

"Going on twenty."

"Well, you realise I'm a stranger here, and I don't need any help. But I will tell my husband. Where are Kenneth and Edwin now? I haven't seen them in a long time."

"Kenneth is going to Moeng. Edwin is in Lobatse. He is doing Standard 7 over again."

"Where is Vivian? I haven't seen her either."

"She is here. Going to school in town, Leshedi. The boys are sometimes here on weekends."

We did see Edwin soon after that, but only to wave to as he went by on the road. Their lives and Joel's blended for a while then gradually, each went off in another direction. Thomas is in school with Joel, though, and is the student Soccer Coach.

Joel has a new friend, Zylla, a boy with a black father and white mother, who surprised us when he said he was from East Berlin. I couldn't figure what people from East Berlin would be doing here and why. Joel eventually found out that his father was originally from South Africa—but they are refugees from East Germany. His father had shot a guard in his escape. We were perplexed for a while about him. He's a good kid; tall and has an unusual voice. He speaks German but has made quick progress learning English and is placed in his own grade at school. He is constantly expanding his vocabulary, questioning words and expressions in general conversation.

Zylla learned his Scout Law and Promise so fast Joel was amazed and started to work harder on it himself to catch up.

The sunbirds are back—en masse! They are a joy to see swarming through the blossoms outside the dining room window whenever we are eating any meal—from breakfast to dinner. The other day I heard a whack and then the excited screaming of one of them. I knew what had happened, for often birds fly straight into the big kitchen window panes, where they reflect the trees and big plants, just like a mirror. Sure enough, there lay a little female sunbird, stunned to insensibility, with her mate excitedly screaming and dancing around, in low plants, right next to her. I picked her up and stroked her neck. For some unknown reason I feel if you pat and stroke them, they'll feel better. The male squawked and flew off a bit, and I kept the little one in the sun and waited. Soon, she reached around and pecked at something in the feathers near her tail, stretched her neck and glanced around. She closed her eyes again and rested some more, and I set her on the lawn chair cushion. Later I took her off and put her down near where she had first landed, and she stayed put for ages, it seemed. When I did go to lift her up and pat her again, she perked up and flew up into the thorn tree. I was happy about that, but then there was no sign of her squawking mate. I hope he hadn't abandoned her permanently, after that short a while.

Joel is packing his bags. He's really excited about the week's expedition on the Kalahari. The man in charge came to school last week and showed slides of where they'll be and gave them a good background for the trip. Radios are outlawed, but they may take tape recorders for taping night sounds. Joel has a problem. His is a combination, so he is taping down the antenna and covering the radio knobs so it can't be turned on.

Pauline's house had been full and brimming over for a while, then this noon, she asked if Roy would take them to the station on his way back to the office. He said O.K., and they were ready so he didn't have to wait. And guess what—Tandi got into the front seat with him and snuggled up against him for the whole ride. He told us all about it, so I guess he was as pleased as I was when she snuggled up to me. We are both accepted by her. At long last!

Aunt Lois arrived on the 15th of March. One year to the day from our first setting foot on Botswana. We all celebrated the anniversary, and her arrival, with dinner at the Inn with the Pahls.

As Aunt Lois got acquainted with the city and the villages nearby, Pauline couldn't believe this lady was eighty-three and had come all the way "from over that side" as she refers to America.

She met Pauline's family in a dramatic way. One evening shortly after her arrival, we were having coffee when there came a parade, single file, down the drive past our big front windows like a scene on a movie screen; Lillian with Lovemore on her back, Catherine with a suitcase on her head, a cousin with a sack of groceries on her head and another sister with a suitcase-satchel on hers! Some parade!

A Safari materialised the next day. Kitty Dunn and Alice had set the date to trek out to the Thamaga Pottery. Bea Henderson (Canadian) and family would go along too, as she was a friend of the lady who runs the pottery, and she had been out before—thus would be a good guide.

All finally fit into the two vans; five women and an assortment of twelve kids, ranging from two years to over fifteen. No one wanted to miss the trip. The boys, smallest girls, Lois and I rode with Kitty and we had quite a ride! She has not had experience on dirt roads and we didn't know what we were getting into. The minute we turned off blacktop, toward Thamaga, it was a new ball game; rough road where we were immediately amongst cattle and herds of goats, with people sitting under thorn trees along the side. Rocky rises and slopes were bad enough but suddenly we were reeling through deep sandy ruts. Sand tends to grab the tires and snatch control of the car from the driver. As the VW is high, it was all the more startling as we snaked through the deep sand. More surprises in store, as we soon came to a rushing brook, rushing over the road with no way to ascertain the depth. Crawling to a standstill, we could soon see that there was a concrete slab under the water which assured a safe crossing. We forded five more of these brooks, and the approach to some were treacherous, as the water had been high and washed the roadbed out to a stone heap. It was tense all the way, with unknown terrain and the question of how bad it was going to get. We passed the turnoff to the village where Livingstone had once stayed a while, then when we thought we must surely be getting to our destination, we climbed and climbed a kopje where, upon reaching the top, we found it dropped away below us, almost straight down. Spread out in front of us was now a magnificent panorama of green valley— stretching as far as you could see—rimmed at the horizon with low kopjes. We slid down the steep incline and were on flat land for the remainder of the way. An hour and a half after leaving home, we drew up at the pottery sales house.

While Alice was plowing along, she asked Bea Henderson, "How fast would you drive on this road?" and Bea looked aghast and replied— "*THIS* road? I wouldn't *DRIVE* on this road!!" No wonder we managed to pack all four families into the two cars.

The kids rushed off to climb on the rocks. A great flat stone surface of about a half acre spread out near by, and beyond that, an odd pile up of boulders. The shopkeeper preferred that not too many be in the rondavel at a time, as so much breakable wares were stacked in close quarters. So the adults did their browsing and purchasing, and later the kids did theirs in relays. Here I found some ostrich egg shell beads and when I held one pair up and asked Alice how she liked them, hanging on my sweater, she replied, "No. They don't look good." I was a bit surprised and so she laughed and said, "Well, I just bought you a string of them for your birthday!"

On over another rocky path we climbed up behind the sales rondavel to the workshop. Work was in progress—with plenty of room for all the kids to watch any operation they pleased. There were products in all stages, and workers were shaping bowls, trimming off plates, painting bands on bowls by holding the paint brush still and turning the bowl on the wheel. An old man was sculpting small animals and some of the workers gave the kids clay. Even when we were ready to reassemble and get started on that return trip, kids were running back in, working on their own bull or elephant and getting the experts to help with the details of it. Joel still has his bull, and it was on display at his school open house.

In the open field in front of the shop was a pretty white Rondavel, with a tall cross set in the yard before it. It is the Catholic "Cathedral" of the village. Father Julian is the person who had the idea of establishing the pottery and the textile operation nearby, to help the village. Workers at the Thamaga Textiles make up dresses, shirts, and skirts of the Botswana cotton. This is a dark print, reminiscent of colonial calico. It was first brought to Botswana by German missionaries, and is still made for Botswana in both England and Europe. The missionaries first mission was to convince the people they were sinning if they weren't covered up. Mary Moffat spent great energy sewing up calico smocks and insisting the women wear them. But this is a *HOT* country. The people wore aprons and skins around the middle—decorated with beads and ostrich egg shell beads, and were not about to cover the rest of them with skins and furs—in this heat. But the cotton was brought in for them—over a hundred years ago, and it's nice that they do have their "own", even though it is all brought in from somewhere else.

We went into the church. The big round room had a round Swaziland sisal rug, and on it were small leather thonged stools—in three concentric circles toward the edge of the rug. All white walls with color at one side where the altar was on a raised portion. Very peaceful.

The ride home was just as long but not so tense, as we knew what to expect and knew we'd make it out to the good road—if we drove carefully.

While Lois rested from our "Safari" I hurried with food, for we were expecting Rat and Susan. We all enjoyed the dinner together, hearing more about Rat's experiences in California. When we urged Susan to have some more food, he said "I will tell you when she is not here why she doesn't want more."

Susan had said she was leaving early the next morning to go to the far side of the desert, for her father was ill in the hospital in Ghanzi. Rat's brother, with Lands and Surveys was going to Ghanzi in a government truck, so she was taking advantage of the free ride. It would take them three days. So we pressed for more information and Rat announced they are expecting a baby. She didn't say much, only grinned.

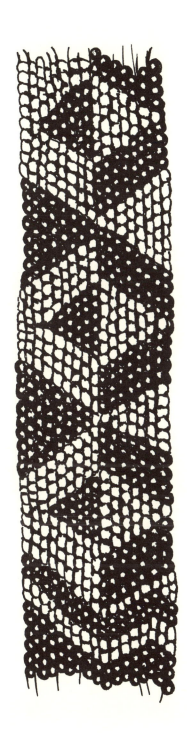

4

Treks North

Zambia

Kazungula

Kasane

Livingstone

VICTORIA FALLS

Chobe
Park

Wankie National Park

Okavango Delta

(Rhodesia)
Zimbabwe

Maun

Bulawayo

Namibia

Francistown

Ghanzi.

Selebi-Pikwe

Serowe

Palapye

Kalahari
desert

Mahalapye

Molepolole

Mochudi

Gaborone

Kanye

Lobatse

Ramotswa

South Africa

BOTSWANA

Lois did not get a South African visa before she came, so she had to be content to "Discover Botswana". Each day of her three weeks we planned something special, but she couldn't quite let go of the desire to visit another country.

Swaziland was out of the question as it entailed an overnight stay in Johannesburg on return, but I wondered about Zambia.

When the girl at Zambia Airways was giving me information on flights to Lusaka she casually mentioned that on Thursday they go first to Livingstone, where you can see Victoria Falls.

"Victoria Falls! Now! Is it safe?"

"What do you mean, is it safe?" I'm talking about Zambia. There are two sides to see the falls from, you know."

Great Day! I was pretty excited. Aunt Lois had mentioned so often wanting to see Victoria Falls.

She was wildly enthusiastic when she heard of the possibility. We applied for visas, purchased the tickets and made reservations at the Intercontinental Hotels, in both Livingstone and Lusaka, and started packing!

When we dropped Joel at the Holiday Inn pool that afternoon, we discovered it was "Botswana Week", and the whole place was one big display of Botswana products. Out on the lawn under the shade trees, there were tables and big mats laid on the grass covered with pottery, leather goods and weaving, baskets, Bushmen products, stones, jewelry, knit goods, drapes, woven spreads, belts, shoes, and hats, just like a fair. Lois would not have been able to "seek out" all this if she'd had months to explore. It seemed a special event, especially for her.

We were at the airport at 9 and found it already crowded. I recognized some people—the pretty Korean girl married to a British Consul. Roy and Lois had played bridge with them on Monday evening. They had two darling children like little dolls, Edward, 6 and Claire, 5. We sat next to each other waiting for loading time, and Mr. Hogarth told me they were on their way home to U.K. for three months leave. They too were going to Livingstone, were staying at the Muse-O-Tunya Intercontinental at the Falls and going on to Lusaka the next evening.

Roy was the last person standing there waving as we lifted off into the sunny sky. He and Joel planned to go out for every meal, go to a show on Friday evening, and both see that the homework was well done that Thursday evening, ready for Friday's spelling test!

We got a good view of Botswana and I got a crick in my neck from watching so hard. Before noon we put down at Francistown. Here I noticed how the women tied the cloth around them to hold their babies on their backs. They made a sling, over the left shoulder and under the right arm. In Gaborone, they wrap straight around, under both arms, the blanket tucked together on their chest or sometimes pinned.

We changed from the South African line here, to a Zambia plane and we watched with keen interest all we flew over.

We saw the mist rising over Victoria Falls as we neared Livingstone. Great clouds rose in the air for a miles. The Native name for the Falls is Musi-O-Tunya meaning the Smoke That Thunders, for the mists rise like smoke above the thunderous roar of the water.

On this trip I decided that we would carry our own suitcases rather than have them checked, so we wouldn't lose them. They were a bit bulky, larger than the usual carry-on luggage.

In the Livingstone airport, after Health check and signing the register, most folks picked up their checked baggage and went their way, but we were detained at the customs desk and a woman opened our bags and went through everything. She even held up the envelope of never-used keys to my bag and wanted to know what that was. There wasn't a thing she overlooked, and felt with both hands into every nook and corner. I couldn't understand why until later, I realised that the bags were sizeable, and we had kept them in hand. I had carried both, most of the time. I suppose two ladies, carrying unchecked baggage, might be suspect.

It was a long drive to the Falls, about fifteen miles and when we saw the signs, not far from the hotel—"Look out for elephants and hippos" like a deer crossing sign at home, our driver explained that the hippos often stroll out of the river at night and graze on the roadside grass. There wouldn't be elephants except in the dry season when the river was low enough in places for them to come over from the Rhodesia side.

The hotel was impressive and the grounds were nicely landscaped with flowers and shrubbery everywhere.

When we went into the big dining room that evening, with all of about ten guests, we saw the Hogarths and took a table next to them. They told us that as soon as they put the kiddies to bed, we could all walk down to the Falls and see it by floodlights.

I never would have dragged out into the dark not knowing where we were going but he knew the way, and we were soon where walks were well lighted.

They led through the woods, and to our right, beyond a chasm which dropped off over four hundred feet, was that roaring plunging magnificent raging water. The wind blew the spray in a constant rhythmic pattern and the lights gave it a green sheen, inasmuch as they were shining also on a mass of foliage. As we walked along the path, and stepped out, here and there between the trees, the picture changed; the water might be more golden, or falling over exposed rock, or the spray deeper and thicker. The spray soon began to gather on the foliage overhead, so we seemed to be walking through the rain, with puddles collecting underfoot. Behind us, there was another gorge with the water raging down through it and on under a railroad bridge.

We left Aunt Lois sitting with a good view where she wouldn't get wet and we went on as far as the Knife-Edge Bridge spanning one of the gorges. The bridge led onto an island like a mountaintop which had a little path encircling it. There was too much spray to venture across it now. Hogarth had seen a man that afternoon, take off everything but his trousers and run over.

There were few safety features in the area except rails on the bridge. The rest was in a natural state and one could step off into eternity very easily. No one kept you from walking into a dangerous area but yourself.

After we had exclaimed over all the sights, realizing we could see only one quarter of the width of the Falls, we walked on back to the hotel grounds, sat by the pool and talked. We were so engrossed, only the dimming of the lights told us it was after eleven.

We were the only ones on a tour of a nearby animal park the next morning. Our van covered a vast network of trails, weaving under thorn trees, over dry streambeds and across open spaces, where we saw Elephant, many White Rhino, Impala and Giraffe. We had a longer ride than we needed so when the driver started on a long search for Zebra, we urged him to call it enough.

Back at the Falls, we stopped at the craft shops at the edge of the hotel lawn where a great store of good carved work, drums, shields and spears was on display. It was fun to look at, but the boys and men were so eager to sell that they were almost a menace. You felt badly that you couldn't get something from each. They were really frantic—as times are not good in Zambia, and food and necessities are in short supply. Lois set a couple things aside, for more money changing and I went and picked them up later. We took pictures at the Falls and sat on benches in different places admiring the views and listening to the roar and marvelled at it all.

I made my dash across the bridge, getting completely soaked from the spray and dripped back to the hotel. I think those clothes were still wet when I got home although they hung on the shower rod in Lusaka one night.

A big monkey ran across the lawn as we headed back to the craft shops, and I was told that sometimes little ones run right into the dining room. Fun to see.

We did enjoy our shopping in spite of the pleading boys. I selected a large Zambian Drum for Joel, and a little one with snakeskin heads, though the scales continue to come off. Aunt Lois bought me a pair of carved heads made from sticks of ebony, and the rough stick is still there, above and below the heads.

As soon as we were aloft from Livingstone that night, heading for Lusaka, there was a frightening electric storm. It was a great relief when the storm finally subsided and I could see some stars out, and later, the lights of the city of Lusaka.

Taxi again here, to the Intercontinental. Fifteen miles into town to it. "I thought I had read it was handy to the airport" she said. "Handy for cab drivers I guess" was my answer.

The hotel was in the area of government buildings, memorials, cathedrals and boulevards.

In our fourth-floor room I could comfortably have showered, had a bite and gone to bed. But we decided to dress and go find the Mokumbah Room—the rooftop restaurant. This turned out to be one of the most elegant we ever dined in. Almost completely copper-clad, the room was impressive, but cozy, with great hammered copper "hoods" suspended from the high ceiling, inside of which light fixtures hung. The columns and walls were all covered in pressed copper, three dimensional. The service was elegant too, and the food the best.

When we were having dinner, Lois said "It's too bad we weren't here on your birthday", and I said, "Today is still Friday. It *is* my birthday." Too many things had been happening to realise it was still the same day that we had waked in Livingstone, for breakfast.

When we got back to the airport the next morning soon after 11, and went to the gate "Francistown" to check our luggage, a girl impertinently informed me we had been cancelled and put on standby, "You didn't confirm that you were still travelling".

"We just came in last night—only bought our tickets a day ago."

"Well you should have confirmed. You'll have to wait till after one o'clock and check back."

That took the pleasure out of things. Not the end of the world but I wasn't pleased. We waited, but I told the girl at the Zambia Airways ticket desk my sad story that my aunt was eighty-three, and we were among the first who were called at about one fifteen. At least we would get on!

We weren't there yet though. They sent us through a maze, and first thing I knew, we were at a table where we needed to pay a head tax of 3 Kwacha each, to be let out of the country. We didn't have that much. We hadn't wanted them left over, so had spent most and they wouldn't take Pula. It was getting late and I didn't know if I had time to get into the Bank—or if any were open. I glanced back into the big waiting room and saw a man in a red shirt who I thought had just been ranting too, that his reservation had been cancelled. I ran up to him and asked if he were going to Botswana, did he want to buy some Pula. "We need Kwacha to get out of this place!"

"No. I'm *never* going to go to Botswana. Here take this", and he handed me a Kw2. Such a nice guy. As it turned out, it was a case of mistaken identity, for the one in the red shirt who had been growling got on after all and sat in front of us!

Well, almost on our way, we ended up at the foot of a non-working escalator with directions to go on up. We had no more than climbed to the top than we had to proceed to the staircase and descend six flights of stairs to come out onto the field. I saw a huge Zambia Airlines plane in front of me "This isn't ours! Francistown isn't large enough for this to sit on", and someone pointed way down to the left where Air Botswana (our size) was loading. Good thing Lois was still in good walking shape. On we went, carrying the drum, but this time we had checked the bags!

When we landed at Gaborone, good old home airport, there were Alice, Jerry and all the kids, Roy and Joel, hanging over the guardrail and waving. I beat the drum for them and then went in to paper our way into the country, and declare our goods. We all came home here and I talked a steady streak until Aunt Lois had to say, "Well! If *I* can get a word in edgeways here!" and I let her.

We couldn't settle down to anything as mundane as getting our own dinner, so Roy said, "Come on. We'll all go to the Gaborone Hotel out at the railroad station. That's where Joel and I've been having our good dinners."

We had a caller. At first I thought she must be going next door but she struggled with her car and finally got it safely into the yard, and I went questioningly out onto the porch to see if she were looking for Pauline, or what. No, she was coming to see us, and Aunt Lois. It was Mrs. Gabakke from the Tax Office. She was reporting to Roy that no one in the Tax Department had been a winner of any of the prizes in the recent Maru A Pula School Fete. Her daughter, at the school, was upset because the Tax Department had supported them so well, and she thought her mother should have a party for all of them, inasmuch as none of them won. She said she couldn't do that, but she wanted them all to know how much their help was appreciated.

She is a charming woman and is a ball of fire. She is an officer of the Botswana Council of Women and has travelled extensively for them, such as to Zambia, through the copper belt (from Lusaka to Khola to Kitwe) in both urban and rural areas to see how the women fare—how active they are in community affairs and social work. She has also been to Israel and lived with a family—"There, the women really *WORK*, and after work, they all go to school."

She said that the older women here are more active than the young ones. Some representatives of women's clubs in the U.S. came to Mole-polole and gave money to the leader of the women's club there, a woman of over eighty, and she used the money to have water brought nearer for household use.

She told us about her family. Her husband was the first teacher of the Thornhill School, when it was in a residence in the Village, before they built the buildings over near the Mall. Mrs. Gabakke is on the committee with Jerry, planning the changeover to Private management of the school.

She is on about every committee there is, President of the Co-op Store on the Mall, the only local member of the Corona Club (overseas women) so perhaps she has come from South Africa—she has all the energy of ones from there.

She wanted to see if Lois would like to come visiting the Council of Women offices and projects and nearby villages, but we had to tell her that time has run out. It was a pleasant visit with her though.

After she left, we went down to the Holiday Inn to sit under the trees and watch Joel swim. There was a treat in store that we didn't expect. Botswana Week was winding up, some displays were still out, and we heard that there were some National Dancers performing.

As we sat there, a large group of boys and girls (who would later dance) filed out from the side door of the dining room and grouped themselves along the edge of the pool. They were about ten to fourteen years old, most were barefoot, and they stood a long while watching, longingly, until they began dipping in their feet, holding up skirts from the splashes. Splashing started and more wading until some couldn't resist, and pulled off their dresses and flung them aside. This began a flurry of activity. Squealing and laughing they raced around and tore their clothes off and jumped in with great joy. Some ran to the small wading pool and filled it while others flung themselves into the big pool.

People sat around fairly bug-eyed, for the happy girls swimming were in all stages of budding beauty—up to full-blown!

Margaret Rowe suggested we might be interested in going to Parliament to sit in the Public Gallery, as today was the last session. She was taking her son, who was home on school leave from U.K., and suggested Joel might like to come along too.

So, Parliament was what we decided on. It gave Aunt Lois an opportunity to dress up in a new winter-white suit she hadn't yet worn. Joel had to go to swim class, and went his way on his own.

We were the first ones in and immediately the Speaker entered with his white wig, opened the session and they were underway. We couldn't hear too well, but it was interesting to watch. Shortly, President Sir Seretse Khama entered and sat in his big chair off at the front. Margaret was late getting there. They had had a big snake episode at her house. The maid had called her at school to say one was near the kitchen, so Margaret told her to stay inside and wait. The snake moved into the trees at the front by the time she got home, so they ate lunch on the screened porch to keep an eye on it. It crossed the lawn in front, and by then I guess, the garden boy had called a neighbor boy and they beat it to death with something. Another boy came in a hurry from a few blocks away, disappointed they had mangled it as he would have liked it for his collection (dead or alive?). Margaret said it was a very thick snake and very long. The skin is hanging now from their clothesline. When the boys dissected it, they found a frog in it.

So much for that—we got a little sleepy in the Parliament, so left after an hour and headed on home.

On Aunt Lois' last day, Joel said his goodbye and dashed over to school. Then, it was a good thing we got out to the airport as early as we did for we just beat the rush. The ticket line stretched clear out the door and was embellished by a dog barking and rebelling, for the Ambassador's secretary, husband and family were leaving, complete with dog, who didn't want to get into his box.

The embassy staff was there for that farewell and the Ambassador soon arrived. Lois had seen the President on Monday, and now saw the Ambassador and Mrs. Norland.

We hung out there, leaning on the wall, watching until the plane finally took to the sky and faded from view. That's when I went home and went to bed for a nap!

APRIL 22

The Pahls stopped by with a six-page typed letter from Ann Neil-son. Very amusing with descriptions of their trip to Cairo—arriving at the height of riots, a cruise up the Nile and then a rough sixteen hour train return trip—with facilities so bad that "John didn't empty his bladder for sixteen hours". They missed their flight, consequently, to Istanbul, and would not settle for waiting for a week for the next, especially with what they had already experienced. They refused the Tour man's enthusiastic suggestion that they go to New York! for a week and happily decided on London, to which there was a flight each day. So they spent a great week in U.K. (of all places, after working with British for five years!) and are now settled on a thousand acres out in Idaho. We read the letter aloud and all got a good laugh when Ann reported that her father said "You got out just in time!!" When she tried to explain what life was like here, he countered with "Well, you didn't know what was going on."

MAY 2

"Look at this! It's a Steenbok horn—I found it—one guy found a pair of them still on the skull. Look at this, it's salt from the pan near where we camped. And THIS—I got this from the Bushmen", and he held up a huge ostrich eggshell—smooth and shiny and rich cream color. "Wait—where are my tapes? Listen to this. This is the Bushmen dancing. The men are dancing. The women sit on the side and clap their hands together—like this, with their fingers bent back so only the palms pop together and make a loud crack"—

He couldn't run down. It was one thirty in the morning and Joel's belongings were slowly boiling out of the confines of the canvas bag and zip case and spreading all over the living room, and a repulsive stink was penetrating the whole place.

"Oh, that must be the Steenbok horn—smell the end" and when I did, it about knocked me over. I put it into a plastic bag for the moment.

At least he was home! We had begun to despair that we'd ever see him again when our waiting at the designated hour of "about six p.m.

at the school grounds" extended to seven, to eight, and then the decision to eat our supper. It was a special one; chicken and a chocolate layer cake decorated with "Welcome Home" and a picture of the Safari truck they started out in; with 9 kids in the back in their big seats, the sleeping bags rolled and tied on the top, and the water tank trailing behind.

Roy kept driving back to the school, searching for some news from other parents. One had a message from the girl at Holiday Safaris, that they'd be along sometime, possibly not until seven thirty.

I kept dozing off, reading a book in bed to pass the time—and kept waking every time he came in with a new story.

Toward eleven Roy went down to the office and called a man, Nicholson, whose son Johnathan was along on the trip. He reported that the last news from the girl was that it would be much too cold for the children to travel in that open truck at night, so if they were held up, no doubt they all camped out and would be in come morning. He wasn't concerned and was going to bed. We did likewise.

Out of a deep sleep we jumped up at the banging on our window at the head of the bed—repeated knocking and "It's me! Joel!"

We answered and he dashed back out the driveway, in bright moonlight, to get his luggage from the truck out in the road. Checking the clock, we saw it was one twenty a.m!

So here is where the jumble of luggage hit the living room and we heard all about their adventures.

I asked one of the mothers the next day if she had been worried before that truck finally got back, and she replied,

"Worried? Terminal Hysteria would be a more apt description!"

Well, the culprit in this whole situation was the truck. Although it looked beautiful, with a new paint job and fancy seal of the Holiday Safari on the door, it had some internal problems—a little ignition trouble, some carburetor trouble, and on the way home, some wiring breaks and shorts. By the next trip it will probably be in fine shape. The kids didn't mind, but Joel reported "that was the scariest trip back I was ever on. I sat up in front with Mr. Youthed, and he had the cover off the motor right beside us, and sparks were flying and it sounded awful and I was worried it was going to blow up!"

When one goes out onto the Kalahari, one registers his "flight plan" with the wardens. There are check points at certain villages, with messages sent back to the headquarters, so they always know where you are. On the return trip, they checked from each place, but when the check-in at Molepolole didn't materialise within a reasonable time, the rescue team went right out to locate them.

The rescue team was a warden, his wife and baby, in a Land Rover. After he had helped with the repair, they all went to his home in Molepolole and stayed there while more drastic repair was made by a crew of mechanics.

Joel was excited about this home. They had bat-eared fox rug on the living room floor, and zebra skin; big buffalo horns mounted on the wall. Shelves held horns and many interesting articles connected with the wild life of the country. He exclaimed over it and kept saying, "You should have seen it!"

We shall probably never hear all the details of the week on the desert but we have heard enough to know it was a complete success.

Joel was up-tight just before take-off time; really getting nervous about it, as when the "Radio man" was here, he stressed that Joel should be careful *NEVER* to go out alone from the tent at night. *NEVER*—for animals circle the camp at night just waiting for someone to stroll out alone. Then he told about an old man out there that Joel might see if he went to the Kutswe Reserve. He was grabbed in a lion's mouth one time, the lion having him by the buttocks. Another man at the camp grabbed a burning stick from the fire, ran after the lion and jabbed it at the lion's rear end, so he howled in pain and dropped the man.

The man was treated by the Bushmen with their herbs and desert "medicine" for nine months, eventually recovering.

Then, a few nights before take-off, Rat was here for supper, and he gave Joel advice. "You'll hear lots of night noises. They'll be so loud they make the sides of the tent rattle back and forth." (His teacher had already suggested that they bring along tape recorders to tape the night noises.)

Mr. Youthed had come to school, talked about the trip and showed slides, and when Joel got home he croaked, "I don't think we're going to be *IN* a tent! We're going to sleep on the ground—in sleeping bags!"

Well, this was something to worry about, after all the other warnings—but someone said that probably they'd have a ring of bonfires.

When the group climbed into the big Safari truck, with the water tank trailing behind, there were Joel and two other boys, six girls and Mrs. Hamilton, his teacher.

The bedrolls were on the roof, the luggage under the big high seats. From where the kids sat, they had a great view as the truck was open, except for a bar on which they could rest their elbows. All the parents, brothers and sisters were on hand to wave them off, and before eight a.m. they were on their way. The Pahl family happened to be driving toward the mall as the truck headed out of town and they said they thought Joel would fall out of the truck in his enthusiastic waving to them!

The Molepolole road is rough, as I pointed out before, but it is a smooth highway in comparison to what they went over later. Beyond Molepolole, heading across the desert, the "road" was one-way, deep sand, passable only by a four-wheel-drive vehicle. They met a tractor hauling some cattle, and had a difficult time getting past each other, with scraping of sides, neither wishing to get far off the safe area. The wheels were spinning and digging into the sand—but they made it! From then on the travelling was at snail's pace, and it took all day to reach the camp place.

A truck had preceded them with George, Robert and Moffat already there with provisions. I have to smile at people here still naming their children Moffat—after Robert Moffat the Missionary who came here in the early 1800's, and whose daughter married David Livingstone.

The camp was a safe place, naturally. There was a thorn brush stockade within which they had the fires, the tent for Mrs. Hamilton, the supplies stored under a thorn tree, and the sleeping area. All safe from the night noises and animals. When I mentioned to Joel that I thought perhaps the kids might sleep in their bedrolls up on top of the truck, he said "Oh, no. That top of the truck was what we stood on to see long distances, when we drove out on trips."

Joel has notes which I am checking into for some details. The first day he found he was in the midst of Ostriches. They saw fourteen by the time they had stopped. The Tswani Pan was near their camp. Pans are depressions in the earth which are only full of water in the rainy season—thus are places that draw much game, then. Presently, both pans near them were dry. One served as a race track for one day's competition. They ran the two and a half mile width of it on hard packed salt. He brought home a piece—like a smooth piece of coral. This pan was five miles in length.

The third day they began to visit the Bushmen Villages. I had no idea this was in store for them, and I guess they didn't either.

The Bushmen demonstrated how they make a fire spinning a hard wood stick in a hole in a soft wood stick and setting fine grass afire.

The women showed how they make rope. They get one foot on a wooden "knife", on a stone; lean over and scrape a sansevieria leaf across the sharp edge of the wood until it breaks into fibers which they take up and roll with their hands along their right thigh. They keep

adding fibers and rolling it—the way you make a "snake" with mod-
elling clay and continue to extend the rope.

The men then showed how they use this rope to make a trap for
birds, and traps for different animals.

The Bushmen are small and wizened. Their skin dries and wrinkles
from the exposure to the intense sun. Their shelters are small grass
"igloo" shaped huts, but they live around the fires, as they can be
warmer there through the night than inside the hut.

A friend of mine asked a doctor who had lived with the Bushmen
about whether they are adjusted to the heat and the chill of the night and
the cold season. He said, "Don't kid yourself. They suffer from the heat
and from the cold just as much as we would if we were there."

The men danced their native dances, with the women furnishing
the rhythm through their clapping—with fingers spread back and the
palms making a loud cracking when whacked together. Joel demonstrated for us and added that the women also sing and make other
noises—some like whistles or trills. The women do not dance.

"One thing was sad" Joel said, "A Bushman baby had fallen into
some hot water and had a badly burned leg. It was awful—all crusty and
bloody. Mr. Youthed cleaned it, sprinkled it with white powder and
bandaged it up."

Each one got to buy an ostrich egg shell from the Bushmen. The
eggs are collected by them for food. They empty the egg through a
small hole in one end and the shell then is used to store water. Water is
precious and some seasons of the year—from April to late October or
even November, there is no rain at all, and moisture is found only in
roots for which the Bushmen dig all day. They can recognize the plant
which has a bulbous root deep underground and dig it with the wooden
"digging stick", sometimes their only means of survival. They also use
the egg shells, broken, to make beads which are used to decorate their
"aprons" and to wear around their wrists and ankles.

They had bows and arrows, but not enough on hand at the moment
to sell. Mr. Youthed promised he would get them some at a later date.

One Bushman liked Joel's green and yellow hat he had bought in
Florida, so put his fur hat, with dangling tail, on Joel and wore Joel's hat
all day. He said he would trade, if Joel gave 2 Pula extra to him. Joel
hadn't taken extra money along, as they were told there would be no
shops and no need for money. Mrs. Hamilton forwarded the money for
the eggs, and she bought ostrich plumes for each, which she will give
them when the next school session opens. They can look forward to
getting the bows later too.

Mr. Youthed gave them instruction in using the bows and organised a competition one of the last days. First they had to gather wood
and build a fire, then they had shooting with the Bushman bows, and
target shooting with his rifle, on which he had given instruction to each.

He gave instruction at night on how to find the Southern Cross. It's
the constellation you hear the most about around here, but not too easy
to locate. The sky is always clear and massed thickly with bright stars
from horizon to horizon. There is never pollution between you and
them, and most of the time, no clouds or moisture, so it's layer after
layer of stars. A beautiful sight.

They had daytime instruction—using your watch to make yourself
a compass. One day he drove them several miles away, said, "Hop out.
There's something here I want to show you." Then the truck drove
away and he said, "Oh oh, we are lost. Now let's see you get back to
camp." So they did, of course.

There was book work every day, with all animals and birds noted,
described and pictures drawn. On a drive one day, they saw thick
circling of vultures so investigated and found a recently killed Hartbeest
probably killed by a lion. Mr. Youthed cut off the horns and the hind-
quarters, which they took back to camp for Robert, George and Moffat
to cook for themselves.

George the cook, gave them a treat one day. He mixed bread, and
set it in the desert sun to rise. At night when they were sitting around
the fire, George shovelled coals into a hole in the ground, set in a pan,
put shaped loaves onto it and covered it, then shovelled coals on top of
that. After about a half hour, he opened it up and "We all had fresh hot
bread!"

"We got points for our work and things we found", Joel explained
"And one day I was writing and found a beetle on my book. I got five
points for him. He had a back like a plastic dome, and each of his feet
had a suction cup on it—you couldn't move him if you tried.

"We saw lots of different kinds of grass. Some was turpentine
grass—and some was 'loving grass'—you don't know what that is, do
you? It has funny burrs on it with feelers on them that love to stick onto
you. We heard the jackals alright. They came around the camp and
made an awful lot of howling. When we started home, we dressed early,
but first went back to some of the Bushmen Villages. All the water that
we hadn't used, Mr. Youthed divided up between the villages. Robert
even dipped out all the water from the cooler he had under the tree. I
think we had about three barrels full to give them. They were happy to
have it. Oh, I forgot to tell you that he also gave the men tobacco when

we went the first time. The men smoke it through hollow bones—they don't have pipes. Anyway, we emptied all the water and then headed toward home. It was a long bumpy trip—and then we had the trouble on the way. Robert is the mechanic and he does the work on the truck when it needs it. He used to work here in town at the Caltex station, but now he works with Mr. Youthed. From eight o'clock in the morning to after one o'clock the next morning was really a long trip."

All in all, it was a great trip. The Bushmen and their hard and primitive life is now very real to these modern-day kids. They are also more informed about the wild life of the desert and survival. They all had a fun time and as Joel said when he crawled into bed about three a.m. Sunday,

"This all seems like a dream."

"What, getting home?"

"The whole thing. The week's trip and getting home, too."

MAY 4

We took Rat and Mongope to dinner last evening. They and the Commissioner will leave in a few days to go to the far edge of the desert, on a Taxpayer Education Trip. Their speaking at the Kgotlas and answering people's questions, will begin at Maun and continue through all the villages until they reach Kanye. When they return home by Lobatse, they will have completely encircled the country.

Travelling by truck and cooking their meals at campsites will not make it a luxury excursion. But Rat is looking forward to it. He is a hunter and he will hunt, instruct the others, and if they have no luck, he will use their permits to cover his take.

Susan went to Ghanzi two months ago to see her ailing father and she hasn't returned yet; Rat has been looking for her. He may see her in Ghanzi if she has not left for Gaborone before he arrives there. She will have to get back soon as Rat has been promoted to Office Manager at Francistown and must move, bag and baggage, the first week in June. He is pleased to be going there.

"That's where I started my work, in Lands and Surveys. Susan will like it too, as she went to the Shashe School not far from there."

Joel has been wanting to go up by train to visit Juan, so now when he gets the chance, he can also visit Rat and Susan.

After dinner I had Roy drop me at home as the men went on to a movie. I read and slept and thought about all Rat had told us.

You can see that households are fluid. Men are away often. Many of them work in mines in South Africa. Many of them work in distant places, coming seldom to the home villages. Rat was away from June to December, now is off for three weeks when Susan may be back here alone, closing up the house. Maybe they'll get together a while, when they settle in Francistown where they'll have a nicer home and will have electricity and a bathroom. That will be fine for them, and Susan plans to work some—I suppose to get more "things". Time will tell how that works out, with her expecting.

Joel said when he got home from the Safari, "I can't imagine Rat being a Bushman. He seems more like a Black American to me."

MAY 5

The yard is full of reclining "work" men in coveralls, jabbering, smoking, throwing dice once in a while, and relaxing in general. Since Tuesday morning, and this is Thursday, the whole house has been painted. This was a surprise. A man came Monday morning and looked it over and said the painters would be here in the morning. The parade of bicyclers began while we were at breakfast, and they went right to work so before the day was over the main part was done. The peeling eaves and troughs had been scraped and painted with a special coat to prevent future peeling and even some of the trim had been finished. Yesterday they were just as industrious, and the doors and screen doors, and the baseboards were done. The gang arrived today, and the only thing they had to do was a bit of trim, but a number of them seemed determined to put in a full day, even it it means just sitting. I shall keep my eye out for the truck when it comes to pick up the scaffolding and box of supplies, and I shall not let it out of the yard unless they take their waste paper and scraps with them. Their mess spreads like a fungus when they're "working" anywhere a while. A man knocked on the front door this morning with a slip of paper for me to sign that the man who patched the cracks began work on Friday and completed his job in two days.

I told him I saw no one until Monday—no workers of any kind until Tuesday. I made him take off the Friday, adding that I had never seen a "patcher"—and eventually I signed the paper.

Well, the truck came, and they did pick up the paper! The last four men stopped at the door when all was gathered, and I gave them each a glass of orange squash and told them how good the house looks now. They didn't have any more papers for me to sign, so that was a relief.

Yesterday I was working on the bedroom floor, basting together my Botswana skirt. Joel was sick in bed, watching me, as I worked nearby to keep him company. Squatting on the carpet, I was pinning the ruffle on, pleating it here and there, when he commented, "You should be using your feet as you go. You could be holding part of it down with your feet. The Bushmen use their feet almost as much as they do their hands, in the work they do."

He keeps coming up with references to what he saw on his visit to the Kalahari.

Alice went to the doctor yesterday. What a laugh! She says, "Well, he knows now, whatever I told him."

"Did he examine you?"

"No."

"Did he take your blood pressure?"

"No."

"Did he ask how many times you've been pregnant?"

"Did he say to take any vitamins?"

"No. No. When I asked if I shouldn't be taking some vitamins, he agreed, and gave me a prescription. When I picked it up at his little medicine room there, I found he had given(?) me 15 vitamin pills and 15 iron pills! I told the girl I'd have to have more than that, I wasn't coming back every week or two, but she said I'd have to talk to the doctor about that. So I waited and saw him again, and he did increase it a little."

"How much did he charge you? 10 Pula?"

"No, 12."

"Well, I guess if you'd taken the P12 and had gone to O.K. Stores and bought vitamin and iron pills, you could have got a six month supply. It's a good thing you know how to take care of yourself!"

"I asked him to recommend a doctor down in Rustenberg. He said they have a good hospital there. I can stop later this month, when we drive to Pretoria. It is three hours away, but I'd be relieved if I can go there."

MAY 9

One day Alice said Shanda, her maid, had asked her if she had some medicine for her girlfriend who was bothered with earache. Alice advised her to have the friend go to the doctor. Then she found through more enquiry about the circumstances, that the girl's husband beats her every day.

"How can you live that way and put up with that all the time?" she asked Shanda. "My husband and I have been married more than 17 years and he has *NEVER* beat me. Mrs. Brown has been married twice as long and her husband has never beat her."

Shanda was struck dumb in amazement. It couldn't be!

Shanda's brother had come last week from the home village way up near Rhodesia, and word had also come that her older brother in Johannesburg had been stabbed and is in serious condition. But she is still in school and exams are scheduled, so she can't leave yet.

Thursday, doing the ironing, she looked up to see someone opening the gate at the driveway, and after watching a few seconds, she gasped.

"That's my Mother!" She was too stunned to move, so after a few minutes, Peggy said to her, "Go let her in!"

"Mama" had never been to Gaborone before, but concern for her injured son had given her the courage to venture forth, with the intention of going on down to Joburg, getting him and bringing him home. She speaks no English, Africaans, or Setswana; her language is Kalanga. Her passport had run out, though she found from someone they would give her a letter. This perhaps would get her out through the Botswana gate, but not likely to let her into the South African gate.

Her arrival, in spite of the reason for it, led to much pleasant activity. She was carrying a huge fowl when she arrived, that someone at the Police Station (Shanda's boyfriend?) had given her. All the Pahl kids watched to see the chicken getting its head cut off and the dipping into hot water before pulling off the feathers and the extraction of the various innards, with eggs in all stages of production. It was a big hen weighing about eight pounds. To the kids, chickens or parts were something that came in plastic wrapped trays from the grocery store.

Shanda told her Mother that she would have to wait until after exams; there was no way to salvage anything from the course if she didn't take them as scheduled. They must wait.

She had more details of what had happened to her brother. He had been set upon by three men, as he returned from work with his pay of Rand 165. He is an electrician with a good income.

Word has come that he is in the Joburg Hospital, hitched up to machines, badly stabbed in the chest. "You would not want to come and see him", was the message to Shanda. "But, the Dr. says he will survive."

JUNE 13

Before this whole trip recedes into a vague blur I shall have to get it down on paper. I've been circling the job for days; waiting for the cold that I had to ease up, waiting for Pauline to come back to work after about a months leave, waiting until all the letters I owe are written, waiting for anything—to put off sitting down and getting to it.

I've told so many people about the thirteen day trip that was so packed with events, mostly unplanned; told them of the highlights in a few minutes skimming-over. But I shall have to refer to my log now, and tell you about all the details. Maybe you'll feel you've been along on the trip; at least you'll know something of how we felt and what we learned.

Our plans for Roy's leave, scheduled for some of the time that Joel was on school vacation, were to drive to South Africa, to Swaziland and down to the coast to Durban and possibly to Lesotho and the Draken-burgs and back up home. Quite an undertaking, but we do want to see Swaziland and the Drakenburgs. In spite of those being the plans, I was not too keen on the old road down to South Africa again. We had just gone to Pretoria to leave our applications for visa renewals, and that same five to six hour drive would be the start of this trip.

It was questionable if the visas would arrive on time; I began to hope they might not come at all. If they didn't, we'd go north and see Serowe, Francistown and possibly go on to Chobe Game Park. While there, we could drive across to see Victoria Falls.

"Aren't you all excited about getting away?" This was Alice, en-thused about leaving the same day for Serowe, to visit the Webbs.

I hadn't done a thing about packing and Roy planned to leave at four-thirty if the mail showed any visas at four. The clocked reached four and four-fifteen and then four-thirty and I began to relax and begin packing. Now I knew we wouldn't start until morning and we'd be seeing the rest of Botswana.

We got an early start, as I reminded Roy we didn't want to get to Francistown after dark on account of the road blocks.

By nine a.m. we were a hundred kilometers north and watched the Rhodesian Railroad trains going north and south beside us; as the road follows the track.

Joel noticed the Monogogo bushes with the grey leaves. "When you see those growing on the Kalahari, and you don't have a four wheel drive, you should turn around and get out. They mean deep sand."

The road soon began to have some rises—up hill and down we went, with twists and turns. A nice change from the level terrain near Gaborone. We had been travelling on blacktop all this while, almost to the town of Mahalapye.

But it ended—we were on dirt again—and as we wound out of

town on a dusty trail that seemed too small to be the main track to anywhere, Roy stopped at a little shop to enquire if this was the right road. It was and when we moved on, he asked, "Did you hear Tennessee Ernie Ford singing? The radio there was loud, did you hear him?" He thought it was a funny place to hear Ernie Ford.

The road was so sandy and dusty that if you saw a car coming, you rolled up the windows until the dust somewhat subsided. Thus, we spent all the time rolling windows up and down, but eventually didn't bother as we were getting so dusty and grimy anyway. We crossed a dry river bed on one of those slab bridges; always a little scary with no posts or fence along it.

Cattle in the road held us up at one point and we soon had small hills on either side. The few huts we saw had a different type of thatching; stepped down in a series of concentric circles. The road flattened again and as we rounded a curve, Joel yelled,

"Look at that bridge!" It was startling because it was a normal bridge, with railings.

That seventy kilometers was some of the worst road we had been on, and worse was yet to come.

At Palapye, the highway ran along the crest of a hill. The rondavels of the village ranged all down the hillsides to our right, and off through the valley beyond. Many family clusters were edged with a green hedge and here again, I was impressed with how ideal their homes are; how they blend into the hills and fields. Being round they are graceful to start with and the thatched roofs are so natural looking, they blend in with the thorn trees and the rolling hills. They have achieved what the west never has; a city of thirty to forty thousand inhabitants, and every bit of it like a country village. Green open spaces, families in clusters, and the whole town barely visible, blending in with the landscape.

The worst road was from here for the next seventy kilometers, at which point we saw a new blacktop running off to the right, to Selebe-Pikwe, a mining town. Such lovely blacktop, but not going our way.

We took another rest stop, in the sandy road, and soon crossed the Sashe River. It was a river of sand, dotted with huge boulders. The sand swirled along, in great dunes, and there was just a trickle of water down among some of them. Women were out on the rocks, washing clothes in what little they could find, and spreading wet blankets and skirts in the sun.

Here we saw trees with the weaver bird's nests clustered all over them. Nests ranged from top to bottom of the tree, but only on one side. Joel pointed out that the weaver's nests that were all sloppy and scraggly were Sparrow Weavers. The nests are just as secure as the neat ones of the yellow and masked weavers, with an entrance at the bottom of the nest, but the overall appearance is "thrown together".

We plowed through the herds of goats which trotted off toward the river as we approached, and from here on, there were more villages, thus more goats and cattle.

The road block was no surprise. The Police promptly motioned us through. Our car was formerly owned by someone in Francistown; with its plates, we were fortunately deemed to be local residents.

I had seen Francistown from the air, but you can't know what a place is like until you walk around in it. The center of everything is the railroad station and the high point of each day is the arrival and departure of the train. The shops and the two hotels are ranged along the street opposite the station and open markets operate through blocks and blocks which entails driving around the block, or in the opposite direction of anywhere you're heading. Very complicated.

We went to the Grand Hotel. There are two hotels; the Grand, that isn't, and the Tati, that is. Roy called Juan Kudo our Japanese-American friend who runs the Francistown Tax Office. He said, "Sit tight—we'll be right down."

Soon there came a bright new yellow Toyota and out popped Juan, Susi and Mimi, their eighteen year old daughter. They were surprised to see us.

"My gosh," Juan said. "A couple weeks ago the Webbs came up for a weekend, now you pop in. If the Pahls come on up, we'll get it all over with!" and he laughed. We sat around for a coke and a little talk and then Juan said, "Say, you want to see some animals, Joel? Come on, follow me." Joel rode with them in the new car and we did the following.

We drove around through housing areas, past the Police Mobile Unit establishment, where a great drape of camouflage net hung over the open dark porchway, and the rest of the white buildings stood out starkly; past the State Prison, wound out dusty roads a mile or so and then Mimi hopped out of their car and opened the gates to Animal and Bird Farm.

The driveway led up to what appeared to be a southern mansion, low and sprawling, amid wide green lawns, shadowy with huge trees and shrubs, with gardens around a pool. Juan said it was a place which sends animals all over the world. They trap and catch them, feed them here on white mice and rabbits. A guide seemed proud of all he had to show us; bird cages filled with finches and love birds, masses of cockatoos, huge Secretary birds, crested cranes and ducks. You name it, it was there. There were individual cages, pens rather, with a small peep hole in the door. You put your eye close to that and it was as if you were looking at a slide show. Dozens and dozens of different kinds of birds, even Ostriches.

Mice were scurrying around in some of the pens, food for the various animals and snakes. I most enjoyed getting into the pen with a couple dozen ostrich, who ran around and posed nicely.

Joel was delighted with the "barn" full of rabbits; every size and color imaginable in tier on tier, pretty as could be. He wanted to buy one to take home, but we put him off.

"Vi Webb couldn't stand this," Juan said, "She was here at feeding time, and they throw live rabbits to the vultures, which just tear them apart." I couldn't blame her.

Outside Juan urged the man to round up the Zebra and we walked out where he indicated they might be.

Zebra are still hard to believe, no matter how often we see them.

Juan then took us over to the Mophane Club where we all went in to see the place where the hand grenade exploded, killed two people and injured so many—the first Friday evening in May.

When we got back to the house, Juan showed us where all that shooting had been one night at his house. He's only half a block from the Police Mobile Unit. Police and stragglers wander up the road in front of his house all the time. Later, I found that the refugee camp is also located there, between the prison and the PMU. Not the most desirable location for Juan.

It was Rat who mentioned they assigned Juan a house, not in the "European" section, and when we asked if he objected or moved, Rat replied, "No, he just got used to it."

There is supposed to be no discrimination here in Botswana, but some evolves. Juan took us to the Tati Butchery the next morning. I have never seen such a store before in Botswana; clean and filled with products from Rhodesia; nice cream and milk, cheeses and good looking meats with not one odor of a butchery.

Juan stepped to the left and was waited on by an English speaking European. They always say "European" instead of "white". While his order was being prepared, he stepped over to us and said, "Notice, the locals all step to the right and are waited on by locals, and the whites step to the left and are waited on by whites. No reason for it—it just is that way." Juan and Suzi had had guests for dinner at noon; a big meal. I realised how big after I'd had one of her meals. So they weren't interested in our treating them to dinner that first night, "Later".

So after our tea and visiting, we went back to the station armed with a map from Juan—drawn hastily on a scrap of paper, so we wouldn't get lost— and went to the Grand Hotel. Roy found they were all booked up—even all the rondavels in the rear.

So it was off to the Tati. I never did get a picture of the Tati. When it was swarming, the sidewalk packed with locals streaming out of the bar next door, or cramming in after a train had arrived, it was either dark, or the sun in the wrong direction. When the light was right, or I had time, there wasn't any crowd and it didn't look like anything but a scruffy building and I skipped it. I shouldn't have.

The room was clean. We went to the dining room for supper and the food was good. Not only was it good, but there was a lot of it. You have no choice at dinnertime; either you ate the dinner or you didn't. Juan had mentioned something about the dinners—"Start at the top and take everything."

We were puzzled by the long menu, though we started with the soup. Roy tried to find out what the choice was and the girl kept saying, "You can have it all. Everything from here to here. You can have the soup, and then the fish, and the savoury, and the chicken and rice, then the meat and the vegetables and potatoes, and the dessert and the coffee and the cheese and biscuits. You start here and you can have it all".

Well, we weren't up to it all! Roy had the savoury, I had the fish and Joel the chicken and rice. We couldn't eat the "everything" by any means.

Juan's Tax Office was a surprise. A pleasant place, nicely arranged; flower beds and lawns in front all clean and bright. The Tax Department used three or four rooms, but other parts of the building, which enclosed a courtyard, were occupied by the Town Council and businesses. Roy said, "Now I see why Rat is pleased about working up here." "Yes", Juan said, "It's pleasant, as there is none of the friction you have down in Gaborone. All goes smoothly."

Mimi took Joel with her to play tennis. Not many eighteen year old girls would be that nice to a thirteen year old. A Canadian Boy, about sixteen who lives nearby, joined them and they found a fourth for doubles.

Juan, Suzi, Roy and I were off then to Bushmen Products factory. Juan is a ball of fire and had been on the phone making the appointment for our tour. "Factory prices here—so buy something" he told me. I hadn't thought of buying anything—but after he had taken us on the tour I felt I had to! It wasn't hard.

The man who owns the place, having recently bought it from Botswana Game Industries, showed us around, described the skins and materials and showed us how they made handbags and a variety of other products. It was a place I could identify with. "They used to spend too much time picking up and cleaning up and putting things away. It looks kind of messy, but we're getting things done." He was right, it was a hap-hazard place, but there was a lot going on. Alice and I had wondered and discussed it once, in Ushma Shop on the Mall as we looked over a neat elephant hide bag.

"It says 'another Bushmen product', but what Bushman would be making these? You know they're not stitching these up out there on the desert." So I had my answer, they were made in Francistown.

I asked if I could come back and take a picture of them all at work. Surely. He went on to tell me that National Geographic Photographers had been in last year, and he had never been able to get the workers to concentrate on their work and ignore the photographer. "He brought in pictures later to show me, and in every one of them, every eye in the place was looking straight into the camera!"

Juan now said he would take Susi on home as she wanted to start her dinner for noon. Mimi soon came in his new car—still unscathed—with Joel, after their tennis. Mimi took Joel and me next door to BGI—where we were to shop. I didn't know I was supposed to do all this shopping.

In Botswana Game Industries Shop, they sell everything from carved ivory and whole tusks to five-cent polished stones. Zebra skins and full lion skins too, if you want them.

I had to force Joel into making a selection—a carved wooden "knife" with a head on the handle—and then we discovered some small skins, or halfskins, under a pile of full ones, and we selected a Kudu—our favorite.

Back at the house, I asked Roy if he had checked in at the Grand, or stopped to see how much the rondavels were. "We can go right down now." So we rushed off and found there was no way we could stay a night for under about $45.

We drove back down to the Tati, with the dust rising and the trash swirling around in the gutters, and found he could get the same room we had had the night before—but he didn't reserve it.

Just before we got to the house I asked "Why don't we drive over to Bulawayo? There'd be a clean hotel there at reasonable price, and we'd have the whole city—for car attention and whatever." He couldn't believe his ears. "I'm going over with Juan some day, when we get back from Chobe".

"I mean go over and stay the weekend—even go up to Wankie instead of Chobe."

"My Gosh. You sure are loose!!" was Juan's reaction later. We were about through with our dinner, and as we had our coffee, Juan was on the phone again—making reservations for us at Grey's Inn in Bulawayo. He had assured us that all is well in the daylight—but get there before five p.m. So we hurried, and he wrote down addresses—got some Rhodesian dollars from Mimi for us to have on hand going in, and that was a good thing, as we had to purchase Rhodesian car insurance at the border post. By twenty after two, we were out of the yard and on our way. A little nervous, but anything seemed better than more nights in the Tati and five hundred more kilometers on a dirt road north to Chobe.

We were hurrying and wondering what we would find when we got to the border. Would they question us or search us? But it was no different than if we were going into South Africa as usual. Just made out the same papers and away we went, to the Rhodesia post. This was a pleasant surprise. We were warmly greeted by the gentleman in charge.

"Would you like me to stamp your passport or would a piece of paper be preferable?"

"A piece of paper will be fine", I replied, and he smiled and said, "Well, it might be better—you know how some of these other countries are."

We were issued gas stamps—as many as we wished—for gas is rationed, but sufficient is available for any tourist. He asked how much and what kind of money we had along "Declare it all, for if you have it coming out, there would be a question. Whatever you have, we'll be happy to have you spend it here".

Soon we were in Plumtree and on blacktop road. After a few detours, we were on a good highway and we sped along, getting to Bulawayo outskirts well before five p.m.

Juan had given us good directions and we had no problem locating Grey's Inn on Grey Street; right on the edge of the main downtown shopping district. The streets from Main, are Abercorn, Fife, Rhodes and Grey—four of the first officers of the South Africa Company.

The manager of the Hotel was an American—Frank something, assisted by his wife Cathy. He was from New Jersey and had worked in Norwalk, Connecticut at one time. He had been in the Far East, and when he came through Francistown, one time, hitch-hiking, he had met Juan and stayed over for a while. So, Juan calling him resulted in our having a fine suite off a foyer. Clean—Clean—Clean! Carpet on the floor, hot water, fluffy towels and also a balcony with a view of tulip trees and street traffic. Joel had a room for himself down the hall.

We enjoyed a seven course dinner—the waiters all dressed in white with red Fezes, the black tassles dangling.

Coffee in the morning at seven along with the newspaper. Both before we were out of bed. Such luxury! It was fun to read a newspaper with another view of happenings.

We had heard often enough that everything is all right in the daylight. The terrorists only do their stuff in the darkness. So, the first night I had only dared peek out from the balcony, hesitatingly, to see if the streets were deserted. Much to my surprise, traffic was thick and everything looked normal.

In the morning we walked downstreet together—first locating Hopeley's Market where Juan said we could get vegetables to bring back to them. We passed the Jairos Jiri Craft Shop, an outlet for all kinds of native work, benefitting the handicapped. The Art Gallery was next door to it, and the big City Hall in the next block. Parks surrounded that and at night it was lighted by amber lights. The department stores were only a block or two away and we visited them all. It was pleasant; you might think you were back in the States. Everyone spoke English and they didn't have any British accent. One way you could tell you weren't in the States, was by their traffic system. They had intersections where the big downtown streets met and everyone had to yield to everyone else. Rarely were there any lights, you could go whenever you felt it was safe. We heard several screeches of brakes and metallic crashes while we were there, and inevitably, it was in the middle of one of those big intersections. There was left-hand-side of the street driving, too. Nothing can go right under those circumstances.

When we called Juan as soon as we arrived at the Hotel the night before, I heard Roy tell him that we might not go any farther north, in light of the reported activity. "We'll see."

On the way to the Tourist Office, I stopped at the Post Office and wandered in and out, using several different doors, trying to find the right place for me. I was surprised to find that everyone was being served, black and white alike at all windows, and in and out of all doors. Then, I woke up to the fact that I wasn't still in South Africa. The last time I was in Rustenberg, I rushed to the Post Office and approached it on the side street, went in and found myself in the black section, hurried out, went in the front door and waited ages to be served. Post Offices handle so many things, the stamps and mailing is a bit incidental. Afterwards I thought, "Why didn't I just stay in the black part and ask for my stamp?" and someone said "Probably they wouldn't have served you, though, they'd have sent you around where you belong."

At the Tourist office I got folders galore, information on everything in and near the city and asked questions.

"How about going to Wankie?"

"Would you fly?"

"No. Drive."

"Oh, you have transportation?"

"Yes. My husband is here too."

"Well, some people still drive up. You'd be all right if you get off the roads before four. Here's a map."

Not knowing any better, we decided to go up to Wankie Game Park on Monday, and we stayed in the city for the weekend.

Stores close resoundingly at one on Saturday, as in all the rest of South Africa, so I then walked down to the parks, a few blocks back of the hotel, while the men had the car worked on.

Never had I seen a more beautiful park. Walks led you up hill and down, onto terraces, beside pools to sunken gardens with borders of Bird of Paradise flowers, great spreads of zinnias, rose trees, palms, white columns, rose arbors and bright sunshine. People lolled over the lawns, lay in the sun and sat at tables.

There were as many black as white, all at home in their own park. I talked to many, and I had no fear of any blacks anywhere I went.

Passing a big playground and a roller skating area, surrounded by hedge, I went on up walks, through gates and under rose arbors, to the National Museum, a huge round building built around a large courtyard. I can't remember ever being in such a fabulous museum.

It was packed with wondrous things. Delving into the History of Rhodesia and the Tribal History, I discovered that the Matabele throughout the Bulawayo area are the Tribe that Robert Moffat had much to do with when they were down near Zeerust and Rustenberg, in the early 1800's. Moffat and Chief Moselaketse struck up a deep and lasting friendship which had a great bearing on the history of this part of the country. I remember reading about the Chief moving on up past Bulawayo (of course Bulawayo wasn't there) and how Moffat went up there and spent almost two years trying to get him to let a group of missionaries come settle there. Remember I mentioned the lilac-breasted Roller, the beautiful bird with bright Alice-blue feathers on its wings, a big bird like a pigeon? Well, Moselakatse reserved the right to use the blue feathers on his own clothes and "decorations"; no one else could use them. On the way home, ten days after this, we were nearing Gaborone at a fast rate of speed, and as we whizzed by, I saw a lilac-breasted roller lying at the side of the road; probably had been hit by a car. How I wanted to stop and pick it up, and pick off the feathers. Where would I ever get another chance at them!

Well, I skimmed through the Museum and realised that Joel and Roy would indeed enjoy it the next day, and I walked on home.

We ventured out to a movie in the evening, so I must say, I have eaten my words; that I would never visit Rhodesia, "while there's still time".

And to think, the week before when Roy mentioned running over to Bulawayo with Juan I had replied, "You two can go, but I'll stay in Francistown."

When we left Francistown, heading for Bulawayo, Joel wasn't pleased.

"I'm not keen on going to Rhodesia, you know. I don't think we should." Later he said, "I thought there'd be tanks on every street corner, and that we would be getting shot at."

As he spent the week in the city and up north, his eyes were opened to the fact that Rhodesians are nice kind people, just like any of his neighbors at home; that all the black people he saw there were kind and friendly.

The next day was the "Day of the Park". It was idyllic, as if everyone were on another planet, removed from all the problems of the present.

The Park rules out radios, tape recorders or any noisemakers, and the ice cream peddlar has to stay out on the sidewalk. The park extends over an area equal to the downtown—and wends out into Camping and Caravan areas, swimming pools, woodlands and zoo, but we stayed in the center, where Joel discovered the Railroad. This is something built and run by "The Round Table," a charity organization. About a kilometer or so of track wound down through "forest" and around a lake filled with duck and black swans, under and over bridges. There was a train shed, and a round house, where the different engines were brought out and connected to the cars. An electric engine, then later two different steam engines were put into use. The engineer, in his railroad outfit, sat there in front of his coal supply and shovelled it in as needed, tooted his steam whistle, and chugged around, time after time. The steam engines cost six thousand pounds each—and that was a few years ago when the pound amounted to much more than it does today. Joel at first looked it over yearningly saying, "Sometimes, I wish I didn't get old so fast."

"What's the matter. Do you think you're too old to ride on it? Look here. Here's a list that says 350 thousands of adults have ridden on it and 750 thousand children since it opened. It's not just for kids. I'm going on it myself."

So, he was on and off the rest of the day, trying rides when different engines were on, watching some of the trips from the overhead bridges and riding both behind the engineer and at the tail.

Well, before the riding started, we wandered down to circle the pond and see the swans, and on the far side reached a high hedge. Peering through, we could see lawns and people, so walked on further to the entrance and hesitatingly went in, picking up speed when we saw a sign "Everybody Welcome—The Bulawayo Bowls Club".

This too, seemed out of time and place. One could only think of the word "elegant". It was quiet. Very quiet. I hardly dared to make the click of my camera.

We were on a raised grass walk, to the right of which, enclosed by high clipped hedges and tall palms, were dozens of men in white, with white straw hats, banded in dark blue, bowling on closely clipped, billiard-table smooth lawn bowling alleys. The alleys were separated by a stretched line, imperceptible except from certain angles. A gentleman (what else could you call him) came over and said, "You should go up onto the upper level. You could get some colorful shots there. There's a Women's Finals Tournament underway."

We thanked him and followed along the lawn path, climbed stairs to the upper level where there was a Club House. We went up a few more steps and were in a bowls area twice the size of the one below. Women were in action at this end, the men on the far end.

Separating the two areas was a raised walk, on which were covered pavillions, long and narrow, with benches facing in both directions.

It was still so quiet, you only whispered if you *HAD* to say something. We sat and watched the action long enough to see the point. All the women wore white dresses, white straw hats with brim turned up at the back, hat bands denoting what team they were on, and all wore identical brown bowls shoes.

The Bowling "balls" were not round, but shaped as though a bowling ball had had opposite sides sliced off. They were rolled, as a wheel, but could topple over then they stopped, or stay upright.

A white ball, small, was rolled down to the far end. Then, in turn, the women rolled their bowls, evidently trying to get as close to the white ball as possible. As the number of bowls accumulated, there wasn't much space for another. A coach (one from each team) stood near the white ball and she would indicate by placing her foot and making a few motions, the path that the bowler should attempt, to curve around and bring the bowl in through some little available space. Marvellous how some could do it too.

They seemed to be unaware of the rest of the world collapsing in certain ways—so close to them—but I guess it's a better way for a little "escape" than many others.

We wandered on. The great Museum and the fun in the park kept us until after the sun had set.

Monday was the *BIG DAY*. I didn't realize how big it would be until we were into it. I had maps from the Tourist Office and we had no problem getting out of the city. Wankie National Park was 265 kilometers up the road to Victoria Falls.

Almost as soon as we were out of the city, we were really *OUT*. There was one little petrol station and a small hotel as we crossed the Umguza River, and then it was like driving the Maine Turnpike. Wide shoulders and open roadside spread up to forests on both sides, and the hills rolled on, but there wasn't anything else in sight.

Once, we spotted an abandoned farm with glass broken out, later two small occupied farms, and a petrol station. All these places were banked with brilliant poinsettia, big shrubs in shimmering white, and Bougainvillaea.

Then I looked at my map with a new eye and saw that it wasn't a map of the road to Victoria Falls; it was of western Rhodesia, and there were no other roads!

All of a sudden we caught up with a fast moving car which had a shotgun sticking out the window, on the drivers side. It maintained its high speed and we stuck close behind it. Once in a while an army vehicle came down the road and we'd see the driver wave to it. Several African buses were headed south, and in front of each was a pick-up truck, with a soldier standing at a machine gun mounted over the cab. In the rear was another, the same.

This was a little nerve shattering. Reassuring, in that patrols were on the road and frightening, in that there was a reason for them.

We hugged that car and by noon arrived at Halfway House, midpoint between Bulawayo and Victoria Falls.

This was the stopping place for our escort car too. He pulled off to the left near some big Army trucks where soldiers in camouflage suits were unloading. One got in with him and they turned and went back down the road.

I wasn't keen on stopping but we got gas and looked over the run-down establishment. There was an arbor dripping with Bougainvillaea in bloom, under which we sat to have a snack. A souvenir shop was closed, a few dusty trinkets on the shelves in disarray and the door locked. A game room with ping pong table was empty. The few workers in the dining room didn't dispel the pervading air or abandonment about the whole place. We hurried on and were again alone until the turnoff to Wankie Park. Now we relaxed. We had been pretty tense all the way up that barren road.

Main Camp, a cluster of thatched buildings, was a delight. Lawns were green, flowers bright and the air filled with colorful birds. We had our choice of the lodges as the place was practically empty.

It seemed an unbelievably modest fee for our spacious double rondavel with two porches. Shades of Francistown, the railroad station, swirling dust, dirt and 40 Pula a night.

We hurried off to see some animals. The lady at the office had marked a map for us and said that most of the game in this 5,432 square mile park was in the immediate area. There were forty different specie we might see. We didn't know it, but mid-afternoon, the time we started out, was the perfect time to see them.

First we had to go through a gate into the Park. The Camp was actually "outside" although game roamed there and around a couple of pans out toward the highway.

The guard took our car number, we wrote down the make and color and to what place we were headed. If we were not back through the gate by six p.m.—a search party would go for us, but at our own expense.

We registered as going to Nyamandhlovu Pan, to the platform and in we went. Not far along we rounded a curve and there was a great Kudu, with about six females posed right in front of the car. They stood still too, and didn't run until we drove toward them. As we watched them, a pair of Water Buck appeared to the left. The male with his regal horns, and the female with big round ears! Zebra, Wart Hogs, Storks, Hornbills and Baboons were in sight before we arrived at the viewing platform.

Here we climbed steep stairs into a thatched roof pavillion—long and narrow, with chairs, where we sat comfortably, watching the animals come to the water and rested our camera on the ledge to take pictures. It was quiet here—no one made a sound. A windmill keeps this pan filled year round, so it is one of the best places for viewing!

We sat and counted the Giraffe, the herds of Zebra, Wildebeest, Kudu and Baboons, and saw Giraffe at a distance, against the sky.

On our drive back to camp, Roan and Sable antelope were in sight and a huge Kudu posed; his spiral horns seemed a meter long. Giraffe wandered across our road in an ungainly gait, while the delicate Springbok and Duiker bounded away into the bush. We felt saturated. There were so many animals that it was difficult at times to catch sight of everything each one was exclaiming over.

I asked Roy if he had seen many people around the restaurant building when he had ordered our dinner. "Two guys came in—both carrying guns."

There were two other couples when we did have dinner and that was the most we saw, at any one time.

That night when we got to bed—early—the wind began to blow; it howled and made the doors rattle. Joel was down the hall in his own big room, and I went down once to see if he were wakened by the unearthly roar and the rattles.

Our car was parked right by our lodge and I began to think—as long as everything else was empty we should have parked over at the office, and no one would know that anyone was in here. I began to wonder what we were doing way up here. After all, we were on our own. If anything happened, we could expect no help from the U.S. to get us out. We weren't supposed to even be here. Well, I mulled away and then was startled by lights from a truck driving up in front of the office. I peeked out the drapes but couldn't tell what was going on. It was about eleven and Roy said later it was the milk truck. I finally got some sleep and woke to happy sunshine.

Off we went, armed with three picnic lunches and our cameras, for a six-hour drive to new areas of the park. The game wasn't as thick as in our first area, but there was always some new bird or animal to exclaim over. All of a sudden, four elephant lumbered across the road in front of us. What a thrill! We had seen "piles of poop" in the road for miles; Roy had told me he wished I'd study the wildlife more and the piles of poop, less!

They moved in single file. Joel ventured they were young ones as they were quite dark, almost as if they were wet. They hurried off the road into the bush where they quickly blended in. That sight was worth the whole long ride. We soon began to recognise the terrain we'd be apt to see them. One sign was broken-down trees and bushes or broken branches in the road. They are not considerate of trees but trample them to shreds.

We reached the Ngweshla Picnic Area at eleven, and as long as we were there, we ate. One doesn't get out of a car except at the viewing platforms and the picnic areas. This one was fenced, and we went in the gate and closed it after us. There was a thatched roof pavillion and many stone-topped picnic tables and benches under the trees. Also, a bird bath over at one side, filled with blue waxbills.

A woman attendant came over with a log book, and we signed it and read the names and remarks of visitors to the park, skimming over the past few months. They came from the world over and had interesting comments—"saw a leopard at Boss Long Pan—wonderful", "Great time, but where are the Lions?"

The lady apparently lived there, in the little house at the rear. I wondered how long she had been in that fenced-in lonely place, but our only communication was smiling, nodding and then waving good- bye.

After we got home Joel found big trees to climb in, and all the trees were *FULL* of birds. The Sparrow Weavers were all around, singing like mad. I sat a long time out under a tree where they had their scraggly nests, and watched them fly in and disappear up through the bottom entrance. There were grey Loeries in the trees, squawking—and none of them paid any attention to us.

While Roy rested, Joel and I explored all the rest of the camp; tenting area, small rondavels and lodges, caravan park and community building, and found it absolutely empty.

Wandering back, we met three people out for a walk too, and stopped to talk. The lady was from Salisbury and her friends from London. They had flown in and were going on up to Victoria Falls in the morning.

I told her I was anxious that Roy and Joel see the Falls, and she said, "What a pity not to, when you're so very near!"

We talked a while longer. She mentioned the flying, as "that road, that lonely drive, is so dangerous now." I replied that we had come up from Bulawayo, and yes, it had given me the creeps.

"Oh, I wouldn't want to be in Bulawayo! Too near the Botswana border!"

"Too near Botswana! I'm from Botswana, and we'll feel safe when we get back inside Botswana—it's home!" So we all laughed. But again, it was something to think about—I added, "You know the people down there don't want to go up north to be near the border—'Too near Rhodesia'!"

"Roy—Guess what! There are daily flights from here to Victoria Falls. You can find out about them over at the office."

"There are? I'd about given up on the idea," and off he went to the office, Joel tagging along. It wasn't too long before he was back—not obviously elated—saying it was easy to get up there, but one would have to stay overnight in order to catch a return flight. We mulled it over a while and decided we'd get up early in the morning and make a fast dash up the road, see the Falls and head right back!

After an early breakfast and an hour of watching game at the viewing platform, we checked out the gate at seven thirty and were off on our fast trip north to Victoria Falls, 195 kilometers away.

The roads were hilly and winding and we maintained a fast pace. There were little villages here and there, and women walking from water sources with filled cans on their heads. There was fencing all along the highway; cattle fencing type, and at intervals a stile for the convenience of these people who had to get across and back to their homes and lands. The stile was metal, and didn't have "Steps" but was a bit like a ladder, angled out on each side.

Here is where we began to see the Baobab trees and they are as startling as some of the animals; look like they have been drawn by a kindergarten child. "Now, when we come back, I want to take a picture of some of the Baobab, and of the villages, as their thatching is different." We were travelling too fast to stop for picture taking now. We crossed the Lukosi River and saw a Lukosi Mission Hospital and some soldiers on the road, but still no cars. We were quite alone.

Wankie is a city surrounded by three huge Collieries, so named, No. 1, No. 2 and No. 3. The hills looked well-mined and smoke was pouring from the stacks. Seven or eight baboons crossed the highway in front of us and scurried into the bush. Joel missed them for he was asleep. Guess he figured it was the best way to escape being nervous.

Another long forty-five kilometers and we crossed the Matetsi River, the bridge well sand-bagged, and we fell behind another road patrol. I wasn't unhappy about that and we stuck to it the rest of the way.

The village of Victoria Falls greeted us with a brilliant display of flowers down the middle of the two-lane, David Livingstone Highway leading straight through the town and to the Falls. Perhaps we were no safer here than out on the highway, but I have to say we certainly *FELT* safer. General small-town activity, Wimpy Bar crowded with people sitting out at cafe tables, flags flying, shoppers bustling about and tourists in the Post Office mailing cards. Nothing could have been more normal. It was nine forty-five a.m. and here we were.

We went straight to the Falls. Roy was amazed at the completely natural setting. There was not one thing commercial. We saw a thatched-roof stone entrance gate, a big map painted on a huge wooden signpost, and inviting paths leading into the "Rain Forest" and to views of the Falls. There were no entrance fees or sales places of any kind.

We followed one of these paths and it led us to the Livingstone Monument which towered over us and we read the inscription, standing there on the very edge of the Zambesi River. Roy and Joel walked up along the riverside a ways and Joel stuck his foot in the water, just to be able to say he had done it!

Our first sight of the Falls, was The Great Cataract plunging down hundreds of feet in a swirling mass of water which was constantly flying back up in great breakers and gusts of spray. Joel discovered some stone steps near here, and we went to the bottom for a closer view.

Climbing up those steps was harder than the descent and we were a bit damper when we got to the top, but not as damp as we were going to be.

The path followed the edge of the gorge and we looked across at the Falls, stepping out at intervals where a viewing spot was paved and safe.

The "Rain Forest" here was created by constant dripping of the clouds of spray rising from the dash of the water against the rocky gorge, hundreds of feet down. This spray never stops; it rains over the trees and drips constantly. We dripped too, as we walked through it, and then, when we got as far as the main Falls, we just stood and gaped. We went on farther, but the spray was so thick we couldn't see anything, sky or water, so came back, along the same path, watching again the unbelievable fall of water. Top flow was measured in 1958 at 16,000,000 gallons per minute. Needless to say—that's a lot of water!

Stopping for lunch at a place well patronised by men in uniform, I picked up a newspaper to glance at. A boxed notice on the front page jumped out at me and I read it aloud—

"Notify Police before starting your trip. Travel in Convoys. Check the Police Station for info on convoys and patrols. Notify Police of any drive on remote road."

"Roy," I asked, "Are you going to stop at the Police Station? It's right across the street."

"No, I'll just stick with the traffic."

So off we went at 120 kilometers an hour and there was no traffic to stick with. After sixty kilometers we could see a car ahead of us, but it was travelling too fast for us to catch. It kept disappearing over the crests of hills, about two or three hills away from us. Eventually, that car caught up to one, and he passed it, just disappeared, and we stuck behind the car he had passed. It was a patrol with several armed men.

We had decided that we might as well turn off the main highway onto a road leading into the northern part of Wankie Park, and return home through the Park, watching animals on the way. We got this fairly well settled before I studied the map and saw there was about forty kilometers of back road through hills between the main road and the park.

But we plowed on into it and it really was barren and windy and dusty, up hill and down over almost mountainous trails. We had missed the Baobab Trees after all; they were on the main highway we had left. We wound on and I was happy, when we crossed a railroad track, to see that there was a sand-bagged section, manned by a group of soldiers. Just fifteen more kilometers to get through and if we don't hit a mine before then maybe we'll be all right. At long last, after forty-five kilometers with not a soul seen except the soldiers, we arrived at Sinamatella Camp.

The guard at the gate seemed surprised at seeing a car come in. I wonder how long since anyone had been there. He no more than made out the little ticket, than we heard a horrible sound, and saw six or seven donkeys grazing among the bougainvillaea blossoms in front of the office building. They had gone into wild hee haws and Joel was almost scared out of his wits, never having heard such a sound before. I doubt that I have ever heard one as horrible either.

Roy checked in at the office. If it had been past two o'clock we wouldn't have been allowed to continue through the park. They know how long the drive takes. We were early enough to get to Main Camp by six p.m., so she gave him an exit ticket for that gate. While he was busy, I looked over some of the camp and admired the neat white cottages, bright with flowers everywhere. There wasn't a soul in any of them and I didn't enquire how long it had been since there had been.

We travelled fairly fast on the dusty twisting roads for about an hour and came to the Shumba Picnic Site. In we drove, and I'm sure the young man there was more than surprised. He came running out of his little house, at one side, all smiles and we settled in and inspected the site. There were sand areas that he had all raked in a design; some stoned areas, and the whole was dominated by a huge Strangler Fig tree in the center, which had enveloped a Rhodesian Ebony, leaving it lifeless. A network of roots intertwined each other and ran up the tree six or seven feet. Naturally, Joel lost little time in clambering up as far as he could. Each tree was labelled, that's how we knew that the huge tree, split into two trunks part way up, was a Rhodesian Ebony.

Well, before we started all this exploration, we had our lunch. We had brought everything left over from yesterday's boxes and as I took out the food, I selected an orange and walked over and handed it to the man. He accepted it in two hands and was profuse with "Thank You, Madame" and bowed and rushed away and ate it immediately. Knowing that we had a sack of oranges at camp, I took two others and a couple apples and gave them to him too. Then we ate what we could and I still had food left over, so packed it in one box and gave it to him, asking "Do you stay here all alone?"

"Yes. I am all alone." He popped into his little house and I guess he was busy looking over all the food in the box and arranging it on some of the shelves I could see inside.

A little farther on, now on black top, we bagan to see mountains of manure! The road was the favorite spot for deposits and the more we saw, the more we were encouraged that there was game all around.

At one place I said it looked like fourteen elephants had come out side by side and decorated the road, for just one animal could not have walked straight down the road and left so much. I guess here was where Roy again suggested I look more at the animals!

We stopped at White Hill Pan where there was a viewing platform. Here was another car, so our isolation was over. We viewed a great convention of Ground Horn Bills. They are ugly, like big black turkeys, but their wings are striped with white that shows when they fly up. Off to the right, in the almost-open field, was a small Springbok that fascinated Roy. It stood immobilized—just like a little statue of Rudolf the Red Nosed Reindeer—and never moved a muscle the whole time we were there.

It was now four p.m., and we paced ourselves, from pan to pan, stopping a while but aiming for the old standby—the big viewing platform. Seven zebra appeared just before we left one pan and then as soon as we started up the main road, there was a *BIG* elephant!

Game was thicker all the time and I had to write fast to record all my statistics! But the most fun was when we saw our Warthog family.

Joel had been trying his hand with the movie camera; he was in back and when we saw some animals, he would sit up on the ledge of the rear window and shoot. At one spot we saw this great big Daddy of a Warthog, staring right at us, so Roy stopped and Joel hiked up out of the door on the left side, "aiming" the camera over the roof top at it. Immediately he was joined by "Big Mama" and Joel kept shooting saying, "Where did she come from?" and then about a dozen little ones swarmed out and trotted around their parents. "What's going on" Joel kept hollering. "Where are they coming from?" Well, we were parked right on top of a culvert so the whole family in turn had run right out from under our car!

A few minutes before this, we had come on a herd of lovely antelope, in a grassy spot under trees to the left of us.

"Kudu", I said at first, but soon knew I was wrong. They were
fawn colored instead of grey, although they had the white streakings of
Kudu. Their horns were different too, and we realised they were Nyala—
with a little ruff of a mane to help us identify them. They began to run
across in front of us as we were parked there, but they didn't "run".
They dashed for the road and then sprang into the air, almost making a
jackknife dive out of it. It seemed we could hear their hoofs clicking
together. One after another, and several at a time, they sprang and raced
over the road.

The next day, Thursday, was check-out day. Now, "all we have to
do is get to Bulawayo!". We didn't add—"safely" although it was understood.

Baboons were playing on the roadside as we turned out onto the
highway and barrelled down to Bulawayo—265 kilometers without
stopping. It was good to see the outskirts of the city, and we checked
into Grey's Inn in time for a huge lunch.

Now we were free; were acquainted with the city and had all afternoon and the next morning to do as we liked.

We called Juan and told him we'd see him Friday afternoon. He
couldn't believe we had been north, as he has visualized us staying in the
city.

The next afternoon, driving again in a dust cloud and watching for
cattle and goats in the road, we knew we were nearing Botswana. We
were indeed a long way from Bulawayo, but not in miles. Through the
dust and over the bumps into Francistown, we stopped at the Police
Roadblock, waited for the "soldier" to rouse himself from his napping,
brush off a bit and dawdle over to the car. He looked us over and
pawed through things, and seeing me looking at the Bulawayo
Chronicle, he asked, "Is that today's paper? I only have yesterday's.
Can I have it?" Well—what would you say? He could have kept us
sitting there as long as he liked, so we handed it to him and he waved
us through.

We went straight to Juan's office, as we wanted to call the Webbs
in Serowe, telling them we'd be at their place on Sunday afternoon. As
we waited for some results on that, we told Juan all about what we'd
been doing and seeing and he accused us of working for the Bulawayo
Chamber of Commerce.

The next day we were about an hour down the road, when we heard an ominous flop, flop, flop, and realized we had a flat tire.

"Gotta get off the road" Roy said.

"Why?" I asked. "There's no one in sight and if someone comes along, they can see us for miles. We don't want to get stuck in that deep sand off the track."

"O.K." and we stopped right where we were, opened the tail gate and began piling luggage, boxes, sacks of oranges and extra coats onto the roof and eventually disinterred the jack and spare tire. Miraculously, we found a big stone nearby to set the jack on.

Joel stood guard up the road, in his bright yellow shirt and waved traffic, what little there was of it, by and had his nose down in the sand of the road, saying "Hartebeest have been across here!"

Repacked and rolling, we soon saw an inviting expanse of new blacktop leading off to the left. We couldn't resist a piece of good road this time, no matter where it went, and got on it, headed to the Selebe-Pikwe Mining Center. When we reached the city, about an hour later, it was sight that brought mixed emotions.

Right in the middle of nowhere rose this alien settlement and at the crest of a hill was a huge new mall of modern office buildings and a big Barclay's Bank which looked like it had been picked up from some California city and set down here, all out of place.

The city was so new that there were no rondavels, just rows of little white concrete block houses, thus it has no "atmosphere" as far as I was concerned.

Back on the "main" road, more than an hour in the dust brought us to Palapye where we looked for gas and something cold to drink. As it was Sunday, nothing seemed to be open, but we prowled around until we located the Palapye Hotel, down at the station. Here we at least got a coke, and sat a while on a screened porch.

Off again on the last lap. It was now after three thirty but within an hour we were in Serowe and had no trouble finding the Webb's house. The road from Palapye off straight to the west to Serowe was some of the best we had travelled—almost like blacktop—a hard stony surface.

Serowe is the largest African village anywhere, I've heard. It didn't hit us, as Selebe-Pikwe did, blaring its existence. Serowe grew on you, beginning with a sprinkling of rondavels and thickening into groups of them. Green open spaces relieved the density of the low homes which blended into the rolling hills.

We kept to the main road and soon saw a unique hotel, spread up onto the steep hill to our right. It was a cluster of rondavels and the entrance door to each was above the thatched roof of the one in front of it. Barclay's Bank and Standard Bank marked the center of the village and we passed a store or two, but there was no "downtown".

Beyond the Hospital we veered off to the left over a gravelly shoulder of the road and through an open lot toward three of the very few western-style homes in the village. One was mauve, one green and the last one, the Webbs, also mauve.

We had a good time looking their place over; Ben's generator and Vi's oil lamps she had used until the generator had been secured.

They decided we couldn't see all of Serowe and still get back to Gaborone the same day. A garden boy appeared who wished a ride to Gaborone so Ben insisted we stay over another night and leave Tuesday morning to take the boy along.

We had a grand tour of the unique valley throughout the next day. The Catholic Mission school where Dammy had classes was a bare building with a dirt yard. We climbed the hill at the hotel with rondavels on the heights; visited a farm where they get their milk. Geese, two flocks which have nothing to do with each other except when they need to squawk at a common enemy, honked and raised a ruckus so the kids understood why they made good "watch-dogs".

Just as we wandered out under the Bougainvillaea arbor to the car, we saw three mounted cowboys galloping down the road, urging a herd of cattle toward Palapye, fifty kilometers away. One cowboy looked like Ghengis Khan with fur hat and dark wraps. He led an extra horse on whose back were bedrolls and supplies. A small pony followed one of the other riders. This was the first time I had seen mounted drivers, in Botswana.

Ben wanted to show us the President's home, and took us there, way up past the Tax Office and well outside the village.

"Whenever the President comes up to his house here, they get out the machinery and scrape the road, all the way from the air strip to his house." The house was impressive, built on the crest of another hill. Ben turned left here and went up yet another hill over some of the rockiest non-road we ever drove on. "You didn't drive the Pahls up this did you? Not Alice, in her condition?"

"Yes, we came on up, and we got back all right."

He stopped and let the kids out to play in the sand. They tore around and scared the goats who were grazing among the trees, and startled the guards that wandered around, I suppose, protecting the President's property.

The precarious descent over the rocks was as trecherous and tense as the ascent, but we got safely down, and then Ben wanted to take us to Swaneng Hill. My cold was getting worse by the minute and we were starving, so urged him to postpone that, and go on back to the house.

I rushed around early Tuesday morning and rearranged everything in the car—packing things so they wouldn't get too dirty and beat up. Finally had it about ready when I noticed some boys milling around, and one had a huge bag, a satchel-suitcase. "Oh, you've got a bag too! I thought there was just going to be a rider. Well, I guess I can put it in the back seat, and you can sit on one side of it and Joel on the other."

Joel was out scouring for Botswana Agate, and we had to send a boy to call him, as it was time to Hit The Road. I told the boy to get in and then saw that one in a blue plaid shirt was already in.

"Well, which one is going, you?" I asked the blue shirt.

The older one in the sport coat spoke up, "I am going with him!" and indicated he was getting in too.

"Now, you can't do that", Ben shouted at him. "You can't do that. We said only one. There isn't room for two!" and so on. They didn't give, and both wanted to go—had their clothes in the bag. So I had Joel sit in front between us and they had the back seat.

That was a good "hitch" for the boys as it was well over three hundred kilometers to Gaborone.

We broke the long drive by stopping at the Tropic of Capricorn. A small monument at a roadside park had a plaque showing that on December 22, at eleven a.m., the sun would be directly overhead. Joel thought he and the Pahl boys should go up on that day and see if it is true.

The pile of mail accrued on Roy's desk urged us on, and we headed directly there before going home to unload. Roy delivered the two "passengers" down to their home in the village. They were lucky to have such service.

So, we were home. It was hard to believe all the things we had done and seen since we had left it, thirteen days before.

JUNE 26

I was writing in the bedroom, when Pauline rushed in excitedly motioning for me to "Come here!"

"Look, he is destroying that car."

She led me to the living room window through which I can look directly into the yard next door. There, just over the fence, stood a bright deluxe yellow VW bug, with stripes. A huge black man was moving around it and it took me a while to see what was actually going on.

"See, he has broken out the windows," and then I could see that every window in the car had been broken out or smashed to the extent a man could do it, wielding a meat cleaver.

"Well, isn't he an idiot. What's he doing that for? Is he mad at it because it won't go or something?" I commented.

"I don't know", replied Pauline.

Then, the big guy calmly proceeded to lift the hood at the back of the car, exposing the engine, and be began to whack at that with the meat cleaver, with all his strength. If anything came loose, he tossed it behind him and reached in to grab something more. Wires, pipes, tubes and pieces flew out behind him and collected on the ground.

Then—I vaguely remembered that a yellow VW had figured in that altercation in the road on Easter Sunday, when the police had been called and the Radio Man and his wife had come to watch the activities from our living room. I checked and could see the license plates were TJ—Transvaal Johannesburg—so it was a South African's car. It is often in the yard next door; the man comes up to visit. I realized that this must be the injured husband at work here demolishing the car of the guy who has been fooling around with his wife. He was taking it all out on the car.

There were several people, and a number of youngsters in the yard while this was going one, but they stayed well back in the far corner. One wouldn't tangle with a man wielding a meat cleaver, even though he looked very calm and matter-of-fact. After chopping until he was tired, or must have been, he sat on the edge of the front seat and took all the papers and documents out of the glove compartment and casually strolled out to the garbage can near the road and dumped them. Later, he thought better of it and retrieved them. He did some more chopping and whacking, and soon Mr. Yanye and a woman came out of the house. He followed them to the pick-up out at the roadside; they all got in and the truck turned around and headed off.

Later—a truck came and six uniformed Policemen strolled over and stood gaping. They just stood in a line and looked and looked. The rest of the day, at intervals, cars arrived and men got out, strolled over and stood gaping.

Late in the afternoon, Roy noticed that several men were standing, still gaping, and Mr. Yanye was demonstrating, with great waves of his arms and pounding motions, how the man had done it. Cars continued to come and men wander around. We didn't see the big man who had demolished it.

"Well, if that guy wanted this fellow out of town and gone—he sure doesn't have any wheels to get out with now!" was Roy's remark.

Yesterday I noticed the yellow car was gone and I never did see if it were worked on and went of its own volition or if a wrecker had come and pulled it out.

Rat and Susan arrived from Francistown on the early morning train. Roy picked them up but found they had been waiting some time in the cold and they had about frozen on the way down (July is mid-winter here). So, Susan wrapped in a wooly blanket in front of the heater while I got breakfast on the table for them.

She wanted to know what we hear from Aunt.

"I have brought something for her." She poked into a suitcase and came up with a small parcel. When she unwrapped it and held up the gift I about fainted. It was just what I had been looking for—ever since we arrived here; a multiple-string necklace of ostrich eggshell beads. This had four strings, tied with soft brown leather, the beads spaced here and there with short lengths of deep-brown shiny grass. She had been out on the desert with the Bushmen and bought this gorgeous necklace there. I shall have to ask Aunt Lois to will it to me!!

Susan had arrived in Francistown directly from her home in Ghanzi, soon after Rat had moved up there, the first week in June. They hadn't seen each other since late in March; her father had died, had been buried, and Rat had packed up for himself here in Gaborone and moved to the new job.

They had time now to come down to their old house to finish packing. Roy drove to their house and picked up all the packed cartons, so when we took them to the train the next evening, we piled the last of their household goods into their compartment with them and waved them off for another cold night on the train.

"There's a house way up on top, way up by all that stone", Joel shouted. It disappeared from view as we wound among the rondavels but eventually it emerged and proved to be our goal.

We were in the small village of Gabane to visit the Hopkins family. We had bumped across the flatland for half an hour, with the tall buildings of Gaborone against the horizon behind us, and a rim of kopjes off in the distance ahead of us.

We knew we were on the right road when we saw a sign, "Pelagano Village Industries" and we made a quick turn to the left, over a little bridge, aiming toward the house Joel had sighted.

We found a cluster of buildings when we got there, including three small rondavels near the main house. We heard music and as we climbed the paths to the house, found Heidi, who is in Joel's class at Northside, playing a recorder as she sat in the doorway of her own Rondavel.

Alberta came to the door to greet us and reported that Ben and Ruthie were both down with some phase of the flu so were sleeping in the house and not in their rondavels. She showed us around, from the steep solid rock behind them to the gardens in the front, and pointed out that the rondavels were stone and mortar at the bottom, but the upper parts were mud, as solid as concrete. They were finished in a coating of mud and cow dung, giving each a hard non-dusty surface.

These were decorated in traditional designs by an old woman using a feather to apply the various shades of clay, available all around here.

Joel asked if he might climb on the rocks at the back. Alberta had shown us where they had built a little wall on this rock to channel the water during rainy season. Joel and Heidi used this wall as a guide to run up the hillside where someday the water will be surging down to a holding tank.

Dick, the architect of this establishment, was hampered by a cast on his leg, having fallen through the roof of his latest building, so Alberta showed us around and explained their projects, saying, "Dick is teaching the men of the village to build, supervise building, to keep records, handle payroll and to estimate jobs, so they will be able to bid on jobs at other places."

We inspected an outdoor work-center with machinery for making fencing, a warehouse, a shop where women make cornhusk dolls and decorate gourds, a concrete-block plant, and the new building with the hole in the roof where Dick had fallen through.

Then there was the chicken business, the building in which they are raised and the slaughter house. We admired a new structure ready to house the ovens of a Bakery.

A pretty little thatched-roof rondavel nearby, trimmed with geometric designs, was the present office. We peeked in the windows at the orderly and cozy place. Nearby, a new office was being laid out; the footings were being poured for an oval rondavel. Blocks were nearby for the start of the walls.

"This is a brick maker" Alberta said, "see, it compresses the mud into good solid brick." Dick is teaching them to use rock at the base of their rondavels and mud bricks above, so they won't wash out in the rainy season.

On the way back from these projects I looked up to that stony face of the mountainside to see Joel spreadeagled against the smooth surface of the stone, hanging on by his fingertips and digging in the toes of his Adidas, here and there, trying for a foothold.

"Don't look. Don't look" was Alberta's advice—and sure enough, miraculously, by looking away a while, he suddenly appeared at the top scrambling to his feet and running down the channels of rock leading to lower regions.

It was great to visit with these folks from home and see how much they are accomplishing in this little village. Alberta sent us off later with a warm,

"Now, don't be strangers. Come out again on a Sunday afternoon and bring a picnic. You know Joel wants to climb on the rocks again!"

We had the farewell party for Zylla, the boy from East Berlin. He didn't register for school this session; said he was going to West Africa to stay with an uncle and go to school there. I saw him around quite often, at movies at night, walking the paths to the Mall during school hours. I talked to him one of these times and thought he was not very happy about going away. I suggested to Joel he have a party for him. This grew to be quite an affair—with seven boys for a big chicken dinner, two of them overnight and all of them off to the movies. It extended into the next day, with the overnights for breakfast and others back to play some more. From then on, Zylla appeared here the minute school was out each day, and he began to be a permanent fixture. Some days I began to wish I'd never suggested the party!

There began to be complications. He was on his Mother's passport and had to get a new one through the President's Office, then his ticket came in the wrong name, as he now has the name of his Mother's new husband.

It wasn't until this Sunday morning, July third, that he did get everything together. Roy and Joel went out the Airport then to see him off and Joel came home teary, but Zylla will be back at Christmas time. Roy said Zylla's mother did well. She waited until he was on the plane and gone until she broke down and cried. He's about 13 I guess. He just learned English this past year and now, in Guinea, I wonder if his schooling will be in French. He's a tall boy, quite dark and you'd never know he had any connection to his Mother, for she is a short German girl with very white complexion.

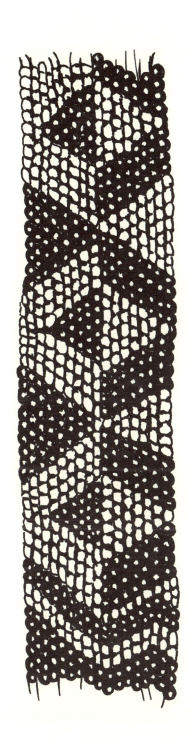

5

Enter, the
Peace Corps

As we set our food out on the table at the second Fourth of July picnic, a couple young fellows strolled up. One noticed our "Connecticut" name tags and excitedly asked, "Where? Where?" He had arrived from Connecticut himself just two weeks before.

"We're from Canterbury, about twenty-five miles north of New London."

"Yes, I know where that is. My home is in Hamden, near New Haven."

Roy went on to tell him that he had worked in Hartford for several years, but had gone down through New Haven for many more, working with the Tax Department.

"My father works for the Connecticut State Tax Department. He has the Waterbury Office."

"Your name is Julianelle? Well, your Dad must be Les Julianelle. I've known him for twelve years!"

The Peace Corps boys said they were doing their "Village Experience" now — staying out near Molepolole, but would be in town on Friday. We gave them our address and they promised to stop by.

On Saturday noon they all came for lunch; Tony Julianelle, Paul Storey of Boston, and Bill Johnston of Tacoma who is to be posted here at the Princess Marina Hospital, as an X-ray technician.

Bill had already been in to see the hospital and couldn't believe what he saw. "The equipment seems to be O.K.—but the rest!"

Tony told us he would be posted up past Palapye, off toward the South African border, way out in the boondocks (six hours away, with no phone connections), at Moeng College—a secondary school. He and Paul are both math teachers for secondary schools but Paul will be in Mahalapye which is about three hours up the road on blacktop.

Tony wanted to know what we missed here that we had at home. I told him you could get anything here that you could think of.

"How about chocolate? Good chocolate. I haven't seen any."

"Chocolate? Cadbury's everywhere—the best."

"But pizza! Is there any possibility?"

"Alice and Jeannine here make the best pizza in the world. You can find everything to make it, right here.

"Any place you'd like to go?" Roy asked as we finished our apple pie.

"Well, when we flew in from Joburg, we met Hazel and Larry Parker who were coming back from leave in Wyoming. They told us to come see them at the Ag College if we could" Tony said.

"Pile in. It's only a short drive to Sebele. We'll surprise them."

Dr. Parker was out raking his lawn and was glad to stop. It took him a few minutes to figure out what this delegation was. Six people in a station wagon with two sitting on the tailgate.

We all trooped in and Hazel joined us as soon as she finished kneading her rolls. She is a gray haired "country girl" who had three majors, but her real love is chemistry. She tutors, supervises the studies of children using correspondence courses, and works at the college.

"Hazel puts in more hours at the library than the faculty. Hours and hours, and she contributes her time" Larry told us.

Larry, a geneticist, teaches more than academics here. He instills proper hygiene practise, insisting on showers and proper attire before entering his classroom. He is good to the boys and collects clothes to have on hand for those in need.

As he showed us through the campus, he gave much good advice to Tony and Paul who would soon be starting their teaching.

Leaving Sebele, we passed the Pony Farm and Tony recognized the daughter of the Peace Corps Director riding there, and leaned out the window yelling, "Hey, we're having a party at the house tonight. Pizza. Come on over!"

Home again, I gave him a recipe for the crust and some yeast, but they needed cheese and I reminded him the stores all closed at noon.

Exception. We found one shop open in White City. Bill and Paul glumly reported, "No cheese" but Tony came out grinning, triumphantly waving a huge bar of Cadbury's chocolate!

Bill Johnston came in the other evening, just as we sat down to supper. He had had his first week or two on the job as an X-ray technician at the hospital and he was wound up over the things he has seen and the conclusions he has drawn so far.

"Boy, I've decided one thing. No one here moves fast. They just never do anything in a hurry." We had to laugh at this; it hadn't taken him long to find this out. They don't move fast and what's more, they don't care if they don't.

"The day is from 8 a.m. to 5 p.m. How they drag it out. They stop for a half-hour mid-morning for tea; the whole hospital comes to a screeching halt. Then it closes down completely for lunch from one to quarter after two. Then they all stop again for a full half-hour for the afternoon tea. I could do with a ten minute break mid-morning, just to sit down a while and relax, and the same mid-afternoon. Other than that, I'd like to get the work done."

"Another thing I can't go along with. There's a dressing room there at the X-ray area, but they never use it. They don't give gowns to the women. My assistant knows what that room is for but says they don't need it."

When I told Alice what he said, she expressed the opinion that it doesn't really matter to the Batswana; it's embarrassing to him, a young man, but probably doesn't mean a thing to the women. Then she said, "Why, the other day I looked out and there was a woman squatting in the gutter, across the road from the house. She evidently had to go, so she went. Her skirts were down around her during the process so it didn't matter too much, except that she was in a deep conversation with some man all during the time she was squatting. That was all right but when she was done, she stood and tossed her long skirts up over her head, then reached down and pulled up her little light blue underpants and adjusted them, so for a few minutes, she stood there all exposed— and calmly continued her conversation."

"You should see the filing system of the X-rays" Bill said. "I said to my assistant, 'Where can I put this now, so it'll be safe?' and he took it and tossed it up on top of the file! They have a file cabinet, but it isn't used. They don't really care if they can find X-rays again or not.

"I have been so busy. I'm doing IVP's and a lot of things they haven't been able to have done. There hasn't been anyone there but a couple of med service people.

"One thing I found out, and that is I can't work very well with the British doctors. My boss didn't give me five minutes time. Didn't tell me what he wanted or what he didn't want. Just nothing, like I wasn't even there. So, I just work around him, but the African doctors are fine to work with."

Tony says he won't be going to Moeng until next week sometime. He'll be here through the Trade Show and then some. They're trying to get word to the Head Master at the school to let him know Tony is coming, but that is difficult. I guess they depend on Police Radio.

He said there is nothing there except this secondary school. Not even a village. The school was started in the thirties. I wonder why one was set up in such an isolated spot. I guess it serves a large area, and may be in a central position. Students board at the school. It's a good thing Tony likes to read and seems the type who will manage in an out-of-the-way place. We wish him well.

There was a tap at the front door the other noon and Joel and I reached it at the same time. There was Zylla's little brother grinning and handing a paper toward us.

"This is for Joel—from Zylla."

Joel opened it hurriedly and read the typed letter. It was dated Luanda, Angola! and we thought he had gone up to Guinea. He had done fairly well with the writing—the English was quite good, but the typing like any kids who hadn't used a typewriter before.

Joel was glad to hear from Zylla, but we couldn't help wondering why in the world anyone would send his child to Angola, at this point. Of course, the point in sending him somewhere was to escape the new fees for school here. When he started they were eighteen dollars a session while now they are a hundred.

Yesterday as Joel passed his house, Zylla's little brother called out to him, "Zylla's coming home pretty soon."

In talking to him, Joel found there are lots of riots going on and it isn't safe for him to be there.

Bill Johnston came over again the other evening. He was disturbed this time that now in the one X-ray room there are four people! That day, Opa Rompa had appeared and Rompa intends to run the show.

This was amazing!

"Rompa is just back from two years training in Maylaysia. He is good—very good, fantastically trained. But he is going to run the place and there's no use in my being there. I have the two assistants; one is excellently trained and has had a lot of experience, the other well experienced, too, so what are we all going to do in that one room—especially now when all the equipment is broken down? Even the Mobile Unit is on the fritz and today, they blew a tube—just when the guy was X-raying a pregnant woman. It'll take P2000 to purchase a new tube."

When he ran down, Roy was able to interject the fact that we know Rompa's father—that he had told us last fall about his son being trained in Maylasia and wishing he could be home for Christmas—but that he wouldn't.

"Rompa's daughter is a nurse out at Livingstone Hospital in Molepolole, and her husband is Conference Lokomo, who works in the Tax Department," he added.

"Well," Bill replied, "They forgot all about him. The government, the Ministry of Health and everybody. They forgot, I guess, that he was being trained for this spot and that he would be available right now. In fact, he told me he had been sitting home a month waiting to be called in. Do you know what other hospitals there are in the country that might need me? I want to get transferred to somewhere where I can work!"

Funny how these characters eventually move into the same picture. We never expected when we talked to Rompa about his son that someday he would have an effect on the life of a young American Peace Corps worker whom we would accidentally get acquainted with.

Bill appears now and then, to borrow a crescent wrench to tighten up everything on his new bike, to sit and talk or play cards a while, or to catch a ride with us somewhere.

This morning when Joel went to school he carried his sleeping bag and a sack with sweater, jeans, old shoes and other overnight essentials. Mrs. Hopkins picked it up when she dropped her children off at school and took it back to Gabane with her. At noon, she will pick him up, along with other boys and girls who are invited to celebrate Heidi Hopkin's birthday in an overnight out in the village about twelve miles from town. Joel is enthusiastic about the expedition as they will get to climb on the big rocks and rocky walls of the steep Kopje against which the Hopkins' home is built.

Joel's friend Ross is along, and I don't know how many others. I was glad Ross was going, because this is scheduled the same evening as another Disco, at Thornhill School. Discos come and go, but one doesn't have the opportunity to go camping out in a village very often.

The fun part of the Trade Fair was the ten mile race. I wouldn't have known a thing about it except that Tony has been running daily since he arrived here, and he asked if we were going to come watch.

We did, and he finished in fifth place. We took pictures as he passed the end of Zebra Way and later at the Awards ceremony, to send to his Mom and Dad.

It has been Peace Corps time for us. We had Bill here a couple evenings, and gave him a special invitation for Friday evening dinner as Joel was away at Gabane.

He reported things going as usual at the hospital. Too many workers in the one X-ray room, so he showed us the letter he had written to the Ministry of Health asking to be sent where he could be of more use.

He pointed out that Rompa, being a Motswana, can be more effective as a teacher here, for the medical assistant's classes. He is hoping to hear within a few weeks that he will go to Maun, Serowe or somewhere.

He told us more anecdotes of his days there at the Hospital, and commented on the fact that modesty is an unknown word. The girls are not hesitant at all of being exposed down to the waist, and don't catch on to putting on the gowns for the X-rays.

"One girl came in the other day, and she was just huge in the bust—really huge. I took her to the dressing room and with a lot of pantomime told her to undress down to here, and put on this gown and tie it up in back, here, and closed the curtain on her. I waited and waited and when it was long past time she should have been ready, I called and then went and pulled back the curtain. I almost died—for there she was, stripped to the waist, and *RECLINING* on the little bench in there for dressing purposes, one only about a metre long, and narrow. I had to pull her up and put the gown around her and tie it—and have her come and sit for the X-ray. I guess that was one time my instructions and my pantomime wasn't enough!"

So Bill is looking for his new assignment and is not taking any housing assignment here.

AUGUST 22

Joel's trip to Gabane was a decided success. When we got back from the airport Saturday, we found him sleeping on the couch; his bedroll and dusty bag of dirty clothes down the hall. He was about as dirty as he had been when he came home from the safari onto the desert.

There had been seven kids. They had slept up on the hillside, had had a bon fire and didn't get to sleep. Mr. Hopkins had yelled at them after midnight and said if they didn't keep quiet, they'd all have to come down from the hill. Joel had ridden a motorbike of some kind down the road and back; once with another kid on it, and they had tipped over and he'd bumped his leg. He had burned his hand when he set it down on the top of the gas stove—or just after it had been turned off. It raised a nice big blister. He had climbed again on the face of the Kopje and had almost slipped down, hanging by his fingertips. They had seen the new ducks brought to keep the old Drake company and had gathered eggs from the new layers.

On Saturday, Ross MacCrae's Mother and Dad had come for them, along with a friend, and Ross' two younger brothers, and a picnic lunch. The MacCrae's drove them to Manana, where the Livingstones lived the years he was in this vicinity. They looked over the stone foundations and saw the big tree. Bill told us about the tree—that as many as fifty can meet under it. They had a fun picnic and a fine time but Joel did a lot of sleeping from then until the next evening.

This morning he discovered he doesn't have his school shoes. Ben Hopkins is going to look under his bed, in his rondavel and see if he can find them.

We have definite word from our daughter Susan that she will be arriving on September 28th. That is just a month away and we will start to mark our calendar with possible holidays and plans.

When we go to meet her in Johannesburg, it will be on a long holiday weekend, giving us time to explore the city and make stops at an animal reserve on the way home.

We wish she were to be earlier, to join us on a trip to Durban during school break, first week in September, but she won't, so we will proceed anyway; through the Drakenburgs, perhaps to Lesotho and Swaziland, and the beaches of Durban. We have to go when the days are available.

This day will be memorable—as the day when I first saw a Lilac Breasted Roller rolling!

Just as I got to the first tee this morning, having walked over alone, I noticed some movement of birds but didn't pay much attention until I suddenly saw one of them, with wings outspread, begin to dip first to the left and then the right. He didn't go far enough to quite tip over completely, but almost. As soon as he was almost upside down, he flipped up and dipped in the other direction, all the while flying straight ahead. I could see there were two of them putting on the same performance and I don't know whom they wished to impress. I thought it might be a courting procedure—"Look at me! See how I do!" Both of these might have been males—practising for the date they were looking forward to, now that Spring is almost here.

One of the nice things about going out, especially early in the day as we do, is that we always see rare (to me) birds. There are shrill or melodious songs from tiny or huge birds, in all the thorn trees we pass. There are cranes and herons in the boggy or grassy places off to the sides or between the fairways. Yesterday three huge blue-grey herons flew over us and lighted on the green ahead. They stood there a long time as we worked our way towards them.

August 19

Yesterday Pauline showed me this composition she had written for class. She was disappointed the teacher had marked her 27/40. She couldn't understand the low grade and wanted me to read it. I gave her a few suggestions on the use of English, as "The people who are" instead of "Those people who are in", but I assured her that I thought she had done a good job, and asked if I might copy it.

The Village I Know

A village I know is Molepolole. It is a big village. Those people who are in Molepolole are called Bakwena. It is 70 kilometres from Gaborone. The chief of Molepolole is Mr. Bonewamang Sechele. The chief stays in the middle of Molepolole. The chief's house is one the left of the main road from Gaborone.

It is divided into five big areas. There are five Headmen. The first ward is Kgosing. The second Makgalo. The third one is Gontloedibe. The fourth is Ntlhayatlase and New Town. The inhabitants are of mixed tribal origins. Some are originally from Tsabong others from Kgalagadi. We have got so many building in Molepolole.

There is a hospital in Molepolole. Its name is Scottish Livingstone. There is Kgari Sechele Secondary School near the hospital. There is United Christian Church on the right side of the road to the hospital. The home craft and the Brigades buildings are on the left side of the road. About five yards, is Mayenyatlala Hotel. With other camps, are the Police camp, the Post Office, Immigration, and other offices. The shops are not in the same area.

I like Molepolole because it is my home Village. Since I was born there I have never got into trouble. Those people in Molepolole are very good and they respect each other. The chief respects his people.

She also had as a lesson, a friendly letter.

Lesedi School
P.O. Box 84
Gaborone
3rd August 1977

Dear Dorcas,

    I am here in Botswana. I am attending school at Lesedi School. Our school started at 7:30 up to 1 o'clock. Our Headmaster is Mrs.

Mmonono. We have nine teachers in our school. We have a nice building. Our school builds with bricks.

> My school is near Community Centre. It is in the middle of the roads North Ring Road and Independence Road. We have interesting games at school. Our class teacher used to teach us many subjects. In our class we are forty-four. Our class is the third flat from the right.
>
> Your friend,

Her school hours are 5:30 P.M. to 9:30 P.M., but she said they were to write the letter as though they were regular day students. I advised her that one would say "at the intersection of", the two roads, also, "the school is built of bricks", and "There are 44 in our class". Only little things, and I assured her she wrote very well—that I would never be able to learn Setswana the way she is mastering English.

We were just starting a game of Hearts when Joel strode across the porch—with his torch—home from Bill's and an evening visiting with the Peace Corps guys. He said Paul had much to report about Mahalapye. They turn off the electricity at will—pull the master switch for the town, any time after four p.m. They have him teaching English instead of Math. There are five people in his apartment, all trying to get breakfast at once on a single stove plate. I imagine he's wallowing in the comfort of Bill's apartment here in town this week. Tony is expected down from Moeng this weekend, and perhaps he'll drop in today and tell us all about his area.

As I completed my shopping this afternoon, I headed down towards the Museum and home. Just then, two huge Herero women appeared in their brilliant dress. All Herero women seem to be huge. These two had voluminous bright patchwork dresses, which are not designed to minimise the fat bottoms that protrude in the rear, almost shelf-like, or the expanse of the front. Both looked as though they were expecting, and had oval "bibs" decorating and emphasizing the bulge. The oval, brilliant yellow with embroidery, extended from under the chin to shooting off the precipice about where the waist should be. The full shirts were the most bulky at hip line, where they were gathered on and the gatherings extended upwards in another ruffle. Both were tall, wearing bright head wrappings in a triangular shape, and one carried a twenty-five pound bag of flour on her head. They were laughing and happy looking, but evidently tired, as all of a sudden, they decided to sit and rest. They sat right there on the sidewalk in front of the hardware store—one of the busiest places; sat with their backs against the low wall which separates the walk from the open mall in the center, and extended their feet straight out in front of them. Pedestrians would have to step high and at their own risk.

I was somewhat mesmerized by this operation and I was irritated that I did not have the camera along. When I do carry it, nothing exceptional comes up and now here I was missing something good.

Just then someone grabbed my arm, panting and calling "Mrs. Brown!" Here was Tony. He had run after me.

"Hey, I've been looking for you. The guys said you were down. News travels. I hear you like the place and that you are off to Swaziland!"

"Yes. Leaving tomorrow morning."

"Do you have some time today? How about dinner tonight?"

"Great. Then I can tell you all about the school and all."

So I left him, telling him to come anytime toward six, and wondering what I would get for dinner. I was too tired by now to go back to any stores to get anything special and went on toward home.

Tony came just before seven. He had some things to leave here, such as his duplicate passport, shoes, and a few books. We stowed them away, and then sat down to hear about his school.

"It's going to be fine. It is a lovely valley—nothing there but the school compound. Over five hundred students, all boarding. The nearest village is a small one about five miles away. The Headmaster is great. He has been there eleven years. Extremely fine Headmaster. That's going to make all the difference. He is South African educated."

"Where are you going to live?"

"I've decided to share a house with another teacher, an Indian who teaches science. I could have had a place of my own, but I figure if I lived alone for two years, I'd get too fussy and want everything just to suit myself all the time. This way, it'll be good to share the quarters, cooking and all, with someone else. It's a large house with large screened porches on two sides, and doors into the bedrooms off the porches."

Then I asked him about his supplies, food.

"A truck goes to Palapye three times a week, so I give the driver a list to buy for me at the store. They keep an account for us."

"You'll owe your soul to the Company store! Huh?"

"Oh, like Sixteen Tons." and laughed.

"Well, if the truck goes to Palapye three times a week that means you can get out of there if you need to."

"That's an hour and three quarters ride—and doing that in the back of a truck on that rough road in the dust is no way to go."

Roy added, "Well, we'll come up and see you some weekend, perhaps in October."

"You will? Boy, when visitors come it's a real big deal. We'll have a place you can stay."

"If you have that big house with the porches, there would be a place as long as we brought along sleeping bags."

"Visitors wouldn't have to do that! There'll be a place for you."

He described the location as a beautiful valley and said he had a pleasant surprise when he got there. Rick, one of the teachers, is a Peace Corps man from Bethany, Connecticut—about six miles from where Tony grew up and they found they had mutual acquaintances.

Everything works out well for Tony. Rick too, is interested in mountain climbing, and was planning to go to Swaziland for the rest of the school leave, so Tony is to go along. They have arranged to get a ride all the way, with the Peace Corps Doctor who lives here in the village. The Doctor serves Botswana, Swaziland and Lesotho.

So, Tony seemed happy with everything. Said he would send for his ropes, though, for mountain climbing. He is the kind of person who likes people and makes friends easily, yet enjoys being alone and reading. He doesn't mind the prospect of being in that distant school compound for months at a time. It won't be dull and may have many advantages over being here in the city.

AUGUST 29

There was a note from the Pahls on our door Friday evening when we got home from the movies. "We arrived home safely this eve from Francistown. See you tomorrow!"

We lost no time in the morning getting over to see them-carrying their mail which Roy had collected from the office.

The kids rushed out, talking a mile a minute, telling about zebra skins, wooden canoes, carved heads, and live elphants they had seen.

Skins were spread on their big coffee table in the living room, and a few were being dragged around by loving hands! Patty had appropriated one for herself, having asked her mother after they started home which one was "hers".

They had riotous tales to tell. When I told Jeannine I was anxious to sit down with her mother alone and hear all the stories of their travelling with Ben and Vi Webb and Dammy, she said "They aren't stories! They're all *TRUE!*"

The two families had met in Francistown and the next day they all went on to Chobe Game Park in the northwest corner of Botswana. The first hundred kilometers was paved, then there was about eighty kilometers of detour—very bad road, and the rest was the new Nata-Kazungula highway built with U.S. A.I.D. funds.

Chobe more than fulfilled their expectations. In driving the road along the edge of the Chobe River, they saw more game than they had expected. Elephants by the hundreds—Kudu, Rhino, and some with baby ones, which were really babies. "I expected a baby rhino to be big," Alice commented, "This was actually tiny-so cute."

"Well, Ben did have a little trouble one time driving near an elephant that had a young one. She gave him a good trumpeting and waved her trunk at him ominously—but didn't charge the car."

"You'll never believe what happened when we went over into Zambia to Victoria Falls. After seeing the Falls and taking pictures, and shopping in the craft stalls, we allowed plenty of time to get back to the Kazungula Ferry. Soon after five we drove up ready to line up for the six o'clock ferry. Just as we stopped, we saw all the crew leaving the ferry, and the customs men closing up shop.

"'Diesel is finished' was their explanation. 'No ferry until tomorrow.'" Here we were on the Zambia side, without much money -in fact, no Kwacha, our clothes and camping equipment over on the Botswana side, all twelve of us stranded."

"So, guess where we spent the night?" Alice asked. "At the Musio Tunya Intercontinental!"

"There was a motel up the road a ways—couldn't you have stayed there?" I asked.

"The problem was the money, we had to stay somewhere that we could use an American Express card."

Earlier that day when they got off the ferry, they chose what looked like a good restaurant, and as they went in, there sat Dr. Curry. He was so surprised to see them. He said he was doing studies in Zambia and to send regards to all. He also told them that they would get a much nicer lunch for less by going to the buffet at the Musio-Tunya, so they took his advice. Alice said it was probably the best meal she had eaten since leaving home. Little did they realise as they were enjoying it, that they would later, that same day, be back for the night!

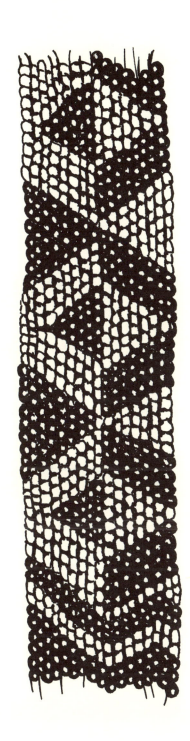

6

Far and Wide

SEPTEMBER 15, 1977

During our holiday trip to Durban and back through Swaziland, I was wondering as we rode along about how I would start my written commentary on the expedition and concluded that the only good lead would be, "Thank God it's over!!"

Now, later, with a little perspective after being home again, relaxed and happily caught up in our pleasant routine, it is easy to recall all the pleasant episodes, all the wonders we saw; the sights and sounds and smells that will always be there in our minds, to pull out and relive.

Swimming in the Indian Ocean at Durban's South Beach where we had a holiday flat just a block away, it was hard to believe that India was off across and beyond that perpetually breaking surf. There were great ships off in the distance every time we looked up, either anchored or moving slowly in around the point to Durban's big bay. The thunder of the surf never stopped, and it was so loud, one had to shout over it to be heard. The swimmers moved up or down the beach, each day, to new sites marked by the lifeguards and their bright flags; kept in an area where it was reasonably possible to keep an eye on them as they rode the waves. Resounding announcements came once in a while, warning surfers to move out of the swimmers area, or to move at least forty-five meters from the jetty. Great waves crashed constantly into the jetty, and one wondered how the surfers managed to escape slamming into the pilings too, but I guess they knew their waves.

The beach had fine sand, few stones and few shells. We decided the water must be fairly warm, as people walked into it without the preliminaries of shivering and gingerly moving ahead sucking in the stomach or drawing away from splashes of others running in. Surprise! When we stepped in, we found it icy. It didn't take long though, to be tossed about by the breakers and to find yourself comfortably adjusted to the temperature.

Behind the hotels was the big city, rushing along with business as usual. First time we had been at a beach area where such a large "normal" city was right against the play area.

Luring us on to the very end of this beach was the building, or wall rather, on which we could read "Snake Park". I loathe snakes, but it was there and we were ready to see something about African snakes.

It was as gruesome as I expected. Repulsive snakes of various degrees of venomousness! Snakes like the black mamba and green mamba were completely enclosed behind glass. The worst was a huge hooded cobra which watched us with bright and evil eyes—moving and moving and glaring, with it's hood flared out, its head a good twenty inches in the air. You could almost read its thoughts. Thank heavens for the glass between us!

Well, Joel and I turned back after the snake park; walked the far side of Lower Marine Drive, seeing new parks, amusement areas, walks and gardens. We stopped at a Wimpy Bar next to the Aquarium for a hamburger, and were surprised that while seated we had a view of one of the big fish tanks. Fun to sit there and watch the sharks and other exotic fish hurrying by.

Well, we went on past this, walked out on a couple jettys which are a bit scary—that surf is so mighty. Out at the end of one huge concrete jetty, on which we felt safer than on those of wood, we saw schools of bright puffer fish—cream and brown striped. We were out far enough to be beyond the breakers, so the water was smooth and clear. A delight to see such fish in their natural habitat—not in an aquarium.

On the way down to Durban, mile after mile, from the edge of Joburg, where we left the great mountains from the gold mining, all the way down to where the foothills of the Drakensburgs began, there was farm country as far as you could see, and it seemed you could see farther than any place I'd ever been before.

Along here, the Bantu homes were delightful, all decorated in their traditional designs. Small square mud houses and a few rondavels, were entirely covered with geometric designs, in a bright or pastel scheme. Once in a while there would be one done in beige and brown, and instead of geometric, the design would be floral. Huge blossoms and leaves, one blossom reaching from ground to roof.

Houses fascinated me, for there is a decided difference in construction in different areas. As we drove north through Zululand later, away from Durban and going toward Swazi, you could see that the basic structure of the native home was a framework of thin wooden poles. The corners and some posts were oversized, but the rest was a mass of cane poles only a few inches apart. When this grill of a house was tied together, it was filled from the inside with mud and stones. Perhaps they were to be covered with mud on the outside, and smoothed off, possibly decorated, but it appeared that once the framework and one layer of mud and stone was applied, it was put to use. These were square buildings, with a sloping roof—also of closely laid cane and weren't much higher than a man could stand.

Then there were the grass huts, quite large, that resembled igloos; perfect domes of grass, sometimes smooth, sometimes with some edges of layers of thatch. These we saw throughout Zululand, and in Swazi. In other places in the Transvaal, there were clusters of both rondavels and square huts, just as the families have here. All along the road from Swazi to Pretoria, we saw them gayly decorated in lovely designs.

Something caught our eye as we first drove into Durban, and our entrance was right down the main street, straight to the beach. Just as I thought we'd be driving onto the sand, the road turned into a street parallel to the beach. As we reached this point, we saw a cluster of Rickshaw men in bright Zulu costumes, ready to give any tourist a ride. Each rickshaw was decorated; the wheels run through with bright strands, like bikes in a Fourth of July parade. But the rickshaw was nothing compared with the gear the man was wearing himself.

It was hard to locate his face at first, for only a small part of it showed. A huge headdress rose three or four feet above, spreading out on either side, draped with wide bands of bead work. Huge cattle horns, brightly painted, curved out and held some of the trimmings. Cloth and straw medallions, zulu dolls, decorated strips of straw matting, ribbons and yarn fanned out and hung down—some sweeping as low as his waist.

A skirt of fur tails hung from his waist to the ground, flapping in all directions as he walked or ran along with the rickshaw which was as large as a regular old-time buggy, without a top. It did have a third little wheel, on a short leg, in the rear and he would run along for a while then give a leap and sit up on the front between the "shafts" and let the vehicle ride along on that little wheel in the back. This way, the occupants got a roller-coaster ride.

They were very commercial-minded though, and it was almost impossible to get a picture of them; it had to be on the sly, for if they saw a camera coming, they rushed at you—tails flying, huge headdress wagging and tipping, threatening to flop off, in all its glory, as they reached out for money, and rattled off how much they wanted for a picture. In fact, each was so boisterous, I couldn't figure out if he wanted me to take his picture, for me to get in and ride, or to pay him for posing. After our first encounter, we steered clear of them and enjoyed them from a distance.

We arrived in Durban shortly after noon on Sunday, and after a drive along the beach, began to study the hotels and holiday flats. There

were plenty available and we soon found where they began to get tacky
and in which direction they began to be too high priced (comparatively).
Armed with a page of ads from the Rand Daily Mail, we narrowed our
choice to a few places a block off the beach. Then, I found the Impala
Flats—fully furnished, beds for four, T.V. included, with a view R10 a
night, without the view, R9 a night. We took one with a view, for four
nights, got the car tucked into the garage, our suitcases brought up and
then looked out at our view. Roy said, "There's the Dunns."

"What do you mean?"

"There's the Dunns. They just parked their car and are walking
along by the park."

I'll be darned, he wasn't kidding us. Joel opened the window and
called to them and I opened another and waved. Joel then ran down to
meet them and bring them up to our flat. With all the thousands in that
city, how did we see them the first few minutes we located a place? Even
not looking out at that minute would have meant we'd miss them. Well,
we had a good laugh. They didn't stay long because they were headed
to the Dolphinarium to see the afternoon show, so Joel and I went along
and didn't get back until toward six. I enjoyed it as much as their three
little girls, but all the while it was on, I felt I was down in St. Petersburg
or back at Mystic, Connecticut.

The evening before we left, I realised I hadn't bought any of the
Zulu articles that were spread on the sidewalks near the beach during the
day. The women sat there with the bead work laid out in rows, the little
dolls, beaded or dressed in lambs wool, arranged among the strings of
seed beads and crocheted work. I remembered that late each evening, as
we walked through the amusement park where Joel had his choice of
one ride each night, we had seen women cruising around with an arm
strung with seed necklaces and dangling dolls, so I scraped up a few
Rand and ventured down. It was well after dark, and I went the back
way through the garage and across the alley, the road, and a bit of park,
down the street towards the cinema and the center where you pick up
the motor tours. Sure enough, there were three women still around and
I chose two dolls and some beads from one, using up all my money.
Then a lady offered me a doll which I fell in love with—lambs wool
dress but beaded bodice and big hat. Cute as could be, but I held up my
empty pocketbook and shook it at her to make it clear I had finished.
Though I still wish I had that doll.

Well, reading the paper Friday, I saw that on that evening, a man
had been stabbed on the beach right by that cinema—so badly he was in

intensive care, and another couple had been assaulted—the woman stabbed in the chest. Just at the time I was wandering down there by myself! Well, our guardian angels are on the job, or maybe the robbers had seen me shake that empty pocketbook!

Reluctantly, looking longingly at the beaches, we drove out of Durban and headed north.

We were soon in the midst of sugar cane fields. They rolled on, hill after hill. We had the ocean off to the right and the low hills to the left, the cane being thicker and shorter than I imagined it would be. Cane cutters were busy and we saw them working all the way from here to Swaziland.

Trucks of cane, train loads of cane, piles and stacks of cane, narrow gauge railways carrying toy trains loaded with cane. Cane, cane, cane, and sugar mills. Cane cutters and cane cutter's villages. There was no end. We put off stopping for lunch at a hotel in Salt Rock, where we veered off to find a restroom, as I pointed out there was a large town coming up, on the map. We went on to find the big town, Darnell, with cane, cane, cane. The mill, the store, truck loads of cane coming and going, Hewletts Mills, Hewletts School, Hewletts Club and no sign of a tea room or restaurant.

On we went as far as a town with the fascinating name of Gingind-lovu. This was sugar too, with a railroad running parallel to the main street. We turned into a short street on which there was a huge old Dutch-style Imperial Hotel, draped in so much bright cerise Bougain-villaea—we had to stoop to miss the blossoms hanging over the entrance. It was a huge hotel, with lounges and rooms and verandas in all direc-tions on the first floor—plus clean, clean, well appointed rest rooms—always of prime importance on trips.

The dining room had just closed and the chef away, but we were served hot toasted ham and cheese sandwiches and coffee in one of the lounges.

We had a good view at the same time, and could watch the antics of the town "halfwit" who danced around the area, happily visiting with all who passed, and we also saw an albino black. She was cream colored, her kinky hair luminous cream. We felt sorry for both, more so for the Albino as one could imagine how difficult her life must be.

This area we had driven through was Shaka's territory. We had passed Shaka's Rock, Shaka's Kraal, and many plaques and signs de-noting battle places. There was Ultimatum Tree, Coward's Bush,

Cetshwayo's Grave and later, beyond Richard's Bay, "Bulawayo, site of
Shaka Kraal". I was surprised to see a Bulawayo down there. It must be
what Bulawayo, Rhodesia took its name from, later.

I could escape more writing now, by dashing down to the Library
and looking up some correct information on Shaka. I know he's the
Great Zulu Chief who defeated the British. He also was instrumental in
driving the Bantu up across Africa—that's why they came up in this
direction. He supposedly warred and slew so that tribes and tribes
moved on and away from him. I think he was about the only one who
ever got the best of the British—that is, except for us!!

We were in Natal, in Pietermaritzburg, where we stayed one night.
From there, in the Valley of the Thousand Hills north, it is Zululand;
referred to as Kwa Zululand (I don't know what the Kwa means) and it
was some of the most beautiful land I ever drove through. I would have
loved getting into some of the area off the big throughway, but what
we saw gave us a good idea of their country and some idea of how they
live.

Often we saw groups walking toward us along the roadside and
girls only had on skirts. They were young though, and the sights
weren't so startling that Roy ran off the road. The houses were grass
domes and often the square cane houses, filled with rocks and mud. We
were sorry eventually to have the road go inland and lose the views of
the ocean.

Late in the afternoon, almost evening, we decided we'd pull off on
one of the crossroads, and see what a village would have to offer in the
line of snacks or petrol. We chose Hluhluwe, and as we turned toward
it, we found ourselves driving between acres and acres of Aloe. The
blossom stem was tall, taller than corn, and you could see the fields had
been planted with them—all in neat rows. From then on we saw thousands of acres of it.

Well, peering through the aloe about three kilometers up this road
I saw a familiar sign and said, "There's a Holiday Inn!"

"What are you talking about?"

"There's a Holiday Inn."

"Quit kidding. Oh—you're right! There is a Holiday Inn!"

Sister to our own Holiday in Gaborone, there it was. We stopped,
had more toasted sandwiches out by the pool, Joel looked over the
tennis court and Roy read his newspaper. Joel was all for staying here,
but as there was still some light, Roy wanted to go on further. There
was a huge animal reserve a few kilometers from this, but it was about
closing time so after getting petrol, we reluctantly left the Inn; out in the

nowhere, lost in a field of aloe—an oasis for travellers going from Durban to Swazi.

We were told there were no hotels in Canover, up ahead, but there were, at Mkuze. So we went on, thus passing by the Umfolozi Game Reserve, the St. Lucia Reserves and Take, the Hluhluwe Reserve and the Mkuze Reserve. I then realized the reasons for the Inn location.

By the time we neared Mkuze it was dark. Black dark, but lighted ominously in the distance by fires; great fires sweeping along at a fast rate. I thought we had reached a lighted town when we discovered that what we were looking at was a burned over area, with trees of different heights and tree stumps, still all burning and bright with coals. The fire seemed to be on all sides of the town and this seemed less than a relaxing situation. We followed signs through the town when we did finally get there, and eventually found the Ghost Mountain Inn.

"Now why did you have to tell me the name of it?" Joel wanted to know. He was already nervous about the ring of fire.

In the daylight we found we were still surrounded by cane fields and numerous signs warned motorists to watch for the narrow gauge cane trains whose tracks ran across the highway at intervals.

More fires sweeping over hills and through forests were to be seen on our left from the highway. It was a scenic route; mountains, forests, deep valleys, rolling cane fields. Many changes from the flatland, and from the coastland we had just been through.

We circled under Swazi staying on the big road, and entered at the Border Post after reaching Amsterdam. It was the first time we had been asked for our vaccination record at a South African border post and as we had not before had to show the shot record, I had left it home. She didn't fuss, just advised us to carry them along with the passports.

As Larry Parker said last evening, "Swaziland is overrated". The first part was exciting, for we were in the forests as soon as we crossed the border. Tree farming is the big thing in this area. All the forests were planted, in rows, and were in various stages of growth. Some hillsides were cleared, some covered with young trees. Roads led into the deep forests, marked with the name of that owner. We were soon on very winding roads with steep descents and advice to travel in second gear.

Good thing we had our new brakes. After much descent—we spotted the huge sawmill in the valley below. Wood was chipped or chopped and blown into great mountains of this coarse "sawdust"—so high that a huge bulldozer was way up on top—pushing it around. And he was dwarfed by the height. Dangerous I'd say, pushing around on a sawdust pile—not pile—mountain.

After the beach and coast at Durban, this seemed a letdown and there didn't seem any reason to stay a day or so. It was a holiday anyway and everything dead. So we agreed to head toward Pretoria and see what we'd run into.

The route was a good one, but it was well past dark when we got as far as Witbank. We were familiar with this city, it being one where we had seen for one of the first times, apartheid in action, in a big way, with black (I mean non-white) taxis and buses and parks.

It didn't take long to get to Pretoria in the bright sunshine the next morning, barrelling down that big thruway. Miraculously we sped through the city, without getting off the route. Once you make a wrong turn in that city and lose your bearings, no map is worth a thing and the exit route disappears completely. We were through the city faster than ever before, assured all the time by familiar landmarks that we were right and headed for Hartebeestport.

This lovely cove and resort, which I described last year as having big homes hanging up the mountainside above it, is a sad sight now. In just a short time, water hyacinth has grown a solid floor completely across the "lake" in the river, leaving all the boats landlocked—or so they look. Dark brown and greenish textured repulsive plants are all you can see where last year was blue sparkling water with boats zipping around and pretty sails moving in the wind.

We knew we could make the border gate before night, so passed up another overnight and went on.

Joel was all for it and had said to me, "Let's get on home. I'm sick of this dragging around. Let's go home."

We took our shortcut from the Marico River across to the Tlokweng Road, but it was so rough and so dusty, Roy said later he's not going to take it again. He'll stick to the blacktop road, right down to Zeerust, even if it is a lot farther.

This area near the Marico is always pleasant for it is a farming area with irrigation systems. The fields are so green you can't believe it. Looking off to some of the patches as we went down, Joel protested they weren't real. They looked as though they were filled in with bright lime and green chalk.

Along this back road I saw the loveliest picture. A field on the left, close to the road, of tall waving grass; light, and dry and shimmering champagne color. The thorn trees, dotted over it, were already bright green and they cast black shadows on this pale grass which changed shape a bit as the breeze moved through them. I wish I could paint it, or had had a chance to take a picture of it.

There was a letter for Pauline in our accumulated mail and the next day she excitedly told us that her sister Vivian had had a baby boy. It had been born on the fourth; this was the 11th. Pauline had stayed here in her house all the while we were gone, so hadn't known about the baby arriving. You don't get mail here unless you have a Post Office box, or get it through someone's Private Bag.

She said, "I told Vivian that if it was a girl, she should name it Elizabeth and if it was a boy, it should be Roy."

"What did she name it?"

"I don't know."

She didn't go home until the next weekend and she reported Monday morning that the baby is all right. "Very small."

"Smaller than Lillian's Lovemore was?"

"Oh yes."

Well, that's a baby for each of the girls in the family except for Katherine, the youngest. I haven't seen any fathers, but there is no such thing in Botswana as an illegitimate baby. Babies are welcomed and loved and somehow, they are provided for.

Later this afternoon I was working out back trimming some plants and all of a sudden Lillian and Lovemore appeared. I walked toward them and Lovemore grinned and reached out for me to take him. What a friendly baby he is. I asked Lillian how the new baby was and she said "Fine", and then I asked, "What did she name him?" and she replied, "Roy". I couldn't believe it. Joel couldn't either when he heard about it later and said, "You're kidding, aren't you?"

I told him it was an honour and he puzzled over that and then said, "Oh yeah. Charles is named for Daddy and Susan for you."

SEPTEMBER 21

Pula! Pula! Pula! The rains have come in September! Earlier than we expected but perhaps this is normal and last year was the exception. That turned out to have sprinkles in October and November and nothing heavy until late in January, too late for crops.

We are happy about the rain, but right now, we are elated that within a week our daughter Susan will be flying in from Maine, to stay a few months. We are primed for the trip to meet her and have reservations at a resort in Rustenberg for a couple days before coming home.

OCTOBER 28

It was rainy when we started out for Johannesburg a month ago to meet our Susan's plane. Rainy isn't descriptive enough. The afternoon we drove down past the Holiday Inn, off past the Village and out toward the Tlockwieng Road, we were surrounded by rainbows.

There was a fine mist of rain and a gleaming sun and huge double colorful arches looped over us and dropped their colors down in front of the rim of kopies, beyond the flatland. You swore you could see right where they touched the ground. As the road twisted and turned, we had different views of the rainbows and they increased and decreased in brilliance, all the way to the border gate.

There were glimpses of them later, but we were soon mired in handling the car on the slippery roadway, and all concentrated on watching for deep mud, helping to choose the best route among the ruts and mentally keeping the car straight. We didn't look up much until we were at last on the blacktop and coming through the mountain passes above Zeerust.

Climbing the last rise to where you break between the mountains and look down on the lush green valley, with more mountains in the distance, is always thrilling. You know as soon as you see the valley why people settled there. But this afternoon, it was the most beautiful sight we ever saw. Far off to our left, arching way up over the highest hilltop, sweeping across the sky, and dropping down into the village, was the most huge rainbow we had ever seen in our lives. It touched down among the houses, with the purple hills way in back of it and the big arch had a replica of itself, reflecting its colors in almost as bright stripes. We marvelled at the size and color. We seemed to be near the top of it, and all the way down the big highway, almost five miles of descent—we watched it, exclaiming over the once-in-a-lifetime sight.

"Beats any MacDonald's arch we ever saw!" commented Roy.

The sight was some compensation for our mud-coated car and the treacherous drive. Without the rain, we'd not have had the rainbow.

We stood at the rail in the airport in Johannesburg straining for a sight of Susan among all those processing their way out to the waiting room. Doors slid open once in a while and we'd stretch and search for the short time there was visibility. It seemed to take forever, but eventually she came through the sliding door and we rushed to hug her. She was very tired, as she had been sick when she stopped in Luxumbourg and the crowded flight from there had been fourteen hours in seats not roomy or comfortable. So we dragged her around to see the city the next day while she was in less than sightseeing shape.

A stop at the Wildlife Reserve in Krugersdorf with a speedy whirl past the animals grazing contentedly as a herd of cows didn't leave Susan feeling that she had seen Africa's animals in the wild.

We went on to the Rustenberg Kloof, the ideal place for a family weekend. The chalet was lovely, with windows all across the front where you could lie in bed, with your head on the window sill in the morning and listen to the raucous and shrill concert of the birds with a few monkey squawks thrown in. The little houses, one occupied by the Pahl family, were high on the hillside, with a sweeping view of the valley and hills beyond.

We climbed the mountain trails behind us, but there was a limit as to how far we'd go. The boys went on up the treacherous parts and in behind the waterfall, but it looked like only mountain goats should try that.

Susan, Jeannine and I had a good walk and found a huge rock to sit on, removed from the world, and we talked for hours.

Joel met a girl from Orange Free State who teamed up with him and the Pahl boys for tennis. She wasn't soon forgotten.

If Susan was looking for "wild", she found it; our trip the rest of the way home!

We tore up over the bumpy road, barely missing cows and donkeys in the tracks; we even saw a donkey's head in the road. We did make the border post in time and an hour later, were in Gaborone.

Pauline was happy to meet Susan and as the days passed, the sisters all appeared too, to see her.

Lillian's little Lovemore appeared with a bandaged right hand. He had caught it in a "swimming pool machine" which had taken off the end of the fourth finger. It took off the top part of the finger from the last knuckle to the tip. The nail is gone completely; awful looking. I soaked it and then bandaged it with a generous amount of Terramycin salve. Poor little guy. He was a year old Monday, and is still grinning happily even with the injured finger.

Vivian also came down, with little Roy and he's a different appearing baby. Big squirrel cheeks, flat little nose and bright eyes that are always focused somewhere else!

We had bought gifts for Vivian's Roy when in Johannesburg so took them with us one Saturday morning on a drive out to show Susan Molepolole. Pauline couldn't go because she had finished school exams the day before and was busy planning a celebration party.

The road to Molepolole is being improved, which means that in the process, it is all worse than usual. We travelled on the detour, parallel to the old road some of the time and urged Roy to take his time—there was no rush. It is a long ride, and much sameness. Thorn trees, dust, donkeys, herds of cattle wandering across the road, little villages, or kraals in sight across some of the sandy, brushy fields, bus stops with huddles of people waiting in the sun—or sitting in the shade with the luggage left at the stop as a signal for the driver. Weaver's nests decorated the trees, all hanging on one side, like handfuls of hay caught by the thorns from a passing hayload going to a barn. They look that way, but are a masterpiece of construction.

At long last we saw the big village in the distance, and were soon on the blacktop that runs through the center. We went the full distance, ending at the entrance to the Livingstone Hospital—drove in around the grounds and down through the village to Pauline's home stand. We stopped in front, surprised to see it had a new wall of concrete block (was that where the building blocks had been used?). We went up into the yard where several children milled about, but none that I recognised. A young woman came to greet us and I introduced her to Susan as "Catherine, Pauline's sister".

"Where is Vivian and the new baby?" I asked and handed her the package with the blanket, booties and rompers.

"She is at the hospital. The baby is sick, since yesterday."

"Where is Thandi?"

"She is far, at her Daddy's."

So, we went on and stopped at several stores. Susan was amazed how well they were stocked. Everything one needs, and some extras, are on hand, in neat Indian shops spotted throughout the village.

We didn't find any vegetables or fresh fruit, so that gave Roy an excuse to race back to town before the stores closed at one. He was happy glancing at his watch between bumps in the road and slithering between loose cows, all the way home.

The Webbs were down the end of the first week Susan was here. They asked, "When are you coming to Serowe?" and Susan took them up on the invitation to go back with them for a visit.

OCTOBER 30

I had given up "taking it easy" and "getting a lot of rest"; still wasn't my normal self with any energy, so the day that Susan came in from Serowe on the early train, she went to bed and I walked down to Dr. Lentsentyane's office.

"Is there a crowd ahead of me?"

"No, only three. Come in."

So I sat down and leafed through some magazines and spent time glancing at the people also waiting, when suddenly a man rushed in, saying to the receptionist, "Back again. My secretary called and I was told I could come right away."

"Come in. What's the problem?"

"A scorpion bite. I was told to come right away."

The nurse disappeared and he came and sat on the chair near me.

"How did that happen?" I asked.

"It was on my sock and bit my arm when I picked it up."

He rubbed his arm where the streaks were working up toward the elbow.

"Well, you go ahead of me. I'm in no hurry."

"Thanks. They did tell me to come right away, but now I'm here, nothing is happening. This is the second one I've had in the matter of weeks. I was in this morning, on something else, and didn't bother about the bite, but then it kicked up."

"The second bite? Are they in your house all the time?"

"This heat has brought them out. You have to be careful. The snakes are coming out now too. You have to be careful on the golf course. Watch for those puff adders. They lie perfectly still all curled up. They blend in the path and you might not see them at all, or might think they are a cow-flop. Have to be careful."

"I hear there's a python out at the far end."

"Python? That's nothing to worry about. It's not poisonous."

He had an accent and I was wondering what it was—German? Scandinavian?, and finally asked him, saying I couldn't place it.

"I'm Swedish. I can tell you're from New England. I've visited there. I did a study on resorts. Went on up to the Maine border and all over Vermont and New Hampshire. Say, I didn't even know about the Trapp family until I got there. Up there, they build the chalets in the mountains just the way they do in the Alps. Then I went out to Aspen and to Lake Tahoe."

He went on to say the Tahoe is one of the clearest purest lakes in the world, second only to one up in some mountains in Russia.

I told him we had been in Sweden briefly, having driven down to Malmo. I tried to pronounce it correctly—missing by quite some, and he said it properly and noted that aside from the umlatt in German, only the Swedish and the Turks use the little rounds over their letters denoting special pronunciation.

It seemed no one was very anxious to treat the scorpion bite, and we covered several other subjects before someone finally called him in. We were wondering how fast they'd have moved if it had been a Black Mamba bite—but of course, they wouldn't have had to bother at all then.

The next night as we took our seats to see the opening night production of "The Mousetrap", I spied him two rows in front of us.

"How's the scorpion bite, better?"

"Yes. How's your . . . your . . ." he floundered, for I had not explained why I was in the Doctor's office—naturally!

"Oh. I'm fine!" I said and laughed.

He motioned toward the woman sitting beside him, and she twisted around and smiled as he said, "This is my wife—this is Mrs. . . ." and knew he didn't know me.

"Brown", I filled in and Susan laughed and the lights went out as the curtain opened on the first scene of the play.

Sometime later that week I was quoting another interesting bit of information I had got from the "man with the scorpion bite".

Joel remarked, "Say, you must have had a real good time when you went to the Doctor's office."

He was so right!

Bill Johnston came Friday with "Good News"—he is sure he will be transferred to the Hospital at Maun. He is not needed here and is delighted that he was able to talk with the Director of the Maun Hospital who was in Gaborone last week. He is assured he is needed up there. If there is not enough X-ray work, he can serve in other ways. He says he'll teach classes for the Red Cross, and he can do wiring and electronic repair. He may be a Jack-of-all-Trades for them.

He was grinning from ear to ear, and I asked him to stay for lunch. He asked if he could leave some of his things here while he was away; he'd start on Sunday evening for a trip up there to see what the situation is and planned to be back in about two weeks. I told him O.K.

Bill brought over a mountain of stuff. We found him, Sunday, sitting on the front porch, surrounded by three suitcases and three card-board cartons, and reading the newspaper when we returned from a visit to the Pahls.

"I hope you haven't been here long. The invitation to the Pahl's came unexpectedly and I debated leaving a note for you—but thought you might be coming over a bit later. How long have you been here?"

"Only about an hour."

I made it up to him by storing away his stuff and then having him to dinner, and Roy and Joel drove him over to the train, with his big backpack, and saw him off to Francistown. I gave him Juan's address, knowing Juan could point him in the right direction for transportation to Maun when he arrived up there the next morning. He asked us to tell Susan to make an effort if she gets to Francistown, to get a ride out to Maun. "There'll be plenty of transportation out there so she can get around to see the area." When I inquired about the bus to there, he wasn't enthusiastic. "It takes twelve hours, starting about 3 p.m. Only time to make the trip is when the sun is down. The bus is packed in—including chickens and a few goats so she should try for some other kind of ride."

NOVEMBER 1

When Susan went up to Serowe with Ben and Vi Webb, she met some of the young volunteers working in that village. Some of them told her about making the trip to Dar es Salaam on the Tan–Zam Rail-road from near Lusaka. They told her the second class fare was seven-teen dollars one way. That seemed almost incredible, but I remembered that Mike, a good friend of the Pahls, had gone to Dar last May; so we looked him up where he works as a Regional and Town Planner on the fourth floor of an office building on the Mall. The elevator was out of order and the climb left us a bit breathless. Mike was full of information, even said he had a copy of the railroad schedule. It was indeed seventeen dollars for a one-way ticket. Just twice that for first class; the only difference being a few less in the compartment.

A Tanzanian visa can be secured in Lusaka, at their embassy. There was some question about having it granted when Susan revealed that her South African visitor's visa for a year was stamped into her passport. "Be sure and tell them you're from Botswana. That might help. If you get the visa, then you can get the train ticket at their office in downtown Lusaka. Then you get a local bus for a two hour ride out to Kapiri M'Phoshi. There you walk a half hour to the Tan–Zam Railroad station, where the express train leaves at 9:30 p.m. Halfway to Dar you cross the Tanzania border and use different currency on the train. You can take a local bus a couple hours from Dar to the Ngorongoro Crater to see the animals. There it is under government control and no one goes into the crater except in the government land rovers, driven by the guides. It takes forty dollars for the trip, so it is best to team up with other tourists and split the fee. As many as five can go together."

Other details were covered, and he promised answers to any other questions, if she had them. Later he dropped off a copy of the train schedule.

Susan's decision to try the trip entailed a lot of dovetailing. It would start with our trip north to visit Tony on the weekend of October twenty-second and twenty-third. She and Joel could then go on to Francistown by train. Joel had school vacation Monday, and he could return that evening. Susan could get a flight to Lusaka on Thursday. In the meantime, she could fill Tuesday and Wednesday with an overnight stay in Bulawayo—riding the train in and out from Francistown. I knew Juan would help with the arrangements there.

She wanted to get to Lusaka with only enough time to make her arrangements and get the Friday evening train to Dar es Salaam; she planned to get into the airport late at night and stay there till morning when she could buy some money and get on into the city. The return trip was something else, again. She would take the train from Lusaka to Livingstone (twelve hours) and then would not have a flight out of Livingstone to Francistown until Tuesday. So she would have several days there to see the Falls.

I'll be glad when she gets out of there though and lands again in Francistown. I guess we nagged her enough about the place, so she will be very careful.

The trip started, as I said, with Roy, Joel, Susan and me going up to Moeng College to visit Tony Julianelle. I had promised him we would come on this holiday weekend which gave us time to drive up one day, stay overnight, spend another day on the return to Palapye for train connections and have Monday to drive on home. I wrote him the week before, to expect us. There are no phone connections with his valley up there and mail delivery is erratic, so there was no way of notifying him if our plans were changed.

Thus, we were aghast to have Joel get sick the day before we were to start. He slept most of the day but had a fever. As soon as Roy got home that evening, we shoved him into the car and took him to the Doctor's, then we poured medicine into him and talked him into think-

ing positively, assuring him he would feel better by the time we got up
to Moeng. Such was not the case. It was a hot ride. We went right
through Mahalapye, not stopping at the open gas station. "I'll get it at
Palapye when we get there." It was just about noon when we arrived
there, but the town didn't look normal. Stores were closed and everybody was in one place—down in the center listening to some politician
speaking over a sound system. Tries at two stations were futile. They
sent us up the road. A few kilometers up the road the man made motions that he had no key; the boss was down at the center. Back we
went—"How much gas do you have?" I asked.

"I'm down to less than a quarter tank."

And we had one and a half hours to go to Tony's—and the return
trip—all in barren country. Back we went and our angel was with us.
Way up on the corner was a Caltex station, or spot with pumps, that we
had passed coming in without noticing. He had petrol!! What a relief!
Then we found there was no water in the radiator and there wasn't any
there. Down to the railroad station we went and Susan let Roy use her
water bottle to fill and refill.

In Palapye, Susan, Joel and I went to the railroad station to get
tickets to Francistown and there were told we should have booked a
week in advance. Nevertheless, he condescended to sell us some; a great
and complicated process. Susan commented, "Some different than in
Germany where they whip the ticket at you before you've had a chance
to pull out your money to pay for it!"

Out of Palapye we turned east onto a poor road across the brushy
desert. There were kraals here and there along the way and soon we saw
some little stands out near the road with furs and carved animals displayed. We passed several of them and then decided to stop and find out
how much the wares were. After we sat a while, people started towards
us, all ages. I think a whole family finally arrived to stand and look at us,
and tell us what each article cost. The hides were stiff and the carving not
that great and nothing any of us really wanted. But I felt badly at not
buying something from them—they were all so eager and I knew how
they'd appreciate the income. I salved my conscience by handing the lady
some bananas and giving the kids handfuls of candy and Roy gave the
man some cigarettes and they all seemed happy and we made our getaway. Susan said, "Don't stop at another of those places. I can't stand it."

We knew we should drive straight east and that sometime, there
would be a road off to the left that would take us up over the hill to
Moeng. It seemed we travelled a long time with the only left turns being
little trails to villages, but eventually we were relieved to see a big new

green and white sign, just like the new ones down around Gaborone. Moeng and Moeng College to the left, Martin's Drift and Sherwood straight ahead. Also, we learned it was twenty-seven kilometers to Moeng College, the last lap.

The last lap was the "mountain", a steep incline which Rat, when he heard we were coming here, warned us was "So steep you might slip right back down the road". It wasn't that bad.

It was fun as everything was different. The trees were huge and tall, the grass was green and the forest dense and green. Cattle by the tens lay in the middle of the road sleeping, some refusing to stir. There were swampy areas just off the road and huge birds flew up as we passed. Trees in the forest and fields along the road were heavy with blossoms like lilacs; the leaves dusty pale green and the flowers pale lavender and sweet. Clouds of perfume floated into us constantly.

It was slow going here, and soon the road entered a narrow gate, and we figured we must now be on the school property. Several kilometers later, we did come to the main entrance. Nothing spectacular; the road ended and we drove on a trail, onto the main "campus".

Here was a field of about ten acres, flat and green, and green forests rolled up onto the hills on the perimeter. Straight ahead were the main school classrooms. We sat and analysed for a few minutes. It appeared to be dormitories off to the far right, the main buildings at center, sports fields between us and them, and off to the left, a cluster of houses we agreed must be staff homes. We followed the trail along this side of the soccer field and wound toward the houses, looking for one similar to Margaret's as Tony had described. Our guess was right and we stopped in a few minutes, nearby, and saw Tony coming to greet us.

We had no more than shaken hands and introduced Susan then up walked a young black boy, grinning.

"Kenneth! How are you?"

"Yeh, that's Kenneth all right—How are you?"

We all shook hands and I gave him a hug. Tony stood there with his mouth hanging open, listening to us introduce Kenneth to "Joel's sister".

"What's this Kenneth bit? How do *you* know *him?*"

"Oh. Kenneth lived next door to us. He was Joel's first friend in Botswana. Oh yes, he has another name—Tutume. That's how you know him?"

"Yes. Tutume is in my, er, homeroom as we call it at home. He's in my Maths too, one of my star pupils. When I get in trouble, I call on Tutume!"

Kenneth went along to play and we said we'd see him later. Tony noted that the Headmaster is really strict about pupils being in the staff homes. It's a "no no". But he said he'd talk to him and explain the situation, and see if he could get permission for Kenneth to come over to lunch the next day.

We were amazed that he had recognized our car the minute we had driven in and amazed to see him, as we hadn't known he was up in this part of the country.

So, we unpacked and settled into Tony's house. We had a well stocked cooler; a big chicken casserole, an eggplant Italian casserole, a carrot cake, fruit jello, rolls, cheese and whatnot. We goofed about fresh stuff. Too much commotion getting Joel to the doctor the night before and we didn't stop in Mahalapye where we saw oranges and vegetables. Our ice block was still pretty solid (frozen in an ice cream plastic container) and as Tony had no refrigeration, he was thrilled just to touch it and drink some cold water from its melting.

We called the other two Americans; Rick from Bethany, Connecticut, and Larry from Iowa. Tony asked them to bring their enamel plates and coffee mugs and join us for supper.

What fun! *FOOD!* Poor guys really enjoyed it. There was a whole big roaster full of the chicken and noodles, but Tony went for the Italian eggplant. In fact, everyone gorged! They can't get any meat. There are only a couple of refrigerators around and the trip out from town on the truck is so long, perishables don't keep.

Tony was explaining about the truck. It's a Government truck, so those rules and hours apply. If they pick up groceries, and then the mail mid-afternoon, they might not get back to school until after end of work hours. If so, they drive the truck into the garage, close the doors and don't touch it until working hours the next day. If it has a load of meat on it, that would be available for any dog, cat or rats about the place to get at. So, there's no point in trying to have anything brought out except canned goods and staples. Tony bakes all his own bread and uses rice, potatoes and eggs.

We ate and talked and ate and talked. I had brought a can of instant coffee mixed with Cremora, and that can just lasted through our stay. We had many a cup. Larry invited us to go to church services the next day at ten thirty and Rick invited us to go on a hike up to see the dam, at eight, a.m., so we had that to look forward to when we went to bed.

Rick arrived on the dot at eight, complete with Boer Hat.

"Everybody ready for the hike?"

"Haven't had breakfast yet. Tony just came in from running. Why don't you sit down and have some bacon and eggs too?" He didn't need a second invitation.

Tony had never been to the dam so this was interesting for him too.

We crossed Moeng Bridge, a trail of stepping stones across a wet running ditch. This little stream came down through the valley a short distance from the main building. Wet and swampy and running with water. What a treat to see. Down in Gaborone we are parched and baking to concrete. Here in Moeng there is green grass—tall grass, tall trees, running water through a real jungle up in the valley above the school.

Ricky was an excellent guide; I began to think he had one of his classes on a field trip. "Watch very carefully for snakes. This grass is tall" he told us like school children, but that was all right. Everything seems so normal you have to keep reminding yourself that in this grass, among these normal rocks and bush, can be lurking black mambas, puff adders or other unfriendly specimens. You are in Africa.

So, carefully we went—sticking to the path as it wound uphill beside the stream among the rocks. Some of the time we walked in the sandy bottom of a former stream bed. After we passed the gardens of the agricultural classes, off to our left, we came to our little jungle. A huge palm tree in the center was hemmed in by masses of elephant grass, rooted in the swampy bog.

Elephant grass grows tall. It's somewhat like bamboo. As the new grows, the old dries up and hangs down, soon to blow around and make a mess, but it grows thick and is scratchy, so planted as a fence, it is soon impenetrable. Many people plant it around their property and it is good except for the dry leaves constantly dropping and accumulating.

Anyway, we were heading up the mountain along the stream to see the dam. The dam almost does its job, but it settled at one point so it has a good healthy leak which keeps the area below it wet and green, but doesn't help to conserve as much as was planned, up above.

We reached the dam and Ricky warned us to be quiet so we wouldn't scare away the baboons which are usually on the cliffs above.

Sure enough, we soon heard some "barks" and saw a baboon out on a ledge.

"That's a scout" Rick said. "He's letting them know we are coming."

Then we heard some answering barks, and as we stood quietly on the top of the dam, we were rewarded by the sight of dozens of baboons of all sizes rushing back and forth over the rocks, where they blended out of sight as soon as they stopped moving. The best sight was the Grand Daddy of them all, up in a tree taking a good look at us. This huge baboon must have been over six feet tall. He looked huge even from a distance.

As we left the dam there were barks again, and the messages flew from the scouts that we were moving. As we tunnelled through the brush and came out onto a lovely open meadow, with rocky hills rising on all sides, Susan and I saw a baboon up ahead, peering at us and giving a bark, telling the rest where we now were. He dashed up into the woods at the left and though we walked clear up to there, and peered in, we couldn't see a sign of him or any other baboon.

Rick said there were often Kudu here in the meadow, but all we saw besides the baboons were some Rock Rabbits. We turned back after a while, heading toward the dam, and I glanced back just in time to see that scout bounce down out of the woods, and give his bark signal that we were now leaving. He disappeared again, his duty done.

Rick said the scouts are always on duty—but once he surprised the pack completely, coming on them so quietly, he shocked them by his presence. The scouts had been goofing off.

Tony had taken us across campus the afternoon before. The main buildings reminded me of California campuses. Big solid buildings, with a wide porch and pillars running along one side so there was coolness even at mid-day, and shade to aid in keeping the classrooms cool. This huge building was original, perhaps thirty years old. Further expansion of the school was not in such a grand manner, and the classrooms were like the house I am living in here; pre-fabricated and metallic, not conducive to being cool. Tony had a homeroom in the big building, but some classes in the hotter ones.

Roy said the dining hall reminded him of Jefferson Barracks. Tables and benches ran the full length on either side; enough so that five hundred could sit down together. It was gaily decorated with ferns and flowers and a big "Welcome to Moeng College" on the front wall over the stage. The day before had been awards day—prizes for academic and sports excellence.

At the end of each table was a stack of metal plates—deep enough to be called soup plates. Beside them were stacked tin cups with handles. As we watched, boys were bringing out big pots of mealies, proceeding from table to table where they poured some into a big basin at one end of the table. Tony assured us they had some variety, some vegetables and meat perhaps once a week, but I guess the staple is mealies, just as it would have been for them at home.

There is much adjusting for the kids when they come here from a rondavel in the bush. They have to learn to sleep in a bed and to sit on a toilet. Tony said the Headmaster, in assembly one day, reprimanded the upper classmen for leading the newcomers astray, by telling them you climbed up onto the toilet seats to squat. The seats were being ruined.

Outside the dining hall, to the rear, we saw three great big ovens where bread was being baked. They were beehive shape, over ten feet high. Down beyond was the new Post Office—"the center of our interest" for which they make a bee-line in anticipation of some kind of mail. Out of sight, off beyond the hostels was another area of staff homes, and a small primary school for children of the staff.

A wire fence surrounds the main school buildings to keep the cattle out. As it is fenced off, the grass inside grows tall and green and the cattle on the overgrazed open spaces peer at it with longing. They are afraid to pass over the pipe bridgeway on the road where it enters the fenced area, but Tony described the time the cows hunger got the better of their fears.

"They really wanted to get into the high grass, so they got up plenty of speed and ran the road to the pipe barrier and leapt over it, one after the other and then gorged themselves. They couldn't leap the fence but could manage a broad jump over the supposedly cow-proof pipe barrier."

After church, which is mandatory for the students, we found that Kenneth had permission to join us for dinner and Susan spread out everything left from the day before. I called all the boys for one last "gorging".

Tony was reluctant to have us leave but it would take several hours to reach our next stop, the railroad station at Palaype and we wanted to be there before dark.

After we got down from the "mountain" area, there was a stretch of fairly level land where Roy began to pick up speed. Just at that moment, Susan and I both glanced around and saw an unforgettable scene. We were mesmerised by it a while—too long to put in a request for Roy to stop so we could take a picture; we were late as it was.

I don't think we'll ever forget it though. The sun was setting—off behind the huge Kopjes, but red light was splashed onto a cluster of thatched rondavels, just off the road. A family group was milling about and strung between two huts, was a line on which several brightly patterned blankets were snapping in the evening breeze. The whole was composed as if by an artist—background, flashes of red highlighting, the blanket-wrapped family and the accent of the patterns on the line, under the thorn trees.

"Maybe I can get it when I come back again," Susan said, but there won't be another time for the same picture. The people would be in a different place, the bright blankets might not be blowing and there would not be another sunset just like that. But—it's nice we've got our heads for remembering such a scene.

It was dark long before we got back to Palapye, which makes driving that much more hazardous, in the cattle country, but all went well and we sat down to a good dinner in the Palapye Hotel, went to bed and got up in the early hours of the morning and put Joel and Susan on the train to Francistown, a few hours north.

We expect our Susan back on this Wednesday or Thursday. We received a wire saying "Home Nov. 17". There has been no follow-up letter and now it doesn't matter as it's almost time for her to head back into Botswana. The wire came from Dar es Salaam, so we know she got that far all right. I hope it was something interesting and enjoyable that kept her the extra week. We'll soon be hearing about it.

Joel came down on the train after a three day stay with Juan. The expected recovery did not materialize as soon as we'd hoped. Good old Juan—he takes care of everybody.

At ten after six on Tuesday morning the sixteenth of November, we heard a crunching on the driveway and I dashed out to see a taxi stopping and Susan piling out with her backpack, carved canes and two drums. The drums she was carrying were the Webbs' she had picked up for them in Livingstone where they had left them in a hotel room last September. We were so pleased to see her. She had been away since October twenty-second, when we started for Moeng.

When we had gone to bed the night before, Roy had said, "Don't you think I had better meet the train in the morning?" and I had said, "Oh, no. She said the seventeenth."

Then, here she was. She didn't have even one purchased trinket. She had her camera with one film, which a Zambian Policeman had asked to look at, and had opened, exposing the film to light. Time will tell if it was all ruined. That was the only heartbreaking part of her trip—not having more than one film—not being able to buy more and not having got any in Francistown or Bulawayo before starting. There were gaudy, regal Masai men posing at the Ngorongoro Crater for her—and the film was at the end. "I could have cried" she said. We had

had film on hand. I just forgot to give her some. We consoled each other by saying you have difficulty getting people to look at your pictures, but it's still in your head. You can remember it all without pictures. We hope.

We were so confused and talked so much, Roy was almost late for work. Joel went off without his snack box and juice; Susan rushed over to school with that, his teacher saying "Well, if he didn't remember it, he deserved to go hungry".

Susan relayed much of her experience through the morning as she cooked, cleaned out her luggage, washed clothes and hung out the small tent and sleeping bag in the bright breezy sunshine. The tent had been wonderful. She slept in it four nights in Lusaka at a good camp (though quite empty) on the edge of the city. It was a nice place and she was soon acquainted with a couple who ran a nearby restaurant and had a big farm out farther. The only fear she had was of snakes. It had been rainy and that had brought them out into the warm roadways. The tent didn't have a zipper across the bottom front, although all the rest was tight, so she went to great lengths to stay secure.

This is Thanksgiving Day and I realise now that I haven't sent any special Thanksgiving greetings to any of my children or other family. I shall have to write some letters this afternoon, telling each how thankful I am that he or she is part of my family.

Looking over my sketchy resumes here, I find I did not include much about Susan's long trip. We heard many riotous episodes, but don't know quite how they fit in chronologically—or geographically.

This letter from Susan which arrived after she got back here, does sort out some of it.

Lusaka, Zambia
12th, November, '77

Hi Folks,

Well, travelling in Africa is not for the weak of body, soul, mind, and spirit. Unbelievably hot in Tanzania and Zambia. I got the visa for Tanzania on Friday October 28 with no problems. Two days ride in train to Dar. So *hot* and *muggy* there, *unreal!!* Not a very nice city, either!

Wednesday, Nov 2, flew to Zanzibar (stayed in Hotel Ya Bwawani) on Friday, Nov 4th flew back to Dar early in the morning. I wanted to see the Ngorongoro Crater (since Dar es Salaam wasn't nice) so I travelled north another 500 km to the crater.

Absolutely Fabulous! Lions and elephants walk around the Lodge. Also, the Masai Tribes all over the hills. Naturally, I ran out of film and could shoot myself. You can't buy any film in Tanzania.

Monday afternoon, Nov 7th, I started back to Dar to catch the train. Naturally all the buses were broken down so I missed my first train. Took the train on Wednesday (Nov 9) and got to Lusaka yesterday morning.

At the campsite the other kids told me the border was closed between Zambia and Botswana. Many people are stranded with campers and trucks. Anyway, the plane is full for Nov. 15th so I must wait until *Nov. 22nd*. Ugh! I wish I had stayed in Tanzania. Lusaka is not too much fun. But will stay in the campsite here rather than Livingstone because it is nicer and cheaper. Some kids are flying this Tuesday to Francistown so I'll have them take a message to Juan Kudo and to you. Relax and don't worry! I'm fine and have plenty of money. I think I lost about 5 pounds carrying that backpack in the heat. And so many mosquitoes! I take medicine right on time for Malaria. I hope you got my telegram from Tanzania; also my post cards from Rhodesia and Zanzibar.

So, I guess I'll see you on the *23rd!!* (bet I won't bother with the Webb's drums) that's the least of my problems.
Love,
Susan (sweaty) Brown

The best laid plans. . . . When Mike told her about getting to Dar and up to the crater, he mentioned that "you took a bus for a few hours;" sounded like it was not too far. When Susan began to enquire after getting to Dar, she found it was over five hundred kilometers away—all the way up to the Kenya Border. In fact, it was not far from Mount Kilimanjaro. This is when she fired off the three word telegram to us. No way was she going to work that trip into the days she had allotted between trains.

Ready to head north, she found the bus was not ready.

"Where is the bus?"

"There", they pointed. A completely dismantled vehicle was spread out in various heaps and piles beside the road.

"That? When will it go again?"

"Maybe tomorrow."

So there was when she joined some other backpackers waving an arm in a motion that we'd take to mean "Bye Bye" but here means, "Going my way?" and one back-of-a-truck ride went on for sixteen hours.

The crater was more than she had expected. Three fabulous lodges on the rim; a village at some distance for the staff and the wardens. Animals everywhere. Water Buffalo peered in the window as she enjoyed her Zebra steak dinner!

She teamed up with other tourists for the Land Rover trip through the crater. Supposed to be five in a car, but they squeezed in six, to split the forty dollars fee. Only the Land Rovers go into the crater, where once the Masai were free to graze their cattle, thus, the animals are used to them and have long since realised that no harm comes to them when a Land Rover drives through. They calmly go about their business and ignore the tourists.

Herds of Lions were one of the thrilling sights. Susan said a huge black-maned lion with his harem of five lionesses practically posed for them.

She had her fill—full satisfaction—of seeing these wonderful animals in their own habitat. The world was tropical and lush up there. Just as you dream of Africa. She had a great view of the Serengetti, although it was not surging with wildlife as at some seasons. She saw Kilimanjaro, Arusha and a lake pink with Flamingoes.

It was sparsely populated with tourists though. Kenya and Tanzania are feuding and have closed the air routes. One must backtrack from either Niarobi or Dar to Lusaka to reach each other. Ostensibly the border is closed to traffic too, but many were getting through. "Just took a lot of nagging and waiting" Susan said.

Because she missed the train for which she had bought a ticket, no amount of arguing would convince anyone the ticket should be used on another day. Good thing it was only a twenty dollar loss.

The train ride was something. She travelled second class, six to a compartment instead of four, as in first class. Six, did you say? Six women, *PLUS* as many kids and babies as they happened to have, and bundles and bags and cases of belongings. All piled in together. All absolute strangers, but they struck up an earsplitting conversation that never stopped. They ate all the way; bones and scraps and trash was tossed to the floor. They asked for Susan's water, and she did share some, but it was her lifeline. The men were herded to coaches by themselves, and the women to theirs. Even if you were married, you'd not travel together.

When they hit the border between Zambia and Tanzania, there was a wild changing of money, in and out of windows and back and forth. Great screams and waving of paper and general confusion.

When she first arrived in Lusaka, having flown from Francistown, she had to take a cab—there were no buses from the airport—seventeen miles out of the city. So, she asked the driver to take her to a campsite, and after much insistence, he finally did. The camp was in the suburbs, and was fine. Only one Kwacha a night. It had a fine community house, with good big bathtubs and showers, a good fence around the area, which was only about twice the size of our yard, here, and it was rimmed and dotted with trees so was shady and pleasant. There were many retired couples there living in caravans. They had once worked in Zambia and since its independence, there's no way for people to take their money out of the country. So these people were living on the money they had accumulated there, taking trips once in a while—to Singapore or wherever else their fancy struck—and would return.

The first time in camp was just for overnight. The next day was frantic, locating the Tanzanian Embassy—having the proper pictures for her visa—which happened to be in her luggage—and getting the train ticket and then finding that the bus for the town up in the copper belt from where the train loaded—was broken down. No bus. Once again it was waving to passing trucks—and four hours later getting to the train.

"No problem. Everyone was great. No one dares touch you."

"Well, if you say so."

While staying at the camp later, this couple took her out onto the Kafue River. While they were sitting on the river bank in the evening, a motorboat whizzed past with a water skier skimming the waves.

They were aghast!

"We've been here thirteen years and that's only the second time we've seen such a sight!" they gasped. "Crazy!"

"The river is full of hippoes" they explained. "When the boat goes by, the hippoes walking on the bottom are curious and they will rise to the surface. They could come up between the time the boat passes, and the skier reaches that point—and wham—gobble. He'd crush and crunch and spit out the mangled body! Just last week a hippo bit a dugout canoe in two, and of course that was the end of the man in it. They just take a big bite for the fun of it. I guess the crocs do the eating up of the remains."

In Livingstone, she retrieved Webb's drums and carved wooden head. The lady at the desk remarked, "That lady wanted us to mail these to her!!" sounding like it was the most amazing request she had heard in her career of running a hotel. Packing and mailing merchandise is a monstrous project.

Susan shook the dust of Livingstone as soon as possible. Got into that airport and nagged for a seat. She only met with rudeness, but she persisted, especially when she heard three had cancelled—insisted they take her name as a standby (even though she had booked this flight weeks before and tried to confirm it early)—her persistence paid off and she got the flight—on Tuesday, November fifteenth!

She called Juan and he popped over to pick her up—took her to the house where she cleaned up, had a light snack—one of Susi's delicious omelets and got the seven thirty p.m. train to Gaborone. That was why we heard the crunch of tires on the drive the next morning and found her getting out of a cab. Home again for an interval of rest, washing, relaying tales, and planning the next expedition.

Susan left again last evening in the midst of a heavy downpour punctuated by great rolls of thunder and constant brilliant lightning. She took the evening train, this time going third class. "I'd rather spend my money on a hotel room in Palapye than on a sleeper going up. I wouldn't sleep anyway, anticipating being awake and getting off at the right time."

She planned to check at the Post Office about what time the truck for Moeng came for the mail, finish shopping and then catch the truck ride out to see Tony, Ricky and Larry. She was loaded with three cakes, fresh cucumbers, Cadbury's chocolate bars and Time magazines. They'd be glad to see her.

Susan didn't get my letter at Juan's telling her that Bill wanted her to come over and see the Okavanga. But when she got home, we explained more about it. Everyone she met while travelling, if asked about Botswana, mentioned going to Maun and the Okavanga; they weren't interested in Gaborone or any other area, except perhaps Chobe. That made Susan realise it would be a worthwhile trip and she began to lay her plans.

First, a phone call had to be made to Johannesburg, to find out flight days and to register a reservation—as near to December twenty-fifth as possible; that is the ninetieth day—the day by which she has to be off and away.

She actually got through and found that the twenty-first is the flight for her; that she must mail in her ticket to them, and then check again shortly before take-off.

We were so elated at getting that settled that we ignored the heat and the noontime sun and walked down to the Museum and the Mall.

The Basket Show was on, and we'd looked in on it two afternoons before. Susan bought five baskets and I spotted a Serowe rug that I liked very much; nice scene of family life and cluster of rondavels. I was armed with Pula enough to buy it and for a few minutes, thought I had—as I had it rolled up under my arm and was counting out the money to a young man who had taken it down from display—but . . . a young lady spoke up that it was already sold—and she leafed through her receipt book to find the slip to prove it. I consoled myself with a few baskets and we went on to the Mall.

The ticket will be photostated by Roy before being sent off to Johannesburg—Susan is not taking a chance on its getting lost and she is relieved to have the date set, so plans can be made in between.

First, to Moeng and Maun, but before she took off, we drove yesterday afternoon, to the Oodi weavers, off in a little village six kilometers off of the Francistown road. We were surprised to find about three kilometers of new road leading in, which made the trip a bit quicker than last December.

There were at least seven tapestries underway on the big upright looms. None of them was near completion, and each had a distinct style. Herds of cattle wended their way into most, but we smiled to see VW bugs in the streets between Kraals in one, and trucks as well. Most were strictly rural or had some story.

The looms with tapestries were out on the porch of the work building and the doors were open so we could wander among the many others, bright with hanks of multi-colored yarn knotted overhead, to inspect the weaving in progress. I'm sure each are "one of a kind", for each weaver "does her own thing". A name plate hung at each loom, identifying the worker and her language—labelled English only, Africaans, or Setswana. I assume this was for the convenience of the supervisor. Several of the shoppers wandered in and we all wondered when the sales room building would open. An energetic black woman soon appeared and bustled off to get the key, from some inner regions of the work building, and then she let us into the double rondavel with thatched roof.

"Hey. I never saw one like this, with ventilation openings up in the top", Susan exclaimed.

"I haven't either", I said.

Inside, the woman said, "My husband built this building. He

wasn't a builder and hadn't done one before, but . . ." and she intimated that someone supervised him and he did it. All the workers are residents of the two small villages there, and perhaps they called on some men of the village to do the construction too.

There was a nice selection of rugs, tapestries, spreads and runners, but again, I chose a woven spread (or table cover or wall hanging); this one was not "mild" like the Christmas present last year. It was hot pink—in fact, coral warp that gives it all a glow. It looks Scandinavian; all stripes with no added designs. I like it.

We noticed a poster on the wall and a booklet nearby, telling of an exhibit of Oodi weaving held in Malmo, Sweden. Always notice Malmo, as it was the only city in Sweden we visited.

Susan bought Oodi posters; one for a former teacher, who is a weaving bug. We resisted everything else.

As we reached the highway on return, Roy suggested we go north to Pilane and Mochudi. Susan was game and we decided we could stop at Rompa's Store and service station for a cold drink.

I sat in the car—after we had pointed out the thorn tree to Susan, under which we and Aunt Lois had had a picnic, and she and Roy went in to meet Mr. Rompa who relayed the latest news of his family.

Off we went, finally, to Mochudi—up to the Kgotla, and through it and on into some of the inner areas of the village, and back again. Past the Barclay's Bank, and Standard Bank—always present in every village, but a far cry from the huge modern buildings of the city here. Tiny white concrete-block buildings are all that's necessary.

We looked off toward South Africa—across a great expanse of Veld stretching on and on to the horizon, no hills in sight here, except the rocky kopjes against which the village rondavels were sprawled.

Names are interesting and we have become acquainted with the names associated with the history of the Union of South Africa, and then the Republic of South Africa, some of the early explorers and missionaries.

These names of course are given to children, of both the whites and the natives. Moffat is popular and Robert, and I suppose there are some Livingstones though I haven't heard of any. But the other day, Roy had some tax returns to deal with, and the name of the taxpayer was Cecil Rhodes Joubert Stanley. How's that for a bit of history to carry around with you?

We had some prints made of Zylla, his mother, brother and Joel at the airport the morning he flew off to what we thought was Guinea. Later we found he had gone to Angola. I told his mother we had the picture and asked if Joel should mail him one. "Oh, don't mail it! I have sent the ticket for him to come home but we are having much trouble in getting him home again." And later that day, the little brother came tapping at the door asking for the picture.

We saw his mother on the Mall Saturday morning and she told Roy, "We have sent the ticket for him, but we are having much difficulty. They have changed his name and his citizenship."

That says a lot. They may not want to part with a young healthy male. But Zylla was only thirteen, even though he looked older. How much better off he would be if he had stayed here and continued school at Northside, no matter how high the fees were. I wonder if he will ever again be back here with his family.

NOVEMBER 23

I worked out front of the house yesterday a little while, after coming back from a round of golf. An old lady whom I have seen the past few weeks working in the yard across the street strolled over to talk with me.

"You like to work in the garden, huh?" I asked.

"It's all I can do", she said. She's somewhat bent over and had her left leg wrapped in Ace bandage.

"It's play for me. I like to putter along at it".

She laughed and said, "You're an American. I can tell by your talk."

She tapped her lips with her fingers.

"My daughter-in-law is in America. She went for three weeks training but now it's going to be a month."

"She's a nurse?"

"Yes." I had often seen a nurse coming and going at that house. I guess this Grandmother had come to stay with the household while she was away. But perhaps she had come down for her health. She indicated her bandaged leg and said, "When I came down, I had to use a walking stick. I wanted them to cut it out, but they only cut out big ones, not small ones. I have some medicine and some salve to rub on." I assumed she was talking about varicose veins. Then she added, "You have BA plates on your car. Are you from Francistown? That is where I live."

"Oh, we bought the car secondhand, and it had been registered by the former owner in Francistown."

She asked, "Was that your daughter that came in the cab the other morning?" I had told her that Susan was visiting.

"In a cab? Oh yes, but that was at six o'clock in the morning last Wednesday—early in the morning."

"Yes, I know. I was out in the yard then."

We don't realise how we are watched and that everyone in the neighborhood knows all our comings and goings.

Batswana tend to rise early. I don't blame them. Early morning is the most beautiful time of day. The air is clear and clean and the birds are shrill and it's cool and breezy. I'd enjoy getting up at five and traipsing off to the golf course, but regular routine starts here soon after six and it's seven thirty before I am alone. But I can get out for a pleasant solitary cup of coffee about six. The birds know I'm coming. They can hear me moving in the kitchen and are alert for their breakfast. At first you can't see a single bird, but if you look hard into the inner recesses of the thorn trees just outside the door and peer under, you soon can discern that it is alive with birds, like decorations on a Christmas tree—blue waxbills, dull sparrows, bright masked weavers, yellow with their black eyes banded, a pair of wydah birds with their long long tails and pretty coral collars, and an army of doves, waiting to boss the whole operation after the seed is scattered. I can sit there and watch them eat. They scatter if I get up for a coffee refill, rushing up into the safety of the thorn tree, but if I just sit still they ignore me and gorge themselves as long as the seed lasts. By the time they are through, I may hear the blare of the radio, and my morning peaceful time is over and we will now have details of the world news. I try to have Pauline come late, so I can have another quiet cup of coffee after the exodus to school and the office, but she likes to get started on the day too, when it's pleasant and cool, and I don't blame her. Anyway, I scramble to be out the door right on their heels, heading for the golf course before the heat begins.

NOVEMBER 25

In spite of the heat of summer, we had a traditional Thanksgiving Dinner last evening. We were pleased to find after we got to the Pahl's house that they were expecting Bishop Murphy for dinner too. He is the Catholic Bishop of Botswana and has made his home here for twenty-six years. He did come, and we had a rare opportunity; a whole evening to listen to his experiences and to get information from him on various aspects of the government, the courts, the traditions, and the present batch of culprits in trouble with the law.

We concluded that there isn't much of consequence within the country that he isn't aware of.

Alice had everything well in hand with six adults at the dining table, where all the food was on the sideboard, four youngsters in the breezeway, and four big boys, outside on the patio. Each one told what he was thankful for, and then we enjoyed the delicious turkey, dressing and all, topped off with homemade pumpkin pie—made from the Botswana white pumpkins. Strangely enough, the finished pie looked just like one from our "regular" pumpkins.

Shanda, Alice's maid, had dinner too, for she was to do the dishes for the crowd afterwards. She is forthright and says whatever she thinks. She'd already told Alice she thought it was crazy for her to take good bread and mush it all up like that, to put in the turkey.

As she was serving herself at the sideboard, Bishop Murphy spoke to her in Setswana and she giggled, and he continued to talk with her. Then she was very excited, for he had discerned where her home was and talked to her in her native Kalanga language. They went back and forth for some time.

"It is good to be able to talk all languages," she said, "So you can know if someone is saying something about you."

After she left, he told us how smart the people are from her village. "We have many applications for St. Joseph's (a secondary school out on the edge of town), but when we get one from that village we accept it with no further investigation, for we know he will do well."

Later, in the kitchen, Shanda spoke to Jeannine about the Bishop. She was so pleased to be able to talk in her own language; sometimes she is discouraged that she can't understand what people are saying here in Gaborone, unless they are speaking English.

"He is so nice. Where is his wife?"

"He isn't married."

"Then he has girlfriends?"

"No. He is a Bishop and he can't get married."

"Can't? Who says he can't?"

"The Church."

"The church? That's not right. No girlfriends? You mean he has no feelings at all? They must give him injections, that's it. They must give him injections."

The Catholic mission has been in the country for twenty-six years and she had never gleaned the information that Priests do not marry.

We discussed the uniqueness of Botswana. A rare Democracy in Africa; ten years of independence and it is still stable.

The next election is in 1979 and publicity is on, encouraging everyone to register. I even asked Pauline the other day if she were registered, and told her she should do it right away, so she could take advantage of a privilege that few people here in Africa have.

Then we got onto Witch Doctors, medicine murder, herbalists and prophets. Some of us had been reading about medicine murder and how ingrained traditions and superstitions are not easily eradicated. There are ominous goings-on right out in Tlokweng, on the edge of Gaborone. The Bishop agreed that something is there, and Shanda had told the Pahls some details. Coming from different sources, there must be some truth about a witch man working out there. Fear is what perpetuates his activities for anyone who knows anything is afraid to report it; he or some of his family may be the next on the list.

Bishop Murphy came first to Francistown but his parish was the whole of the country from there west to Maun.

"I had a bicycle. That's all." He did get from one village to another by someone's truck, but once there, he rode his bike.

"You should have seen the road from Francistown to Maun, then. It wasn't a road, but a track. And it was a wondrous ride, for game was thick everywhere. You saw herds of elephant, herds and herds of springbok, and Kudu, and lions."

"Like driving through a game reserve?"

"Oh, there wasn't any reserve. It was just the natural wild country."

"I was reading about the problems the villagers had a long time ago up in the area between Francistown and Rhodesia, with the herds of elephants swarming in and demolishing their homes and tearing down the forests."

"Yes. That's true."

The road from Francistown to Maun may have been a track then, but even today, you don't drive it in a regular car. A truck with four wheel drive is a must.

We told the Bishop that we had all just finished *Trinity* by Leon Uris and that he would enjoy reading it. Susan brought it with her and after I read it, lent it to Jerry Pahl, who had a hard time keeping it away from Danny, Jeannine and Alice.

While reading *Trinity*, we were also passing *Cry, The Beloved Country* by Alan Paton, back and forth. Everyone cried over it. Joy

Packer's *Apes and Ivory* which I finished last evening, dealt with that book and with the making of the movie, down in the Natal Valley in which the story is set. I didn't even know it had been made into a movie, much less that it was an Oscar winner. I wonder, in the light of present developments, why they don't get it out and redistribute it.

I found interesting information in Joy Packer's book—about the school where Seretse Khama went—Lovedale, in the Transkei, and the Fort Hare University in Cape Province where "Tshkedi Khama was the greatest student of his time". Joy Packer was the wife of an Admiral of the Royal Navy and this book is the diary of her two years in Africa. It's chock full of information and impressions—all from her point of view, naturally. It is interesting to read her descriptions and predictions—as it was written in 1951 and 1952—so we "know how it all came out"—so far. It's a book I don't want to part with.

That Thanksgiving dinner was indeed unique. We may never have another as hot either. The next day, Shanda the maid ate one of the rolls I had taken to the dinner, and she remarked, "Good, but I think she put too many eggs in them." Jeannine gets exasperated with Shanda, as Shanda always has to have the last word and prove she is right. She thinks Alice should go down and get vegetables from the prison gardens—something she hasn't done and won't start now, at this late date. "They have everything. They have every kind of vegetable there is!" she said.

"Oh, do they have sweet corn?" Jeannine asked, "White mealies?"

"No," Shanda said. "They do not have corn. But . . . corn is not a vegetable!"

"You'd better go study your vegetables," Jeannine muttered.

I met Lillian as I was walking to town the other day and asked her how Lovemore's finger was.

"It is better. Thank you for the medicine." She had bought herself a tube of the salve and used it after I showed her how and had bandaged it several times. Yesterday, there was a tap at the front door and there was Lillian with beautiful Lovemore, to show me how well his finger was. I gave him some cookies and admired him again. I still think he is half white—just a lovely soft coffee color. Danny and Joel almost embarrassed me one day when they were admiring him and asked Lillian, "Why is his hair so straight?"

It's a nice soft halo around his head now, although once in a while she clips it down short; it is not tight woolly curls. We are very happy his finger is so well. The way it looked for a while, I wondered if he'd lose it; all a mess and him crawling around in the dust and dirt!

We heard one disturbing newscast the other night on the late news after we came home from Thanksgiving dinner. Terrorists in Wankie National Park. All the time I was in Rhodesia, I felt that if I just got into the park, I, and we, would be safe; no harm could come to us.

Well, how silly. The point of terrorist activity is to assure all that no place is safe.

DECEMBER 1

Susan has been away for six days; was to be in Moeng last Monday and then go on to Francistown. Two men from the Tax Department were in Francistown during the week and reported to Roy that Susan had called Juan and he was arranging transportation for her to Maun. What day this was to be, is a mystery, but we know, at least, that she was on her way. I imagine she'll be back by the end of this week. I wrote Bill Johnston at Maun, that she might be arriving and to see that she took all precautions concerning the tsetse flies!

Along with the tension of the Rhodesian action north, the refugees pouring in, and constant news of action or inaction in the Republic of South Africa, there's now a new crisis.

Hoof and Mouth disease has broken out in Botswana. This is a real crisis, for the economy is largely based on the beef industry. The abattoir in Lobatse is closed. No cattle can be moved in the north.

Roy had recently learned of a large operation underway up north where a man is using huge trucks to transport cattle as an alternative to their being driven hundreds of miles—so now his trucks and business is idled, too.

All available government vehicles have been sent out with teams for innoculation of cattle. This week, reports are that one whole section is absolutely quarantined, another next to it, is designated as a buffer area and nothing can move in or out of it either. Thus, only the south will be moving any cattle to Lobatse, and the Meat Commission will be handling only thirty percent of its usual load for the year to come. This is very serious for everyone in the country. Coupled with the late rains, they may be in for harder times.

Susan has kept in touch on her wanderings. A letter from Moeng written on Thanksgiving eve.

Nov 23, '77
Moeng College

Hi Folks,

Had a very nice time here for three days. If only there weren't *so many mosquitoes!* I have twenty bites on each arm.

I met a lovely Botswana nurse on the train. She was going to Bulawayo but will be back on December 8th. She's going to come visit at *Elephant Road!* I managed to get inside the Palapye Hotel and slept pretty well. Had a nice breakfast and then bought eggs, on-ions, tomatoes, bread, etc. in Palapye (more goodies for Tony). I also found some single sheets (light blue) to make curtains.

It was a rough ride across to Moeng on that truck. Jiggled me to death. *Destroyed the elastic in my bra!*

We passed Tony running, so I didn't get to surprise him at the door. His chocolate bars made it safe and sound and he loved the cakes too. Just like *Christmas!*

I made fried rice, spaghetti, and "quiches" tonight. My pie crust was Terrific! Made one pie with peaches and custard.

Also, today I went to visit the Home Ec. Class. Six periods of making chocolate pudding!! The kids are darling. Anyway, the teacher is Danish (Eleanor); is finishing on December 7th. She is interested in going to the Cape. So perhaps I can fit that trip in my schedule before we go to Joburg. I'll go if you don't mind. I could meet you in Joburg the 17th. Is that O.K.? Think about it!!

Anyway, tomorrow I'll go to Francistown and maybe I can even get to Maun for Saturday. That would be wonderful because Bill could go canoeing with me.

I should be home by Friday, Dec 2nd, anyway.

I ate too much tonite! Ugh!

Hello Joel!!!! Study Hard.

I cut a nice stencil for Christmas Cards.

Love, Susan

So life moved along without her and I busied myself with a surprise baby shower for Alice. Only a few weeks till arrival time.
Another letter from Susan today.

Maun

Friday, November 25

Dear Mom,

This paper just got sprayed with Insect Repellant!! Too many mosquitoes in Moeng, but not many here.

My LUCK has been *wonderful!* I left on the truck from Moeng. Got to Palapye at 11 A.M. Got a ride with a man to Francistown who was going to Maun in the morning. Walked to the Tax Department and talked with Juan and Rat. Went home with Juan and stayed overnite.

At 10:30 A.M. Friday, I met my ride for Maun in front of the Tax Dept. Also, one other rider worked with *Bill* here in Maun. Got here at 6 P.M. Threw my luggage in a window (at Bills) and got a ride to Maun Village. I got to see a *wedding!* Fabulous. People dancing outside and 4 couples (girls in white and guys in suits) sitting inside hut (very serious and pious). Very lucky to see all this.

Maun is beautiful. All pretty huts (rondavels) and green grass. Bill's house is very nice. But has *outside toilet.*

Anyway . . . tomorrow, Bill and I and a Danish couple are taking a *week long* Landrover ride to all the hospitals in the *Chobe Game Area.* So, I won't leave here until Sunday or Monday (Dec. 4 or 5) Will try to get home soon. Thanks for the letter here. Bill enjoyed it. I had a tour of the hospital tonight. Very *Primitive!!*

P.O. Loads of Herero women in nice outfits! Love, Susan

I'll have been here two years by the time I leave and never will have seen Maun, Chobe and a dozen other places Susan is taking in in a whirlwind tour. She'll see more of the Chobe area than an ordinary tourist after this trip in the Landrover. The Danish couple may be the same med couple who looked after Susan Sethantsho's father when he was ill out near Ghanzi—that's south of Maun, but I wouldn't doubt that they cover the same area. Funny how the puzzle fits together.

I think I will include here, the letter we had the other day from Bill, up in Maun. I had written him that Susan was late back from Zambia, that she might not head his way at the tail end of that trip. He replied— on a folded sheet of the bright orange paper from the X-ray film; it makes a good letter and envelope, combined with a bit of scotch tape.

Nov. 20, '77

Dumela,

Well, I made it up here alright. The driver stopped off in Francistown for three hours to see his girlfriend but guess she didn't
invite him to spend the night because we ended up leaving Francistown around 9:00 p.m. By the time we got about 100 km from
Nata, he began to get tired so I drove from Nata in. The generator
went out on me and the lights became dim but it was almost dawn,
so pulled off the road to wait until it got lighter, and spent the time
trying to check for loose connections. It was a ten ton Bedford
diesel and would run forever without a generator, but the driver
woke up and wouldn't listen to me and turned the engine off. There
wasn't much power left in the battery and they tried to push a fully
loaded ten ton truck—but it was so heavy, and too much sand. I
finally talked them into pushing it down into the ditch and luckily,
got enough momentum to start it. Got in to Maun at 7 a.m. and
found no house set up for me. The new D.C. (District Commissioner) has a new rule that all medical people from me on, will live
on the Hospital compound. After two weeks of waiting, I got a nice
two bedroom house next to the Hospital and on the Thamalakane
River with crocodiles and hippos in my backyard. The house has a
wood stove and fireplace and because of the heat, I cook on a gas
burner. Also have a Rhodesian boiler out back for hot water, but in
the summertime, the last thing I want is a warm bath (104–115 F
daily). No fridge yet but am working on one that needs some parts
and should be Making ICE CUBES by Christmas. I have a screened
verandah all along the back of the house but no lawn or shade trees.
(The Botswana before me pulled everything up to keep the snakes
away.) The only bad thing about the house is that it does not have
a flush toilet. Just an outhouse in the front yard (of all places!) and
am getting used to it. The hospital is 3 km from the nearest store
and 5 from the govt. camp where all the other white people live. I
therefore bought a motorcycle. It is just too hot and far to walk here
and without a fridge, I must shop every other day. I am down to
140 lbs., and think I am levelling off. I could stand to lose another
five, but no more.

My job is going fine. I get to do a lot of different things.
Reduce fractures and apply the P.O.P. (cast), Suture, give the anaes-
thetic in surgery and scrub in when necessary. They are in need of
a blood bank here so I am trying to talk Peace Corps into sending
me down to Port Elizabeth to learn to type and cross match blood.
I am supposed to do a two week training in whatever I want after
six months and thought that would be a good trip.

I will understand if Sue can't make it up here. She should spend some time with you before she leaves, I don't plan on coming down to Gaborone until I take my 6 month training, sometime in January. I plan on spending Christmas at one of the Safari Lodges with friends. They expect a big function here and looks like it will be a lot of fun. Got to go now. Running out of paper.

Later, Bill

Alice Pahl went to Rustenburg last Thursday, December 1st, and she had her baby—Matthew Christopher, 9 lb. 9 oz., on Sunday morning. Jerry had a phone call on Saturday to come on down, and he made it through the border gate in plenty of time—as the baby took its time. He is a beautiful healthy happy baby. Jerry went back on Friday and brought Mother and baby home, and that evening, Susan, Roy, Joel and I went over to visit, especially because Susan was taking off in the morning and wouldn't see them again.

She had broached the subject of going to Capetown, but when she popped out of a cab Saturday morning at six (Dec. 3rd), she was going on nerve. She was worn out and sick but hadn't given in yet. Of course we had a run-down on her travels, taking up where she had arrived in Maun.

The morning after her arrival there, they all piled into a land rover, with tents, food and various equipment, plus, an imperious British nurse from nearby (been in Botswana four years and couldn't say Dumella) who insisted there was room for her to go along. Staring her down was useless. She insisted, "I know there's rooms for me"—so settled herself into the front seat. It was rough riding and after rains there was much mud. Susan was the first one out to help push and test depth of puddles to see if it were safe to drive through them. She did get a few tsetse fly bites, but so far, it seems they were harmless. They travelled through the Chobe area and camped two nights. Susan said "I didn't sleep all night. Just sat up, tense, listening to the snuff, snuff, snuffling of the hyenas pacing around the tent, only a sheet of mosquito net in the end of the tent between them and me. She was dying to go to the bathroom but didn't dare. That was wise, as warnings to Joel before his safari was that animals wait for just that, "If you have to go out to 'go'—don't". The ground shook from the tromping of the elephants and hippos there on the river bank. When I asked why she didn't pitch her tent right up next to the truck, she said they were warned that there must be plenty of room between everything—no criss-cross of tent ropes to trip up an elephant; must be lots of stepping-around room for them. The two Botswana girls were afraid of everything and they stayed in the truck.

At Kasane, they all decided to get Zambia visas and go over into Livingstone; they crossed on the Kazengula Ferry and went on through town and out to the Falls, sixty kilometers from the ferry. This time, rains had come and the Falls were at their rushing heights. When Susan got there the first time, she could hardly see any water; it had been dry for so long. Now she saw it in all its glory.

The man who had given them a ride in, the owner of the Southern Suns Safari Hotel at Chobe, near Kasane, said he would be going back at two; "Just be out by the road". They got to their appointed spot an hour early and waited and waited. Another young person said he had been waiting since seven a.m. . . . . There was no traffic, the man evidently had changed his plans or schedule. Susan and Bill had been laughing about having been able to go to Livingstone, see the Falls and all, on about five dollars, in contrast to the Pahls and Webbs getting stranded there and having to spend a mint!

They laughed too soon. No one went by and they had to rent some rondavels at the Rainbow Motel, where Susan stayed the other time.

The next day, no problem getting to the Ferry and back to Kasane.

Susan took leave of the group after their almost-a-week's trip, and she came down the Nata Road, to Francistown. She was nearer Francistown at Kasane, than she would be after the long trek back to Maun— so she did the wise thing. She dropped in on Juan again, and Susi gave her a light supper and Juan put her on the evening train.

She had a great time at Shashe when the train stopped at the station. I think she bought twenty-nine different animals. Carved turtles by the family, small pairs of antelope of different sorts and some birds; she took all they had. She puttered with them all week, removing the white paint they had added for eyes and various touches—and trimming down some of the horns. They have already been packed and mailed.

Well, Susan dragged along and slept a lot. She took aspirin and slept some more and finally got some of the aches out. She sorted her belongings and studied all the brochures of Capetown.

Eleanor, the Danish girl arrived and had lunch with us. She and Tony had bounced in the back of the truck from Moeng to Palapye, and hitched down to Gaborone. Eleanor is rugged and has done a lot of travelling.

Tony dropped in after lunch to say good-bye as he is off on a long trip north through Zambia to Malawi.

D-Day was the next day—Saturday, December tenth. We set 6:25

as exit time to get to the border gate early. Susan had her second cup of coffee on the run and in the car, and we found Eleanor waiting outside her flat and were off down the road.

I don't even want to write about this—it's too much.

Roy loves to fly, on the unpaved roads; they are some kind of great challenge to him. He has to go at a great speed and when he's home report about how fast he got back. Having Eleanor for an audience made it a greater challenge, and about thirty kilometers from the Mafeking Gate, he was flying along with the car shaking and pounding and rattling, and I was tempted to say "Slow down. This car has a lot of travelling to do yet", but I thought better of it. A second later, we flew off a big bump, so fast there was nothing to do about the rutty rocky section we had just come to, and we came down with a crash, dust flying out all around and an ominous "*CRACK*" setting us all on edge. We kept going though, and it's a good thing we did, for once we stopped at the border gate, that was it. We stopped with wild crunches and rattles and Roy looked up with amazement saying "I haven't got any clutch!" I was only amazed that it was only a clutch we didn't have.

Roy fiddled with things, hoping for the best and we went in and made out border exit papers—shaking and nervous.

Back at the car, Roy said he didn't think it was going anywhere right now, so the girls had better pick up a ride and go on. There was a nice Mercedes on the scene just then with only a man and his young son in it, so I asked if he'd take them along, as our car had broken down. He said fine, but that he was only going to the other gate—into South Africa, but that was enough. They went on, and then I was sorry I had hustled them off so soon, as within five minutes, Roy got things hauled together enough that he could get into gear and move. We opted for heading straight home—not going through this border after all, so turned around and retraced our route. The housing from the flywheel had been broken and was flopping, but he had poked it together a bit and we did make it home—non-stop.

After getting into the kitchen, he looked at the clock and said, "Well, we got to Mafeking Gate and back before nine thirty. That's only three hours!"

The part for the car has not come. If it doesn't by Monday, we'll have to try having it welded, as we must be in Joburg Thursday.

After we see Susan off on her plane, we three will go on down to Capetown.

Joel had a letter today from Karin, the girl he met in Rustenburg at the Kloof. He had written to tell her he was going to drive through

Bloemfontein, and could he have her phone number. She wrote today that she moved this week to the Cape, to Stellenbosch, so she would see him there. He is quite pleased.

"The lovely nurse" Susan mentioned meeting on the train going north, came to visit yesterday and she was disappointed that Susan was not here, and wouldn't be back again.

"She said she'd be here, now!"

"Yes, but a friend asked her to go along to Capetown for this week and she couldn't resist the opportunity."

"Oh, I see," and she wrote out her name and address for me. Susan was right when she said "lovely". She is tall and very thin, with her hair close cropped; is light brown with a long face and delicate features. Very beautiful. She works at Princess Marina Hospital here.

She had been to Bulawayo and said she went to the park, and the big round Museum, and to Salisbury and the Kariba Dam; that's what backs up the water from Victoria Falls, making a many-hundred-mile-long lake; and she had seen Victoria Falls from the Rhodesian side.

"In the daytime, in the cities, you never feel anything is wrong. All is safe. It's just in the dark-time things happen."

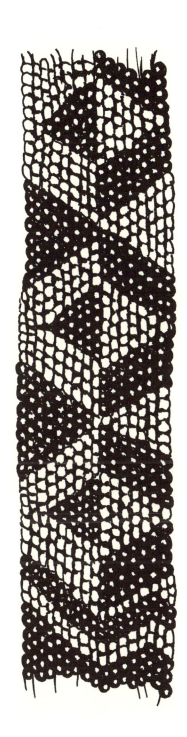

7

Capetown and
Ostrich

We are home from the holidays. It was the most unusual celebration of Christmas and New Year's ever.

A Christmas tree and gifts in a Johannesburg hotel room with our Susan, a city of Christmas lights in Kroonstad in the Orange Free State, a blistering drive through the Great Karoo, another Christmas gift time in a hotel near Capetown, our first view of Table Mountain with Capetown wrapped around its base, a boat ride out to sit and watch the seals, standing on the Cape of Good Hope, swimming in beach after beach, exploring the Garden in Capetown, visiting an Africaner family, standing on the southern most point of Africa at Agulhas, seeing thousands of Ostrich in the Little Karoo valley, stopping to look at "The Big Hole" in Kimberley and seeing Secretary birds stepping through the grass as we drove past. All these are some of the things which made the holiday unique.

When we drove into the garage at our Joburg hotel, Susan was waiting, back from her stay at Capetown, and helped carry our luggage up.

What a surprise when we opened the door to our room. A tiny green tissue paper and cellophane Christmas Tree, decked out in colorful serpentine streamers, surrounded with some little packages, a fruitcake and candy, was spotlighted by the reading lamp, with the rest of the room in darkness. It was very festive and was the first time that any of us had felt "Christmasy".

I felt badly that I didn't have a thing wrapped for Susan, and Joel said afterwards that he felt bad too, and guilty. Life had been so hectic, all I had done was to take care of Pauline and her family. Susan's gifts had to be some cash, to help on her travels and shopping for things she needed the next morning.

The dreaded hour arrived to head for Jan Smuts Airport. Susan was getting butterflies realising that in a few hours she would fly out, and in a few more, would be up in cold Europe and later, in cold Maine.

"I don't want to leave Africa!" she said with much feeling.

The week in Capetown had been a good wind-up for her stay. Perfect weather, lovely beaches, a decent hotel, the tours to every point of interest on the peninsular, and doing it all with a friend, made it very satisfactory and added to her reluctance to go.

Eventually, we had to say goodbye, a teary one. Susan's plane wasn't to leave for hours so there was nothing for her to do but sit there and wait until she could check her luggage. We settled her on an upper balcony with a view of the take-offs, but after we went downstairs and found it so pleasant and cool, we went back up and told her to come down to the lower level.

"After I just recuperated from saying good-bye, I have to go all through it again!" But she laughed now, and we waved to her and hoped she'd be all right. We were off in opposite directions as we drove straight south for four hours, stopping for the night at about the time she would fly straight north.

Kroonstad, in the Orange Free State, was a Christmas City. Besides lights down the main street, the bridge leading out of town was festooned with multi-colored lights, and an archway at the left, just before the bridge, led to Kroonstad Park. We drove into the park, through which the river wound, and the water reflected and multiplied the lights that were looped across it. It seemed as though we drove a kilometer and the river was festooned all that way, with lamp posts along the road holding ornate lighted designs, as huge flowers, bells, fountains, and windmills. The park was a veritable Tivoli; the most ambitious lighting scheme I had ever seen. But I couldn't help think of the energy use.

We had a surprise the next morning, after breakfast, when we stopped at a Shell station across from our hotel. We were descended on by a group of uniformed attendants—lively and cheerful and energetic who hopped around, washing windows, greeting us with good mornings, and opening the hood to check the radiator and serve the gas. Our mouths fell open and Joel and I kept saying, "They're so lively!" We even told the men themselves that they were a lively bunch. Blacks in South Africa live in a society almost as fast moving as the States. It's a moving and doing, up-to-the minute modern and mechanised world and they move right with it. Such a contrast to the ambling, relaxation, generally, in Botswana. As I said before, if you see someone speeding here, and lively, they come from South Africa.

Another surprise for us was to see huge Secretary birds in a field just outside of town. They were stepping along in rather high grass and it took me a few minutes to realise what I was seeing. It's like seeing your first elephant or giraffe in the wild.

The farther we went, the nearer we were to the Karoo and there is nothing there but sheep and windmills. There must be some ranches, but they're out of sight. We wondered how far the people had to travel for their supplies, for we drove all day, and after passing Bloemfontein, all we saw was open space and sheep and one ostrich, until we drove into Beaufort West.

Roy couldn't imagine why it was there, but I think it is one of the early towns of South Africa. Van Reebeck landed on the Cape in 1652 and I'm sure land was settled as far north as Beaufort West before too long. It has lovely old Dutch Colonial houses. It may have been the jumping off place for Moffat going north, with his ox teams from the Cape to see what was up there, the other side of the Karoo.

A hot wind was blowing and our eyes burned and all the while I was wondering how the Moffat family did it, moving along at a snail's pace in the heat—without the National Throughways to follow!

The Great Karoo was great. Scruffy, windswept, barren, hot, dry and nothing but sheep on it, though we did see some huge red grass-hoppers. By huge, I mean about five inches long. Many on the road hopping up and crashing into the windshield with a "crack" and crunch. Here is where we saw truckloads of sheep coming and going. They looked hot in their woolly coats.

We began to see mountains and soon the soil changed enough so there were some small wheat fields, and later larger and larger fields, running up toward the mountains.

We were soon running up the mountains ourselves, going up through the Aex River Pass. We were 350 km from Beaufort West when we headed up off of the barren Karoo. Up and up we wound to scary heights in switchbacks, and looked down on an unimaginable sight. A green valley, ten kilometers long, green, green, green, with a stream winding through it, and the fields rolling with vineyards and dotted with reservoirs. After almost two days of heat and desert, it was a sight to behold and to feast our hot eyes on. I didn't ask Roy to stop at one of the lookout stops to take a picture of the lovely valley, I'm too scared of heights and just wanted to get through the second half of the pass safely. DeDoorn was the green valley town and it was a sample of lovely things to come. From here on to the Cape, it was lush and green and pretty all the way. The desert was behind and the beautiful Cape Peninsular ahead.

The reason we had been moved to make this trip to the Cape after not seriously considering it at all, was my reading the book by Joy Packer, *Apes and Ivory* telling of her two years in Simondstown, as the wife of the Admiral (British Royal Navy), describing the beauty of False Bay and Capetown. This whetted my desire to see the Cape—more than any reports of friends who had been down.

We studied the calendar a bit, dovetailing Susan's departure and

Roy's leave and the numerous holidays; an extra two days after Christmas and two after New Year's, and decided to go.

Other friends planning to go in the Spring had sent for brochures
and maps, so they let us study them a week or two, and Susan brought
back some folders and maps, giving them to us in Joburg, along with
some good advice on where to go and what to see.

Having this bit of a preview, we knew somewhat what to expect;
nevertheless, the first sight of the big port city dwarfed by the looming
Table Mountain behind, was spectacular. We headed straight toward
the mountain but stopped first for some lunch snacks for a picnic up
there somewhere. We found an open space off the road with an almost
terrifying view of the depths below, where we could look upward, too,
to where the cable car was carrying people to the heights above. We
could see a road lined with parked cars, and when we went up, we
found there were hundreds standing in line in the heat. We drove on
past and wound along the road on the side of the mountain, thinking it
would eventually descend, but all of a sudden we came to the end and
had to turn around.

We had so many views of dizzying heights that Joel said he didn't
care about going clear to the top in the cable cars—and naturally, I
didn't. We didn't go back later in the week when the holiday crowd had
thinned; just kept doing other things with our feet on the ground.

They weren't always on the ground, for by mid-afternoon we were
on the choppy waters of Hout Bay!

Joel and I talked Roy into going on the boat excursion, when we
happened on it, on our exploration drive. We bought tickets, joined the
long line, hopped on the boat and in a few minutes, were moving out
into the walled harbour, nosing through its opening, heading around
toward Chapman's Peak, the huge mountain that guards the left of the
Bay.

All of a sudden the water began to be choppy and I wondered what
I had done! Here I'd been so busy insisting we should come I had
forgotten how scared I get on rough water. I asked the young man at the
wheel, "Is it always as rough as this?"

"Only when the wind blows. This morning it was as smooth as
glass, but a Southeaster has come up."

"Well, don't you hesitate to turn right around and go back if it gets
worse!" I told him.

The water got choppier. Here I stood with the camera around my
neck and my purse on my shoulder in which were our passports, shot
records and reserve resources and I wondered—"What have I gotten us

into? No one will know where we have disappeared to!", but the water calmed down, and so did I.

We nosed out of the Bay to circle the big peak and then headed back across the opening. Here a boy of about fifteen was at the helm; the bigger boys and the men of the crew were downstairs, casually chatting. I didn't feel they were giving our safety their full attention. Looming up at the other corner of the bay was the Sentinel; a sharp lopsided pyramid of stone. The boy at the wheel called down below—"We're coming to the island", and one of the older ones came and took over the navigation. Skimming along past the Sentinel, we saw a mass of rocks ahead, lapped by waves, and they appeared spotty and black. As we neared them we saw hundred of seals; sitting in the sun, diving all around, flipping their tails and brushing their whiskers. The boat moved in closer and closer, turned for full views on every side and then sat there in the middle of all those rocks to let us watch the seals of all sizes and ages.

We saw one that was wounded, flipping a bloody tail and barking. We moved away from the rocks and cruised back into the Bay and the harbour, where already another line had formed for the next excursion.

Roy returned to the hotel by way of the impressive southern suburbs; the highway bordered for miles with huge beds of blue and white amaryllis.

Joel and I finished setting up Susan's crushed little paper tree again, and ranged our pile of gifts around it. He had other ideas and after we were asleep, got up and strung colored serpentine all over the room. It was a festive sight when we woke on Christmas morning and we couldn't see how he had done such an artistic job in the dark!

"Are you Karin's American friends? Come in. Come in and have coffee." Karin's young mother ushered us through the cool tiled entrance hall, across the living room onto the patio overlooking the swim pool. Karin, a big tall girl with short curly hair, appeared with her younger sister and little brother Cornelius. Grandmother was also there, having come down from Bloemfontein the week before, in the big move to a new home.

Karin had written "See you at the Cape!" and when Joel called her on arrival, she had said, "Come out and see us Christmas afternoon". So here we were in Stellenbosch, having been kindly escorted right to the house on the mountainside, when we showed someone in town the address we were looking for.

We had our coffee while the kids swam. Joel said later that Africaners used to do nothing on Sunday after church but sleep or visit friends, but they are not quite that strict now. Her mother let Karin swim because he was there, but they couldn't play tennis until the next day. This Christmas had fallen on a Sunday.

The father of the household soon appeared—roused I guess from his Sunday afternoon nap. He wore a Rugby shirt. He had been a Rugby player all his life. We found that this new job which he was to undertake on January third was Coach for all of South Africa.

He and Mrs. Smith spoke good English, although they had to search for a word to express themselves, once in a while.

"We have no intimate friends who speak English, so we rarely have a chance to use it. It takes a while for the tongue to loosen." Mrs. Smith said.

Cornelius didn't speak English although both girls spoke beautifully. The girls are studying three languages, Latin, French and English, besides Africaans and both are accomplished pianists.

The Smiths explained why they had chosen Stellenbosch over a home in the southern suburbs of Capetown. There was no Africaans school in Capetown so Mrs. Smith would have had to do a lot of transportation. Then, too, Stellenbosch University is the most sought after of all the Africaans Universities; here they would be close to it. Even though living here would entail a thirty-five minute drive to Capetown for Mr. Smith, he could put up with the drive for the benefits of living out on the mountainside. The high schools were at the foot of the hill—"just three minutes to get to them or a half hour to get back", he joked.

Roy and I left Joel there and went to explore the town. Stellenbosch is nestled in among towering mountains and is noted for its beautiful architecture; old white Dutch homes and wineries with dark wooden doors and shuttered windows. It was much larger than we had thought and we found the great University, the old wineries, the Wine Museum, the Rembrandt Museum, all closed tight because of Christmas. There wasn't even a restaurant open those three days except in spots on the beach; one of the drawbacks of having a holiday on a holiday!

We drove out behind the mountain—through vineyard after vineyard.

The vineyards were started in the 1650's, in both Constantia and Stellenbosch and Stellenbosch has been a wine center ever since. Curriously enough, an American, William Charles Winshaw of Kentucky, a Doctor, happened to get to South Africa when he met someone buying four thousand mules to deliver for the British Army, in the Boer

War. He came along with the mules, fought in the war, practiced med
icine and late in life got involved in the wines at Stellenbosch. In fact, he
is the founder of the Stellenbosch Farmers Winery—which now, in the
70's, employs 6,000 people, and markets over half of all the natural
wines in the Republic of South Africa.

Joel was reluctant to leave when we went back to pick him up.

"We're going to play tennis in the morning!" he said.

Before that tennis, we moved into the Garden district of Capetown
into "the most interesting hotel I was ever in" as Joel expressed it.

The Lenox was indeed an interesting place. It was old. It looked
related to something in New Orleans for it had balconies here and there.
Stairs ran up from one porch to another, lounges opened out onto wide
balconies, inside stairs led you up to a landing where other stairs took
you down again to the outside. Everyone was assigned a table at which
he sat for all meals; an old fashioned boarding-house style.

The day after the tennis session, our goal was to reach Cape Point
and Cape of Good Hope; to drive as far to the tip as we could. This we
did, seeing great vistas of ocean along the way. Miles of the Point is a
Game Reserve and along the highway, way up on the mountainside,
there were numerous big friendly baboons sitting casually on the fence
posts, or rummaging through trash cans at rest stops. They seemed to
take a great interest in all the cars going by and the people watching
them. Some were nonchalantly sitting with crossed legs peeling oranges
with their hands.

The Cape of Good Hope! Just hearing that name made me remember grammar school geography books and stories of the explorers.

The unbelievably great mass of rock stands there as it has for centuries. The same dangerous waters still crash against it. We peered out
at what is still the most treacherous waters in the world to navigate.
There were ledges running up the face of the rock and both Roy and Joel
climbed way up looking off toward the Indian Ocean and then turned
back toward me on the beach of the Atlantic. The great waves crashed
in and the spray rose almost to where they were perched.

We had fun here, climbing over great rocks to watch the surf breaking in different ways over various rock formations. Nothing is so fascinating as surf. Time stands still as the waves break and break again.
We clambered around, took pictures, walked the beach where a man in
a wetsuit appeared with a supply of abalone he had harvested in the
deep. Another man bought the whole lot from him and went off to his
car happy.

We stayed almost an hour then retraced our route, but stopped off at Buffalo's Bay for Joel to swim. It was one of numerous safe beaches within the Reserve. The surf was good and there were plenty of youngsters riding the waves.

Baboons were out enjoying the passing traffic, sitting on the fence posts as if they hadn't moved since we passed before. The sight of them was a good finish for the special expeditions of this day.

I got a surprise when window shopping downtown on Adderly Street. One minute I was part of a jostled crowd in front of a big department store and in the next, I was facing an old Dutch Colonial house which turned out to be a cultural museum and one step away from that I found myself on a wide brick walk leading in where huge trees drooped overhead and flowers and shrubs closed in on either side.

I followed it through this "enchanted forest" and soon saw the parliament buildings and the President's home, off to the left. All the rest was the wide expanse of the Public Gardens. It covered about six blocks, one of them a huge rose garden. Several museums were on the fringes and a snack bar nestled in, so I sat in peace and quiet with a cup of coffee, none of the sounds of the city reaching me.

The great open area in front of the Art Museum was graced by a rugged statue of Jan Smuts, set against the backdrop of Table Mountain towering above.

As I emerged from the garden at the top, another surprise; Roy and Joel coming to find me. Our hotel was just a few blocks from here, and I had discovered the garden from the city end!

Everything has to end sometime, and so on Friday, a week after our arrival in the Cape, we had to pack up, check out one more last time and head down the throughway and up the Eastern Coast.

This was a pleasure, for the throughway carried us into the lovely southern suburbs and past the Strand on False Bay after which we began to climb. We were so high we could see the beach curving on off toward the inner edge of the peninsular, for miles.

Joel had been reluctant to give up the beach the day before, and even when we were through swimming at Camp's Bay and at the big pool in Sea Point, we had hung around Bantry Bay, watching the surf on the rocks and admiring the delicate maneuverings of three surfers, zipping precariously over the huge breakers, not far from the jagged monstrous rocks. I had promised him then we could stop at the Strand on the way out the next morning, but once we started, he wasn't interested in an early morning swim after all, and we swept past, and admired the view only.

It had now begun to rain. When we left the hotel, there had been an ominous cloud, completely obliterating Table Mountain. Now, the drops were falling and before long the downpour was heavy and the wind strong.

Now we began to see huge Horse Farms. Neat green pastures fenced in white held dozens of horses grazing. It looked like Kentucky. Then there was an orchard area, with big Apple Co-op and many road-side stands. The hills, were soon rolling beyond each other in an endless expanse, all in shades of tan and brown. The last of the good water sources must have been back in the green valley with the horses and orchards. The ground cover was scruffier now and had nothing on it but sheep. The rain came down and as the wind blew harder, we laughed when we saw that every sheep in the fields was standing tail to the wind, thus they all faced us as we passed. They looked like an audience waiting for the show to begin.

Roy had agreed that we should go on down to Cape Agulhas, in that it is the southern most point of Africa, where the Indian Ocean rolls in from the East and meets the waves of the Atlantic. This entailed turning off the main road at Caledon and dropping down 125 kilometers. So we stopped in Caledon for coffee.

Good thing we had this recuperative stop—for later we needed all the composure we could muster. Little did we know what was ahead!

The land got more barren, as it does near the ocean. We followed the water for miles, raging on the rocky coast to the left of us. Rain and wind dashed against the tents and caravans in a number of parks and I wondered why anyone would come to this desolate place to camp.

"Agulhas, the southern most town in Africa" was the sign at the entrance to the little town. Just as we passed, I said, "Oh, I should have taken your pictures in front of that sign!"

"Yes," Roy said, "we'll be sure to stop there coming back."

We were so shook coming back I didn't remember about it till hours later.

The ocean has an ominous air about it, to say the least when a storm is at its height. Nothing stops. The waves slam onto the rocks, no matter what. I wasn't too keen on being even this close to it.

At the end of Agulhas' main street, we pulled up near the lighthouse. The gate was open and a sign fallen over flat on its face. A huge sign, Pad Werkes Ahead—Road Work—was plain enough and a big earth mover was busy in the middle of the way. Roy pulled around it, ploughed through a deep puddle and went on. I wished the operator of the big piece of equipment would call or motion to tell us to get out, but no black man is going to say, "Master, it's not safe for you to go in there".

On we went on the narrow way, with scrub brush and the raging ocean on our left. I was scared to death, for where would the road lead? It was so narrow and things so wet how would we ever turn around? We dove into a big lake across the road which stalled the car and it was some time before we got started again — but we ploughed on. Even when it looked like the end had come, a little turn brought us into more desolation.

We must have gone five kilometers at least, and in some places had to climb up into the roadsides to get around puddles. Coming down a slope, we could see muddy lanes leading off over the scrubby seaside hills, but below, was mud and a water-flow over the road, and Thank God—some equipment and men.

Before Roy could drive off onto some other trail—"It must go around and come out somewhere", I jumped out of the car and ran down to where the men were working. Of course I could hardly talk and the foreman, obviously, as he was the only white man, had to ask me twice what I had asked. Then he said "Agulhas? There's only one way to that. That's the way you came in. This is the end of the line out here. We're building a resort."

"But that road has big lakes across it."

"I know."

"But there's a place with a sign that says 'No Entry'. I saw it as I looked back."

"That's all right. Pay no attention to that. Just go back the way you came."

This information was relayed to the driver, and we began the tense return.

We plotted, carefully, the attack at the deep places. Roy hesitated at some places, saying, "I can't go through that!" and Joel and I had to convince him we could, such a short while after he had convinced us, by doing it, that we should plough down that road. What for, I don't know except to say that we had ultimately reached the southernmost point of Africa. We got out without being stranded and we appreciated beyond expression, the reappearance of the lighthouse at the end of one of the worst rides we ever had. But all thoughts of taking a picture at the Agulhas sign left our minds.

The car coughed and sputtered and hic-cupped for the next fifty kilometers but eventually dried out and acted normal. I can't be sure I can say the same about us!

"Wow! We got back to Botswana in a hurry, didn't we?" Joel joked as we turned onto a rough detour off the Garden Route we had been following. The road was cut through rock, and as we went through the cuts, we were amazed to see the colors—purple and lavender, gold and yellow, in great streaks.

Sheep by the hundreds grazed in the rain all over these hills. They still turned tail to the wind, and so did the cattle we saw, for the land was getting richer as we drew away from the ocean. We were a hundred kilometers inland when we returned to the main road, and stayed inland until it brought us to the wild ocean, at Moussel Bay.

That day's papers had huge headlines about the great mass of oil spilled at the time of Venpet-Venoil collision a few weeks before, some-where off Port Elizabeth. The storm and the wind was blowing it into the coast and already surfers had their boards covered and the oil was slopping onto the rocks and some of the resort beaches.

We drove down to the point to see if we could see the oil, but in the raging mass of dark roiling water, I couldn't have recognised oil if I'd seen it.

By the time we got to George, we were in the real Garden Route area; lush and green, hilly, full of flowers and trees. The city itself was clean and neat; rich and flower decked. The main street, perpendicular to the ocean in back of us now, lead us straight toward a great wall of mountain.

These were the Outeniquas, and by now we had found that if you see three little dots, on either side of a road on a map, it means a Pass. A Pass means to get ready for a climb that seems never to end, for soaring views from the heights and for a treacherous descent. This, the Outeniqua Pass was one of the longest and scariest, but it did end, and somewhere on the tail of the descent, we looked down onto fields dotted with Ostrich. We were in the Little Karoo.

All the way into Oudtshoorn, fields were filled with hundreds of Ostrich; both black and white, (the males), and brown (the females), contentedly milling around, heads on the ground, constantly eating.

We were headed for Oudtshoorn for the express purpose of seeing the Kango Caves; were being real tourists and going to the advertised sights. We hadn't realised that the biggest treat was to fall into the Ostrich center of the world. We didn't leave Oudtshoorn for three days.

Roy spotted a municipal park as we drove through the city, and exclaimed, "There are some Rondavels. They would be great!" So one of these was our home for the rest of our stay; civilised camping for a small fee.

That evening, just as we parked our car by the theatre and stepped out, a piercing squeal-shriek hurt my ears. I looked around to see if someone's T.V. had gone berserk or what siren it might be. It was an "other world" sound in a high frequency range. Then I remembered Susan explaining how her ears had been almost hurt by a high piercing sound and that she had found it was from a type of caterpillar in the trees, chomping the leaves. Several times the rest of the way, we passed a lovely drooping willow tree and it would shriek back at us! At home we had experienced the messy onslaught of the Gypsy Moth caterpillars but they were quieter about their destruction.

As we drove north a half hour, to the Kango Caves, we saw field after field of the birds. One setting had sheep, cattle and ostrich together; all seemingly content.

The cave entrance was high on the mountainside, reached by a series of switchbacks and the parking lots seemed stacked on top of each other. We were dismayed to see one labelled "Non-White Parking Only," and later found that tours for Non-Whites were limited to certain months. I wondered if they would be shown the same route as I, or one less interesting.

The Caves were intriguing and the humorous guide reeled off all his descriptions and explanations in both English and Africaans.

He gave us permission to turn back at about the halfway mark saying the going ahead was more rugged, tight or slippery-pathed. Some turned back, but we stuck to the bitter end. It was rough, and soon we squeezed through such a small "doorway" that anyone much bigger than I would not have made it. The passage here could be gone through only on all fours, or by squatting and scooting along. I began to get a little claustrophobic in the inner recesses and was relieved when we slid down a well worn passage to an area where we could stand. Roy came along holding his aching back and dabbing at the top of his head. He'd left a little scalp on the stalactites.

Returning to camp, we stopped at one of the fields of Ostrich. They all trotted over to see us and stood batting their eyelashes. They seemed shy and gentle. We found out the next day, that was definitely a misconception.

"Come on," our guide at Highgate said, "We'll go down to the egg shelters in the field."

We had just concluded an hour's lecture on the Ostrich Industry which thrives in this valley. We had sat under a huge willow tree (which did not screech at us), nibbling Biltong (smoked ostrich meat) as we listened to him stress that the birds are mainly raised for the feathers. There's a good chance that the feathers you see on costumes in Las Vegas or Paris come from these farms on the Karoo.

Highgate was founded in 1850 by the Hooper family who emigrated from London. The fifth generation of the family is here, still raising ostrich.

The egg shelters were in the fields at some disance and we all hopped into our cars and followed the leader. We sat under another tree where benches were ranged and he told us many tales, and gave us advice.

"An ostrich will claw you if you tangle, and your best defence is to lie down on the ground. If he tries to claw you then he will lose his balance and topple over. One time two men got in, trying to steal some eggs, and tangled with the birds. One man got away, but the female sat down on the other and stayed there the rest of the night and the next day, until someone happened to see the fix he was in."

We viewed a pair of birds nearby; an old married couple with rare likes. One enjoyed swallowing match boxes and the other snapped up any two cent piece within reach.

Each of the egg shelters was a thatched "A" frame, about six feet high, open at both ends. Under it was a pile of eggs soon to be taken to the incubator. Eggs are strong and can stand two hundred fifty pounds pressure on them sideways, and five hundred pounds endways. Some of the men stood on the eggs to prove the point—and so did Joel.

"We'll go down to the plucking pen now", our guide said and we drove to a little "rodeo" corral.

The whole place was jammed with ostrich and we spectators quickly found places up in the covered bleachers at one side. Several workers kept the ostrich on the move and when the guide asked for one, they reached out with a long hook, catching it around one of the long serpentine necks where it slipped up to the wide head and stayed there. The ostrich tried to back away, but to no avail. He was hauled up to the small stanchion in the center. This was a "V" of wood on posts, into which he headed while a bar was passed in back of him and fastened, thereby pinning him in. A strap was also fastened across, under his wings and over his back, to further secure him. Now, anyone who wished could climb up some steps and sit on his back.

"Have you noticed the ostrich's eyes?" the guide asked. "See, he has three eyelids. The quick flashing one that keeps it moist, the big heavy one that comes up from below which he closes when he sleeps, and the third, a heavy one from the top which he uses as sun glasses. His neck skin is so loose and pliable, it's a help if he gets into any sort of tussle. It just stretches and pulls around and keeps him from getting hurt. Want to see me reach down his throat?"

With only a little coughing and resistance from the bird, he stretched the mouth open and slipped his hand down inside the loose skin of the neck. You could see his whole arm down, almost to the elbow and he waved his hand around as though saying "Bye-Bye."

"This means you can readily get down there to retrieve something he has eaten that needs to come out."

He let loose the bird who had been in the stanchion, and asked if anyone would like to ride an ostrich—"at your own risk", and Joel went bounding down from the stands, ready to climb onto one. There was a bit of a problem catching one from the milling mass of grotesque birds, and they happened to get one that didn't want to stand still for the mounting, but Joel stuck there and didn't give up. They proceeded to put a sack over the bird's head. He looked more grotesque than ever, hooded, but at least they got Joel hoisted up onto it, with instructions to hold to the wings but lean backwards, and they snatched off the hood and away the bird went—round and round the pen—charging through all the rest of the birds. Joel hung on for a good long ride and then took the advice of the guide—"just let go and slip off the back when you've had enough."

Later I found I had left my camera case there. Dismayed at my negligence, though I did find it, I decided my excuse was "seeing your son ride around on an ostrich can be undoing!"

As we left Oudtshoorn the next morning, reluctant to leave our Rondavel in which we could have stayed on, we saw thousands more ostrich; so many we began to take them for granted, not with the great wonder, as seeing one alone, on Cape Point.

Watching them kept my mind off the six little dots on the map. Another pass coming up. The mountains were with us now and we wound around one bend after another, following a stream on our left where cranes and storks stepped high among the grass. There were tent and caravan parks on the edge of the stream, with rocky heights towering overhead.

We snaked between mountains of rocks, some bending over us, but we never climbed. We expected each bend to reveal an ascent, but we lucked out. The whole pass of five to ten kilometers was flat and beautiful. One blight on this beauty was the designation of White rest stops, and Non-White rest stops. How far can you go?

Later we compared notes with others who had made the trip to the

Cape and the Ostrich Valley, and invariably each had raved over the beauty of that Pass. At first I'd think they were talking about the one which carried us to great heights on the way up from the coast, but "no, no, the one that took you through the ravines with the unusual rock formations—the great high overhanging rocks". We found that our friends, the Pahls, had camped in here along this stream when they made the trip. What a lovely spot to tent and stay a while, but, we are always in a hurry—checking the time and keeping with pre-set deadlines.

So, on we went, out of the ravine now and onto the scraggly Karoo—beginning of the Great Karoo. The last ninety kilometers before reaching Beaufort West were absolutely barren; hardly any sheep even.

This was Sunday, New Year's Day, but we weren't really aware of it. One loses all track of structured life in traveling. It was just a day of driving.

While Roy and Joel were getting a snack, at Beaufort West, I sat in the car studying the map. Suddenly there were two dirty little boys at the window asking for ten cents. It so happened that I didn't have one cent in change, just some Rand 10 bills, so I gave them each a cookie. They dashed off across the street and I saw them join two men—also dirty, scraggly and tattery. One man had a baby in his care. They were light brown, not black. I felt terrible and looked around for something more for them—a big bag of rolls. So I whistled to the boy to come back and gave him the bag. The little group looked it over. The man tied the baby on his back—and they sauntered away, chewing on the cookies and carrying the rolls. I tried the rest of the trip to get them out of my mind.

Coming down, Joel had said, "I don't see how we're going to have a Merry Christmas with all these poor kids around. Makes you feel awful!"

Just out of Beaufort West, we turned left toward Kimberley. Immediately we found ourselves on a gravel road. Then we began to see the huge red grasshoppers and it passed the time noticing them on the road and crunching on the windshield—and wondering about them—and what harm they do.

Some of this road was reminiscent of the horrible trek we had covered on Cape Agulhas. We drove through several "ponds" but at last, a fantastic expanse of new blacktop appeared. A great wide road so new it hadn't yet had the white lines painted on it. Hours and hours we drove seeing no cars whatsoever. We saw no more than ten cars during four or five hours driving, going either way.

Kimberley the Diamond City is noted for "The Big Hole." Here, DeBeers in the past had used an open mine system. The big hole is left and is supposed to be a great tourist attraction. As we drove through the city, toward evening, there was the big hole to our left, just a wire fence between the traffic on the street and it. That's all it was.

There seemed no reason the next day to linger in any of these cities, shut tight for the holidays, so, like a horse smelling the oats in the barn, we were off at a gallop for home.

We stopped in Zeerust for a few vegetables at the perennially open take-out place, and headed toward the Tlokweng road to Gaborone. There beside the road in the driving rain was a big hitchhiker and Roy pulled over quickly. The guy started to put in his backpack as I said, "Hi, Paul!" but he didn't realise for a few minutes that friends were picking him up. It was Paul Storey of Boston, Peace Corps volunteer who came the same time as Tony and Bill Johnston. He laughed and laughed when he found himself in our car and I said, "Boy, you really lucked out! All this rain and we're taking you straight to Gaborone!" Another two and a half hour drive.

Little did we know that the rain had been coming down constantly in Gaborone, and the northern regions of the country, since Christmas. We found that out when we got to the dirt road. Once again it was slippery and conducive to fishtailing. We slopped along toward the border, listening to Paul tell of his travels.

He too had been to the Cape; had gone to Joberg first to hitch down, and had come back the same way. We knew why—because of the sparse traffic on the Kimberley route. He had stayed in a Hostel above Camp's Bay, where we had spent so much time on the beach so we compared notes on all we had seen.

"I really planned to get to Mahalapye by this evening", he said, "As I'm anxious to see my Christmas mail. I've been gone for three weeks."

"Well, you're not going to get to Mahalapye tonight," I told him, when we got to the house after dark, "So you might as well bunk in Joel's room tonight and go up in the morning.

He agreed readily, and helped unload the car and we all had a good dinner after inspecting the place and finding everything fine—except tall grass where there used to be lawn.

Later I told Paul he could go ahead and take a hot shower and he could hardly believe it. "I haven't had a hot shower in weeks", and he kept looking at the bed in Joel's room saying, "That's the best bed I've seen in weeks, too."

While Joel and Roy went to the Pahl's for our mail, Paul and I sat and rehashed the various aspects of the South African race situation. He said he and friends had discussed it constantly and he did the same with any Black, Indian or White who had given him a ride. We did agree that the more we see of the country and the more we learn about it from various points of view, the less we understand the whole picture.

All we know is that it's great to be back in Botswana. That's what you hear from every returning traveller, "I never completely relax until I get back to good old Botswana!"

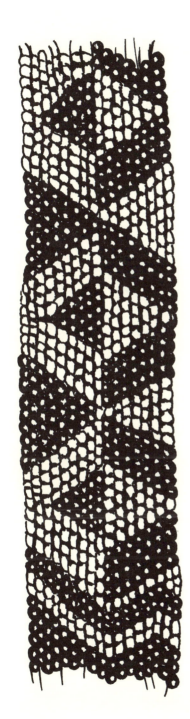

8

Winding Down

We have had a pleasant surprise as far as this "summer" goes. It hasn't come! No searing burning heat and stifling house where you have to close yourself up in the bedroom and put on the air conditioner just to exist until the evening coolness comes. No lethargy from the heat; you plan a day and have some ambition. It is cool. There has been more rain than any other December or January in history. It is a pleasant surprise and we hardly give a thought to what it was like last summer. It's a help, when I'm beginning to clear things out and organise for our packing.

In just eight weeks, our stay here will be over and we'll head north by leaps and bounds, with long stops between. We can stop as often as we please, anywhere along the Gaborone to Hartford, Connecticut route, just as long as we don't back-track. So, we shall take advantage of that opportunity and spend about six weeks in travel. Time will tell what the final itinerary will be.

I went out Friday to use a phone; calling Joburg for information on some package stopovers in Greece. Later, that noon, Joel casually mentioned, "Pauline seemed pretty upset when I told her you were making a phone call about our going home soon."

"You told her that? Why?"

"I don't know. She wanted to know where you went."

So, as soon as she came up to do the lunch dishes, I went and told her that we had finally learned that our contract would not be extended. We definitely would be leaving in March; not very soon.

"In March—Oh?"

"I will try to place you in another job before I leave. I'll keep looking for someone new coming in—perhaps you could work for some other Americans. You don't have any other place you know of, do you?"

"No."

She went home to Molepolole that afternoon which is unusual for her. When she came in this morning I asked her if she had gone home and how baby Roy was.

"He is all right. They are all worried that you are leaving."

I explained again that we were here on a two-year contract and that there would be no further financing of any Tax Team. I suppose she'll

get used to it. I've softened the blow by beginning to give her things—
like Joel's outgrown clothes to keep for Fred, and a load of my things.
No doubt she is worried, for she has a good home here, for herself and
various and sundry relatives who need a bed.

Neighbors have come in to put their names and deposits on some
of our belongings. Most of the big items are already spoken for. Roy
will take shoes and clothes to the office to give them first choice.

I have some packages of books and pamphlets and stories from
South African papers ready to mail, along with a wealth of amusing
items from the local Daily News, I can't part with.

Tony Julianelle appeared last Tuesday afternoon, back from his trip
to Malawi. It was good to see him and he came in and visited a while and
then later came back for dinner. We were going to a show at the Town
Hall but he asked if it were all right if he stayed here, read the Time
magazines, listened to records and took a hot shower. When we got
back about ten, he looked like he had thoroughly enjoyed himself, and
Roy gave him a ride out to the village.

He had enjoyed his trip, but he didn't like Zambia, through which
they had to drive to reach Malawi, and on the return trip had not even
stopped within its borders; just kept going. "I don't like to be where
people are pushing guns into my face."

He said again, "As usual, I don't really relax until I get back to good
old Botswana. This is home, now."

Being relaxed in Botswana is often discussed. A bank executive's
wife from Washington D.C. and I were comparing notes on Capetown
when one of us commented on the fact that people at home think we're
in the midst of danger here in Botswana, and in reality, we're in one of
the safest places in the world, if not *THE* safest.

She laughed and said, "Oh, my yes. I'd never dare do the things at
home I do here. You can walk anywhere here day or night and be
perfectly safe. If I were out on the street in Washington, a policeman
would come and tell me to get off the street."

The wife of another Tax Department man commented, "I'd never
spend a night alone in Jamaica when we were there. You just couldn't do
it. Here, David can go off for a week at a time—he's going to Francistown on Monday—and I stay here perfectly content and safe. My family
at home can't believe it. They write and say, 'I know better. I read the
papers and I read the Time magazine and I see the T.V. and I know that
what you say isn't true.' They don't understand how far we are from the
incidents. The four hundred kilometers to Francistown is so much far-

ther than if there were throughways; the whole desert is between us and South West Africa and Angola. Nobody can get across that. It takes hours to get to Joburg—and we don't go to Soweto. What happens there has no effect on us way up here where the people are quiet, peaceful and guns are outlawed."

"Yes, it's hard to understand, when what you hear is only the blow-up of the incidents in the urban areas of South Africa. When you're down there and travel the vast vast areas, miles and miles of varied terrain and cities all so different from each other, even there, the incidents in the urban area of Joburg are minimized. They are almost tiny compared with the size and magnificence of the whole big country."

They aren't tiny, though, and we are more chagrined every day at the trends in South Africa, and the increased stubborness and self-righteousness of the Nationalist Party. Every day's paper tells of new discouraging developments.

Just be happy you aren't a Black in South Africa—even though you might be better off than Blacks anywere else in Africa. Another of those ironical situations. Tony reported there was nothing on the shelves in the stores in Zambia. Nothing. We had been told that. That's why Susan carried so much with her as she went through. But, trucks go to Zambia, via Botswana; go up the Nata Road and across the Kazangula Ferry, taking needed supplies into them. All these countries are surviving on what is raised and made in South Africa. If South Africa is slowed down through boycotts, it's the Black countries surrounding them that are going to suffer.

I was talking to an English lady the other day—about visiting South Africa—about its being such a wonderful place to holiday.

"My yes. Never in all the times we have been down, has there ever been one person, black or white, that wasn't gracious, kind, pleasant and helpful. Never once has anyone ever been rude or snapped at me for anything. They are all exceptionally gracious. That's not the picture the world is getting. It's too confusing."

The trunks are in the "spare" bedroom—spare now as I guess we've had our last guests.

Juan and Suzi were down. We had a fun week with them and took them to the theatre one evening. Suzi had seen all her movies in Francistown in a hall where the chairs are set up for the evening and you sit and wait for the reels to be changed. She was impressed with our huge theater, enjoyed the Interval, a pleasant time of visiting with friends, milling around in the lobby or out in the cool of the sidewalk, buying cokes and sweets, before going in for the feature.

They were the first of our group to leave for home. We saw them off to Hong Kong and Japan, with their first stop being the Seychelles and then Columbo in Sri Lanka; a circuitous route to Stockton, California.

Then Rat and Susan appeared one day to show us their little son. Pabana (Little Rat) with his deep black eyes and high forehead, was alert and bright; a large baby for three months. When the electric fan was turned on, he craned his neck to search out the source of the whirr.

Susan did nothing but hold him, stroke him, bathe and fuss over him. When she had to have her hands free, she slung him on her back where he nestled in contentment. He seemed the most loved and fawned-on baby in the world.

Rat beamed as Susan said, "I shall have a houseful of Rats" and laughed with pride.

Life has changed. It has taken a new turn in that activity is now all in the direction of winding up here and looking ahead to the trip to Athens, to Rome and the rest of Europe.

So, the bedroom is filled with trunks; three are fully packed, the others designated. The closets have been gone through and I told Pauline she would have to get her sister and cousins to help cart the stuff to Molepolole. I have given her everything that Joel has outgrown; but Fred will eventually grow into it all, and there are many cousins who will share. I have parted with loads of my things, too, and I see Pauline going up the drive in my old blue jeans shorts.

One evening we drove into our yard just as Pauline and her boyfriend were starting out for the evening. We picked them up in our headlights and Joel said, "Hey! Look at Pauline!" She was wearing a dark green dress and had a gold lame stole over her shoulders, which picked up and reflected the light.

As she passed the car, Joel said, "You look nice Pauline!"

Her escort is always a fine appearing person, I don't keep close track of her and rarely see her going out with anyone, but she gets a lot of mail—some post cards from all over the world; someone is in Tripoli, Nigeria or Spain sending fond greetings. I don't hesitate to read post cards—they're interesting!

I have been working on the project of getting Pauline placed in a good home. I realise that I can recommend her enthusiastically. She can be completely trusted, she always has our interests in mind and keeps close watch on the place if we are not here. I have two ideas and I'm banking on one of these places. Pauline can move the first of March and spend a couple weeks getting settled in her new place, for a pleasant transition. She's getting used to the idea of our going and today she offered to take a pile of shoes that I have for sale to "show" her friends.

The Radio Man and his wife have been here to buy things. I see she is expecting again. He has not yet returned the 20 Pula he borrowed so early one morning a year ago last October, and Roy told me they couldn't be buying stuff unless they paid the 20 Pula first. But, she came with a friend from Mochudi a few Sundays ago, and wanted to make a list and have things reserved, paying for them in installments.

She introduced her friend as from a Mission in Mochudi. Well, when you say "Mission"—that's the wrong introduction for me, for pricing and making sales. Like a fool, I asked Pula ten for spreads I paid eighteen for and ten for the matching curtains which had cost more than twice that, for the material before I had started making them. Once the price was written down—that was it. Then she wanted to know about the curtains in my room and I said they were expensive, but the Radio man's wife piped up-"Money is no object. She can get what she wants. The congregation is going to pay for it all."

Well, Mrs. Radio Man came back, with him, Sunday evening, with cash in hand and left carrying some. I missed my chance though when he began asking about tools. I told him Mr. Brown would be handling that later, but I should have added, "Yes, Mr. Brown wants to see you!" Maybe it would have jogged his memory.

The Pahl's had a sale on the past weekend, and many interesting stories floated over to us about it.

One middle-aged man came looking for games. Tony showed him what they had and his interest grew. He was fascinated by one in which dice automatically jumped around inside a plastic dome, and he was soon down on his hands and knees finding out how the game went. "The directions are there on the box", Tony said, but he replied, "How can I play it with someone else if I haven't played it myself? Let's try it," and for some half hour or so, this big black man and Tony were on the floor, trying out the various games in close competition.

The gas stove was a sought-after item. Too bad they only had one stove to sell, for they could have sold fifteen. It was promised to someone at Pula 250, but someone else still wanted it and said, "I'll give you Pula 300 for it!" They decided perhaps they should have arranged an auction.

The maid, Shanda, who incidentally is expecting a baby next

month (yes, fathered by the boy friend who persisted in beating her up, a dapper gent who we saw at the Holiday Inn Saturday night with two other cute girls—where was Shanda?), has been getting cheeky, as the British say, and a bit insolent. She was actually sassy to Mrs. Pahl when they had dinner guests one evening, and had to be spoken to about such behavior, the next day. Also, things have begun to be missing—from money to wristwatches, so there came a point where action was called for. Alice feared to keep her on and lose more in the confusion of selling and sorting out and packing—so they told Shanda to pack—gave her a month's pay and were happy to see her go down the drive, even though in helping her boyfriend steer his loaded pickup, she did run into the front fence a couple times. The Pahls are delighted to be alone and relaxed.

The rain is pouring down, so the shrubs continue to get more dense and lush, the marigolds are approaching hedge size again, and the grass gets thicker and taller as you watch it. The heat of the summer has not yet materialised so we are all thankful and keep telling newcomers not to expect this to be the usual February. It is a relief, for you can stay energetic and accomplish much.

Everyone who stops in tells us what a beautiful place we have created here—in contrast to the overgrown dilapidation for more than a year before our arrival. I realise, that in spite of the grass being a little high, it is a lush and attractive ground. All the labour has paid off, just when we have to leave it. That's why I'm enjoying giving loads of plants to friends who stop.

Zylla's mother and dad and little brother Candy came yesterday afternoon. They went to work, loading all my filled window boxes and ornamental concrete block. Three or four trips to their home around the block did it, and she added all the cannas and ferns she could dig before the rain began.

The last time I saw her she reported that Zylla had written that he was sick, he cried all the time, the man he lived with didn't give him enough to eat. Can you imagine a boy of thirteen missing his German mother's cooking while he has to make do with mealies and whatever those people over in Angola have? The man had had Zylla's name changed, given him a new passport and placed all manner of obstacles in the way of his getting out of the country. "He says Zylla must stay there until he grows up."

She said she was thinking of going to the U.N. High Commission on Refugees to see if they could do something and I asked her if she had gone to the Red Cross. "Lady Ruth Khama is President of the Red

Cross—and after all, the President gave you the passport allowing Zylla to go over there." She said she was going to try something, for now he had written that he had stomach sickness. "He has parasites. Is that bad? Can it be fixed?" We assured her that many can be treated, but after she went home, I could have sat down and cried.

"How, after their experiences with East Germany and their escape from there, could they have been so casual about sending their son into a place like Angola, now?" This is getting on toward a year since he went over there for some "free schooling".

But now, the news is better. Zylla has had his passport restored and a visa, and he may be able to get out of there the end of this month or early in March.

"I want to get home to see my good friend Joel before he goes to the States", is what he wrote to his mother.

We took the plunge and posted our list of articles for sale, on the Board at the Mall.

In anticipation of payday, some local people came in the next afternoon, and contracted for a number of things. One man prowled around and found my good laundry basket in the bathroom. He wanted it but when he carried it to the living room, a lady latched onto one side of it and they almost came to blows. What a tirade in Setswana! They went on at a great rate and when another man with them saw that I was disturbed, he said, "Don't mind them. They are brother and sister."

He hung onto the basket, filled it with a pair of sheets, two pair of shoes, two pillows and a blanket. "I will come on Monday" he said after I told him he could take it after he paid for it. Days have passed and he hasn't shown. I'll have to sell it all over again.

Pauline is in the middle of all this; she's doing a great job and will have to have a commission.

She has shoes and coats and shirts and suits down at her house and each day brings me bills in payment, and we laugh as we see the traffic down the driveway and people going up again carrying a plastic sack, or a pair of shoes, with happy contented smiles on their faces.

This evening, two men came to look at the sewing machine. They were sent by the man who was here with the couple who fought over the laundry basket. They have a great advantage as they can stand and discuss just what they think, in Setswana, and we can't tell what they are saying. After lengthy conversation and discussion and looking over what else we had, they took their leave saying they'd have to discuss it with the wife of one of them.

"When are you going?" one asked as he went out the door.

"In March."

"Going to the United States? Well, when you get there, tell them to do something about the MPLA. We don't like those communists."

Evidently they may have come from Angola; it seemed uppermost in their minds. The regular run of Batswana aren't too likely to mention the MPLA or even Mugabe or Nkomo.

Our days continue to be pleasant, though some wind and rain often blows up in the afternoon. And, in this pleasant coolness, our preparations for exit are going well. Most of our things are sold except three rugs. I also have to untangle my situation with the Radio man and wife, and their friend from Mochudi who has everything tied up and hasn't appeared with a cent. As she is a pastor's wife, I should be able to trust her word—that she will appear soon.

I went over to the Radio man's to tell her that the lady *MUST* come with some money or I will sell things to someone else, and found the wife was not at home. A skinny lady standing at the ironing board in the open patio between two wings of the house, where two little boys were underfoot, motioned off saying, "Hye!" In Horpital. Baby."

"She had a baby? When?"

"Marnday"

"A boy?"

"Aye. Aye." I suppose she thought that was to be expected, as those two little ones were boys, and there was an older boy in the yard who helped ward off the snarling dogs I felt were going to eat me.

Keeping my word to her has done me out of good customers and delayed the completion of this unsettling process. We still have the big living room rug. Everything left after one more payday, I shall give to Pauline.

MARCH 8

I thought I had Pauline all set in a new home! It didn't work out. She came home mid-morning in tears, on her third trial day, saying she couldn't work for "that lady". That lady had laid down the law that she could have *NO ONE* come to her quarters to see her. No sisters staying overnight or other family or friends, staying or visiting. Well, I don't blame Pauline for rebelling. After all, she is a person and one would not expect her to be practically banned from a normal life—as part of a Pula 30 a month job as maid.

I have another lead though. The lively Mrs. Gabaake of the Tax Office and the Botswana Council of Women says to have Pauline stop and see her. She can help place her.

So Pauline is now happily puttering in the kitchen, getting the clothes on the line—putting off thinking of next week.

The house next door is very quiet, where Kenneth and Edwin, Shinga, Vivian and sisters along with Thomas and Charla used to make it a perpetual noisy playground. The house is dark at night, the yard empty and drab in the daytime. Kenneth is off at Moeng, the younger boys at Lobatse, in school, the girls spread around among relatives, and even Mr. Yanye seems to have two homes— living "way off there" it's reported, and only coming here once in a while.

Zylla finally made it home! He had been in Guinea all this while; had not stayed in Angola, and is now fluent in French. It was hard for him to pull out English words when we had a farewell dinner with him, at the Inn.

Inasmuch as I've got to the point where I am inserting my carbon the wrong side up and doing myself out of a copy of these happenings, I think I must draw them to a close and soon pack the typewriter into its case and into a trunk. That's going to be hard to do. Things will be happening that I'll wish to record and I seem to have lost the knack of using a pen.

It seems too bad to just peter out on this two-year log. There should be something overwhelming and crisis-like to top it off. Maybe I'm getting blasé if I don't think that tearing up a home and household, bidding farewell to good friends and taking a six week tour through Europe is not "crisis-like!"

MARCH 14, 1978

Our homes are now only houses and the Pahl and Brown families are settled in the Inn, almost ready for the flight out tomorrow; the first leg of our long journeys home.

But, Pauline and I have spent one final afternoon together—working. The big rug had at last been sold and when it was dragged out the front door this morning, just before the house was to be inspected for check-out, it left a sorry mess which had to be dealt with.

Strips of wood had to be pried from the perimeter of the big dining-living room, and the holes left from the prying, filled. The floor had to be swept, scrubbed and even scraped, for the fuzz of the rug pad stuck to it, here and there.

We both worked hard at it, although theoretically, she was no longer in my employ, and I was supposed to be having lunch at the Inn. We were exhausted by the time we finished but were glad to have had the chore, for it post-poned again, facing goodbye.

Before we left the house, I handed her a paper and said, "Here's my address, Pauline. As long as I live, even if I'm travelling elsewhere, you can reach me here. Don't lose it. Come on, I'll walk with you," and we went out the gate together, down Elephant Road to Zebra Way and wound off on one of the green pathways that lead to town.

When we reached a fork where the path lead toward her cousin's house, she cried. I put my arms around her and we stood a while, with no words to soften the separation. I gave her a big hug and a kiss and she hung her head and turned away.

She moved slowly down the path and I watched until she was out of sight. She never looked back. So, I turned then in the opposite direction and took my first steps into my life without Pauline.

Epilogue

Pauline never again worked as a domestic maid. She secured a position with a government agency handling procurement of supplies and is still working for Water Affairs, making her home in Mahalapye. She married, some time after our departure, and in 1983 had a baby girl, Sethunya, which means Flower.

She writes often, telling how Fred, almost ready for University, Thandi, in Secondary School, and Leng, in training at Princess Marina Hospital, are progressing.

Rat Sethantsho was promoted to Deputy Tax Commissioner in 1981 and later assumed the office of Commissioner. After a term, he resigned to open his own Consultant's Firm, with Susan. They and their four children make their home in Gaborone.

A letter from Rika came out of the blue one day in '83.

Kirkland, Washington

Dear Mr. and Mrs. Brown,

It's been seven years since Roger and I stayed with you in Gaborone, but I've often remembered your kindness and hospitality. I only recently stumbled on your address, and I wanted to let you know what it meant to me (us) to have some clean sheets, friendly, trusting faces, and some fun (going to the movies with you) after the long dusty roads we had been travelling.

After Gaborone, we went to South Africa where we were, unfortunately, divorced. However, I have since remarried and have two beautiful little girls. I also run a preschool and childcare facility in my home which keeps me busy.

I don't know where Roger is or what he is doing. I spend my time raising Camille and Liana, working in the garden and playing with our dog, cat, bunnies and one East African Chameleon (remember, I'm a wildlife biologist in disguise).

Thanks again for all you did for us in Gaborone. I'll always remember it and offer the same to other travelers on the road.

Rika

Jerry and Alice Pahl and the younger half of their family came to Connecticut for a long weekend in the summer of 1986. The four college students stayed with their jobs in Minnesota, but the rest of us renewed our friendship and reminisced at length about all the good days we had together, in Botswana.

E. W. B.